South-East Asian Social Science Monographs

Marriage and Divorce in Islamic South-East Asia

Marriage and Divorce in Islamic South-East Asia

Gavin W. Jones

KUALA LUMPUR
OXFORD UNIVERSITY PRESS
OXFORD SINGAPORE NEW YORK
1994

Oxford University Press

Oxford New York Toronto
Delhi Bombay Calcutta Madras Karachi
Kuala Lumpur Singapore Hong Kong Tokyo
Nairobi Dar es Salaam Cape Town
Melbourne Auckland Madrid

and associated companies in
Berlin Ibadan

Oxford is a trade mark of Oxford University Press

Published in the United States
by Oxford University Press, New York

© Oxford University Press 1994
First published 1994

British Library Cataloguing in Publication Data
Data available

Library of Congress Cataloging-in-Publication Data

Jones, Gavin W.
Marriage and divorce in Islamic South-East Asia/Gavin W. Jones.
p.   cm.—(South-East Asian social science monographs)
Includes bibliographical references and index.
ISBN 967 65 3047 6:
1. Malays (Asian people)—Asia, Southeastern—Marriage customs and rites.
2. Muslims—Asia, Southeastern—Marriage customs and rites.
3. Marriage (Islamic law)—Asia, Southeastern.
4. Divorce (Islamic law)—Asia, Southeastern.
5. Malays (Asian people)—Asia, Southeastern—Social life and customs.
6. Muslims—Asia, Southeastern—Social life and customs.
7. Asia, Southeastern—Religious life and customs.
I. Title. II. Series.
DS523.4.M35J66 1994
306.81'0959'0917671—dc20
93–38170
CIP

Typeset by Typeset Gallery Sdn. Bhd., Malaysia
Printed by Kyodo Printing Co. (S) Pte. Ltd., Singapore
Published by Oxford University Press,
19–25, Jalan Kuchai Lama, 58200 Kuala Lumpur, Malaysia

Preface

I first developed an interest in marriage and divorce among Muslim populations of South-East Asia when working with the Demographic Institute, Faculty of Economics, University of Indonesia. In 1973, we conducted an ambitious Fertility–Mortality Survey, covering some 54,000 households in Java, Sumatra, Sulawesi, and Bali. The survey included a marriage history, and the results showed that female age at marriage during the few decades preceding the survey had been very low throughout Java and divorce rates very high. Subsequently, Peter McDonald and Kasto developed a questionnaire for use in the Indonesian Marriage Survey, which they co-ordinated in 1978, to examine in much more detail the factors affecting marriage and divorce in Indonesia, including areas such as South Kalimantan which had not been covered by the Fertility–Mortality Survey.

Around this time, I spent a year (1978–9) as a visiting professor in the Faculty of Economics and Administration, University of Malaya under a UNFPA project. Some of my students covered aspects of marriage and divorce in their graduation exercises, and near the end of my term I helped design the Malaysian Marriage Survey which was subsequently conducted by the Population Studies Unit of the University of Malaya, using a questionnaire which owed much to that developed for the Indonesian Marriage Survey. Later, I collaborated with Tan Poo Chang in some analysis of the Malaysian Marriage Survey data.

Despite these studies, Muslim marriage remained under-researched in the region, especially in peripheral areas, including many provinces of Indonesia, Southern Thailand, and the Muslim areas of the Philippines. However, Yawalaksana Rachapaetayakom had included marriage as part of a broader study of the Southern Thai Muslim population conducted in 1976. I had the opportunity to assist her with questionnaire design and with the early stages of fieldwork.

I have had the good fortune, then, to be associated in one way or another with much of the survey-based research on marriage and divorce in Islamic South-East Asia. The trends emerging from this research were fascinating, but nowhere had they been examined comprehensively for South-East Asia as a whole, utilizing available census and registration data and ethnographic studies to supplement and deepen the analysis of survey data. With this need in mind, I started working on this book. Because of the strong competition from other research interests and increasing administrative responsibilities, progress was slow, but finally—*syukurlah*—it has come to fruition.

Particularly because of the pressures of other activities, I owe a great debt of gratitude to those who have helped in the preparation of the book. Pat Quiggin has been a marvellous research assistant, on whom I have relied heavily. Lulu Bost designed a computerized bibliographic data base and Wendy Cosford assisted with the final preparation of the bibliography and with other wise editorial advice. Elia Zulu and Bob Hogg prepared a detailed data base on state- and province-level marriage and divorce data. The Cartographic Unit at the ANU prepared maps and diagrams. Colleagues at the ANU commented on two draft chapters presented in seminars, and I have also presented seminars on sections of the book at the University of Southampton, London School of Hygiene and Tropical Medicine, Universiti Kebangsaan Malaysia, and the University of Adelaide.

I have benefited greatly from discussions over the years with colleagues from outside the region who have worked on marriage and divorce in the region—Peter McDonald, Terry and Valerie Hull, Peter Xenos, Philip Guest, and Richard Leete. Terry Hull, Peter McDonald, and Richard Leete gave suggestions on particular chapters. I have also profited from pioneering work by colleagues from the region, notably Sutarsih Muliakusuma, Yasmine Al Hadar, Budi Suradji, Masri Singarimbun, Tuti Djuartika, Yahya Asari, Tan Poo Chang, Che Hashim Hassan, Yawalaksana Rachapaetayakom, and Jutamas Wayachut. Officials involved in marriage and divorce registration in West Java and Kelantan were generous with their time, and I particularly appreciated discussions with Abdul Razak Yaacob in Kota Bharu.

Progress on the book was greatly expedited by two periods of outside studies granted me by the Australian National University. The first, for four months in early 1990, was spent at the Institute of Southeast Asian Studies in Singapore. The second, for five weeks, was spent as a Scholar in Residence at the Rockefeller Foundation Study and Conference Center in Bellagio, Italy, in May–June 1992. My gratitude goes to these institutions for the facilities and collegial atmosphere which they provided.

Finally, to Margaret, for her understanding and patience as work on the book cut into other activities, and to Andrew, Tanya, and Greg, always tolerant of their father's sometimes inexplicable priorities, who reached adulthood as the book progressed.

Canberra   GAVIN W. JONES
June 1993

Note

In the text, RM refers to the Malaysian ringgit. In 1990, one Malaysian ringgit was worth US$0.37, down from its 1980 value of US$0.46.

Contents

    and Remarriage   163
    Incidence of Widowhood   163
    Incidence of Divorce   165
    Characteristics of Couples Who Divorced   202
    Rujuk (Reconciliation)   211
    Remarriage   213

6   **Influences on Stability of First Marriage**   218
    Factors Traditionally Fostering Divorce   218
    Effects of Divorce   234
    Factors Fostering Greater Stability   237
    Case-studies of High-divorce Regions: Kelantan and
        West Java   249
    Summary and Conclusion   264

7   **Polygyny: Trends and Influences**   268
    Introduction   268
    Polygyny in Traditional Society   269
    Trends in Polygyny   271
    Correlation between Polygyny and Divorce   277
    Living Arrangements in Polygynous Marriages   278
    The Malay-Islamic Context: Arguments for and against
        Polygyny   278
    Factors Underlying Decline in Polygamy   279
    Community Attitudes to Polygamy   282
    Conclusions   286

8   **The Effect of Changing Marriage Patterns on**
    Fertility   288
    Historical Analyses of Other Regions   289
    A Demographic Accounting Approach to Nuptiality–
        Fertility Relationships in Islamic South-East Asia   291
    Proportion of Reproductive Span at Risk of Conception   293
    Marriage and Fertility: Aggregate and Individual-level
        Relationships   295
    Measures of the Net Impact of Marriage Change on
        Fertility   299
    Conclusions   302

9   **Conclusions**   304

    Appendices   312
    Bibliography   322
    Index   342

Tables

Figures

Maps

Plates

13 Another Javanese wedding in Yogyakarta. The parents of the bride and groom pose with them.
14 In Malaysia, marriage courses have become very popular in recent times with young Malays about to marry.
15 The marriage registration office in Gabus Wetan, in the high divorce regency of Indramayu, West Java.
16 Syed Mohd. Zain, aged 50, of Kampung Patani, near Kota Bharu, Kelantan, with his four wives, whom he married in 1962, 1969, 1972, and 1987 respectively. (The first and fourth wives are seated next to each other on the left of the group.) He has 27 children. Syed Mohd. Zain's situation is hardly typical; fewer than five men in every thousand in Islamic South-East Asia have more than two wives.

Appendices

1
Introduction

The South-East Asian Malay-Muslim World

THIS book is about marriage and its dissolution among the Malay populations of South-East Asia, or stated differently, among the Muslim populations of South-East Asia. But neither of these terms is precisely correct in describing the populations the book deals with. To a large extent, the Malay population, an ethnographic term, is synonymous with the Muslim population. In Malaysia, a Malay is by definition a Muslim, and a decision by a Malay to become an adherent of another religious faith creates consternation and newspaper headlines. But in Indonesia, 13 per cent of the population (about 23 million) in 1990 were non-Muslims, of whom over 4 million are Chinese but the rest belong to the broad ethnographic 'Malay' group. Again, if the Philippines is considered to be a Malay population, then it is a predominantly non-Muslim Malay population.

Malay, the language whose core lay in the area around both sides of the Straits of Malacca (Prentice, 1978), represented a lingua franca throughout the region in the form of a trading language, and Malay dialects stretch from Southern Thailand through the Malay Peninsula, Sumatra, Kalimantan, and into eastern Indonesia (Adelaar, 1985). The three main languages of Java (Javanese, Sundanese, and Madurese) belong with Standard Malay and several others in a relatively close-knit subgroup (Nothofer, 1975). A form of Malay has been adopted as the national language of both Malaysia and Indonesia, and as one of the official languages of Singapore. There is considerable movement of populations across national borders within the Malay realm. For centuries, the Malay population of Malaysia and Singapore has been absorbing migrants from Indonesia: in 1931, one-quarter of the Malay population of Selangor had been born outside what is now Malaysia and Singapore. Immigration from Indonesia continues right up to the present (Lim, 1986).

The Malay populations of South-East Asia do, however, recognize distinct differences between themselves. For example, in Malaysia and Singapore, there has been an admixture of Indian Muslim blood to many Malay families, which is rarely the case in Indonesia. The definition of 'Malay' in the region is fraught with difficulty and inconsistency. In

Malaysia, the indigenous ethnic groups in Sabah and Sarawak are not considered Malay, though they are, like the Malays, defined as *bumiputera* ('sons of the soil'). Across the border, in Indonesian Kalimantan, no such distinctions are drawn. There are basic issues as to whether Indonesian ethnic groups such as the Javanese, Sundanese, and Bataks would be considered 'Malay' by the Malaysian Malays, though many descendants of migrants from such groups are included in the Malay population of Malaysia.

There are also small numbers of Muslims in South-East Asia who are not of Malay stock. The Indian Muslims in Malaysia and Singapore, the Arab Muslims in Singapore, and recent Chinese converts in Malaysia are examples.

However, it is not necessary here to embark on an involved ethnographic or linguistic discussion. The aim of this book is to examine marriage amongst the South-East Asian population of Malay stock (broadly defined) who adhere to Islam: the Malayo-Muslim community, to use Roff's term (Roff, 1974a: Chapter 2). This population is an important one, constituting the main element in the populations of Indonesia, Malaysia, Brunei, and Southern Thailand, and an important element in Singapore and parts of the Philippines. Unfortunately, lack of data for precisely the group that should be included will frequently necessitate tabulations that would not satisfy the purist, through omission of parts of the Malay-Muslim population or inclusion of some non-Muslim population, as, for example, when figures for Indonesia as a whole are presented.

Islam has a history of at least seven centuries in the region.[1] The Sunni version was brought to the region in the late thirteenth, fourteenth, and fifteenth centuries from various parts of India and Arabia by Muslim merchants and Sufi missionaries. Three factors can be identified in explaining the eventual acceptance of Islam in the Malay Peninsula and the Indonesian Archipelago. One is the role of merchants who established themselves in local ports, married into local ruling families, and provided important diplomatic skills, wealth, and international experience for the commercial enterprises of local rulers. Another is the role of Sufi missionaries from Gujarat, Bengal, and Arabia, who came not only as teachers but as traders and politicians and interacted with rulers, merchants, and villagers. They were able to communicate their religious vision in a form compatible with beliefs already held in Indonesia. A third is the value of Islam to the common people, providing 'an ideological basis for individual worth, for solidarity in peasant and merchant communities, and for the integration of small parochial groups into larger societies' (Lapidus, 1988: 469).

The cultural manifestations of Islam differ widely throughout the Muslim world, and in South-East Asia, the influence of pre-Islamic religions and belief systems remains very important.

While many Muslims adhered to the high tradition defined by 'ulama' and Sufi teachings, many, if not most, lived in a mental world defined by the heritage of local cultures. For most Southeast Asian villagers, Islam was an element of a more complex social and religious identity and not the exclusive symbol of personal and collective life. (Lapidus, 1988: 488.)

Of the entire Muslim population of South-East Asia, not far short of half are ethnic Javanese, living mainly in Central Java, Yogyakarta, and East Java but scattered widely in other provinces of Indonesia as well. As far as high culture was concerned, in Java, Islam was moving into 'one of Asia's greatest political, aesthetic, religious and social creations, the Hindu–Buddhist Javanese state' (C. Geertz, 1968: 11). Little wonder, then, if the absorption of Islamic influences was pragmatic, gradualistic, and full of compromises, an absorption leading to definable differences in the religious culture of the upper classes, the peasantry, and the traders (C. Geertz, 1968: 13). The nature of Javanese Islam has been widely discussed, with general agreement that a large proportion of Javanese Muslims follow a variety of religious beliefs that differ considerably from orthodox Islam. This is different from saying that they do not adhere very strictly to the tenets of their faith, although this is probably true of a substantial proportion of adherents to most religions. Rather, it is to say that the faith to which many Javanese adhere is different from orthodox Islam. When pressed, they may say they are 'statistical Muslims' (i.e. Muslims when required to give their religion for official purposes), but whether they mean that they are not serious about religious belief and practice or whether they recognize that their religious beliefs differ from orthodox Islam is often difficult to determine.

Koentjaraningrat follows C. Geertz (1960) in making a clear distinction between two different variants of Javanese Islam, that is, the *agami Jawi* and the *agami Islam santri*, the first term meaning 'Javanese religion' and the second meaning 'Islam of the religious people'. 'The *Agami Jawi* manifestation of Javanese Islam represents an extensive complex of mystically inclined Hindu–Buddhistic beliefs and concepts, syncretistically integrated in an Islamic frame of reference' (Koentjaraningrat, 1985: 317), though the dominance of Hindu–Buddhistic folk beliefs tended to characterize the lower social classes, whereas further up the social scale, more sophisticated beliefs integrating Hindu–Buddhistic concepts of fate, reincarnation, pantheism, and magico-mysticism were prevalent.

By contrast, the *agami Islam santri* variant of Javanese Islam, 'although not totally devoid of animistic as well as Hindu–Buddhistic elements, is much closer to the formal dogma learnings of Islam', stressing observance of prayers, an intolerance for heterodox Javanese beliefs and practices, and a sense of the Muslim community or *ummat*. Based on the dichotomy between *santri* and non-*santri*, C. Geertz (1972) has noted that 'the Moslem community, properly understood, is a minority community in Java—a large minority but nevertheless a minority'.

Syncretistic versions of Islam are not confined to Java. In Kelantan and Trengganu, though Islam as practised by most villagers adheres more closely to the *santri* version of Islam than does the *agami Jawi*, animistic and Hindu–Buddhistic elements are present, as students returning to the region in the 1970s, after being influenced by the *dakwah*[2] movement during their overseas studies, were quick to point out.

While differences in Islamic beliefs and practices within the region are important, it should also be stressed that aside from ethnicity and language, Islamic identity, however understood, is the one shared factor among the Malay-Muslim populations.

Marriage and the Family: The Malay World in the International Context

Marriage and Family Systems

Marx and Weber specified three basic stages of social organization, to each of which a particular kind of marriage system can be considered more likely to adhere. The first is where the lineage (normally patrilineal) is the principal unit of production and consumption. Marriage functions as the recruitment mechanism for the lineage but also as a means of alliance with other lineages, and given its central role in the security and prosperity of the lineage, it is tightly controlled by the elders (McDonald, 1985: 87–8). This kind of social organization is not relevant to the present study.

The second form of social organization is where power is concentrated at a higher level than that of the lineage (perhaps in a feudal, manorial system or in a bureaucratized nation-state) and social differentiation is more highly developed. The lineage may serve as a link in the chain of authority or it may have been largely supplanted; in either case, members of a lineage may be able to gain advantage through the wider power structure without depending on the elders of their own lineage. Peasant agricultural systems are a prominent example. Rights of access to the means of production will be primarily inheritable, so the younger generation will still be heavily dependent on the favour of the older generation. Inheritance systems will affect marriage patterns (Davis and Blake, 1956: 215–18). Primogeniture will tend to lead to high levels of celibacy, whereas in the system of shared inheritance emphasized by Goody (1976) and characteristic of much of South-East Asia, marriage and inheritance are the expectation of all brothers and sisters within families (P. C. Smith, 1980: 77).[3] Alliance through marriage will be important to the ruling class, so marriage will be tightly controlled by the parental generation. Single people of the peasantry may be given more choice in choosing a partner, but this freedom may need to be restricted by the rules of class or caste endogamy.

This basic type of social organization characterizes the Middle East, South Asia, and East Asia, and, further along the continuum towards the third type, South-East Asia, and Latin America. It also characterized Europe up to the Renaissance and beyond. The family in the Middle East, South Asia, and East Asia is strongly patriarchal and patrilocal, while in Latin America it is patriarchal to a lesser degree. In South-East

Asia, however, family organization 'is generally more bilateral in nature; here an individual may look to either or both paternal and maternal kin for assistance, and residence after marriage is not strictly or consistently prescribed. Expediency is often the principal factor in decisions about residence.' (McDonald, 1985: 89.)

The third form of social organization is the advanced capitalist mode of production characterized by urbanization, industrialization, and individualism. Marriage is by free choice, the marriage market is relatively unrestricted, and marriage payments are no longer relevant. The extent to which this type of marriage occurs in developing countries depends primarily on the extent to which the vehicles of Westernization— industrialization, education, urbanization, and perhaps Christianity— have penetrated the society (McDonald, 1985: 89).

A marriage transition is in progress throughout Asia (P. C. Smith, 1980). Basically, it appears to involve the movement of large sections, at least, of the populations from the form of social organization described as stage two above to that of stage three; or from traditional to non-traditional bases of marriage decisions. This is consistent with Goode's (1963) provocative thesis that global industrialization is causing a convergence of family systems around the world towards the conjugal or European form. A range of models of causal structure have been put forward, none of them entirely satisfactory.[4]

P. C. Smith (1980: 61) is undoubtedly correct when he argues that the simple distinction should be maintained

between factors of predominant significance within the traditional Asian village matrix—kinship, land, production, reproduction, inheritance—and those generated by processes in the modernizing larger society, in particular, by expanding educational opportunity, changing workforce activity and urbanization. . . . The village matrix allows little room for purely individual choice; the modern milieu supports and expects it. If the nuptiality transition in Asia is linked to social and economic transition, then the force of the traditional determinants of marriage ought to be receding and the impact of modern influences on the rise.

A key question for the present book is the extent to which religion influences marriage systems. As McDonald (1985: 89) observes, 'While it can be argued that religion is a product of the social organization and one of its supporting planks, in the course of time religion develops a life and structure of its own. The moral teachings of the religion may therefore exert an influence above and beyond the form of social organization.' Goody (1976: 119) also acknowledges that, in some circumstances, religion or ideology can have a dominant effect on marriage systems by extending particular patterns to very different types of society by the process of imperial conquest or religious conversion. This will be taken up again later with discussion of some of the idiosyncratic features of marriage systems in Islamic South-East Asia.

Women's Roles, Marriage, and the Family in Sunni Islam

Teachings about sexuality, women's roles, marriage, and the family differ between different variants of Islam, and in any case become adapted to the particular cultural and economic setting in which the religion is being practised, as clearly evidenced by comparisons between the Malay world, the Middle East, and the Islamic parts of the Indian subcontinent. To compare Mandelbaum (1989) on North India, Pakistan, and Bangladesh and Goode (1963: Chapter 3) on the Arabic countries with H. Geertz (1961) on Java, or Rosemary Firth (1966) or Strange (1981) on the Malaysian East Coast, is to compare different worlds. The Arab and South Asian obsession with 'women's seclusion and men's honour', though not entirely absent in the Malay realm, is present in such muted form as to be almost unrecognizable.

Images of sexuality underlie the legal situation and cultural norms affecting women's life in Islamic societies. The Moroccan anthropologist Mernissi (1975) argues that Islam offers a double image of sexuality. Although the prevailing contemporary view is that men are active in their interaction with women, while women are passive, there is an underlying view (as formulated in the classical interpretation of the Koran by Imam Ghazali) of an active female sexuality casting woman as the hunter and man as the passive victim, unable to resist the cunning and intrigue of women. The disruptive potential and disorder of women's active sexuality require that women be controlled so that they do not tempt men; curbing active female sexuality is at the basis of many of Islam's family institutions (Nicolaison, 1983: 5–6). An alternative view is provided by Haeri (1989: 67–72), who stresses that ambivalent perceptions of women in Islam stem from the multiple images of women in the Koran, and that this ambivalence 'has been reinforced historically through socialization, education, and enculturation, and legitimized by pervasive patriarchal ideologies and cultural beliefs'. Haeri claims that in Shiite ideology at least, the nature of female sexuality is left ambiguous; the strong sense of power imputed to female sexuality is rather because of 'what it signifies to men and the reaction it presumably provokes in them'.

The strength of alternative images of sexuality and of different emphases in family law differs between different Islamic societies and in the same society over time. Nevertheless, there are some basic teachings derived from the Koran and the *hadith* (sayings of the Prophet, of which there are a vast number, of varying degrees of authenticity) which underlie many aspects of marriage, divorce, and polygamy in Islamic societies, including Malay society. The difficult question arises as to whether Koranic texts are normative and specify externally valid rules, as the traditionalists argue, or whether some of them are ethical injunctions rather than legal requirements, thus enabling adaptations with changes in historical and social conditions, as the modernists argue.

Islamic teachings about women are the subject of controversy. Many Western critics and some, especially women, from the Islamic world (e.g. Azizah, 1982) argue that women's rights are suppressed in Islam.

Many of the indicators often used to denote low female status (Mason, 1984)—purdah, polygyny, patrilocal residence, arranged marriage, an emphasis on bridal virginity, male divorce rights, occupational segregation of the sexes, and son preference—have traditionally been associated with Muslim societies. Proponents of Islam, on the other hand, argue that early Islam enhanced the status of women in Arabian society, and that the historical conditions of Middle Eastern societies, and not Islam itself, were responsible for the subordination and segregation of women. Others, indeed, argue that Islam respects women, provides for their protection and security, and guarantees them many legal and property rights. The literature is vast (much of it is cited in Beck and Keddie, 1978; Rahman, 1982; Utas, 1983), and the debate has become so highly politicized and ideological, incorporating broader issues such as secularization versus Islamization and Westernization versus cultural authenticity, that it is difficult to take a dispassionate position.

All that can be done here is to try to identify certain teachings in Islam and aspects of Islamic law which can be expected to influence aspects of marriage and its dissolution, and to summarize briefly the historical development of this law.

The Koran's teachings on the subject of women can be viewed as part of its effort to strengthen and ameliorate the condition of the weaker segments of society in pre-Islamic Arabia, including orphans, slaves, the poor, and women.

It mentions both men and women separately as being absolutely equal in virtue and piety with such unflinching regularity that it would be superfluous to give any particular documentation. (Rahman, 1982: 291.)

The main burden of the Quranic family legislation, it seems clear today, was to stabilize the nuclear family, limit polygamy and divorce, and to protect the interests of wives and children. (Bellah, 1970: 154.)

Insofar as it prescribes rules of behaviour, however, the Quran is not primarily a legislative document, but rather the declaration of the fundamental Islamic ethic.... (Coulson and Hinchcliffe, 1978: 37.)

But a considerable period separated the Koran from the classic formulation of Islamic law, and 'the general Quranic norms and injunctions suffered progressive dilution during this time' (Coulson and Hinchcliffe, 1978: 38). According to Bellah, the main tendencies of Koranic thinking about the family suffered a serious retrogression in the early centuries of Islam.

Unfortunately, in accordance with the way Islamic law developed, it was the post-Quranic and not the Quranic provisions that became the effective precedents in Sharia family law.... Practices tending to undermine inner family equality and solidarity and elevate patriarchal arbitrariness were pronounced legitimate. Traditional Islam thus presented a mixed heritage to the modern family reformers. (Bellah, 1970: 154.)

The ... ethical injunctions of the Quran were rarely transformed into legally enforceable rules, but were recognized as binding only on the individual conscience. Thus, for example, a husband was never required to show that he had any reasonable or proper motive before exercising his power to repudiate his wife. And while the Quran might insist upon the impartial treatment of co-wives in polygamous unions, classical Islamic law did not elevate this requirement into any kind of legal restriction upon a husband's entrenched right to have four wives. (Coulson and Hinchcliffe, 1978: 38.)

Some provisions in the Koran itself stand in the way of legal reforms related to women's status: for example, the specific authorization for men to have four wives, and the provision that a male shall always inherit twice as much as a female (Coulson and Hinchcliffe, 1978: 47).[5] But the provisions of Islamic law inimical to women's interests, which reformers in the Islamic world have been trying to change, have more frequently been based on *hadith*. The Koran does not require purdah or the veil, and the provision that a woman's evidence in court has half the value of a man's is based on a *hadith*, albeit one that is included in the most authoritative *hadith* collections (Rahman, 1982: 290–2).

Provisions of Islamic law with a close bearing on marriage and the family include those dealing with the arrangement of marriage, polygamy, divorce, and custody of children. Relevant provisions will be briefly discussed, stressing the implementation of marriage laws in various parts of the Islamic world. The legal situation in South-East Asia will be discussed in Chapter 2.

On marriage arrangement, all schools of Islamic law except the Hanafi provide that even adult women may be contracted in marriage without their consent and against their will by their father or paternal grandfather, but not by other *wali* (marriage guardians). However, legal reforms providing minimum ages for marriage and requiring the consent of the bride were enacted in Tunisia in 1956 and in Morocco in 1958 (Coulson and Hinchcliffe, 1978: 39; Beaujot, 1986). Traditional Islamic law allows a man to have up to four wives at any one time, and to pronounce *talak* (divorce) without restriction. Although the Koran stresses that a man should not marry an additional wife if he does not feel able to treat his several wives equally, the law regards this purely as a matter for the man's own conscience. Few Islamic countries have been willing to eliminate the right to polygyny and easy divorce: in the late 1970s, only Tunisia, Turkey, Albania, and the Muslim states of the Soviet Union had done so (White, 1978: 57). In Turkey and the Communist Muslim states, this was in the context of replacing religious law with a code of civil law based on European legal codes. More interesting was the abolition of these practices in Tunisia within the framework of an Islamic explanation. 'The abolition of polygamy was explained as being based upon the Quranic stipulation that men must treat their wives equally even though no mortal is capable of being so fair. The contradiction is interpreted to mean that Muhammad was not in favour of polygamy under general circumstances.' (White, 1978: 58–9.)

Divorce law has posed the greatest problem to reformers in the Islamic world, though the problems differed according to the school of Islamic law being followed. Under traditional Hanafi law, women had no right to obtain a dissolution of their marriage, no matter how ill-treated they had been, whereas Maliki law was the most liberal on this issue. However, reformers in the Islamic world have concentrated on the need 'to restrict the husband's unfettered power to repudiate his wife at will, for this power represented an even more serious threat to the welfare of the Muslim woman than her own lack of the right to seek a dissolution of her marriage' (Coulson and Hinchcliffe, 1978: 43). Between the 1950s and 1970s, countries such as Syria, Tunisia, Pakistan, Iran, Iraq, and South Yemen introduced legal changes which in some cases required all repudiations to be pronounced in a court of law and in others specified compensation payments. Iran in 1975 and South Yemen in 1974 totally abolished the husband's power of unilateral re-pudiation, though new legislation in Iran, ratified in 1979 after the Islamic Revolution, reinstated this right (Tabari and Yeganeh, 1982: 236).

The traditional law relating to the custody of children is rigid, stipulating that the woman who is divorced or widowed retains the custody of her children only for a limited period of time, after which they pass automatically into the care of their father or nearest male agnate relative. In Shafii law, 'where ... the mother has not remarried, the custody of a girl remains with the mother until she is married and that of a boy until the completion of his seventh year' (Ibrahim, 1965: 235). The mother, however, loses custody if she marries a man who is not related to the child within the prohibited degrees; in such a case, the father or nearest male agnate relative remains the guardian of the child, and has the right to control the child's education and to contract the child in marriage without the consent of the mother. Throughout most of the Muslim world, however, including Islamic South-East Asia, these traditional rules regarding custody of children have been relaxed.

Marriage and the Family in Pre-Islamic Malay Cultures

Islamic beliefs, when introduced into South-East Asia, had to come to terms with a culture vastly different from that of the Middle East, South Asia, or the Mediterranean, the main regions of Islamic influence up to that time. In a recent study, Reid (1988: Chapter 4) has assessed the testimony of many historical sources on South-East Asia from the mid-thirteenth to the late seventeenth century on the role of women and aspects of marriage in these societies. Islamization was already proceeding in some of these societies at the time to which some of these sources refer. Nevertheless, it is possible from many of these early writings to obtain a picture of the status of women in the region before Islam.

The picture is one of relatively high female autonomy and economic importance. Women engaged in transplanting and harvesting of rice, vegetable growing, weaving, pottery making, and marketing. They were also prominent in larger-scale trade, diplomacy, entertainment, literature, and statecraft; corps of women formed part of the palace guard of major rulers (Reid, 1988: 163–72). The value of daughters was never questioned in South-East Asia as it was in China, India, and the Middle East; and bride-wealth was paid at marriage, the reverse of the European or Indian dowry, and normally went directly to the bride (Reid, 1988: 146–7). Postmarital residence was more normally in the wife's than the husband's village. Women played a strong, rather than passive, role in sexual relations (Reid, 1988: 147–50).

The dominant marriage pattern was one of monogamy, reinforced by the ease of divorce for both sides. Polygamy was largely confined to the rulers. On divorce, the rule appeared to be that the wife (or her parents) kept the bride-wealth if the husband took the initiative to end the marriage but had to repay it if she took the initiative. 'Pre-marital sexual relations were regarded indulgently, and virginity at marriage was not expected of either party.' (Reid, 1988: 153.) On the other hand, European observers commented on the constancy in marriage of South-East Asians.

The broad pattern of sexual relations—relative pre-marital freedom, monogamy and fidelity within marriage (which was easily dissolved by divorce), and a strong female position in the sexual game—conflicted in different ways with the practices of all the world religions which were increasing their hold on Southeast Asia.... The sharpest conflict might have been expected with Islamic law, which made women both legally and economically dependent on their husbands and markedly restricted their rights to initiate divorce. Pre-marital sexual relations (*zina'*) were also punished very severely under Islamic law.... (Reid, 1988: 156–7.)

The conflict between traditional attitudes and Islamic injunctions was greatest among the wealthy urban mercantile class, whose marriages involved both property and status. Among this group, arranged marriage at puberty appears to have spread in reaction to the prevailing premarital sexual permissiveness. Severe penalties for adultery were sometimes enforced as early as 1600 in important Islamic trading centres such as Aceh and Brunei, and some attempts made to impose a more male-dominated procedure for divorce; but in general rigorous implementation of Islamic codes did not appear to make rapid headway (Reid, 1988: 157–8).

There is some conflicting evidence about prevailing ages at marriage, but Reid (1988: 158–60) concludes that among the population as a whole (as distinct from the trading classes in the large towns strongly affected by Islam), female marriages were generally between 15 and 21 years of age.

The Islamic influences which gradually spread through the region from the late thirteenth century onwards influenced family and marriage customs to a greater or lesser degree depending on the strength of the Islamic impact and the resilience of pre-Islamic cultural forms in particular areas. The next section of this chapter will briefly describe Malay-Muslim family and marriage customs in more recent but still traditional times (the 1950s), when there had been ample time for Islamic influence to permeate the customs and legal structures of the region, and before the vast socio-economic changes of the post-war, independence era had proceeded very far.

The Malay-Muslim Family

The Malay-Muslim family in the 1950s still reflected elements of its pre-Islamic past as described in the previous section, and because of these elements it differed greatly in many respects from families in the Islamic heartland of the Middle East or South Asia. Though female roles in the wider society had been constrained, women continued to play significant roles in the economy and frequently dominant roles in the family. Their freedom for independent action increased greatly once they had married and produced children.

Given Goody's stress on inheritance systems in influencing marriage patterns, it should be stressed here that Islamic law knows nothing of primogeniture, but stresses division of property among all children, albeit giving sons twice the share of daughters. Daughters may frequently forfeit these rights as a means of substantiating other rights in natal kinship or on the grounds that they were compensated by bridal gifts at marriage (Pastner, 1980: 157). Inheritance rules in the Malay world varied. Apart from the matrilineal option of Minangkabau society in both Indonesia (mainly West Sumatra) and Malaysia (mainly Negri Sembilan), other systems featured compromises between *adat* or customary law which favoured equal shares for men and women and Islamic law which prescribes a double share for men. Generally, throughout the Malay world, equal shares were favoured, and Islamic law on inheritance was never effectively implemented (C. Geertz, 1963: 47, 81). Children inherited from mother and father separately.[6] Therefore in landholding families, the wife in most cases could be expected to provide roughly half of the new family's land resources (Rudie, 1983: 132–4). *Adat* law frequently provided for the inheritance of the family home by the youngest daughter on the understanding that she would care for her parents in old age.

In one major respect, Islam had succeeded in overcoming the pre-Islamic heritage, namely, in achieving much tighter reign on pubescent girls and ensuring that their virginity was protected through early, parent-arranged marriages. However, in other major respects, it had failed to change the pre-existing pattern very much. One example is the persistence of flexible conventions about postmarital residence; another is the survival of high divorce rates. On the latter, it is not so much that Islam had failed to change the pre-existing pattern, but rather that Islamic law had been appropriated to support the prevailing easy-divorce system. These matters will be discussed in more detail in Chapters 4 and 6.

Marriage was frequently at very young ages, around the time of the girl's first menstruation. Young ages at marriage meant that the couple was very immature, and the custom was that both husband and wife would live with one or other set of parents (or both) for a few years before moving into their own home.

One strong cultural tradition among the Malays was the ideal of marrying relatives, particularly first cousins (Downs, 1967: 139–40; Koentjaraningrat, 1985: 123).[7] The *adat* appears to have differed somewhat from area to area. For example, among Singapore Malays, cross-cousins, children of two sisters, second cousins (except the children of two male first cousins), and third cousins were considered equally suitable partners. However, there was a strong traditional ban against the union of the children of two brothers, on the grounds that such marriages invariably led to family quarrels and divorce (Djamour, 1966: 68–71). In the Kelantanese village studied by Downs (1967: 140), though, there appeared to be no objection to marriages between the children of two brothers, and no such objection is mentioned in other village studies referred to elsewhere in this book.

The preference for marriage with cousins was also a feature of the Arab world (Goode, 1963: 93–5), where the preference was for patrilateral parallel cousin marriage (i.e. marriage between the children of two brothers). This raises the question of whether the similar Malay preference predated Islam or was another effect of the coming of Islam. The answer to this question is that the preference did predate Islam: cross-cousin marriage is a common feature of the Austronesian peoples from Madagascar to the Pacific. For the discussion of cross-cousin marriage among the non-Islamic Karo, see Singarimbun (1975) and among various populations in eastern Indonesia, most of them non-Islamic, see the papers in Fox (1980).

Among Malaysian Malays, the ideal of marrying a relative was not followed very frequently in practice. In Kampong Jeram, Kelantan, only 8 per cent of marriages were between cousins of any kind, and a further 2 per cent between distant relatives (Downs, 1967: 139). In Galok, Kelantan, 14 per cent of women had married relatives, slightly less than half of whom were first or second cousins (Kuchiba, Tsubouchi, and Maeda, 1979: 160). In one village in Negri Sembilan, 12 per cent of pre-1960 marriages were cross-cousin and a further 26 per cent between other kin, but these percentages declined substantially among post-1960 marriages (Peletz, 1988: 238–40). In the Malaysian Marriage Survey (1981), 6 per cent of Malay female respondents had married their first cousin, and another 11 per cent married another relative. In urban areas, 3 per cent had married a first cousin and 12 per cent another relative (Tan et al., 1986: 118). Moreover, when asked whether it is better to marry a relative, more than 60 per cent said no, compared to about 16 per cent who said yes (Tan et al., 1986: 117). In Rusila, Trengganu, marriages between first cousins were definitely not preferred, on the grounds that difficulties between married cousins would have negative repercussions on the social relationships of their parents and other kin (Strange, 1981: 109).

From data collected in the Indonesian Marriage Survey (1978) and other village studies, it is clear that there is considerable variation between different parts of Indonesia in the prevalence of marriage to relatives. The proportion of respondents who had married relatives (according to the Indonesian Marriage Survey unless otherwise noted) ranged from 81 per cent in a village study in Sumbawa (Goethals, 1967: 48–9), 53 per cent in the Banjarese study, 51 per cent and

28 per cent respectively in two villages in Madura (Niehof, 1985: 112), 34 per cent in the Acehnese study, and 30 per cent in the Betawi study in Jakarta down to 15 per cent in the Javanese and less than 5 per cent in the South Sumatran study. The fairly low prevalence of marriage between kin in the Javanese case-study cited above is supported by other evidence that the Javanese are less prone than most other groups in the Malay world to marry kin. For example, Jay (1969: 130–1) found that fewer than 4 per cent of marriages in Modjokuto were between kin, and there was a strongly held consensus that marriage between kin was unwise.

It is hard to tell how much of the marriage to kin in the Malay world was due to a preference for this kind of marriage, and how much simply to the frequent interaction with kin in the village setting, automatically leading to frequent marriage between kin in the absence of any taboos on such marriages. In many studies, it appears that such marriages were more common—and more favoured—in the past. Support expressed for the practice was frequently less than the practice itself, the usual argument against it being that should divorce occur, family relationships would suffer.

The Malay household observed the Islamic principle of *nafkah* or the obligation of the husband to provide adequate food, housing, and clothing for his wife; failure to provide maintenance is grounds for divorce under Islamic law. Where the wife worked, her income was seen as supplementary; her main duty was to provide domestic services and, in farming or fishing communities, to contribute her labour in those activities normally performed by females. As will be discussed in Chapter 4, the wife was frequently given control over the household finances. Husbands and wives held resources separately, and worked not only to improve the economic position of the family as a unit, but also their own individual position within it. Wives held resources in land or gold, and sometimes maintained secret savings of which their husbands were unaware. This was understandable, given the ever-present possibility of divorce (Swift, 1963: 280; Li, 1989: 18–33). 'The actual willingness of the parties to give generously to each other, rather than demarcate their property, save, and accumulate separately and secretly, tends to reflect the current state of stability of the marriage.' (Li, 1989: 27.)

Traditional Marriage Arrangements and Ceremonies in the Malay World

To give something of the flavour of marriage customs in Islamic South-East Asia in the 1950s, the following brief description of the negotiations and marriage ceremonies widely prevailing at the time may be useful. The description draws heavily on H. Geertz (1961) for Java, Niehof (1985) for Madura, Rosemary Firth (1966), Strange (1981), and Kuchiba, Tsubouchi, and Maeda (1979) for the East Coast of Peninsular Malaysia, and Mohtar (1979) for the West Coast of Peninsular Malaysia. There were, of course, regional and social class differences which cannot be fully captured in a composite description.[8] Even in one small region, there could be great variety in the forms of wedding followed (Niehof, 1985: 125).

The early stages of arranging a marriage consisted in discreet enquiries as to whether the girl sought after was available. One or more representatives of the boy's family (usually an elderly and respected person, frequently a close relative such as an aunt or uncle) visited the house of the prospective bride to find out whether she was potentially available. Elaborate and allegorical speech was normally used, referring to whether the beautiful and fragrant flower espied in the garden had yet been plucked, or visited by the bee. Having established potential availability and interest, time was allowed for the girl's side to make further enquiries and if all was satisfactory, the boy's party again visited the girl's house to obtain a formal answer to the proposal and to discuss the engagement date, marriage settlement on the bride, and wedding expenses. At the engagement ceremony, additional matters were discussed and decided on, including the length of the engagement, and the dates for the solemnization and the wedding ceremonies. At the engagement, too, the boy's party presented the engagement ring, along with the money for the marriage settlement, and gifts were exchanged. Agreement was reached on compensation to be paid should either party break the engagement.

Among Malays, marriage was established through two ceremonies: the conclusion of the marriage contract (*nikah*) and the wedding reception (*bersanding*). Normally, the marriage contract was concluded at the bride's parents' home. The *imam* was invited, and in the presence of relatives and two witnesses the bridegroom and the bride's *wali*, or guardian (normally her father), signed the marriage contract. The bride was not present at this ceremony but signed the marriage contract in another room. The marriage payment was made at this time, the whole of which usually became the bride's property. In certain areas, this payment was dispensed with, or used to provide household essentials for the newly married couple (Swift, 1963).

The wedding reception followed the same day or the following day, at the bride's house, and featured the *bersanding* ceremony, where the young couple were placed on an elaborate dais for all visitors to see. The following description refers to Kelantanese rural weddings (Kuchiba, Tsubouchi, and Maeda, 1979: 158–9). Among wealthier families, invitations indicating the day and the place are issued in advance. Among poorer families, invitations are likely to be in person. The wedding feast may be attended by dozens, hundreds, even more than a thousand, guests, depending on the status and wealth of the bride's family. If there is not enough room in the house for the guests to eat together, marquees or temporary buildings are erected outdoors. The guests arrive with gifts about noon, and at about four in the afternoon the groom and his relatives arrive in procession for the reception, which focuses on the ceremonial enthronement of the bride and groom on decorated chairs or a bed. The groom's relatives stay for one or two hours, then return home, leaving the groom behind.

The groom stays at the bride's house for about one month, and then returns to his parents' house with his bride (*sambut menantu*). In better-off households, the groom's parents give a feast at this time, to which they invite relatives and other villagers as well as a group from the bride's family. After this, the couple is free to set up house with one or the other set of parents or separately.

Outline of the Book and Data Sources

Following a brief introduction to the Malay-Muslim world and some Islamic beliefs and practices pertaining to marriage and divorce in Chapter 1, Chapter 2 of this book goes on to look at the economic, social, and legal context in which the Muslim populations of South-East Asia live, stressing the dramatic changes that have taken place since World War II. Chapter 3 will then examine trends and differentials in age at first marriage, while Chapter 4 will assess what is known about the causes of these changes. In Chapters 5 and 6 attention turns to divorce, again focusing first on trends and differentials (both regional and according to the characteristics of individuals) and then on an assessment of causes. Case-studies of the changing divorce situation in Kelantan and West Java, where divorce was traditionally very prevalent, will be presented. Polygamy is then discussed in Chapter 7, and in Chapter 8 the effect of changes in marriage and divorce on fertility. Chapter 9 draws the diverse strands together and reaches some conclusions.

There is no attempt to treat comprehensively all aspects of marriage and divorce. Not much attention is paid to marriage ceremonies, as many descriptions of these ceremonies in the different subgroups of the Malay populations of the region are already available. More attention is given to female than to male age at marriage. In Malaysia and Singapore, where Malays live alongside large non-Malay populations, there is no systematic attempt to assess Malay–non-Malay differences, though this is sometimes done. The main aim of the book is to identify and explain the broad changes in patterns of marriage and marital dissolution among Malay-Muslim populations, and to examine some of their key effects.

This book makes use of a wide range of both primary and secondary sources of data. Much of the background discussion is based on ethnographic, anthropological, and sociological studies conducted in South-East Asia. Newspapers and Malay and Indonesian novels have provided further flavour. The more statistical part of the marriage analysis utilizes censuses and surveys, both large nationally representative surveys and smaller surveys of particular groups or regions. The author participated directly in a number of these surveys. Details of the surveys utilized are provided in Appendix 1, to guide the reader through the labyrinth and avoid cluttering the text with too much detail. Statistical analysis of divorce draws not only on census and survey data but also on registered marriages and divorces among Muslims in the region. The registration data are variable in quality and not readily available, especially in the case of Malaysia, Southern Thailand, and the Philippines. Further details are also given in Appendix 1. The final source is the author's own observations during a total of more than ten years of residence in the region at intervals since 1964, including some years of lecturing in local universities and periods of fieldwork in various parts of the region.

Before launching into the book proper, it may be desirable here to present a thumbnail sketch of the trends on which it will focus: the broad picture before the details. What will be analysed are some of the most dramatic changes in the structure and internal dynamics of a traditional society over a relatively short period to be found anywhere in the world. Certainly, it is hard to find comparable changes elsewhere in the Islamic world. But then Islam, despite its claims to be a revealed religion backed by scriptures and a body of law, is far from monolithic in its daily observance and its impact on the social and family life of its adherents around the world. Malay society and family life is not Middle Eastern society and family life, despite the efforts of some fundamentalist groups to make it so, in the belief that Middle Eastern styles of dress, full application of the *syariah* (Islamic religious law), and female seclusion are more truly Islamic.

What, then, are the key trends to be described in this book? In a nutshell, the main trend is the change from a pattern of fairly tight control over adolescent females and universal, early, or parent-arranged marriage to one of freer female adolescence, much later, self-arranged marriage, and greater options for non-marriage or very late marriage. A parallel trend is observed in the movement away from high rates of divorce, typically soon after marriage, and from relatively common polygamy. The changes are still in process, and they have proceeded much further in some parts of the Malay world than in others. It is unlikely that they will converge everywhere in the Malay world; after all, before the changes really got under way in the 1960s, the Malay world was characterized by wide differences between subgroups and subregions in all these aspects of marriage.

One net impact of all of these changes, along with the decreased incidence of widowhood among women in the childbearing ages, is that Malay women are now spending a smaller proportion of their potential reproductive lives in a marital union. Another is that children nowadays are more likely than before to grow to adolescence living with their natural parents in an unbroken family situation.

In attempting to explain what has been going on, the book will invoke aspects of rapid social and economic change, including educational expansion, the communications revolution, changing labour markets, urbanization, consumerism, Westernization, Islamic reform movements, and new legislation. Change has been so pervasive across these societies that it is impossible to make much progress in sorting out cause from effect; everything has been changing simultaneously. However, there is no doubt that aspects of culture are resilient in the face of change, and this is demonstrated not only by the persistence of wide differences between subgroups of Malay-Muslim populations exposed to similar economic, social, and institutional changes but also by the persistence of wide differences between Malay populations and other groups (e.g. Chinese and Indians) exposed to similar influences within particular national settings.

1. For scholarly accounts of the history of Islam in South-East Asia, see Benda (1970), De Graaf (1970), Roff (1970), and Johns (1987).

2. The word *dakwah* literally means to call or invite, as in missionary work. In the Malaysian context as in many other countries, the meaning has been expanded to include the task of making Muslims better Muslims. In popular understanding, the movement is associated with fundamentalist Islamic teachings and with the adoption of distinctive forms of dress, including, as a minimum, the mini-*telekung* head-dress, but also, among more extreme groups, the *hijab*, an ankle-length one-piece long-sleeved robe, worn with socks to keep the feet hidden, or even the face veil and gloved hands.

3. Goody refers to the mode of inheritance which requires distribution of an individual's property to children of both sexes, thus diffusing it outside the clan or lineage, as 'diverging devolution'. It characterizes many systems of advanced agriculture and hierarchical social order. He argues that such a system would make for in-marriage or up-marriage (homogamy or hypergamy), and that the implications of such a system would be control of the sexuality of girls, prohibition of premarital sex, arrangement of 'proper' matches, monogamy, and low rates of divorce (Goody, 1976: 119–20). All these fit the traditional Malay-Muslim world except the low rates of divorce.

4. Dixon (1971) identifies variables bearing on the 'feasibility' or 'desirability' of marriage, and those impinging on the 'availability of suitable spouses'. Fawcett (1973) distinguished factors influencing when to marry, whom to marry, and whether to marry at all, and outlines a scheme involving psychological traits, immediate situational factors, societal barriers and facilitators to marriage, and the perceived benefits and costs of marriage. Becker's (1991) theory of marriage is based on economists' utility maximization theory. Though envisaged to apply to a situation of individual choice of marriage partners, paradoxically it is probably more relevant to a situation of parent-arranged marriage, where 'extraneous' factors such as falling in love are irrelevant.

5. More specifically, a woman's inheritance is half that of male relatives with the same blood relationship with the deceased. The Koran specifies that a wife whose deceased husband is survived by descendants inherits a mere one-eighth of his estate, but if her husband is not survived by descendants, her share is increased to one-quarter (Coulson and Hinchcliffe, 1978: 46, 57; Lapidus, 1988: 30).

6. The property of husband and wife before marriage remained separate, and on death reverted to the children or parents of the individual, not the spouse (Swift, 1963: 275; Jay, 1969: 63).

7. The present Malaysian Prime Minister, Mahathir bin Mohamad, in his book *The Malay Dilemma* (which continued to be banned even when he was Deputy Prime Minister) argued that the rural Malay stock was rarely enriched by inter-ethnic marriages, and that this was further aggravated by the habit of family inbreeding. Malays, especially rural Malays, prefer to marry relatives. First cousin marriages were and still are frequent, and the result is the propagation of the poorer characteristics, whether dominant or recessive, originally found in the brothers or sisters who were parents of the married couple (Mahathir, 1970: 29).

8. Geographic differences are readily apparent in the description of marriage ceremonies in villages in different parts of Indonesia in Koentjaraningrat (1967a).

2
The Social, Economic, and Legal Context: Influences on Traditional Culture

Post-war Political, Economic, and Social Changes

Economic Growth and Urbanization

PROFOUND political and economic changes have marked the post-World War II era throughout the Malay realm. In Indonesia, Malaysia, and Singapore, the former European colonial powers could never regain their former hold once their prestige had been irrevocably destroyed by their humiliation by Japan before the eyes of their colonial subjects. Independence therefore came—bloodily in Indonesia, peacefully in Malaysia and Singapore.

Singapore then set about achieving an economic growth record that has been the envy of the world (see Table 2.1). The Republic of Korea, Taiwan, and Hong Kong were grouped with Singapore in the developmental and popular literature by the late 1970s as the 'four Asian tigers' or, more prosaically, as the newly industrializing countries (NICs), their economic growth performance an inspiration, or a standing rebuke, to other less successful countries. Malaysia and Thailand, growing steadily though less dramatically than Singapore, were less noticed until the late 1980s, when they suddenly became acclaimed candidates for the title of NIC, or newly industrializing economies (NIEs) as they are now called. Economic growth in the south of Thailand, where the vast majority of the Thai Muslims live, however, has been less spectacular than that in the Bangkok–Central Plains area.

Indonesia's economy was left far behind by the other countries until the late 1960s, owing to disruptions during the fight for independence and economic mismanagement during the Sukarno regime. However, since the late 1960s, guided by a steady policy course set by the economic technocrats in government and assisted by the spectacular rise in oil prices in the early 1970s, Indonesia has also entered a period of impressive economic growth (Booth, 1992).

The structure of these economies has changed, with a relative shift out of agriculture and a move into industry and services (Nayer, 1987).

TABLE 2.1
ASEAN: Economic Growth Indicators, 1965–1991

	GDP Growth (Average Annual)		GNP Per Capita	
	1965–80 (%)	1980–91 (%)	1991 (US$)	Average Annual Growth Rate, 1965–91 (%)
Indonesia	8.0	5.6	610	4.3
Malaysia	7.3	5.7	2,520	4.0
Philippines	5.9	1.1	730	1.6
Singapore	10.1	6.6	14,210	7.2
Thailand	7.2	7.9	1,570	4.0
Lower middle income	6.5	2.7	1,590	2.6
Upper middle income	5.6	2.1	3,530	2.3

Source: World Bank (1990: Tables 1 and 2; 1993: Tables 1 and 2).

In Malaysia, the industrial base remains narrow, with electronics alone accounting for 50 per cent of total manufactured exports in 1988 (Mahathir, 1991: 12), and in Indonesia, manufacturing employment continues to be concentrated in traditional, labour-intensive, small-scale, and cottage industries (Jones and Manning, 1992: 389). Nevertheless, industrialization is proceeding apace in both countries.

As a concomitant of structural economic change, urbanization levels have increased, as shown in Table 2.2. Developments in transportation have brought many formerly isolated areas into closer contact with the mainstream of national life (Leinbach and Chia, 1989). In Malaysia, the transportation infrastructure was already quite good at the time of independence, and the typical village anywhere on the western side of the main range had frequent bus services to larger towns. The East Coast states of Kelantan and Trengganu were nevertheless quite isolated until the mid-1960s. There had been a very slow rail connection from the West Coast since 1931, and the road trip remained long and arduous, with frequent ferry crossings of rivers. In the monsoon season, Kelantan was sometimes cut off for weeks. By the late 1970s, all ferries had been replaced by bridges, and the road trip from Kuala Lumpur was down to about eleven hours (Jones, 1981: fn. 34). The far south of Thailand was also quite isolated, although it had been linked by rail with Bangkok since 1917. In Indonesia, the transport infrastructure left by the Dutch, which was seriously deficient outside of Java, ran down during the 1950s and 1960s (Dick and Forbes, 1992). In Sumatra, Sulawesi, and Kalimantan, land transport systems were embryonic and communications very difficult indeed before construction of sections of the Trans-Sumatra and Trans-Sulawesi highways led to some improvement in the 1970s and 1980s, especially in Sumatra. Even in Java, the road system deteriorated badly in the 1960s

TABLE 2.2

Singapore, Malaysia, and Indonesia: Economic and Social Indicators for Selected Malay Populations, 1960–1985

Country/Indicator	1960	1970	1980	1985
Singapore Malays				
Malay population ('000)[a]	197[b]	311[c]	352	381[c]
Malay population (%)[a]	14[b]	15	15	15
Level of urbanization (%)[d]	100	100	10	100
Per capita GNP (current US$)[e,f]	n.a.	763	3,600	5,900
Per capita energy consumption[g,h]	492[i]	901[i]	1,710[i]	2,165[i]
Percentage of female employment in non-agriculture[k]	92[l]	99	100	100
Percentage of female employment as employee[a]	88[l]	92[l]	97	n.a.
Female LFPR, ages 15–39[k]	7	22	56	52
Percentage literate of females aged 20–24[a]	33[b]	59	81	n.a.
Infant mortality rate[m]	65	29	15	12
Peninsular Malaysia Malays				
Malay population ('000)[a]	3,127[b]	4,860	6,102	7,349[n]
Malay population (%)[a]	50[b]	47	56	57
Level of urbanization (%)[a]	11[b]	15	25	n.a.
Per capita GNP (current US$)[f,o]	n.a.	273	1,200	1,600
Per capita energy consumption[g,h]	222	390[i]	689[p]	826[i]
Percentage of female employment in non-agriculture[k]	13[l]	20	47	n.a.
Percentage of female employment as employee[k]	28[l]	25	50	56
Female LFPR, ages 15–39[k]	26[b]	35	42	42
Percentage literate of females aged 20–24[a]	21[b]	52[q]	77	n.a.
Infant mortality rate[r]	83[b]	41	28	22

Indonesia

Muslim population ('000)[a]	85,377[s]	103,579[t]	128,316	142,589
Muslim population (%)[a]	n.a	88	87	87
Level of urbanization (%)[u]	15	17	22	25[d]
Per capita GNP (current US$)[f]	n.a	90	480	530
Per capita energy consumption[g,v]	88	130[i]	191	219[j]
Percentage of female employment in non-agriculture[w,x]	29	35	46	46
Percentage of female employment as employee[w,x]	n.a.	29	23	24
Female LFPR, ages 15–39[x]	29	34	36	42
Percentage literate of females aged 20–24[y]	27	47	66	79
Infant mortality rate[y]	150	143	107	75

Sources: Jones (1990a: Table 1).

[a] Calculated from *Census of Population, Singapore*, 1957, 1970, and 1980.

[b] 1957.

[c] Republic of Singapore, *Yearbook of Statistics: Singapore, 1985*: Table 3.1.

[d] World Bank, *World Development Report, 1987*: Table 33.

[e] Malay rates derived from all-Singapore rates by applying adjustment factors to allow for lower rates of Malay to total per capita incomes.

[f] World Bank, *World Tables, 1987*, 4th edn.

[g] Kg of oil equivalent.

[h] World Bank, *World Development Report, 1984*: Table 8 (refers to whole country).

[i] Interpolated or extrapolated.

[j] World Bank, *World Development Report, 1987*: Table 9 (refers to whole country).

[k] Labour force participation rate from *Population Census of Malaya, 1957* and *Population Census of Malaysia*, 1970 and 1980; unpublished data from 1985 Labour Force Survey.

[l] Includes apprentices.

[m] Republic of Singapore, *Report on Registration of Births and Deaths, 1987*: Table 14.

[n] Malaysia, *Vital Statistics, Peninsular Malaysia, 1985*: Table 3.1.

[o] Malay rates derived from all-Malaysia rates by applying adjustment factors to allow for a lower, but rising ratio of Malay per capita incomes to total per capita incomes.

[p] 1981.

[q] Includes semiliterate.

[r] Calculate from *Vital Statistics, Peninsular Malaysia*, various years.

[s] Estimated from *1961 Population Census*.

[t] Jones (1976: Table 2).

[u] Hugo et al. (1987: Table 3.10).

[v] World Bank, *World Development Report, 1984*: Table 8.

[w] Hugo et al. (1987: Table 8.7).

[x] Labour force participation rates from *Population Census*, 1971 and 1980, and the *1985 Intercensal Population Survey*.

[y] Hugo et al. (1987: Table 4.4); Indonesia, Central Bureau of Statistics et al. (1992).

and left many rural areas relatively isolated. But the improvement of roads from the late 1960s on, and the land transport revolution, brought public transportation of various kinds, particularly in the form of buses and 'colts', into Java's villages and therefore made the larger towns accessible at quite low prices (see Hugo, 1981).

The degree of isolation of much of rural Indonesia in the early 1960s would be hard to exaggerate, not only because of the transport situation but also because of limited communications. In one village in Gunung Kidul, Yogyakarta, known to the author, the only radio at that time was owned by the headman; about twenty villagers would listen to it on a Sunday night: not to the news or other outside influences, but to the traditional drama, the *wayang*. Politically, there was much tension in village Java between the Communist Party and Islamic and other groups, but in terms of social and family life, traditional patterns held sway. By contrast, Malaysian villages by the early 1960s were already well served by radio and 'rediffusion'; in late 1964, 55 of the 108 households in one village in Selangor had a radio, and all households in the village were within earshot of a radio (Wilson, 1967: 53). This was probably fairly typical of rural Malaysia.

In terms of both transport and communications, then, the Malays of Peninsular Malaysia were far better served than the Indonesians in the early 1960s. In Indonesia, development of communications since then has played a major role in bringing formerly isolated rural populations closer to the mainstream of development. The transistor radio played the major role in the 1960s and television in the 1970s–1980s; in Peninsular Malaysia, mass TV viewing dates from the late 1960s and in Indonesia from the mid-1970s. In Indonesia, 10 per cent of households possessed a television set in 1980 and 26 per cent in 1990, and a much higher percentage were able to view television frequently by visiting neighbours' houses.[1] Television has increased the knowledge and widened the horizons of villagers (Chu, Alfian, and Schramm, 1991). It has been particularly important in bringing images of middle-class urban life, indeed of middle-class American life, to villagers, along with previously alien values, including a heavy dose of consumerism.[2] These influences have undoubtedly been important in influencing villagers' views of acceptable behaviour, acceptable dress, and acceptable roles for women and young people, not to mention the allure of the towns. Television may have been particularly important in Southern Thailand in working subtly to bring the Muslim minority into closer touch with Thai language and culture.

Peninsular Malaysia was the most urbanized of the large South-East Asian countries in the 1950s and 1960s, but even there, approximately two-thirds of the population was rural,[3] and the Malay population was much more rural still (Hirschman, 1976). In 1970, only 15 per cent of the Malays were urban, compared with 47 per cent of the Chinese, though Malay urbanization proceeded apace during the 1970s and 1980s. Thailand and Indonesia were predominantly rural societies in the 1950s and 1960s, with fewer than 20 per cent of their people in urban areas.

It was not until the 1980s that urbanization really picked up in these two countries (NUDS, 1985; Ashakul, 1990), reaching levels of 31 per cent in Indonesia and approximately 30 per cent in Thailand by 1990. In Thailand, the Malay population is concentrated in the far south, where levels of urbanization are below the national average. The Malay populations under discussion in this book, then, with the exception of the Singapore Malays, were overwhelmingly rural in the 1950s and 1960s, and although changes have occurred since then, particularly striking in the case of Malaysia, they have remained predominantly rural to this day.

For the purpose of this book, the key trends to be discussed are those affecting Islamic populations in the various countries. Largely because of lack of data, not all of the smaller Islamic populations will be covered. Those covered will include the population of the four southern Thai provinces of Pattani, Narathiwat, Yala, and Satun, three-quarters of whom are Malay; the Malay population in Singapore and Brunei; the Malays of Peninsular Malaysia; and the populations of the predominantly Muslim provinces in Indonesia.

The Muslim population of the Philippines, comprising almost 3 million persons or over 5 per cent of the population, will be referred to only briefly owing to lack of information.[4] The same applies to the Muslim populations of Sabah and Sarawak. Islamic populations not covered at all will include, in Thailand, those further north along the peninsula and around the Bangkok area; and in Malaysia, the Indian Muslims. In Indonesia, though 13 per cent (some 23 million in 1990) of the population are not Muslims, the entire Indonesian population will sometimes have to be taken as a proxy for the Muslim population, because of the unavailability of suitable disaggregated data. In other cases, data are available for the Muslims alone. In still other cases, provincial-level analysis will omit certain provinces with a non-Muslim majority. The provinces with large non-Muslim populations (with 1980 percentages in brackets) are East Timor (99.2 per cent), Bali (94.8 per cent), East Nusa Tenggara (91.1 per cent), Irian Jaya (87.9 per cent), North Sulawesi (54.2 per cent), Maluku (44.5 per cent), and North Sumatra (37.3 per cent). It should be noted that where it is necessary to use the total Indonesian population as a proxy for the Muslim population, this to some extent biases the age at marriage upwards and the divorce rate downwards, because the non-Muslim population consistently have higher age at marriage and lower divorce (Muliakusuma, 1976: 19–23). However, because of their relatively small proportion of the total (13 per cent) the extent of the bias is not too great.

Policies adopted in the different countries have differentially affected the Malay and non-Malay populations. In Malaysia, the New Economic Policy instituted in 1970 following race riots in May 1969 was influential in raising the economic standing of the Malay community. Between 1970 and 1990, mean household income for Malays rose from less than 0.7 to 0.8 per cent of overall mean household income. In manufacturing, the Malay share of employment rose from 29 per cent of total employment in 1970 to 49 per cent in 1990, and in manu-facturing and services combined, it rose from 37.5 per cent to 51.4 per cent over the same period (Malaysia, 1991: 45, 47, 99).

Certain policies which showed positive discrimination in favour of the Malays, such as the award of scholarships and places in institutions of higher learning, and the reservation of a certain proportion of jobs for them in different firms and industries, can be expected to have had important effects on marriage timing, fertility, and family life (Jones, 1990a). In Singapore, educational incentives for Malays have no doubt assisted in raising educational levels; however, they were disadvantaged in employment by policies to reduce their role in the police and armed forces, especially in the early 1970s.

Table 2.2 shows some indicators of economic and social progress in the main countries under discussion, and where possible, specifically for their Malay or Muslim populations. Interpretation of such data poses problems. For example, although the Singapore Malays are clearly much wealthier, on average, than those in Malaysia or Indonesia, they have always been seen as a disadvantaged group in Singapore in comparison with the other ethnic groups.[5] Again, while the Malaysian Malays had a level of urbanization similar to the Indonesians', they were far less urbanized than the other ethnic groups in Malaysia. This comparative status could be as important in its effect on behaviour as the absolute levels of the indicator concerned.

Educational Changes

Literacy rates among Malay women in Peninsular Malaysia and Singapore have been increasing steadily ever since the early 1930s (Sidhu and Jones, 1981: 212). The rise accelerated in the post-war period (see Table 2.2); in Peninsular Malaysia, the rate climbed from 15 per cent in 1947 to 29 per cent in 1957, then rose very rapidly from this still-low level to 69 per cent by 1980. In Indonesia, the rise from 27 per cent to 66 per cent between 1960 and 1980 is a remark-able one, suffering only by comparison with the even more spectacular Singapore figures. Expansion of schooling in Indonesia was in full swing throughout the 1970s and 1980s, and by 1985 the percentage of literates among Indonesian women aged 20–24 (79 per cent) had reached approximately the levels attained by Malay women of the same ages in Malaysia and Singapore only five years previously. Illiteracy in Indonesia by 1985 was largely a residual of earlier times, characterizing mainly those aged 45 and over (see Figure 2.1, upper left-hand panel and Figure 2.2).

Literacy has remained much lower in some regions of Malaysia and Indonesia than in others. Table 2.3 shows Malay literacy rates by state from 1957 to 1980, unfortunately not disaggregated by age, and Table 2.4 shows the same data for a selection of predominantly Muslim provinces of Indonesia between 1971 and 1990. In the late 1950s, literacy levels were much lower in Kelantan and Trengganu than elsewhere in

FIGURE 2.1
Indonesia: Indicators of Educational Progress, 1971, 1980, 1985, and 1990

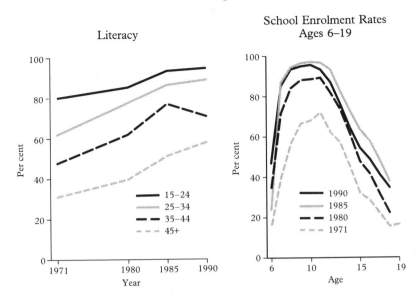

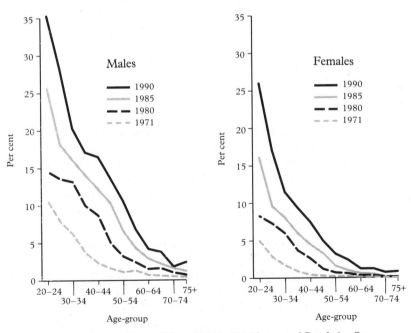

Percentage Completed Senior High School

Sources: *Population Census*, 1971, 1980, and 1990; *1985 Intercensal Population Survey.*

FIGURE 2.2

Indonesia: Percentage Literate of Population 10 Years and Over, by Age and Sex, 1961–1990

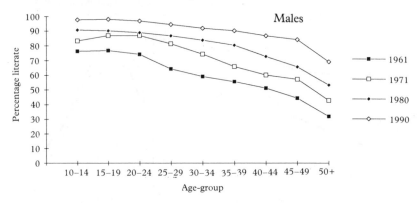

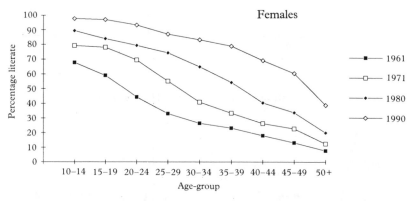

Sources: Population Census, 1971, 1980, and 1990; *1985 Intercensal Population Survey.*

Peninsular Malaysia. Perlis, Kedah, and Pahang were the other states where overall literacy remained below 50 per cent. Females were relatively more disadvantaged in these states than were males, as indicated by the greater 'spread' (in relative terms) in literacy rates for females than for males (Sidhu and Jones, 1981: 217). Literacy, however, rose sharply in all states between 1957 and 1970 and again by 1980, and the relative disadvantage of females in the lowest literacy states was much less by 1980, largely no doubt because of national educational policies which sought to give girls and boys equal access to education, irrespective of where they lived (Unesco, 1972: 115–28). By 1980, the female literacy percentages for Malays in Kelantan and Trengganu were in the mid to high 50s, well above the figure for the highest-literacy state (44 per cent) in 1957. In other words, by 1980, these states were less than two decades behind the highest-literacy states. Moreover, the differences were largely a residual effect of very low female literacy in earlier times; by 1980, interstate differences in literacy had largely disappeared in the young age-groups, although they remained more prominent than the male–female differential.

TABLE 2.3

Peninsular Malaysia: Literacy Rates of the Malay Population Aged 10 and Over, by State, 1957, 1970, and 1980 (per cent)

State	Males			Females			Total		
	1957	1970	1980	1957	1970	1980	1957	1970	1980
Johore	71	77	88	33	56	73	53	66	81
Kedah	63	70	81	23	45	62	43	57	71
Kelantan	40	53	68	15	34	54	27	43	60
Malacca	78	86	92	32	52	69	55	67	79
Negri Sembilan	78	87	93	40	59	73	60	73	83
Pahang	65	73	86	31	51	71	49	62	79
Penang	78	85	92	41	60	76	60	72	83
Perak	79	81	88	44	59	71	61	69	79
Perlis	62	72	83	26	50	65	44	61	73
Selangor	73	85	92	38	65	79	57	75	86
Trengganu	43	56	73	18	39	59	30	47	66
All Peninsular Malaysia	65	73	85	30	51	69	47	62	77

Sources: Population Census of Malaya, 1957 and *Population Census of Malaysia,*
1970 and 1980.

TABLE 2.4
Indonesia: Literacy Rates of the Population Aged 10 and Over in the Predominantly Muslim Provinces, 1971, 1980, and 1990 (per cent)

	Males			Females			Total		
	1971	1980	1990	1971	1980	1990	1971	1980	1990
Aceh	79	82	92	57	67	83	68	75	87
West Sumatra	83	87	94	69	77	89	75	82	91
Riau	77	85	94	54	69	86	66	77	90
Jambi	82	87	94	55	66	85	69	76	89
South Sumatra	85	88	95	64	74	87	74	81	91
Bengkulu	82	84	94	58	65	84	70	74	89
Lampung	79	85	93	58	70	85	69	78	90
DKI Jakarta	88	94	98	70	82	93	79	89	96
West Java	75	83	92	56	68	83	65	75	88
Central Java	69	77	89	43	56	74	56	66	81

Yogyakarta	68	81	88	42	59	72	55	69	80
East Java	66	74	85	41	53	70	53	63	77
West Kalimantan	60	69	85	34	47	69	48	58	77
Central Kalimantan	83	86	94	63	72	87	73	79	91
South Kalimantan	81	85	94	59	70	86	70	78	90
East Kalimantan	70	82	92	53	69	86	62	76	90
Central Sulawesi	77	87	82	61	77	86	69	82	89
South Sulawesi	59	68		44	57	74	51	62	78
South-east Sulawesi	67	79	89	40	59	76	53	69	82
West Nusa Tenggara	49	66	78	28	45	62	38	55	70
All Indonesia	72	80	90	50	63	79	61	71	84

Sources: Population Census, 1971, 1980, and 1990.
Note: Some figures in Table 17 in the Series D Report of the *1971 Population Census* are incorrect; they have been replaced by figures from the individual provincial reports.

The literacy rates of Malay women still remained well below those of Malay men in 1980, but, as with interstate differences, the difference was largely a residual effect of very low female literacy in earlier times; among young Malay women—those aged 15–29—literacy rates were barely any lower than those of Malay males in the same age-group: 90 per cent and 94 per cent, respectively.

In Indonesia, only two provinces, West Nusa Tenggara and West Kalimantan, had literacy rates below 50 per cent in 1971 (thus matching Kelantan and Trengganu in Malaysia), though the rate in South Sulawesi barely exceeded 50 per cent, and it was only in the mid-50s in all of Java east of West Java. Steady improvements took place during the 1970s and 1980s; interprovincial differentials evident in 1971 tended to persist, but there was a narrowing of the 'spread' in the rates. The relative disadvantage of females in terms of literacy greatly diminished by 1990, across the board, reflecting, as in Malaysia, the impact of national education policies applied fairly even-handedly across regions and between genders. By 1990, female literacy in East Java, one of the lowest provinces in 1971, was above the level reached in any other predominantly Muslim province except Jakarta in 1971, indicating that though provinces such as East Java were lagging by two decades, literacy improvements in Indonesia were taking place universally.

In Peninsular Malaysia, the special efforts made to increase the status of the Malays led to quite remarkable advances in the education of Malay women over the 1970s and 1980s. These can be seen in rising school enrolment rates in the relevant age-groups, as well as in increasing levels of educational attainment for Malay women. The proportion of Malay girls aged 10–19 attending school rose from 32 per cent in 1957 to 47 per cent in 1970 and 67 per cent in 1980. (The equivalent 1970 and 1980 figures in Indonesia were 39 per cent and 53 per cent respectively, indicating a lag of only about six years in Indonesia.) The 1980 census data revealed that the modal level of education for Malay women in their fifties was none; for those in their thirties, it was primary education; and for those in their teens, secondary education.

Table 2.5 shows that the proportion of Malay females aged 20–29 who had completed the Lower Certificate of Education or its equivalent rose from 2.2 per cent in 1957 to 10.4 per cent in 1970 and 37.9 per cent in 1980. The ratio of the Malay rate to the equivalent Chinese rate rose from 0.25 to 0.59 and then, remarkably, to 1.13 over the same period. The 'catch-up' successfully performed by Malay women is also revealed by comparing the mean number of years of schooling of ever-married women in two successive Malaysian Family Life Surveys, conducted in 1976 and 1988. In 1976, Malay women had 3.9 years of schooling, compared with 4.6 years for both Chinese and Indians. By 1988, Malays, with 7.8 years of education, were ahead of both Chinese (7.6 years) and Indians (7.1 years). The measure of educational attainment of Malays in Table 2.5 shows much the same ranking of states as does literacy: Penang, Selangor–Kuala Lumpur, and Negri Sembilan in the lead, Kedah and Trengganu trailing. Kelantan, however, scored relatively

TABLE 2.5

Peninsular Malaysia: Percentage of Malay Females Aged 20–29
with Completed Lower Certificate of Education or Its Equivalent,
by State, 1957, 1970, and 1980[a]

State	1957	1970	1980
Johore	3.3	10.6	35.0
Kedah	0.9	7.3	27.3
Kelantan	0.9	6.2	31.5
Malacca	2.0	9.5	37.3
Negri Sembilan	3.6	13.5	40.7
Pahang	1.8	8.4	31.8
Penang	4.1	13.2	n.a.
Perak	2.4	9.5	32.1
Perlis	2.6	9.9	35.1
Selangor	4.3	10.2	50.7
Trengganu	0.7	5.4	29.2
Federal Territory[b]	–	–	64.7
All Peninsular Malaysia	2.2	10.4	37.9

Sources: *Population Census of Malaya, 1957* and *Population Census of Malaysia,* 1970 and
  1980.
[a]In 1970 and 1980, completed LCE or above; in 1957 includes all those who have spent
  at least 7–9 years in school. This will include many who did not pass LCE.
[b]Included in Selangor in 1957 and 1970.

better on educational attainment than it did on literacy.

In Indonesia, various indices of educational advance are presented in
Figure 2.1. The 1970s and 1980s were on all counts a remarkable period
of educational expansion, spearheaded by the Inpres school-building
programme and the programme of compulsory primary education in
the mid-1970s. This expansion affected females even more sharply
than it did males. For example, in the age-group 25–29, the percentage
of males who had completed senior high school exceeded the equivalent
percentage of females by 180 per cent in 1971, but by only 65 per cent
in 1990. Figure 2.3 shows the shifts over time in the proportions of
people aged 15 years and over with different levels of educational
attainment. Although the education of females lagged behind that of
males, the shift out of the 'no schooling' category and into 'completed
primary' and 'completed secondary' levels was even more dramatic for
females than for males.

Finally, Figure 2.4 shows trends in the proportion of girls currently
in school, by age, in Indonesia and Peninsular Malaysia. Detailed information is not available before 1970, although it is clear that the rates
for both populations had been gradually increasing. The 1970s saw sharp
increases in school attendance by age, leading to particularly striking
increases in school attendance by teenaged Malay girls in Peninsular
Malaysia. By 1980, more than half of Malay girls in Peninsular Malaysia

FIGURE 2.3
Indonesia: Population 15 Years and Over by Level of Education, 1961–1990

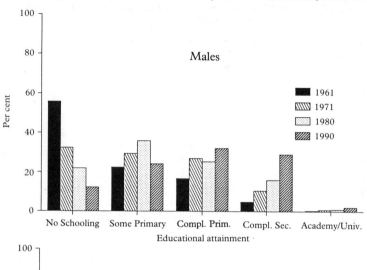

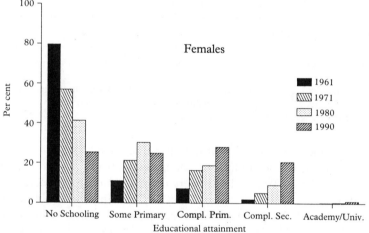

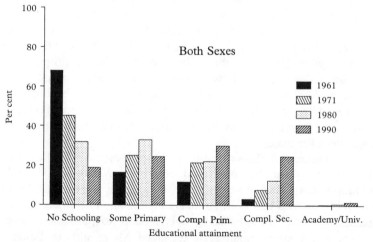

Sources: *Population Census*, 1961, 1971, 1980, and 1990.

FIGURE 2.4
Indonesia and Peninsular Malaysia (Malays): Percentage of Girls Currently
Attending School by Age, 1970, 1980, and 1990

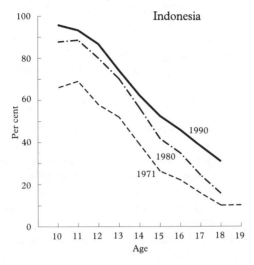

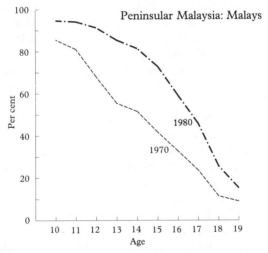

Sources: Indonesia: *Population Census*, 1971, 1980, and 1990.
Malaysia: 1970: Calculated from 2% sample tape of *Population Census of Malaysia, 1970.*
1980: *Population Census of Malaysia, 1980.*

remained in school at 16 and 17 years: ages at which, twenty years
before, most of them had been marrying.

It is worth observing that the timing of educational expansion for
girls in Indonesia and among Malay girls in Peninsular Malaysia differed
according to age and level of education. In Indonesia, the big push
during the 1970s was in primary education. This is reflected in the fact
that in 1980, school attendance rates of Indonesian girls at ages 11–13
were well ahead of those reached by Malay girls of the same age in

1970; in other words, at this level the Indonesian girls were only a few years behind their Malay counterparts. At ages 15–17, however, the Indonesians were exactly a decade behind the Malays, reaching the same enrolment rates in 1980 as the Malays had reached in 1970. Expansion of school enrolments in Indonesia over the 1980s, however, was not as rapid as that achieved by the Malays in the 1970s, with the result that in 1990, from the age of 12 upwards, Indonesian enrolment rates were still below those reached by the Malays in 1980.[6]

Changing Women's Roles: Women in the Workplace

There was a tendency for women's labour force participation rates (LFPRs) to rise over the 1970s in urban areas throughout most of East and South-East Asia (Jones, 1984). The rise, however, was especially dramatic among Malay women in Peninsular Malaysia and Singapore, and has been in evidence ever since the 1957 Population Census (see Table 2.6). In these countries, female LFPRs have traditionally been characterized by large differences between the three main ethnic groups. The differences, however, narrowed dramatically over the 1960s and 1970s. Chinese females, whose LFPRs in urban areas greatly exceeded those of Malays and Indians in 1957, progressively lost that edge over the course of the 1960s and 1970s, even though Chinese LFPRs, too, were increasing; by 1980, in urban areas there was little difference in female LFPRs between Chinese and Malays.

The rising Malay rates are especially noteworthy because they have been associated with rapidly increasing urbanization of the Malay population; they therefore reflect a very rapid absolute increase in the number of Malay women who are working in urban areas. Structural changes in urban areas appear to have favoured female employment over the 1970s and 1980s, with females heavily represented in export-oriented manufacturing, in community and personal services, and in trade and tourism. Malays did particularly well in this employment, partly because of government policies of affirmative action. The changes in employment of Malay females between 1957 and 1980, compared with those for other groups, are shown in Table 2.7.

In both Malaysia and Singapore, the increase in manufacturing employment in the 1970s went very largely to women, and in the 1980s almost exclusively to women; Malay women benefited more than Chinese women from this growth.[7] In Peninsular Malaysia, female employment in manufacturing industries is estimated to have increased from 22,500 in 1957 to 73,000 in 1970 and 290,000 in 1979, while the increase in male employment was much slower. The female share of manufacturing employment rose from 17 per cent in 1967 to 29 per cent in 1970, 41 per cent in 1976, and 52 per cent in December 1979. The largest industry, electronics, was dominated by female workers; in 1980, two-thirds of these women workers were Malays (Jamilah, 1983: 40). In manufacturing as a whole, Malay women workers' share of total employment rose from 6.6 per cent in 1957 to 19.4 per cent (of a

TABLE 2.6

Singapore and Peninsular Malaysia: Female Labour Force Participation Rates of Those Aged 10 and Over in Urban Areas, by Ethnic Group, 1957–1980 (per cent)

	Labour Force Participation Rates					
	1957	1970	1976[a]	1980[b]	1985[c]	1990[d]
Singapore						
Chinese	21.8	20.8	32.4	39.7	n.a.	47.3
Malays	6.3	14.3	26.6	38.3	n.a.	43.4
Indians	7.1	11.2	28.6	38.2	n.a.	51.7
Total	19.3	18.5	31.1	39.3	n.a.	47.8
Peninsular Malaysia[e]						
Chinese	n.a.	25.0	45.7	47.7	45.8	47.2
Malays	n.a.	15.7	37.6	43.2	44.6	45.8
Indians	n.a.	13.5	34.2	37.6	46.1	50.3
Total	n.a.	21.5	41.9	45.0	45.0	46.8

Sources: Cheng (1978: Table 3); *Census of Population, Singapore*, 1957, 1970, and 1980; *Report on the Labour Force Survey of Singapore*, 1988; *Population Census of Malaysia*, 1970 and 1980; *Report of the Labour Force Survey, Malaysia*, 1976 and 1985–6.

[a] For Malaysia, ages 15 and over.

[b] For Malaysia, refers to 1979.

[c] Refers to ages 15–64.

[d] For Singapore, refers to 1988 and to ages 15 and over; for Peninsular Malaysia, refers to ages 15–64.

[e] Towns 75,000+ (1970); towns 10,000+ (1976, 1979, 1985, 1990).

TABLE 2.7

Peninsular Malaysia: Change in the Employment of Malay Females Compared with Other Groups, 1957–1980

Occupation	Employment of Malay Females ('000)			Percentage Change in Employment, 1957–80			
	1957	1980	1957–80	Malay Females	Malay Males	Non-Malay Females	Non-Malay Males
Agriculture	218	346	128	59	11	1	–17
Manufacturing	9	107	98	1,105	625	786	105
Commerce	7	52	45	597	296	726	69
Services	14	139	125	889	259	174	53
All other industries	1	7	6	908	103	28	63
Industry not adequately described	1	11	10	756	336	871	301
Total working	250	662	412	165	82	107	41
Looking for work	2	19	17	700	44	90	–28
Total labour force	252	681	429	170	81	107	39

Sources: Fell (1960: Table 13); Population Census of Malaysia, 1980, General Report: Table 6.4.

much larger sector) in 1980. In services, a sector in which government employment looms large, Malay women did almost as well as in manufacturing, increasing their share of employment from 4.4 per cent in 1957 to 15.5 per cent in 1980. The rise in Malay women's share apparently slackened off over the 1980s, however. Female LFPRs as a whole increased only slightly between 1980 and 1990, from 45 per cent to 47 per cent (*New Straits Times*, 29 April 1992).

The state of Malacca can be used as a case-study of the burgeoning work opportunities for Malay females. According to the 1970 Population Census, 10,000 people worked in manufacturing in Malacca but about 70 per cent of them were engaged in small-scale cottage industries. Between 1972 and 1976, 10,600 jobs, 60 per cent of them in electronics, had been created in factories set up in four industrial estates in the state. Whereas according to the 1970 Census, two-thirds of those employed in manufacturing were men, some 75 per cent of the job opportunities in the new industrial estates were for women, who were considered more dextrous, hard-working, and docile, whereas male workers posed problems of insubordination and theft. Malays were over-represented in the industrial estates' workforce; Malay women were heavily over-represented (Ackerman, 1980: 68–74).

Some authors have made much of the disadvantages faced by women in the Malaysian and Singaporean labour force, and the tendency for them to be segmented towards the bottom of the occupational status hierarchies in the industries in which they work (Wong, 1976: 301–3; Manderson, 1979; O'Brien, 1983, 1984). While these observations are true, the rapid expansion of urban work opportunities for women has undoubtedly had a liberating effect for very large numbers of young Malay women from rural areas, opening up the chance of earning an independent living, and escaping the confines of rural society. Both because of government policies and because the Malays were formerly in a disadvantaged situation, education has tended to bring greater occupational rewards for Malays than for non-Malays, especially in the clerical and professional spheres (Inglis, 1979: 224–5).

The financial contribution of Malay women workers to their families was important and sometimes crucial. In one study in electronics factories in Penang, most of the Malay female workers were migrants from Kedah and Perak; they typically had secondary education and their parents were mostly in rubber and paddy farming. Many of these girls had been withdrawn from school so that their mother could be released to work for money, and their male siblings (sometimes older) could remain at school. The regularity of their income and remittances enabled their parents' limited and insecure earnings to be used for other things, while the daughters bought consumer durables, took over responsibility for educating their siblings, financed house repairs, and bought presents for family members (Young, 1991: 279).[8]

Figure 2.5 presents some more detailed data about changing LFPRs of Malay women in Singapore and the more urbanized states of Malaysia. Whereas the 1980 age pattern of labour force participation for Malay

FIGURE 2.5

Singapore, Penang, and Selangor: Malay Female Labour Force
Participation Rates, 1957 and 1980

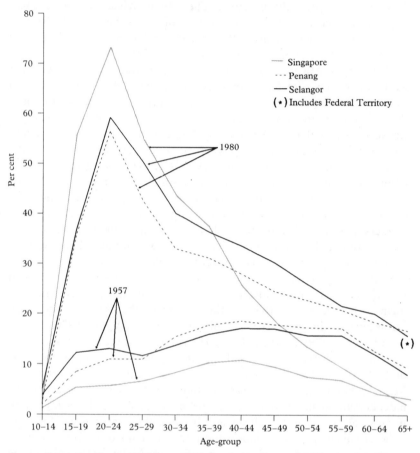

*Sources: Population Census of Malaya, 1957; Population Census of Malaysia, 1980, Census
of Population, Singapore, 1957 and 1980.*

women in Peninsular Malaysia as a whole was a two-peaked one with
the major peak at 20–24 and an extended minor peak at 35–49, in the
cities young women predominate, with a sharp peak in participation
rates at 20–24, and quite high rates all the way from ages 15–19 to
35–39. By contrast, in 1957, LFPRs for Malay females in the towns
were very low, and reached their peak at ages 40–49. The two-peak
pattern characteristic of Chinese women in Peninsular Malaysia at the
time was absolutely missing among the Malays (Jones, 1965), reflecting
the very young marriage patterns and the cultural resistance to young
women working, whether married or unmarried. There has clearly been
a dramatic change in labour force participation of young Malay females
between that time and 1980. As indicated in Figure 2.6, by 1980 the
rates were particularly high for never-married females aged 20–24 and
25–29, in both urban and rural areas.

FIGURE 2.6

Peninsular Malaysia (Malays): Female Labour Force Participation Rates, by Place of Residence and Marital Status, 1980

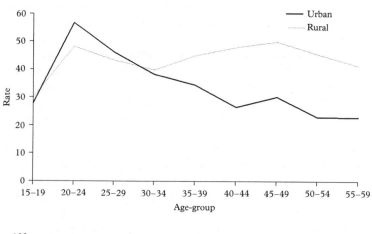

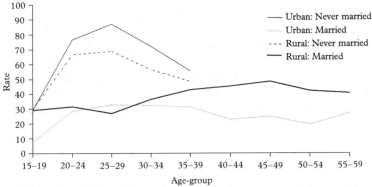

Source: Calculated from unpublished tabulations, 2% sample tape, of *Population Census of Malaysia, 1980*.

In Indonesia, the rise in female LFPRs has been more muted than in Malaysia and Singapore and difficult to interpret because of data inconsistencies (Jones and Manning, 1992: 366–72). In rural areas of Java, over some periods in the 1970s there may even have been a contraction of job opportunities for poor women whose labour was displaced by rice mills and harvest contract teams. However, especially in urban areas the rise appears real enough, and is reflected in a rising share of females in most urban occupations over the 1970s and 1980s (Widarti, 1991: Tables 3.9 and 3.10). For example, the size of the civil service expanded very rapidly during the oil-boom years of 1974–81. Between 1974 and 1984, civil service employment rose from 1.67 million to 2.79 million, or by 66 per cent, and the female share rose from 18 to 27 per cent over the same period (Logsdon, 1985).

New work opportunities for women in Indonesia certainly did not represent an unambiguous improvement in their situation. Factory work was frequently so poorly paid that young women's subsistence needs still had to be met in part by their households (Mather, 1983; Wolf, 1990; White et al., 1992). In factory work and in government service, women were concentrated in the lower-level positions, to an even greater extent than would have been expected on the basis of their lower educational levels (Arif, 1992). In terms of social change, however, this work was of great importance in providing non-traditional work settings, wider contacts, new lifestyles, and some discretionary income.

The patterns of labour force participation by education among both Malay women in Peninsular Malaysia and Indonesian women are very similar. The rates are relatively high among the uneducated, falling to a trough among those with lower secondary education and rising to very high levels among those with upper secondary education and especially those with tertiary education. The reason for these patterns appears to be the economic necessity to work among the lower income groups, who are more likely to have low levels of education; and the strong motivation among those with upper secondary and tertiary education to put their education to use, a motivation fuelled by the rapid expansion of jobs suited to educated women. For young women who achieve only lower secondary education, there may frequently be a 'status frustration effect': a disappointment that the kinds of jobs available to them are not as desirable as they had expected (Jones, 1986: 8).

The rise in female LFPRs throughout Islamic South-East Asia reflects not only changes in economic structure which provided new opportunities for women to find remunerative work (Lim, 1992), but also changes in attitudes to women working, both before and after marriage. This point will be elaborated in Chapter 4.

A Subjective Perspective on Change

So far, the evaluation of social and economic change has been based mainly on macro-level analysis and available statistics. This, however, cannot give a 'feel' for the changes that have occurred. The pace of life has altered with electrification and improved transportation. Greater monetization and higher real income has led to greater demand for consumer goods. In many regions, the water-buffalo of the 1960s has been replaced by small Japanese tractors; the picturesque ox-cart, moving at little more than walking pace, still ubiquitous in the Malaccan countryside in the early 1960s, had vanished by the late 1970s. Children are in school, and in their free time are more inclined to play than to mind water-buffaloes or collect grass as in the past—in fact, the water-buffalo has almost vanished.

Not many village studies give a good summary of changes in the way people live. However, Keyfitz (1985), in his study of changes in an East Javanese village between 1953 and 1985, highlights the rising incomes, the productivity gains in agriculture, the switch from hand pounding to machine pounding of rice, the improvements in diets, clothing, and housing, the remarkable developments in schooling, the prevalence of volunteer youth groups, and the disappearance of *pikul* traders (using carrying-poles with baskets on each end). Perhaps most interesting of all is the change in access to information.

In 1953 contact with the outside world among even the upper level of citizens was confined to what they learned from the headman at a weekly meeting of the village elders. The headman in turn obtained his information from a daily paper that he had brought by messenger from Gondanglegi.

Our recent visit shows that the media have taken the place of much of the earlier face-to-face communication. Everyone can find out what is happening for himself, on his own transistor radio, for instance through the hourly news broadcasts provided by the national radio network.... There are now some 60 ... [television] ... receivers in village homes.

Perhaps the biggest boost to communication has come from the 'Colt Revolution', the passing back and forth through all the villages of Java of vans capable of holding 15 or so passengers.... There are also buses that go short or long distances....

Whereas in 1953 only three of the 51 village elders had ever been to Surabaya, now most villagers have made the trip.... Gondanglegi, 8 kilometres away, visited by only two of the elders in the week preceding our visit in 1953, is now used regularly to shop for food and clothing or visit the clinic.... The increasing worldliness of the villagers is due to schooling, television, and travel, but what the relative influence of these three has been no one knows.

(Keyfitz, 1985: 707–8.)

Edmundson (1977) and Edmundson and Edmundson (1983) describe changes in two villages in East Java since 1971. They highlight the increasing prosperity, increasing inequality, diversification of income-earning opportunities, improvements in housing and water supply, and greater acceptance of government extension agents. The number of daily minibus trips from the poorer village to the regional city of Malang had increased from one in 1971 to six in 1977.

Trends in Islam: Modernism and Fundamentalism

The harsh legalisms of Middle Eastern Islam have been softened in South-East Asia—some would say, by the lush tropical setting and the concern with *halus* or refined social and personal relationships in traditional Malay culture. But the roots of the popular forms of Islam in the Malay world run deep; they include the influence of the pre-Islamic Hindu–Buddhist heritage, the early compromise between Islamic orthodoxy and Sufism in the Malay world, and in the early twentieth century the influence of modernist movements such as the Muhammadiah (Winstedt, 1961: 18–44; Benda, 1970; Roff, 1970). The pre-Islamic high status of women in the region (Winstedt, 1961: 18–62; Reid, 1988: 146, 162–4) undoubtedly also inhibited the enforcement of restrictive rules on women's behaviour. Although in South-East Asia, as in the Islamic countries of South and West Asia, 'women's seclusion and men's honour' have been guiding sentiments for the organization of traditional Islamic family life, female seclusion was not a pre-Islamic pattern and a much larger degree of female autonomy survived the conversion to Islam. Although after Islamization, women adopted modest clothing, covering the arms to the wrists and the legs to the ankles, and frequently adopting scarves as head-coverings, the veil was never adopted among South-East Asian Muslims.

The world-wide Islamic resurgence beginning in the early 1970s has had a profound influence within Islamic South-East Asia. At an international level, the resurgence is associated with disillusionment with Western civilization, social systems based on capitalism and socialism, and the lifestyles of secular élites in Islamic states, as well as with a search for identity and security in rapidly urbanizing and changing societies (Lapidus, 1988: 879–917; Tibi, 1991). This resurgence has been backed by the growing strength of certain Islamic states following the oil price increases in the 1970s, and by an increased self-confidence following the 1973 Arab–Israeli War, the 1979 Iranian Revolution, and the dawn of the fifteenth century in the Muslim calendar (Chandra, 1987).

Among South-East Asian Muslim populations, the influence of Islamic resurgence was strongest in Malaysia, for a variety of reasons, mainly associated with the political and ethnic situation. In Indonesia the government headed a predominantly Muslim country without severe ethnic problems, and in Singapore the Malays were only 15 per cent of the population and therefore lacked political power. In neither country did the government hesitate to deal firmly with any manifestation of Islamic revivalism that it felt was threatening national stability. The same was true in the Philippines and Thailand, where Islamic assertiveness was associated in the minds of government officials with separatist movements. In Malaysia, however, Islam symbolized the identity of the Malays, particularly after the national language policy removed the exclusiveness of that other symbol of Malay identity, the Malay language. The main Malay opposition party, Partai Islam Se Malaysia (Pan-Malaysian Islamic Party) or PAS, espoused a fundamentalist and Malay chauvinist platform, and constantly challenged the Islamic credentials of the political leaders of the ruling party, United Malays National Organization (UMNO). In a context in which it was dangerous to give any appearance of resistance to Islam, 'the antidote to an "excess" of religious zeal ... [was] ... paradoxically more of the same' (Nagata, 1982: 158). Those in power therefore sought to display their Islamic credentials in symbolic as well as more substantive ways: by building more mosques, sponsoring Koran reading contests, increasing the air time for Islamic broadcasts on radio and television, and building an Islamic university; and through a series of laws and regulations designed to placate the Islamic right.

The paradoxes of Islamic fundamentalism in Malaysia were many. Whereas traditionally the villagers of Kelantan, Trengganu, and Kedah were seen as the most religiously conservative of the Malays, the *dakwah* movement had its origins in the universities and by the mid-1970s successful students who had been sent abroad for studies were returning to these states to inform their somewhat bemused village parents that many aspects of their beliefs and practices were not consistent with 'true' Islamic belief. 'Urban and rural parents alike are often startled by the vehemence and seeming arrogance of the assault on their own religious practices (or lack of them) made by their juniors.' (Nagata, 1984: 237.) The Chinese and Indians feared resurgent Islam for its hard-line championing of Malay interests and the possible imposition of *syariah* law. But most fundamentalist leaders claimed they were not pursuing narrowly Malay interests but rather those of Islamic universalism.

Although not accurately described by the loaded term 'fundamentalism', movements have been afoot in other parts of the Malay-Muslim world, particularly in areas such as Java, Southern Thailand, and the Muslim regions of the Philippines, to 'purify' the local version of Islam by bringing it more into the orthodox mainstream. Muslims in these areas have been aware of, and somewhat embarrassed by, the strong role of traditional pre-Islamic beliefs and practices in their version of Islam. For Indonesia, the trend towards greater orthodoxy has been documented by Dhofier (1989): the number of enrolments in *pesantren*, the traditional Islamic educational institution, grew by 74 per cent between 1979 and 1987. Among the Maranao in the Philippines, growing religious feeling 'causes tensions between old and young, conservative and liberal, tolerant and fanatic, traditional and modern in ... everyday life' (Weekes, 1984: 498).

It is not easy to evaluate the effect of Islamic resurgence on marriage and its dissolution among the Malays. As already noted, in Malaysia the movement originated among tertiary students, who were already well past traditional marrying ages for females. Except for the more extreme groups, it did not oppose their continuing their studies, nor did it seem to press for early marriage thereafter, or oppose women's participation in the workforce.[9] Indeed, the spread in the use of the *tudung* (mini-*telekung* or head-cover coming down to the chest; called *jilbab* in Indonesia) among Malay government employees through the late 1970s and early 1980s showed where large numbers of *dakwah* followers were going after graduation. (The use of such clothing was conspicuously uncommon among Malay women working in electronics factories, where the *dakwah* movement has made scarcely any inroads.) However, there is no doubt that a traditional female role as helpmate and mother was held up as the ideal, one that could be combined with, but never made inferior to, paid work.

The *dakwah* movement undoubtedly reinforced the trend towards self-arrangement of marriage, because it both fostered a greater assertiveness by young people towards their parents (whose understanding of Islam they were being taught to believe was very inadequate), and narrowed the range of potential spouses considered suitable by *dakwah* followers (Karim, 1987: 47). Many would therefore not be willing to trust their parents to make a suitable choice, though others did accept the Islamic injunction to respect one's mother and rely on her to make a choice sympathetic to her daughter's desires (see Nagata, 1984: Chapter 5).

With regard to divorce, the fundamentalist groups, in upholding 'pure' Islamic teachings, could—and did—find plenty to criticize in motivations often underlying divorce, the lax implementation of divorce regulations, and the lack of regard for the welfare of children following divorce. The attitude of the fundamentalist movement towards polygamy was somewhat less clear-cut. On the whole, fundamentalists appeared to condemn easy access to polygamy, but at least one group (Darul Arqam) asserted the husbands' right in Islam to be polygamous.

Malay Minority Groups in Singapore, Southern Thailand, and the Philippines

Singapore

In Singapore, the Malay community is in a unique situation. The Malays of Malaysia and Singapore have much in common: they live in close proximity, they have many family links, and they can easily travel between the two countries and watch each other's television programmes. In both countries, they have been the economically weak community compared with the Chinese and Indians. But there are nevertheless fundamental differences in their situation, stemming from the minority status and weak political situation of the Singapore Malays. Singapore, as a small, predominantly Chinese nation surrounded by the massive populations of Malaysia and Indonesia, has been working hard since its break with Malaysia in 1964 on building a Singaporean identity to take precedence over the separate ethnic identities of its inhabitants. Malays, then, are under pressure to be 'Singaporeans' and not to stress their ethnic links with neighbouring countries. They are well aware that their loyalty is considered suspect: the independent Singapore government has followed an unspoken policy of excluding Malays from recruitment into the armed forces and police, where previously they had been strongly represented, and failed to call up Malay youths for national service during the 1970s and into the 1980s (Li, 1989: 109); as recently as 1989 their loyalty was publicly questioned by the Prime Minister's son, Brigadier-General Lee Hsien Loong, and the matter was debated in Parliament.

The other major difference in the situation of the Singapore Malays vis-à-vis Malays in Malaysia is that they must make their way in a meritocratic society in which few concessions are made to their initially weak educational and economic status. Certainly, as in Malaysia they are given a special position by the Constitution (Article 152) and they have benefited since 1960 from subsidized education at primary and secondary levels and waiving of tertiary fees,[10] but these privileges do not match the levels of assistance available to Malays in Malaysia. Neither do the government's 'social engineering' programmes take much account of possible Malay sensibilities. The family planning programme is a good example. By contrast with the low-key approach adopted in Malaysia for fear of religious opposition, in Singapore the programme has taken a very forceful approach and was remarkably successful in that the three ethnic groups reached replacement level fertility simultaneously in 1975. The Singapore Malays were the first sizeable Muslim population in the world to reach replacement level fertility.

The result of all these unique aspects of their situation is that the Singapore Malays are, in many respects, very different from their cousins across the causeway, though this was much less true in the 1960s. City dwellers with high female labour force participation, more Westernized in dress and less influenced by *dakwah*, they are constantly aware of their minority status and are often somewhat condescending towards the Malays of Malaysia, whom they see as failing to take full advantage of the special privileges granted them by the government, as abusing these special privileges through 'Ali Baba' business arrangements and corruption, and as being unwilling to 'take on' the Chinese without the buttress of these special privileges.

Southern Thailand

The Malays of Southern Thailand, although they represent the majority population in the four southernmost provinces of Pattani, Narathivat, Yala, and Satun, are nevertheless a tiny minority in the country as a whole, representing only 4 per cent of the population. They occupy the borderland between the predominantly Malay-Muslim world of island South-East Asia and the Buddhist world of mainland South-East Asia. From the seventeenth to the nineteenth century, they were part of the Kingdom of Pattani, long known as a 'cradle of Islam' in South-East Asia. This kingdom was only loosely under the suzerainty of Siam; the nobility were traditionally required to send the *bunga mas* (gold and silver flowers and leaves of tribute) as a token of vassalage to the Thai king every two-and-a-half years (Pitsuwan, 1985: 33). It was only as recently as 1902 that Pattani came fully under the control of the Kingdom of Thailand, and the status of the Muslim provinces changed from that of mere dependencies to that of 'provinces'.

Thailand is on the whole a remarkably homogeneous society, whose population is predominantly (95 per cent) Buddhist. In government policy and administrative practice, it has found it difficult to come to grips with the need to recognize the special needs of minority groups, particularly the Muslims and the hill tribes, and the result in the south has been simmering revolt and separatist movements up to the present time.

It is now increasingly recognized by Thai government representatives that many officials appointed to the south have been insensitive to or indeed contemptuous of Malay-Muslim culture (see Thomas, 1974, 1982), and that this has fuelled Malay resentments which have found overt political expression in breakaway movements. Greater attention is now being paid to the needs of the Muslim minority, but although the 'forced assimilation policy' of Phibul Songkram during and after World War II has been replaced in recent decades by a basically assimilationist stance, stressing 'development', the tensions remain. Even the attempts to promote secular education in place of, or in addition to, the religious education in Arabic or Malay of the traditional *pondok* (religious schools where students live in) (Haemindra, 1977: 93–7; Thomas, 1982: 170–3) have not met with great success. The reason is not hard to find:

Among the Malay-Muslims in the South, the socio-economic development strategy was employed to weaken the social values and cultural institutions that had for a long time served to resist government penetration into their society.... Thus the more intense the development efforts were being carried out by the government, the more insecure the Malays felt about their own identity and socio-cultural values considered sacred and immutable. (Pitsuwan, 1985: 168.)

A continuing source of frustration has been the lack of a significant role for Thai Muslims in local administration, including a dearth of Muslim teachers in the region's public school system. Muslim intellectuals have called for the introduction of local elections for provincial governors, but most Thai officials view a degree of local self-rule as being a step towards separatism (Handley, 1990: 22–5).

Each of the southern provinces has an Islamic Committee, whose members are appointed for life, and there is a Muslim supreme religious leader (the Chula Ratchamontri) appointed by the king, also for life. These committees have a conservative bent owing to the advanced age of most of their members, and moves were afoot in the Thai Parliament in 1992 to set a retirement age of 70 on both the Chula Ratchamontri and the chairmen of the provincial Islamic committees, and to reduce the term of the provincial committee members to six years.

Southern Thai Muslim society is closely linked linguistically, culturally, and through family connections with that of the neighbouring state of Kelantan in North-east Malaya, and with Kedah–Perlis Muslim society on the western side of the peninsula. Like Kelantanese, Southern Thai Muslims remain very conservative and resistant to central government pressure for change. One good indication is that when contraceptive prevalence rates for 1980 were mapped at the state or provincial level throughout the ASEAN countries, the lowest rates of all were found straddling the Thai–Malaysian border, in Pattani, Narathivat, and Kelantan.

The Philippines

Muslims constitute a somewhat higher proportion of the population of the Philippines than of Thailand. They are fairly concentrated geographically in certain regions of Mindanao and the Sulu Islands, and as in Thailand, most of the Filipino Muslims live in areas where Muslims are a majority: the provinces of Sulu, Tawi-Tawi, Lanao del Sur, Basilan, and Maguindanao. The Muslim population in regions such as Cotabato has been diluted by the heavy in-migration of Christians from other parts of the Philippines, notably the Visayas. But even there, most local areas are either heavily Muslim or Christian (Costello, 1992: 40).

The low regard in which the Muslim population of Southern Thailand is held by other Thais is replicated in the Philippines, perhaps to an even greater degree. The history of Christian–Muslim antagonisms and suspicions was transplanted to the Philippines from Europe by the Spanish, who at the time they took control of the Philippines had only recently driven the Muslims from their own homeland. As in Thailand, the Muslims have spawned separatist movements and their loyalty to the Philippines is suspect. As in Thailand, their levels of education are lower than those of the majority population; in the Catholic Philippines, too, practices such as polygamy are looked on askance. With this background, it is hardly surprising if the failure of the Maranaos, one of the major Islamic groups, to adopt 'quite a number of the attitudes and practices which they are expected to exemplify as Filipino citizens is due mainly to their feeling that there is a conflict between the requirements of Philippine citizenship and the demands of Islam' (De los Santos, 1974: 238).

As elsewhere in the Malay world, the Muslims in the Philippines were organized into sultanates, the most powerful of which, the Sulu and the Maguindanao, carried the brunt of resistance to the Spanish colonizers during the intermittent 300-year hostilities known as the Moro Wars. However, having brought them under central government control after 1905, the government neglected to make use of the allegiance of the Muslims to their traditional leaders, the *datu*, and there was 'a certain degree of indifference on the part of Christian Filipino officials sent to these areas to educate the people and bring them into the national body politic' (Glang, 1974: 281).

Official attitudes of condescension are clear enough in the following quotation from a Congress committee reporting in 1954:

In their ignorance, and in their trend toward religious fanaticism the Muslims are sadly wanting in the advantages of normal health and social factors and functions. Their health conditions, for example, are wretched. The Muslims in Mindanao and Sulu are a superstitious lot. In mixed communities they still look at the Christian Filipinos with the old suspicion and the old anger, refusing to participate in social and charitable works organized by the secular government.... As an individual, the Muslim refuses to concede that he is a part of the entire Filipino citizenry. He identifies himself by his religion. (Glang, 1974: 282.)

That religion is distinctly a folk Islam. 'Especially in rural areas the religion is imperfectly understood, and frequently there is only limited observation of rituals and obligations. The formal religious convictions of rural villagers tend to coexist with strong ancient beliefs in environmental spirits.' (Stewart, 1984: 465.) However, in recent years, 'there has been increased awareness of, and interest in, orthodox Islamic beliefs and practices. This has been accompanied by a growing sense of community with Muslim peoples outside the Philippines.' (Stewart, 1984: 465.)

Many Islamic missionaries from the Middle East came to the Philippines in the 1950s and 1960s, and an Islamic renewal movement swept over Mindanao from the early 1960s to the mid-1970s, a period marked by the construction of more than 1,500 *madari* (religious schools) and a sharp increase in the number of young people receiving a formal religious education (Lacar, 1992: 112–13). The number of young Muslims receiving an education in government and private Christian schools has also been increasing. The traditional secluded life of women in Muslim areas of the Philippines has started to break down with increased participation of women in education and in the workforce (Lacar, 1992).

In the Philippines, the Muslims

have been subject to special laws allowing them to maintain certain of their cultural traditions, most notably the practices of polygyny and divorce. These laws have been renewed or extended repeatedly, but they have always specified a termination date at some time in the near future. The assumption of the central government in granting such short-term exceptions to national laws appears to be that they ... must sooner or later accept the norms of the larger society. (Weekes, 1984: 466.)

Islamic Marriage and Family Laws

In Malaysia, Singapore, Brunei, Indonesia, and the Muslim provinces of the Philippines, a diverse range of *adat* or customary law systems have historically applied to the indigenous populations in the different regions, most of them infused to greater or lesser degrees with Islamic law of the Shafii school, one of the four orthodox schools of law in Sunni Islam (Ibrahim, 1965: 1).[11] In Indonesia, Islamic courts have jurisdiction over most marriage and divorce matters for Muslims, but civil courts, basing their decisions on *adat* law, which frequently incorporates Islamic law, decide marriage questions involving money or property.[12] This section will summarize briefly some of the main provisions of this body of law pertaining to marriage, divorce, and the care of children among the Malay-Muslim population around the 1960s, a task complicated by the differences in legal detail between and within countries. Changes brought about by the Muslim Law Act of 1957 in Singapore, the Indonesian Marriage Law of 1974, and the Islamic Family Law Act of 1984 in Malaysia will then be outlined. The discussion will be kept as brief as possible. Further details on the legislation and its effects can be found in sources such as Ibrahim (1965, 1978), Djamour (1966), Prodjodikoro (1967), Lev (1972), and Katz and Katz (1975). Chapters 6 and 7 will present a more detailed discussion of the legislation as it pertains to divorce and polygamy.

Basically, the provisions of Muslim family law in the region before new or revised laws were introduced in Singapore in the 1950s, Indonesia in the 1970s, and Malaysia in the 1980s were in line with those described briefly in Chapter 1. There was no legal minimum age at marriage, and the consent of the bride was not required if a virgin girl was given in marriage by her father or paternal grandfather, although administrative procedures put mild constraints on wicked or careless actions on the part of the father or grandfather (Ibrahim, 1965: 7–10).

The *mas kahwin*, the obligatory marriage payment due under Muslim law to the wife at the time the marriage is solemnized, normally had to be paid, or the amount promised recorded, in the presence of the person solemnizing the marriage and at least two other witnesses. The *mas kahwin* became identified with the Islamic *mahr* payment and actually represented a compromise between ancient Malay custom, which required a series of presents, and Islamic law by identifying the particular payment with the *mahr* (Ibrahim, 1965: 19). There was no fixed legal minimum, though in the West Coast states of Malaysia it was conventional to pay RM22.50.

Four kinds of divorce were provided for by law in Malaysia, Singapore, and Indonesia. By far the most common was *talak*, or male-initiated divorce.

Talak

A Muslim husband could divorce his wife by *talak* at his own will without intervention of the court, by mutual consent, or by judicial decree through annulment or dissolution. A *talak* divorce is one in which the husband informs his wife, either verbally or in writing, of his intention to divorce her. If pronounced once, it is a one-*talak* divorce, and this can be revoked (*rujuk*) by mutual consent during the 100 days of the *eddah*, during which a divorced woman is forbidden to marry another person. If pronounced three times (a triple-*talak* divorce), it cannot be revoked, and marriage can only take place again after the wife has first remarried and consummated the marriage with another man. Three one-*talak* divorces add up to a triple-*talak* divorce, and the last *talak* is then irrevocable. The official procedure in Malaysia was that within seven days of the divorce, the husband had to report it to the registrar of the locality at which the divorce took place. If the divorce could not be revoked, the registrar would then issue a certificate of divorce, one for the husband and one for the wife (Tan et al., 1986: 250-1).

Some state enactments required that every effort be made at reconciliation before a *talak* divorce was registered. In some states, the presence of the wife or the *kadi* (Muslim judge) was necessary for the registration of the divorce.

Cerai Ta'alik

A wife can apply for *cerai ta'alik*, or divorce by redemption, if the husband breaks the condition that he has agreed to on the solemnization of the marriage. The *surat ta'alik* (referred to in Indonesia as the *talik talak*) was placed at the end of many marriage certificates; it was compulsory in all marriages in some Malaysian states—Kelantan, Trengganu, Pahang, and Perak (see Ibrahim, 1978: 213), and in Indonesia had been standardized by the Ministry of Religion and put on the back of its official marriage contract since 1955. The Indonesian version specified that the wife has the right to seek a divorce if the husband deserts her for six consecutive months, fails to maintain her for a period of three consecutive months, physically mistreats her, or neglects her for six consecutive months (Katz and Katz, 1975: 658–9).

This form of divorce was more prevalent in Malaysia and Indonesia than in the Arab countries or in India or Pakistan. Some Indonesian writers attacked it as giving encouragement to divorce (e.g. Rasjid, 1954); by contrast, women's activists, while encouraging its use, saw it as giving insufficient protection to women because it required the initiative of the bride, the willingness of the groom, and the co-operation of the presiding Islamic official (Lev, 1972a: 143–5). Moreover, the husband still had the right to revoke such a divorce; Ibrahim (1965: 100) argued that this should not be permitted without the consent of the wife.

Kholo' (Chul' or Cerai Tebus Talak)

A *kholo'* divorce is a divorce in which the wife pays compensation to the husband in return for marital release. The wife normally initiates this by applying to the *kadi* and offering to pay compensation to the husband. The Shafii school teaches that the husband's consent is necessary for a divorce to take place. If the husband decides to accept compensation, the release of marital rights would be by a *talak* and it would be irrevocable on its pronouncement. This type of divorce was provided for in Kelantan, Trengganu, Pahang, Penang, and Kedah, as well as in Indonesia, where its regulations were, however, not clearly spelled out (Lev, 1972a: 169).

Fasakh

This is the dissolution or rescission of contract of marriage by judicial decree. The normal ground is that the husband is unable to maintain the wife, but the divorce can also be based on her becoming aware after marriage of her husband's impotence, insanity, leprosy, or elephantiasis. In theory, a husband can also apply for a *fasakh* divorce on similar grounds, but since he has the right to *talak*, such an application for *fasakh* is rare.

Sjiqoq

Though not one of the four legal grounds for divorce, *sjiqoq* should be mentioned. It was basically a formal mediation procedure employed in Indonesia in cases where a couple was irreconcilable but the wife had no legal grounds for divorce and her husband was adamantly opposed to one. The two *hakam*, or arbitrators, appointed (one for each spouse) had acquired the power, by 1940, to effectuate a divorce, if necessary, regardless of the husband's refusal. Though relatively rare, *sjiqoq* cases in Indonesia trebled in number between 1963 and 1965, representing a broadening of the means available to wives to escape unhappy marriages (Lev, 1972a: 169–71).

Summary

Divorce regulations were clearly much simpler for the husband wishing to divorce than for the wife. While the *talak* can be the unilateral act of the husband, it is necessary for a woman to apply to a *kadi* or a court for a decree of *cerai ta'alik*, *kholo'*, or *fasakh*. However, everything is not always as it seems. On the one hand, the legal provisions were frequently flouted against the interests of the woman by what can only be interpreted as a 'male conspiracy' between the husband and the religious officials.[13] On the other hand, the *talak*, though a male-initiated form of divorce, was frequently instigated by the wife, as it was easier for her to persuade her husband to divorce her in this way than to go through the legal procedures required for other kinds of divorce. This will be documented in Chapter 6.

Reform of Marriage Laws

The weaknesses and lack of precision in legal provisions related to Muslim marriage and the family in South-East Asian countries, as well as injustices towards women, were recognized by many, including legal experts, who noted that there had been little attempt to adapt the law to the requirements of modern life, or to make it consistent with the equal rights of men and women, as declared in the United Nations Charter and the Universal Declaration of Human Rights (Ibrahim, 1965: 95). For example, in some Malaysian states and for Indonesian and Thai Muslims the bride's consent to her marriage was not required, although other Malaysian states provided some degree of protection by requiring that the marriage register be signed by both the husband and the wife (Ibrahim, 1965: 7–10, 96). However, legal reform was frequently resisted by the more fundamentalist forces in the Islamic community who were concerned that secular considerations would replace religious imperatives.

Singapore

The Muslims Ordinance in Singapore in 1957 was the first major attempt to reform laws, or more correctly, the administration of laws, related to Muslim marriage and divorce in the region. It did not aim at fundamental change in the Muslim law governing marriage and divorce, but rather at its more effective enforcement and reduction in the very high divorce rate among Muslims. It provided for the setting up of a Shariah Court, which became the regulatory body in the administration of the Muslim law concerning marriage and divorce. Applications for divorces had to be made to the Court, and divorces were not granted until after some reconciliatory efforts were made (Wong, 1976: 297). This 'placed some bureaucratic hurdles and financial costs in the way of quick and thoughtless divorce' (Li, 1989: 35). The Court 'was also empowered to enquire into and adjudicate upon the claims of the married woman for the payment of her "maskahwin", the payment of maintenance and consolatory gifts, as well as over the question of custody of children and division of property' (Wong, 1976: 297).

With regard to polygamy, a follow-up Administration of Muslim Law Act in 1966 required polygamous marriages to be granted by the *kadi*, who must be satisfied that no obstacles, according to the Muslim Law, to such marriages existed. This implied that the *kadi* had to ensure that the wives in the polygamous union would receive equal treatment from the husband, and that he was financially able to maintain both or all of them. The effects of the Muslims Ordinance on divorce in Singapore will be discussed in Chapter 6. These pioneering legal reforms in Singapore were very slow to be followed up elsewhere in the region.

Indonesia

In Indonesia, demand for marriage law reform had been at issue since the mid-1950s. According to Lev (1972a: 138), these demands arose from 'a growing intellectual liberation of upper- and upper-middle-class women, an easing control over women in urban society, the impact of egalitarian ideologies, and the influence of foreign examples'. The Indonesian Marriage Law of 1974, enacted after becoming a fierce political issue between the Muslim and other groups in the Indonesian Parliament (Katz and Katz, 1975; Suryadinata, 1989: 66–9), codified the marriage law and gave Indonesian Muslims a clearer picture of their marital rights and responsibilities. Many of its original provisions—in fact, all those contrary to Islamic law—were dropped, including provisions that would have required use of civil rather than Islamic courts by Muslims for some purposes, demanded registration to validate a marriage, allowed mixed marriages, and given legal status to engagement (Katz and Katz, 1975). Another original aim was to set the minimum age at marriage for females at 18, in the interests of supporting the family planning programme by delaying marriage and hence childbearing. But eventually, the minimum ages were set at 19 for males and 16 for females; consequently the law followed rather than led practice, as few girls were being married before the age of 16 by that time. Moreover, dispensations could be obtained from a court or the Department of Religion for those who wished to marry below these ages (Katz and Katz, 1975: 674; Daly, 1987: 132-4). Since the reason such dispensations were sought was frequently the girl's pregnancy,[14] they were normally granted.

Nevertheless, the Indonesian Marriage Law had some very important effects (Katz and Katz, 1978). First, to obtain a *talak* divorce, a Muslim husband now had to go to an Islamic court and must give a reason for wanting it. Secondly, under the new law, a Muslim husband had to receive permission from a court to take more than one wife, and permission would be given only if certain specific conditions were met, including permission in writing from his other current wife or wives, who must also appear in court. Both divorce and polygamy became less frequent after the law was passed (Katz and Katz, 1978), no doubt mainly because of the greater trouble and expense involved in obtaining a divorce or marrying polygamously, and the possibility that the application will be refused by the court. Other influences on divorce and polygamy will be discussed in Chapters 6 and 7.

Malaysia

In Malaysia, the Islamic Family Law Act of 1984 introduced a number of important changes and a tightening up of various administrative procedures. Although passage and enactment of the law by the different states was very slow, partly because of strong opposition in some quarters to the restrictions it placed on polygamy, by the end of 1991 it had finally been enacted in all states. There were further amendments to the Act in a number of states during the early 1990s. The Act set the minimum age of marriage at 16 for a woman and 18 for a man, as in the case of Indonesia following, rather than leading, this aspect of social change. However, in relation to polygamy and divorce, the Act can be expected to have some real impact, given the frequency with which the Malay wife was formerly left uninformed that her husband had taken an additional wife or even that he had divorced her.[15]

The following description of the provisions of the new Act is based heavily on an article in the *New Straits Times* (12 March 1986, 'Times Two', p. 1).

POLYGAMY

Under the new Act, a man wishing to take a second or subsequent wife is required to submit an application to the Shariah Court. The application has to be accompanied by a statutory declaration stating
(a) the grounds on which the proposed marriage is considered to be just and necessary;
(b) the man's present income and details of his commitments and financial obligations and liabilities;
(c) the number of his dependants, including persons who would be his dependants as a result of the proposed marriage; and
(d) whether the consent or views of the existing wife or wives to the proposed marriage have been obtained.
The application will be heard in court in camera in the presence of the applicant and his existing wife or wives. Permission will be granted by the court only if it is satisfied that
(a) the proposed marriage is just and necessary under the circumstances including such circumstances as sterility, physical infirmity, physical unfitness for conjugal relations, wilful avoidance of an order for restitution of conjugal rights, or insanity on the part of the existing wife or wives;
(b) the applicant has the means to support all his wives and dependants including the woman he proposes to marry and her dependants;
(c) the applicant will be able to treat his wives equally;
(d) the proposed marriage would not cause *darar syar'i* (meaning harm

according to what is normally recognized by Islamic law, affecting a wife in respect of religion, life, body, mind, or property) to the existing wife or wives; and

(e) the proposed marriage would not directly or indirectly lower the standard of living that the existing wife or wives and dependants had been enjoying and would enjoy were the marriage not to take place.

However, an appeal against the decision of the court may be made if the applicant or his existing wife or wives is not satisfied with the decision of the Shariah judge. A person who contracts a marriage in contravention of this section has to pay immediately the entire amount of the *mas kahwin* and the *pemberian* due to the existing wife or wives. He is also considered to have committed an offence under the Act which is punishable with a maximum fine of RM1,000 and/or imprisonment not exceeding six months.

DIVORCE

The Act has retained all the former categories and grounds for divorce. However, for the *fasakh* (application by a woman for an order for dissolution of marriage), the grounds upon which a woman may petition have been considerably enlarged. The grounds on which a woman is entitled to obtain an order for *fasakh* are listed in detail in the *New Straits Times* article of 12 March 1986, and reproduced in Tan et al. (1986: 266–8).

The Act also lays down the procedures for divorce. Both spouses will have to appear in court so as to enable it to enquire whether or not they consent to the divorce. If the court is satisfied that the marriage has irretrievably broken down, it shall then advise the husband to pronounce one *talak* before the court. However, if the other party does not consent to the divorce, and there is a reasonable possibility of a reconciliation between the parties, the court will appoint a conciliatory committee consisting of a religious officer as chairman and two other persons, preferably close relatives of the parties, one to act for the husband and the other for the wife. The committee is given six months to try and effect a reconciliation. If this fails, the court will advise the husband to pronounce one *talak*. Any man who divorces his wife by the pronouncement of the *talak* outside the court and without the permission of the court will have to pay a fine not exceeding RM1,000 and/or face six months' imprisonment.

MAINTENANCE OF WIFE AND CHILDREN

In addition to her right to maintenance during the *eddah* period, or three months following the divorce, a woman who has been divorced without just cause may apply to the court for *mut'ah* or a consolatory gift, and the court may order the husband to pay a reasonable sum. But under the provisions of the new Act, the court may also make an order for the wife to maintain the husband if he is incapacitated from earning a living through physical or mental injury or ill health, if it is within the means of the wife to do so.

Regarding the maintenance of children, the father has a duty to maintain his children until the age of 18 years, instead of the previous 15 years. But where the child intends to pursue higher education or training, the duty to maintain continues until the child's education is completed.

The Islamic Family Law Act clearly makes both polygamy and divorce more difficult to organize than they were in the past. The Act was slow to be enforced in the various states: three states, Perak, Selangor, and Penang, enacted it only in 1989, and three more, Trengganu, Johore, and Perlis, only in 1990 or 1991; so it is too early yet to identify its effect on divorce and polygamy.

Southern Thailand

Marriage laws for the minority Muslim population in Southern Thailand have not undergone any of the reforms undertaken in Singapore, Malaysia, and Indonesia. The legal situation concerning Muslim marriages is therefore closer to the situation prevailing in the rest of Islamic South-East Asia in the 1950s. The Islamic authorities take a very traditional view of marriage and divorce procedures, with more emphasis on the rights of men in marriage, divorce, and polygamy than on their responsibilities.[16]

Concerning the registration of Islamic marriages, before 1947 the fact that the traditional marriage ceremony had been conducted was considered evidence enough that the marriage had taken place; the *imam* would usually be invited anyway. In 1947, Islamic Committees were established in the four southernmost provinces of Pattani, Narathiwat, Yala, and Satun, and now exist in twenty-eight provinces. Islamic marriages and divorces have to be registered with the *imam*, who in turn is supposed to pass on the information to the Islamic Committee. But even if the marriage is not registered with the *imam*, it is still considered legal.

As for divorce, it should be pronounced in front of the *imam*, but there is no penalty if the husband pronounces the *talak* first and reports it later. There is no procedure for counselling. The wife is simply informed later on that she has been divorced.

No barriers are placed in the way of polygamous marriage, which should be registered, like other marriages, with the *imam*. The first wife does not have to be informed that the husband is taking another wife. All that is required is that the husband can provide for his wives and treat them fairly.

A young girl can be married against her will to a man chosen by her *wali* (male guardian). There is no provision for a process of discussion with the *imam* in such a situation.

1. Television was first introduced in Indonesia in 1962 and in Peninsular Malaysia in 1963. By 1966–7, about 10 per cent of married Malay women in Peninsular Malaysia watched television at least once a week (65 per cent in metropolitan areas watched it, 34 per cent in other urban areas but only 4 per cent in rural areas: see National Family Planning Board, n.d.: Tables I.1, I.8, I.15, and I.22). The spread of television in Indonesia was slower; there were only about 65,000 licensed viewers, all of them in big cities, in 1969. New stations were established outside Jakarta in 1969, and by 1971, there were 212,000 receivers, still less than one-tenth the number per head in Malaysia. By 1976, there were about 643,000 receivers. Alfian (1976: 4–5), assuming five viewers per household, estimated the total potential audience at that time as still only about 2 per cent of the total population, most of them better-off urban dwellers. He appears to have underestimated the amount of 'mass' viewing as neighbours clustered around open doorways or outside the veranda in the evenings, watching the television programmes on the set of a more fortunate neighbour. (For a case-study, see Hefner, 1990: 188–9.) But he was correct in arguing that television did not yet have a mass audience. This came with the launching of the Palapa communications satellite in 1976; by 1980, 33 per cent of urban households and 4 per cent of rural households possessed a television set (1980 Population Census figures), and the percentage regularly watching television would have been much higher. By 1983, nearly three million television sets were registered, reaching an estimated total of 95.5 million people, or about 64 per cent of the population (Chu, Alfian, and Schramm, 1991: 43). Viewing time in Indonesia increased from one hour a day in 1962 to five hours in 1972 and eight hours in 1985. Entertainment programmes occupied over 30 per cent of viewing time, and in the early 1970s, over 70 per cent of them were imported, mostly from the United States. By 1985, the foreign share of entertainment programmes had fallen to about 30 per cent.

Thus by the late 1970s, television was already an instrument of mass communication in Indonesia, viewed by all social classes in both urban and rural areas.

2. The author was struck, when staying in rural Kelantan with the family of one of his students in the late 1970s, at the incongruity of family members congregating after evening prayers to watch 'Charlie's Angels'. This programme was also staple fare in Indonesia at the time.

3. The actual proportion depends on the size cut-off used to define urban places; in 1970, the level of urbanization in Peninsular Malaysia was 28.8 per cent using the definition of gazetted areas of 10,000 and over, 41.9 per cent using the definition of gazetted areas of 1,000 and over, and 44.3 per cent using the definition conurbation and gazetted areas of 1,000 and over (ESCAP, 1982: Table 5).

4. The figure of over 5 per cent of the population is from Weekes, 1984: 901. The National Census and Statistics Office gave a figure of 4.32 per cent Muslim in 1975. Muslims in the Philippines belong to seven main ethnic groups: the Maranao, Maguindanao, Tausug, Samal, Yakan, Jama Mapun, and Bajao. Of these, the first three are by far the largest groups (Weekes, 1984: 462–7, 495–9, 654–9, 764–70, 901; Gastardo-Conaco and Ramos-Jiminez, 1986). Philippine Muslims are concentrated in Mindanao and in the Sulu Archipelago.

5. The Malays in Singapore have traditionally been concentrated in the public sector and to a lesser degree as unskilled workers (drivers, messengers, etc.) in transport, storage and communications activities (Jones, 1966: Table 2.11; Pang, 1982: 59–60). Malay income in 1966 was on the average about 15 per cent below that of the Chinese (Pang, 1982: 64). Income growth for employed Malays lagged badly behind that of the other races between 1966 and 1974, as Malays adjusted slowly to the demand for new skills created by industrialization. 'By not accepting them into the military and police forces, their traditional fields of employment, official policy also contributed to the employment problems of Malay youths' (Pang, 1982: 72). But after 1974, Malays enjoyed faster income growth than the other racial groups.

According to Pang (1982: 73), 'Their improvement reflects the impact of sustained full employment in Singapore and changes in their values and attitudes as a result of the spread of education among them and their increased participation in the dynamic sectors of the Singapore economy. The changing role of Malays in the economy can be seen in the rapidly rising labour force participation of Malay women. In 1966, working-age Malay women had a labour force participation of only 8.5 per cent, 20 percentage points below that of Chinese women. The large gap in participation rate suggests that cultural factors by influencing Malay attitudes towards female education and training inhibited female Malay participation in the labour market in the 1960s. In 1980, Malay women had a participation rate of 46.2 per cent, less than 2 percentage points below the Chinese rate.'

Furthermore, 'the sharp rise in the labour force participation of Malay women in Singapore has not provoked negative reactions from Malay community and religious leaders. These leaders support the government's efforts to encourage Malays to compete in the modern sectors of the economy. In contrast, the rapid inflow of young Malay women into the work-force in Malaysia has been criticized by Islamic fundamentalists who argue that modern sector employment of Malay women undermines the teachings of Islam, particularly those relating to the role of women in Moslem societies.' (Pang, 1982: 79.)

6. It must be remembered, too, that if the Indonesian figures were restricted to the Muslim population, the school enrolment ratios would be a little lower than those shown in Figure 2.4, because Muslims lag behind the remainder of the population in educational enrolments and educational attainment (Jones, 1976).

7. In Singapore, manufacturing provided 31 per cent of Malay female employment in 1970, but this rose to 55 per cent in 1979; the rise was offset by a decline in the proportion of Malay women employed as domestic servants (Wong, 1981: 447).

8. In the mid-1980s, recession led to retrenchment of many Malay female workers. After recovery, employment prospects in electronics were less certain, and rising wages, shortages of skilled workers, infrastructure problems, and technological changes within the industry, favouring re-basing of production back in Japan or the United States, made prospects of further expansion of the industry in Malaysia uncertain (Tsuruoka, 1990).

9. The Muslim Youth League of Malaysia (ABIM) recognizes the value of education and the role women can play in appropriate sectors of the workforce, provided the job does not compromise their primary roles as wives and mothers. Another major *dakwah* group, Jemaat Tabligh, however, puts a premium on women's not working outside the home (Nagata, 1984: Chapter 4).

10. These advantages had not resulted in much improvement in the Malays' involvement in higher education: only 2 per cent of Malays had had post-secondary or tertiary education, as compared to 7 per cent of the general population (Chua and Wong, 1988: 214).

11. Outside South-East Asia, the Shafii school of law has a considerable following in Egypt.

12. Law No. 22 of 1946, aimed at unifying the administration of marriage and divorce throughout Indonesia under the Ministry of Religion, transferred the Religious Court systems of Java and Madura, and of Banjarmasin, to the Ministry of Religion in 1946, and in the remaining territories in 1957.

According to Hooker (1978: 99), 'It was provided that all marriages, divorces and reconciliations of Muslims must be brought under the formal supervision of Registrars appointed by the Ministry. Fines were to be levied against persons who undertook to change their status without registration and fees for registration were imposed.... The motive behind the statute was to provide some measure of certainty and stability in marital relationships as well as to assert a political control in the name of Islam.'

13. The male bias in judgements by many *kadi* in Malaysia is widely acknowledged. In a 1991 seminar on the possibility of appointing women as Shariah Court judges, a number of recent cases were cited of 'the indifference of many judges towards the injustices to women' (Ali, 1991). In 1992, the Finance Minister, Datuk Seri Anwar Ibrahim, stated: 'I'm sorry to say that our syariah court used to be a "pro-male court". But this kind of unjust administration had been corrected with amendments made to the law.' (*New Sunday Times*, 26 April 1992.)

14. Based on discussions with religious officials in West Java in 1990.

15. In a parliamentary debate in 1984 on the Islamic Family Law (Federal Territory) Bill, the Deputy Minister in the Prime Minister's Department, Sharifah Dora binti Syed Mohamed, said there had been several occasions when the first wife discovered that her

husband had a second wife and a string of children when he died and the other half of the family turned up at the cemetery (*Star*, 24 March 1974).

16. This section is based on discussions with members of the Islamic Committees in Yala and Pattani in 1991 and 1992 respectively, with Apirat Madsa-I, Judge of Islamic Law of Pattani, with members of the Islamic Studies Department of Songkhla Nakarin University, and with other officials both in Bangkok and in Southern Thailand.

3
Trends in Marriage Timing in Islamic South-East Asia

Sequence in the Arrangement of Marriage

THIS chapter will examine the changing age at marriage among Malay-Muslim populations in South-East Asia. The main emphasis will be on female age at marriage, which is important in signalling entry into the responsibilities of establishing a household, initiation into sexual relations, and the potentiality for childbearing. Early or late marriage patterns and the degree of autonomy a woman has in choosing her marriage partner also reflect fundamental aspects of the roles and status of women in society. But male ages at marriage and age differences between the partners in a marriage also reflect importantly on male roles in family and society, and will be discussed, albeit more briefly.

In the West, however, marriage these days has little to do with the initiation of sexual relations as these have usually begun before marriage; nor is marriage necessarily the precursor of childbearing or the responsibilities of running a household, since both these are frequently undertaken without recourse to formal marriage (Zelnik and Shah, 1983; Khoo and McDonald, 1988; Villeneuve-Gokalp, 1991). In Malay-Muslim societies, marriage may appear to have a more precise relationship to establishment of a household, initiation of sexual relations, and the potentiality for childbearing. Certainly there is very little childbearing outside marriage, and traditionally, strenuous efforts have been made to protect an unmarried girl from any intimacy with the opposite sex except for close family. However, 'illicit' sexual relations are now almost certainly on the increase among young Muslim people in Indonesia, Malaysia, and Singapore.[1] There has been relatively little setting up of households without formal marriage, although enough of it so that the term *kumpul kebo* (literally, 'marriage in the manner of water-buffaloes') is well known throughout Indonesia.

There is a further complication. It cannot be assumed that in traditional Malay society in South-East Asia, the formal marriage ceremony was necessarily coterminous with the commencement of sexual relations or with the setting up of a household. Traditional marriage among the Javanese and Sundanese, which frequently occurred before the girl had menstruated or soon after her first menstruation, required a delay in initiation of sexual relations in many cases. As Hull and Hull (1987: 107–8) have noted, there could be a lengthy delay between the religious and legal marriage ceremony (*akad nikah* in Malay) and the social ceremony; moreover, whether these ceremonies coincided or not, there could be a considerable further delay before the marriage was consummated, and in a not insubstantial proportion of cases it was never consummated. The term *kawin gantung* (*nikah gantung* in Malaysia), or 'suspended marriage' refers to cases where a couple is married in a legal and religious sense, but a more elaborate ceremony, and the consummation of the marriage, are delayed (see also Swift, 1963: 289).

In the Indonesian segment of the Asian Marriage Survey, conducted in Central Java, 22 per cent of girls in the rural sample were married before their first menstruation, though the figure was much lower— around 5 per cent—in urban areas. Somewhere between 5 and 8 per cent of parentally arranged marriages were never consummated, though the figure fell to 1 per cent among marriages arranged by the couple themselves. Delayed consummation in parentally arranged marriages was recorded by a proportion of respondents ranging from 9 per cent among urban middle class respondents to 25 per cent among rural respondents. Delayed consummation of couple-arranged marriages was substantially lower (Hull and Hull, 1987: Table 3). In Kota Gede, Yogyakarta, 10 per cent of divorces registered between 1964 and 1971 were to marriages which were never consummated (Nakamura, 1983: 74).

The Javanese, however, appear to be characterized by greater delays in consummation and more non-consummation than any other major group in the Malay world. Some figures for other groups follow. Among Peninsular Malaysia Malays surveyed in 1981, 8 per cent had delayed cohabitation by more than one month from the date of the formal marriage ceremony (Tan and Jones, 1991: Table 7); among the Betawi of the Jakarta region, 2 per cent of female respondents had done so (Muliakusuma, 1982: 50); among the Banjarese of South Kalimantan, 9 per cent of female respondents had done so, but only 1 per cent delayed for more than one year or never consummated the marriage (Mahfudz, 1982: 46). One West Java study reported cases of non-consummation among parent-arranged marriages (Adioetomo, 1993: Chapter 7). Non-consummation of marriage was formerly common in Kelantan, related to parent-arranged marriages, very young age at marriage, and immaturity and embarrassment on the part of both bride and groom. Divorce frequently resulted (Kelantan focus-group discussions, 1889).

In contemporary Malay society, the formal marriage ceremony continues to correlate less than precisely with the commencement of sexual relations, though these days the imprecision is more likely to result from premarital sex and (more rarely) living together without entering a formal marriage, rather than from suspended marriage (Sarwono, 1981, 1990; Widyantoro and Sarsanto, 1990; Jones, Asari, and Djuartika, forthcoming). Some unpublished studies in Indonesia suggest that about a third of young people marrying have experienced premarital sexual intercourse, and an unpublished study in Perak in the early 1980s showed that about 6 per cent of Malay women had experienced premarital sexual intercourse.

What, then, do we mean when we talk of age at marriage in the Malay context? The data collected in censuses and surveys normally define marriage in terms of the official marriage ceremony. In some cases, this is not the time at which consummation of the marriage, or the establishment of a separate household, takes place. Such marriage data would therefore tend to systematically understate the age at which women entered conjugal relations, particularly in earlier times. Even so, it should be stressed that, although separation of the legal ceremony and the social ceremony are known throughout the Malay world, as is delayed consummation, it is only among the Javanese and perhaps the Kelantanese that the incidence and duration of these delays is enough to cause non-trivial distortions when the age of formal marriage is used as a proxy for the initiation of cohabitation. Elsewhere, it is doubtful if cohabitation is delayed for a year or more in more than 1 per cent of cases.

Trends in Age at Marriage and Proportions Marrying

In the Malay world, marriage has traditionally been universal, for both men and women. Marsden, writing in the nineteenth century about the districts of Sumatra under his charge, did not conceive that it would be possible to find among a population amounting to about 8,000 persons even ten instances of men of the age of 30 who were unmarried (Marsden, 1811: 256 ff.). In Java in much the same period, Crawfurd 'never saw a woman of two and twenty that was not or had not been married' (Crawfurd, 1820: Vol. 1, 86). Universal marriage has continued to characterize the Malay world at least up to the 1970s.

Not only has marriage traditionally been universal among South-East Asian Muslims; for females, it has also been very early. In Indonesia, it has been earlier for Muslims than for Christians; in Malaysia, it has been earlier for Malays than for Chinese, and in Sabah, earlier for Muslim than for Christian groups; in Southern Thailand, it has been earlier for Muslims than for Thai Buddhists; in the Philippines, it has recently been about two years earlier for Muslims than for Christians.[2]

Recent developments may be signalling a sharp erosion of the universality of marriage, though the evidence is not conclusive, as will be discussed below. What is incontestable, though, is that over the past thirty years, there has been a revolution in age at marriage throughout Islamic South-East Asia. The word 'revolution' is no exaggeration in describing these trends, because the changes, besides being dramatic in themselves, reflect fundamental changes in family structure, parent–children relationships, child-raising practices, and expectations of daughters. The root causes lie in the economic and social changes which have swept the region, and although it is tempting to stress one or two factors as crucial—for example, urbanization, the spread of education, new work opportunities for women, the transistor and television revolutions and their role in spreading Western culture, and the growth of consumerism and individualism—there is little doubt that it is the complex of changes rather than any one or two of them that must be invoked. South-East Asia over the past thirty years has in many ways altered almost beyond recognition. The changes have swept the region as a whole, and not only its Islamic populations. One aspect has been a universal trend towards higher female ages at marriage (Smith, 1980; United Nations, 1990: Figure 16), which has also characterized the rest of Asia to greater or lesser degree. In this context, it is not surprising that the Islamic community's traditional practices in marrying off its daughters have not been immune to change.

Period and Cohort Measures

Before the evidence is presented on trends in age at marriage, a brief discussion is needed of the period and cohort measures employed in this chapter. Period measures are those which show indicators of marriage age at particular points in time; examples are the percentage ever-married at the ages of 15–19 and 20–24, or the indirect period indices of median age at marriage and singulate mean age at marriage, calculated from census or survey data on marital status by age and sex. The latter two measures are frequently used to approximate the average age at marriage for the census or survey year (Shryock and Siegel, 1971: 292). They suffer from a number of shortcomings, including a rather vague time reference, because they apply to a synthetic rather than a true cohort (being based on marriages occurring up to forty years before the census or survey); biases when used to study trends in age at marriage during a period of rapid change or to study differences in age at marriage among groups with quite different age distributions; and inaccuracies introduced by interpolation when the calculation is based on five-year age-groups. They will be used very sparingly in the following analysis, as an indicator of general trends.[3]

Cohort rates are those based on the experience of a group who were born in the same time period. Comparing the age at marriage of such cohorts gives a clearer picture of time trends than does the synthetic mean or median estimates, and cohort measures are therefore the main data used in this chapter.[4] In using such measures, care must be taken to avoid censoring biases, which arise when some of the cohort have not yet had the chance to experience the event being analysed. The tables employing such cohort measures contain footnotes indicating censoring problems when they exist.

Period Trends

Table 3.1 presents data indicating the general patterns of change in age at marriage among the populations under study, based on 'snapshots' of marital status from censuses and large, representative surveys. The data for Indonesia cover not only the 87 per cent of the population who are Muslims but the non-Muslims as well. Age at marriage among Christians and Hindus in Indonesia is universally found to be higher than among Muslims (Muliakusuma, 1976: Table II.5; Palmore and Singarimbun, 1991: Tables 4, 5, and 6). Therefore, the Indonesian data in Table 3.1, if taken to represent the Muslim population, will overstate Muslim ages at marriage, but not too seriously given the high Muslim proportion of the total population. In a separate section on Indonesia below, more disaggregated data will be presented.

Five items of information are presented in the table. The first three are self-explanatory: the proportion of women still single at ages 15–19, 20–24, and 30–34. The fourth item, the proportion single among women aged 45–49, is taken as a measure of non-marriage. Although some women may marry after this age, such marriages come too late to have a reproductive outcome. The fifth item is the median age at marriage, already discussed above.

These indicators highlight both the uniformities and the fascinating differences within the Malay world. The uniformities lie in the universal trend towards higher ages at marriage. The differences lie in the timing and speed of this trend. In Singapore, the sharpest rise was concentrated in the late 1950s and 1960s. During this brief period, the median age at marriage for Singapore Malays climbed by almost five years, a rise possibly unmatched over such a short period anywhere else in the world,[5] and the percentages still single at ages 20–24 rose from less than 10 per cent to 45 per cent. In neighbouring Peninsular Malaysia, the leap in age at marriage occurred during the same period: between 1957 and 1970. Again, the rise was dramatic, though it could not match that of the Singapore Malays. In both countries, quite rapid further rises occurred through the 1970s, but slackened off in the 1980s. Different data show conflicting trends for Singapore Malays in the 1980s: census data indicate little change in age at marriage, but annual data on mean age of Muslim brides show that this climbed by almost two more years—from 23.8 in 1980 to 25.7 in 1990.

In Indonesia, the rise began later and, though steady, was modest until the 1980s. Trends among the Southern Thai Muslims appear to have paralleled those in Indonesia. By 1980, the proportion of females still single at ages 20–24 had reached 60 per cent for Singapore Malays, 54 per cent in Brunei, 49 per cent for Peninsular Malaysia Malays, 22 per cent in Indonesia, and 16 per cent in Muslim-dominated provinces of Southern Thailand. There was evidence that the rise in age at marriage plateaued in Peninsular Malaysia in the early 1980s, but that it continued to rise in the other countries, especially in Indonesia and for Muslims in Southern Thailand, where one and a half and two and a half years respectively were added to the average age at marriage for females over the course of the 1980s.

As for non-marriage, the proxy data (percentage single at ages 45–49) presented in Table 3.1 give no evidence that it is becoming any more than an aberration in a resolutely family-centred Malay world. However,

TABLE 3.1

Islamic South-East Asia: Indicators of Trends in Marriage Timing and Non-marriage among Females, 1947–1990

Group and Indicator	1947	1957	1964	1970	1975	1980	1985	1990
Peninsular Malaysia Malays								
Percentage single at ages 15–19	40.8	45.9	—	77.3	83.3[d]	89.5	93.3	—
Percentage single at ages 20–24	6.6	9.4	—	32.4	40.4[d]	48.6	48.7	—
Percentage single at ages 30–34	1.3	1.1	—	3.3	5.0	7.9	9.0	—
Percentage never married[a]	1.4	0.6	—	0.7	0.0[d]	1.7	3.2	—
Median age at marriage	16.6	17.1	—	20.5	21.4[d]	22.2	22.2	—
Singapore Malays								
Percentage single at ages 15–19	32.7	46.6	82.9[e]	89.5	—	95.1	95.3	96.4
Percentage single at ages 20–24	6.3	9.7	31.3[e]	45.0	—	60.4	65.3	62.8
Percentage single at ages 30–34	2.3	1.7	1.4[e]	3.9	—	12.7	14.9	13.8
Percentage never married[a]	2.1	0.9	1.5[e]	1.1	—	1.7	1.4	3.8
Median age at marriage	16.1	17.2	20.2[e]	22.0	—	23.9	24.7	23.9
Indonesia								
Percentage single at ages 15–19	—	—	56.8	62.6[b]	67.9[c]	69.9	81.2	81.8
Percentage single at ages 20–24	—	—	14.2	18.5[b]	23.5[c]	22.3	29.7	35.7
Percentage single at ages 30–34	—	—	-	2.2	2.5[c]	3.4	4.1	4.5
Percentage never married[a]	—	—	1.0	1.0[b]	0.8[c]	1.2	1.4	1.5
Median age at marriage	—	—	18.2	18.9[b]	19.5	19.5	20.5	20.9

Brunei Malays					
Percentage single at ages 15–19	—	—	85.3[b]	89.8[f]	91.8[h]	93
Percentage single at ages 20–24	—	—	44.3[b]	54.3[f]	61.7[h]	61
Percentage single at ages 30–34	—	—	11.1	15.1	15.8	15
Percentage never married[a]	—	—	4.5[b]	6.5[f]	5.5[h]	9
Median age at marriage	—	—	21.5[b]	22.7[f]	23.8[h]	n.a.
Southern Thai Muslims[i]					
Percentage single at ages 15–19	—	43.1[g]	51.4	62.4	—	79.2
Percentage single at ages 20–24	—	—	—	16.3	—	35.6
Percentage single at ages 30–34	—	—	—	1.3	—	3.1
Percentage never married[a]	—	0.3[g]	0.5	0.8	—	0.0
Median age at marriage (SMAM)	—	17.9	18.7	19.3	—	21.6

Sources: Jones (1980: Table 2); Tan et al. (1988: Table 1); Rachapaetayakom (1983: Table 5.2); Various census reports; Brunei Darussalam Population Survey, 1986, Demographic Report, p. 51; Unpublished data provided by the Population Planning Unit, Ministry of Health, Singapore; Computer tapes of *1980 Population and Housing Census* and *1990 Population and Housing Census*, Thailand.

[a] Percentage single among women aged 45–49.
[b] 1971.
[c] 1976.
[d] 1974.
[e] 1966.
[f] 1981.
[g] 1960.
[h] 1986; data includes non-Malay population (31% of total).
[i] The four provinces of Pattani, Narathiwat, Yala, and Satun, where Muslims constitute three-quarters of the population.

if the proportion of women aged 30–34 is substituted for the proportion aged 45–49, distinct trends are in evidence among all these populations except the Southern Thai Muslims. Brunei Malays were the pacesetters, with 11 per cent of women still single at ages 30–34 as early as 1971. Among Singapore Malays, the proportion still single at the same ages rose very sharply over the 1970s and by 1985 had reached the 15 per cent figure already reached by Brunei Malays in 1981. The comparable proportion among Peninsular Malaysian Malays also showed a big rise over its levels in the 1950s and 1960s, and had reached 9 per cent by 1984.

Even these upward trends in percentages still single at ages 30–34 do not prove that non-marriage is on the increase. In theory, most women still unmarried in their early thirties may still marry by their late forties. However, the failure of proportions single among women in their forties to show any rise probably represents the persistence of traditional patterns among older women, whereas the sharp rise in percentages non-married at ages 30–34 appears to reflect revolutionary new attitudes among the younger cohorts now reaching these ages. It seems likely that when these cohorts reach their late forties, the proportion unmarried at this age will begin to rise quite sharply. Confirmation of this interpretation will only come with the passage of time, a decade or so from now. Interestingly, the majority of respondents in the 1981 Malaysian Marriage Survey considered that a woman's chances of marrying declined sharply if she reached the age of 30 without marrying (Tan et al., 1986: 205). Even if it does not, the potential dampening impact on fertility of failure to marry before a woman's early thirties is clear.

Cohort Trends

The Indonesian, Malaysian, Singapore, and Thai census reports for 1980 presented information on age at marriage by current age, from which it is possible to estimate comparable cohort trends in age at marriage for a few decades preceding the census. For Indonesia, the 1990 Population Census repeated this tabulation, thus enabling the cohort trends to be brought forward in time, and also to be cross-checked for most cohorts against the figures produced from the census a decade earlier. The data are summarized in Table 3.2, which shows the age by which 50 per cent of women in each birth cohort had married. Some additional survey information from Singapore and Southern Thailand is also included. It is reasonable to assume that the data are increasingly unreliable the earlier the birth cohort; after all, women born before 1906 were aged at least 72 in 1980, their memories would not always have been accurate, and in any case knowledge of age was worse before 1906.[6] Such factors may account for the higher age at marriage recorded in Indonesia for this oldest group of women, although it cannot be ascertained that there was not a real change. The oldest group of women in Malaysia, by contrast, had the youngest age at marriage.

The key trends from Table 3.2 are shown graphically in Figure 3.1, which brings out the broad similarity in ages at marriage between

TABLE 3.2

Islamic South-East Asia: Age by Which 50 Per Cent of Female Birth Cohorts Had Married

Birth Cohort	Indonesia[a]			Peninsular Malaysia Malays	Singapore Malays[a]	Southern Thai Muslims[a]		
	Total	Urban	Rural	Total	Median	Total	Urban	Rural
1966–70	20.3	–[b]	19.7	–	–	–	–	–
1961–5	19.0	21.0	18.3	–	–	–	–	–
1956–60	(18.5)	(20.6)	(18.0)	–[b]	22.9	17.3	–	–
1951–5	(18.0)	(19.8)	(17.8)	20.5 (21.7)[c]	21.9	16.5 (16.6)	(17.7)	(16.2)
1946–50	(17.5)	(18.9)	(17.7)	19.5 (21.0)[c]	19.2 (19.7)	16.7 (16.3)	(17.2)	(16.0)
1941–5	(17.4)	(18.5)	(17.7)	18.3 (19.8)[c]	18.6 (18.3)	17.0 (16.2)	(16.6)	(16.0)
1936–40	(17.4)	(18.2)	(17.6)	17.9 (17.6)[c]	18.4 (17.8)	17.0 (16.1)	(16.4)	(15.9)
1931–5	(17.4)	(18.0)	(17.5)	17.5 (17.5)[c]	(17.4)	17.3 (16.2)	(16.3)	(16.0)
1926–30	(17.4)	(17.9)	(17.6)	17.3	–	17.3 (16.0)	(16.3)	(16.0)
1921–5	(17.5)	(17.9)	(17.6)	17.3	(18.0)	17.9	–	–
1916–20	(17.7)	(17.8)	(17.7)	17.2	(18.1)	17.2	–	–
1911–15	–	(17.7)	–	–	–	16.9	–	–
1906–10	(17.6)	(17.6)	(17.6)	⎱ 16.8	–	–	–	–
Before 1906	(17.8)	(18.0)	(17.8)	⎰	–	–	–	–

Sources: Computed from Indonesia, *1990 Population Census, Tabel Pendahuluan Hasil Sub-Sample*: Tables 2 and 17 and *1980 Population Census, Series 5*: Table 21; *Population Census of Malaysia, 1980*: Table 3.3; *Census of Population, Singapore, 1980*, Release No. 9: Table 16, and Release No. 2: Table 40; Chang (1979: Table 6.4); Computer tape of *1980 Population and Housing Census*, Thailand; Rachapaetayakom (1983: Table 5.4).

[a] For Indonesia, the three columns in parentheses are based on data from the *1980 Population Census*, whereas the other data are based on the *1990 Population Census*. For Singapore, the column in parentheses is based on the 1966 Sample Household Survey, whereas the other data are based on the *Census of Population, Singapore, 1980*. For Southern Thai Muslims, the three columns in parentheses are medians, based on data from the Southern Thai Muslim Survey, 1976 (for ever-married women who married before the age of 30). Birth cohorts are actually 1952–6, 1947–51, etc. Age at marriage for the most recent two cohorts could be slightly underestimated because older-marrying women had no chance to be included.

[b] Above 20; exact number indeterminate because some members of the cohort had not yet reached ages above 20.

[c] Based on unpublished data from the Malaysian Population and Family Survey, 1984–5. Birth cohorts are actually 1955–9, 1950–4, 1945–9, 1940–4, and 1935–9.

FIGURE 3.1

South-East Asian Muslim Populations: Age by Which 50 Per Cent
of Female Birth Cohorts Had Married, 1911–1970

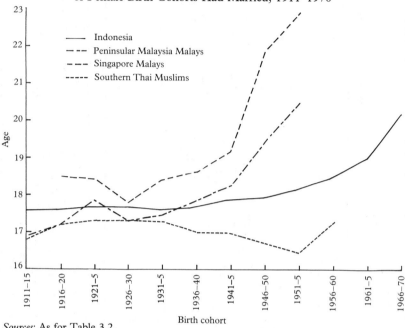

Sources: As for Table 3.2.

countries, the stability in marriage ages over time, and the sharp change in
more recent years. Over most of the period covered (more specifically, for
women born between 1916 and 1940, most of whom married between
1931 and 1960), throughout the entire Malay world over half of Malay
girls were marrying before their eighteenth birthday. Median age at
marriage was almost identical in Indonesia, among Peninsular Malaysia
Malays and among Southern Thai Muslims: a level of around 17.5 years.
Except for the 1926–30 cohort, it was about half a year higher for the
Singapore Malays; interestingly, ages at marriage for Singapore Malays
were very similar to those of Indonesians living in urban areas. During
this lengthy period, age at marriage showed no sign of systematic change
throughout the region.

It is surprising, in a way, that age at marriage appears to have remained
so constant throughout the turbulent wartime and revolutionary period
of the 1940s in Indonesia. This was the period during which the 1921–5,
1926–30, and 1931–5 birth cohorts would have been marrying. Yet
there is no hint of any deviation of the marriage ages of these cohorts
from the long-established pattern. Nor is there any hint of such deviation
among the Malaysian Malays, although admittedly their lives were
somewhat less disrupted by the Japanese Occupation than were those
of the other Malaysian ethnic groups.

Signs of an upturn in age at marriage for Malays were evident in
marriages occurring by the early 1950s in Singapore, and by the late
1950s in Peninsular Malaysia; thereafter age at marriage rose steadily.

In Peninsular Malaysia the rise accelerated between the 1941–5 and 1951–5 birth cohorts; girls in each successive five-year cohort were marrying a full year later than in the previous birth cohort.[7] From the perspective of when the marriages actually took place, the period of very rapid rise in ages at marriage was between about 1957 and 1979 (the period spanning one-quarter of the marriages of the 1941–5 cohort to three-quarters of the marriages of the 1951–5 cohort, respectively). From the 1980 data it is not possible to be sure whether the pace of change continued unabated after 1979, though from other sources it would appear that it did.

Indonesia, meanwhile, was left behind. A substantial rise in age at marriage was delayed by fifteen years compared with the Malaysian Malays, and its pace was not as dramatic. A wide gap therefore opened in median age at marriage between the two groups, reaching 2.5 years for the 1951–5 birth cohort. Nevertheless, depending on whether we rely on the 1980 or the preliminary 1990 Population Census data, between half a year and a full year had been added to the median age at marriage in Indonesia between the 1946–50 birth cohort and the cohort ten years younger.[8] This rise started about five years earlier in the urban areas; indeed, according to the 1990 Census data it was barely evident in the rural areas. The availability of this preliminary information from the 1990 Census makes it possible to trace the trends in Indonesia a further ten years forward, and it is over these ten years that really sharp changes in age at marriage become evident, in both urban and rural areas. The 1966–70 birth cohort, the cohort doing most of its marrying in the late 1980s, was marrying more than a year and a half later than the cohort born a decade earlier. The rise appears to have been as pronounced in rural as in urban areas.

Southern Thailand was also left behind. Its ages at marriage were below those of all the other groups (though not, as will be seen later, below those of the neighbouring Malaysian state of Kelantan). Ages at marriage appeared to rise through the 1930s and then fall again from the 1940s to the 1960s. After that, as in Indonesia, its rise in age at marriage was delayed. In fact, it was not until the 1956–60 birth cohort, marrying in the 1970s, that there were clear signs of a rise.

The differences in onset of rising age at marriage can be plausibly explained by differences in economic conditions between the different countries. In the 1950s and 1960s Malaysia was making steady economic progress and Singapore was its metropolis, whereas the Indonesian economy was in a parlous state throughout most of the 1960s. Southern Thailand was a mainly rural, though relatively prosperous, backwater in the Thai kingdom. It will be an important task of Chapter 4 to explain more fully these differences in the onset of a rise in age at marriage, taking note of regional differences within countries.

In the detailed country sections which follow, the findings of Table 3.2 will be compared with data from other sources for consistency and for more detail. Differences among provinces in Indonesia and among states in Malaysia, and socio-economic differentials in age at marriage, will also be examined.

Trends and Differentials in Malay Age at Marriage in Malaysia

Table 3.3 presents data from the 1984–5 Malaysian Population and Family Survey showing the proportions of birth cohorts of women (Malays and Chinese) who had married by given ages. The figures are most readily understood by looking down the columns and comparing the proportions who had married at given ages among the different cohorts. The striking long-term trend towards later age at first marriage is clear. In general, the younger the cohort of women, the lower the proportions ever-married by any given age. For example, at the exact age of 21, just 36 per cent of Malay women born in 1960–4 had married, compared with 50 per cent among those born ten years earlier and 81 per cent among those born twenty years earlier. The reductions in the proportion of women married at older ages are much less striking, indicating that most of the decline in marriage rates at the younger ages has been due to the trend towards later marriage rather than a strong trend towards remaining permanently unmarried.

Ethnic differences in proportions married are pronounced at the younger ages, especially among the earlier birth cohorts. For example, among women born in 1940–4, 54 per cent of Malays had married by the age of 18 compared with only 16 per cent of Chinese. For both groups, this proportion was falling over time, so that for the 1960–4 birth cohort, the proportions married by the age of 18 had fallen to 14 per cent and 7 per cent respectively. The Malay decline was clearly much sharper, thus narrowing the earlier differential.

At older ages (above 30), ethnic differentials in proportions ever-married almost disappear, reflecting the near-universality of marriage among all Malaysian ethnic groups. However, the proportions ever-married among the Chinese remain a few percentage points lower than among the Malays.

In summary, then, Malay–Chinese differentials in marriage in Peninsular Malaysia have always been mainly a matter of timing. In recent years, the earlier sharp differences have narrowed considerably, because the Malays have repeated, with a considerable lag but within a much shorter time period and from a lower base, the earlier rise in female age at marriage among the Chinese.[9]

Census data for Malaysia enable us to calculate the indirect period measure, median age at marriage, for Malays in different states at different times. These are presented in Table 3.4, which has three striking features. The first is that, although Kelantan had the earliest age at marriage in 1947, the other 'traditional' states of Trengganu, Pahang, and Kedah actually had higher median ages at marriage than many other states. The second is that the 'spread' in median ages at marriage widened considerably by 1957 and 1970, because the delayed rise in age at marriage in Kelantan, Trengganu, Pahang, and Kedah established them firmly as the states with lowest ages of marriage, whereas age at marriage in other states rose considerably before 1957. The third is that the 'spread' in median ages at marriage narrowed again by 1980

TABLE 3.3

Peninsular Malaysia: Cumulative Percentage of Malay and Chinese Women in Different Birth Cohorts Ever-married, by Given Age, 1984

Birth Cohort	Age at First Marriage (Exact Age)								Age by Which 50% Were Married
	15	17	19	21	23	25	27	31	
Malays									
1935–9	23	44	66	80	85	88	89	91	17.5
1940–4	18	43	65	81	88	92	94	96	17.6
1945–9	10	27	45	58	70	79	86	90	19.8
1950–4	6	20	36	50	64	75	83	—[a]	21.0
1955–9	4	13	27	44	59	73[c]	—[a]	—[a]	21.7
1960–4	2	8	21	36	—[a]	—[a]	—[a]	—[a]	—[b]
Chinese									
1935–9	1	9	20	37	53	66	77	91	22.6
1940–4	0	10	20	36	54	68	80	89	22.6
1945–9	1	5	18	32	45	63	76	86	23.6
1950–4	0	5	13	29	46	66	76	—[a]	23.4
1955–9	0	1	11	24	43	58[c]	—	—[a]	23.9
1960–4	1	2	13	—[a]	—[a]	—[a]	—[a]	—[a]	—[b]

Sources: Unpublished tabulations from the Malaysian Population and Family Survey, 1984–5.

[a] Cannot be computed because some or all respondents have not yet reached this age.

[b] Above 21; exact figure cannot be computed because fewer than 50% of the cohort were married at the time of the survey.

[c] Slightly underestimated because a small group of women in this cohort had not yet reached the age of 25.

TABLE 3.4

Peninsular Malaysia: Trends in Cross-sectional Median Ages at Marriage
of Malay Females in Different States, 1947–1980

	1947	1957	1970	1980
Johore	16.7	18.0	21.3	22.7
Malacca	17.5	19.0	21.7	23.9
Negri Sembilan	16.2	17.4	21.1	22.8
Selangor	17.1	17.9	21.1	23.2
Perak	16.4	18.0	n.a.	22.5
Penang	16.4	18.5	22.2	23.7
Kedah	16.6	16.8	20.2	21.7
Perlis	16.3	17.0	20.4	21.5
Pahang	16.8	17.0	19.8	21.0
Trengganu	16.7	16.1	19.0	21.5
Kelantan	15.9	15.8	18.6	20.9

Sources: Computed from *Population Census of Malaya, 1947*: Tables 20 and 21; *Population
Census of Malaya, 1957*, State Population Reports: Table 8A; *Population Census of
Malaysia, 1970*, State Population Reports: Table 27.2; and *Population Census of Malaysia,
1980*, State Population Reports: Table 3.1.

because of particularly sharp increases in marriage ages in Kelantan and
Trengganu.

More detailed data on cohort trends in age at marriage for a number
of states are presented in Table 3.5, along with comparable estimates
for some of the provinces of Indonesia, to be discussed later. Special
interest attaches to differences between the northern states, Kelantan,
Trengganu, Kedah, and Perlis, where age at marriage was the youngest
by 1957 (see above), and the other states. The data show that Kelantan,
Trengganu, and Perlis definitely had the earliest marriage, with Kelantan
younger than Trengganu and Perlis by a quarter to half a year. Somewhat
surprisingly, Kedah, Johore, and Perak were not far apart until the
1936–40 birth cohort; since then, age at marriage has risen faster in
Johore and Perak. Selangor had the highest age at marriage throughout.
The beginnings of a substantial rise in age at marriage occurred two
cohorts earlier in the West Coast states (among the 1936–40 birth
cohort) than in Kelantan and Trengganu (among the 1946–50 birth
cohort). In other words, the real rise in the West Coast states began for
marriages taking place during the 1950s, whereas in Kelantan and
Trengganu this rise was delayed until the 1960s.

The figures for Kelantan and Trengganu confirm the wider
applicability of the early ages at marriage reported in various small-scale
surveys. For example, Laderman (1983: 13) found that in Kampung
Mechang, Trengganu, girls married in their mid to late teens and that
the median age at first pregnancy was 16 years; in Rusila, Trengganu, the
mean age at marriage for females in 1966 was 17 (Strange, 1981: 107);
Kuchiba, Tsubouchi, and Maeda (1979: 159) reported that in Galok,

TABLE 3.5

Age by Which 50 Per Cent of Female Birth Cohorts Had Married among the Malays
in Various States of Malaysia and Provinces of Indonesia

Birth Cohort	Peninsular Malaysia							Indonesia					
	Kedah	Perlis	Kelantan	Trengganu	Perak	Selangor	Johore	West Java	Central Java	East Java	South Kalimantan	West Sumatra	South Sumatra
1956–60	_a	_a	19.9	_a	_a	_a	_a	17.2	18.4	17.9	18.0	19.4	19.3
1951–5	20.3	20.5	18.5	18.9	21.6	22.7	21.8	16.7	17.7	17.3	17.5	18.6	18.9
1946–50	19.0	19.3	17.5	17.9	20.1	21.2	20.5	16.1	17.2	16.8	17.0	18.2	18.4
1941–5	18.0	18.2	16.7	17.1	18.7	19.5	18.8	16.1	17.0	16.7	16.9	18.0	18.1
1936–40	17.7	17.7	16.6	17.0	18.2	18.7	18.3	16.0	17.1	16.6	17.0	18.1	18.3
1931–5	17.4	17.1	16.5	16.9	17.9	18.2	17.8	16.0	17.2	16.7	17.2	17.6	18.6
1926–30	17.3	16.9	16.6	16.8	17.7	18.1	17.7	15.9	17.2	16.6	17.2	17.2	18.7
1921–5	17.3	16.9	16.5	16.7	17.6	18.0	17.7	16.0	17.2	16.7	17.3	17.1	18.8
1916–20	17.4	16.9	16.4	16.8	17.5	17.9	17.5	16.0	17.2	16.8	17.6	17.2	19.3
Before 1915	17.1	16.9	16.2	16.6	17.0	17.5	17.1	–	–	–	–	–	–

Sources: Malaysia: Computed from Population Census of Malaysia, 1980, State Reports: Table 3.
Indonesia: Computed from 1980 Population Census, Provincial Reports: Tables 13 and 30.

(For both countries, a small group of 'not stated' age at first marriage was distributed pro rata.)
aAbove 20; cannot be computed because of overlap with age of respondents.

Kelantan, the female average age at first marriage was 16.5 years and the modal age 15. Hashim (1984: 21) reported that in Mukim Jenereh Tujuh, Kelantan, median ages at marriage for women in first marriages rose from 14.7 for those married before 1958 to 15.7 for those marrying between 1958 and 1969 and to 17.3 for those marrying in the 1970–81 period.

The 1989 Population and Family Survey in Sabah provides some information about the mean age at marriage of women aged 25 and over who married below the age of 25. Whereas for the mainly Muslim Bajau, Indonesians, and Filipinos, this averaged 17.8, for the mainly Christian Kadazans and Dusuns, it averaged 18.6, and for the Chinese, 20.3 (National Population and Family Development Board, Malaysia, 1992: Table 4.5).

Trends in Age at Marriage in Singapore

The dip in median age at marriage for Malay women in Singapore in the 1926–30 birth cohort, shown in Figure 3.1, is hard to explain. It is based on data from the 1966 Household Survey; data from the 1980 Census unfortunately do not permit the identification of separate five-year cohorts prior to the 1931–5 birth cohort. If this dip is ignored, the marriage age remained very steady until it started to rise in cohorts born after 1940.

Table 3.6 shows, for Singapore Malays, a similar set of data to that shown for Peninsular Malaysia Malays and Chinese in Table 3.3. As might be expected of a large city, the Malay age at marriage was higher in Singapore for all birth cohorts. Interestingly enough, whereas there

TABLE 3.6

Singapore: Proportion per 1,000 Malay Women in Different Birth Cohorts Ever-married, by Given Age, 1980

	Married before Exact Age				
Birth Cohort	15	20	25	30	Age by Which 50% Were Married
Before 1931	193	630	822	907	18.5
1931–5	151	666	870	936	18.4
1936–40	140	645	862	930	18.6
1941–5	99	581	817	906	19.2
1946–50	45	377	696	840	21.9
1951–5	10	274	658	_a	22.9
1956–60	6	199	_a	_a	_b
1961–5	1	_a	_a	_a	_b

Sources: Computed from *Census of Population, Singapore, 1980*, Release No. 9, Region and Fertility: Table 16; and Release No. 2, Demographic Characteristics: Table 40.

[a]Cannot be computed because respondents have not yet reached this age.

[b]Cannot be computed because fewer than 50% of the cohorts were married at the time of the census.

was a sharp decline in very early marriage (below the age of 15) between cohorts born in the 1920s, the 1930s, and the 1940s, no such sharp change is apparent in the proportion marrying below the age of 20; it is only with the birth cohort 1946–50 (those marrying mainly in the late 1960s and early 1970s) that the proportion marrying by the age of 20 begins to fall off sharply, and this trend continues strongly thereafter. In other words, it appears that whatever it was that fostered child marriage was already breaking down by World War II and the early post-war years, whereas marriage in the later teens remained the norm until the late 1960s, after which it also lost greatly in popularity.

Trends and Differentials in Age at Marriage in Indonesia

Age at marriage for girls was very low in Indonesia in the 1950s and 1960s. This represented the traditional situation, with very little evidence of change up to that time. The highest ages at marriage tended to be recorded in non-Muslim areas such as Bali, Maluku, East Nusa Tenggara, and the Minahasa area of North Sulawesi.

Age at marriage began to increase during the 1960s (Iskandar, 1970; McNicoll and Mamas, 1973; McDonald, Yasin, and Jones, 1976: 29–33; Muliakusuma, 1976; Al Hadar, 1977; Soeradji, 1979). The conclusion from the 1973 Indonesian Fertility–Mortality Survey was that in urban areas, the median age at marriage rose by one to one-and-a-half years over the 1960s, whereas in rural areas, a slight rise appeared to have begun late in the 1960s (McDonald, Yasin, and Jones, 1976: Table 3.14).

The 1976 Intercensal Population Survey (Supas) and the subsample of this survey used for the Indonesian Fertility Survey were conducted three years after the Fertility–Mortality Survey. Though there was some inconsistency between the two sources (see Committee on Population and Demography, 1987: 54–8), the Supas data support the evidence from the Fertility–Mortality Survey that a rise in age at marriage had been under way for some time in urban areas but had only been clearly evident in rural areas from the late 1960s.

Data from the Indonesian census of 1980, already presented in Table 3.2, permit the calculation of ages at entry into the married state by single years of age for birth cohorts dating back to the earliest years of the twentieth century, and as such are of great value. Comment is needed though, about problems with the data. First, there is a group of ever-married women for whom age at marriage was not stated. These women were distributed pro rata among the age-at-marriage groups. This should not greatly affect the results for the cohorts aged from 20 to 44, in which the proportion not stated is less than 2 per cent. However, the proportion is higher for women aged 15–19 (3.9 per cent) and it rises for older women, reaching 5 per cent for the cohort aged 60–64. A more important bias in the data for such older women, though, is undoubtedly memory lapse and lack of knowledge of age, leading to substantial age heaping in numbers ending in 0 or 5. In general, the older the women, the poorer the quality of the data in Table 3.2 is likely to be.

With these warnings in mind, the findings from the 1980 Population Census data will now be examined in more detail. The cumulative percentages of women married by various ages for different birth cohorts are shown in Table 3.7, separately for urban and rural areas. Summary data for individual provinces are shown in Table 3.5. However, a discrepancy must first be noted between the census data and detailed estimates for the provinces of Java from the Indonesian Fertility Survey (1976) shown in Appendix 2. The median ages at marriage from the latter can be roughly compared with those in Table 3.5 by lining up birth cohorts. This exercise reveals close consistency for the 1951–5 birth cohort, but for earlier birth cohorts the Indonesian Fertility Survey gives substantially lower estimates, reaching a maximum discrepancy of one-and-a-half years lower in the case of Central Java. The reason for the discrepancy is not clear, although the Indonesian Fertility Survey estimates were out of line with both the Fertility–Mortality Survey and the Intercensal Survey of which they were a subsample (cf. Committee on Population and Demography, 1987: Table 19). The latter estimates tally more closely with the census-based estimates from Tables 3.7 and 3.5, and this strengthens the case for concluding that the Indonesian Fertility Survey estimates presented in Appendix 2 understate the real age at marriage. The following discussion will concentrate on the census data.

The highlights of the Indonesia-wide data are the early age at marriage, the extraordinary degree of stability in marriage patterns over time, and the beginnings of a steady rise in age at marriage beginning with the 1951–5 birth cohort (i.e. the cohort doing most of its marrying around 1967 to 1977). Traditionally, one-third of Indonesian women were married by exact age 16, and this continued to be the case until well into the 1960s. By the late 1970s, however, only 10 per cent of girls were marrying by this age. The 1970s, then, witnessed a revolution in marriage patterns after at least half a century, and probably much longer, of near-stability.

The rural areas closely mirrored the picture for Indonesia as a whole, not surprisingly given that until recently they held more than four-fifths of the Indonesian population. It was in the urban areas that the harbingers of change appeared. Clear evidence of a rise in age at marriage appeared five years earlier (among the birth cohort 1946–50) and the rise was much sharper than in rural areas: a 2.3-year rise in the age by which 50 per cent of women married, compared with a 0.9-year rise in rural areas, comparing the 1941–5 birth cohort with the 1956–60 birth cohort. This appears to be a classic case of social change originating in the cities and gradually diffusing. There is evidence of dramatically accelerated change affecting age at marriage among the 1961–5 birth cohort, the cohort whose early childhood was spent in a period of great poverty, uncertainty and, in late 1965 and 1966, bloodshed. Although most of this group had not yet married by the time of the 1980 census, the

TABLE 3.7

Indonesia: Cumulative Percentages of Female Birth Cohorts Ever-married and Age by Which 50 Per Cent Had Married in Rural and Urban Areas, 1980

Birth Cohort	Percentage Married by Exact Age										Age by Which 50% of Cohort Married
	14	15	16	17	18	19	20	22	24	30	
Urban											
1961–5	1	3	–	–	–	–	–	–	–	–	–
1956–60	3	6	12	19	29	38	47	–	–	–	20.6[a]
1951–5	5	9	16	24	34	44	52	66	80	8	19.8
1946–50	7	12	21	31	41	51	58	72	84	92	18.9
1941–5	8	13	25	35	46	57	64	77	87	94	18.3
1936–40	9	15	28	37	48	58	65	79	88	95	18.2
1931–5	8	14	28	39	50	60	67	80	89	95	18.0
1926–30	10	16	31	41	52	61	66	81	89	95	17.8
1921–5	8	14	30	40	51	61	67	80	88	95	17.9
1916–20	8	15	32	41	52	60	65	82	89	95	17.8
1911–15	7	14	33	43	54	63	67	82	88	94	17.7
1906–10	8	15	34	44	54	63	68	84	89	94	17.6
Before 1906	7	13	30	40	50	59	64	82	86	93	18.0
Rural											
1961–5	3	6	–	–	–	–	–	–	–	–	–
1956–60	6	12	23	35	49	62	70	–	–	–	18.1
1951–5	9	15	29	42	55	67	74	85	93	–	17.6
1946–50	11	19	36	48	61	71	77	88	93	97	17.2
1941–5	10	17	35	48	61	73	78	89	94	97	17.2
1936–40	10	18	35	47	59	71	76	90	94	98	17.2
1931–5	9	16	34	46	58	69	74	88	93	97	17.3
1926–30	11	17	36	47	58	68	73	88	93	97	17.3

(continued)

TABLE 3.7 (continued)

Birth Cohort	Percentage Married by Exact Age										Age by Which 50% of Cohort Married
	14	15	16	17	18	19	20	22	24	30	
1921–5	8	14	34	45	57	67	72	87	92	97	17.4
1916–20	8	14	33	43	54	64	68	87	92	97	17.7
1911–15	8	14	34	44	54	63	68	85	89	96	17.6
1906–10	8	13	32	42	52	61	65	86	89	95	17.8
Before 1906	7	11	28	37	46	55	59	81	86	93	18.4
Urban and rural											
1961–5	2	5	–	–	–	–	–	–	–	–	–
1956–60	5	11	20	31	44	56	64	–	–	–	18.5
1951–5	8	14	26	37	50	61	68	81	90	–	18.0
1946–50	10	17	32	44	56	67	73	84	91	96	17.5
1941–5	9	16	33	45	58	69	75	87	93	97	17.4
1936–40	10	17	34	45	57	68	74	88	93	97	17.4
1931–5	9	16	33	44	57	67	73	86	92	97	17.4
1926–30	10	17	35	46	57	67	72	87	92	97	17.4
1921–5	8	14	33	44	56	66	71	86	91	96	17.5
1916–20	8	14	33	43	53	63	68	86	91	96	17.7
1911–15	8	14	34	44	54	63	67	84	89	95	17.6
1906–10	8	14	33	42	52	61	65	85	89	95	17.8
Before 1906	7	12	29	38	47	56	60	81	86	93	18.4

Source: 1980 Population Census: Table 21. The small number with age at marriage not stated was distributed pro rata.

[a] Number could be slightly overstated because of overlap with age-group concerned.

data from the 1990 Census in Table 3.2 shows a sharper rise in average age at marriage for this cohort than for any previous cohort, especially in the urban areas.

As for interprovincial differences, Figure 3.2 and Table 3.8 present some summary figures. Table 3.8 shows the trends in singulate mean age at marriage (SMAM) for the different provinces of Indonesia between 1964 (for some provinces) and 1985. Though unsatisfactory in the sense that it gives a composite picture of marriage age for all women under 50, thus obscuring time trends, it has the advantage of showing, in the one table, interprovincial comparisons of patterns

FIGURE 3.2

Provinces of Java: Trends in Percentage of Women Never-married at
Ages 15–19 and 20–24, 1964–1985

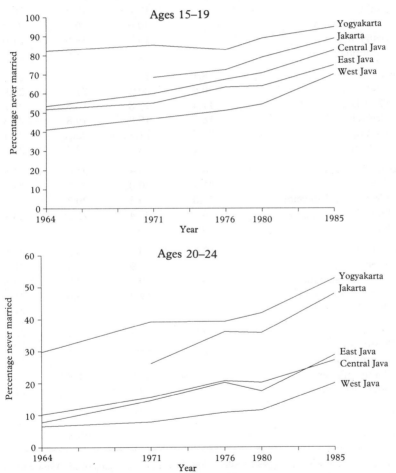

Sources: Soeradji (1982: Table 1); *1976 Intercensal Population Survey* [Supas I and II];
1980 Population Census; *1985 Intercensal Population Survey*.

Notes: 1976 data are from Supas I. For a discussion of differences between the Indonesian
Fertility–Mortality Survey (1973) and Supas I and Supas II results, see Committee on
Population and Demography (1987: 54–6).

TABLE 3.8
Indonesia: Trends in the Singulate Mean Age at Marriage of Women,
1964–1990

Region	Mean Age at First Marriage			
	1964	1971	1980	1990
Indonesia	–	19.3	20.0	21.6
Sumatra	19.9	19.9	20.6	22.1
DI Aceh	–	19.5	20.8	22.6
North Sumatra	–	20.8	21.7	23.3
West Sumatra	–	20.3	20.8	22.8
Riau	–	20.0	20.7	22.0
Jambi	–	18.4	19.2	20.8
South Sumatra	–	20.0	20.7	21.7
Bengkulu	–	19.7	19.6	21.0
Lampung	–	18.0	18.9	20.8
Java	18.1	18.7	19.5	21.1
DKI Jakarta	20.0	20.2	21.7	23.9
West Java	17.4	17.8	18.5	20.2
Central Java	18.2	19.0	19.8	21.3
DI Yogyakarta	20.7	21.8	22.5	24.1
East Java	18.1	18.7	19.4	21.0
Nusa Tenggara	–	20.8	21.6	22.5
Bali	21.7	20.8	21.2	22.7
West Nusa Tenggara	21.0	19.2	20.3	21.0
East Nusa Tenggara	–	22.4	23.1	23.8
East Timor	–	–	–	22.7
Kalimantan	18.6	20.0	20.2	21.5
West Kalimantan	–	20.9	20.9	21.4
Central Kalimantan	–	19.7	19.8	20.8
South Kalimantan	–	19.2	19.6	21.5
East Kalimantan	–	19.6	20.5	21.6
Sulawesi	19.5	20.7	21.6	22.8
North Sulawesi	–	21.6	21.7	22.4
Central Sulawesi	–	20.6	20.7	21.3
South Sulawesi	–	20.5	21.8	23.6
South-east Sulawesi	–	19.9	20.6	21.5
Maluku	–	22.0	21.6	22.4
Irian Jaya	–	–	19.8	–

Sources: Hull and Hatmadji (1990): calculations based on the results of the 1964 Sample
Survey and *Population Census*, 1971 and 1980; author's calculations based on *1990
Population Census*.

prevailing over a period of time. What we have is clearly a pattern of very early marriage in Java and in areas dominated by settlers from Java (Lampung). The only other provinces that can match Java in the incidence of early marriage are South Kalimantan, Jambi, and West Nusa Tenggara. Within Java, West Java (i.e. the Sundanese) leads decisively in the proportion of girls marrying early, whereas Yogyakarta is an outlier for Java in its pattern of later marriage. Provincial differences in urban areas (not shown) mirror those in Table 3.8, though with slightly older ages at marriage (Kasto, 1988: Table 8).

In view of the importance of Java as an early-marriage region, a more detailed picture of differentials within Java is desirable. This is given in Map 3.1, based on the simple measure of percentage of females single at ages 20–24 in 1980. The status of the Province of Yogyakarta as an outlier for Java in its higher age at marriage was clearly shared by some of the adjoining *kabupaten* of Central Java. Somewhat surprisingly, the other area with relatively high ages at marriage was the western part of the island of Madura. Apart from these areas, there were very few parts of Java where more than 15 per cent of women were still single at ages 20–24.

The oldest female ages at marriage of all tend to be found in provinces which are predominantly non-Muslim: East Nusa Tenggara and North Sulawesi (mainly Christian), Maluku (over 40 per cent Christian), and Bali (mainly Hindu). This reinforces the point made earlier that use of all-Indonesia figures as a proxy for Muslim populations in Indonesia overstates the Muslim ages at marriage. It is therefore of interest to show in more detail the cohort trends in age at marriage in six provinces where non-Muslims are a tiny fraction of the population: West Java, Central Java, East Java, South Kalimantan, West Sumatra, and South Sumatra. The trends in these provinces, already shown in Table 3.5, will now be discussed.

As with the all-Indonesia data, what is striking about this table is the extraordinary stability in female age at marriage over time in Java, and in South Kalimantan as well. In West Java, the age by which 50 per cent of girls were married did not deviate by more than one month from exact age 16 among birth cohorts spanning a period of some thirty-five years. Similarly, in Central Java, the age by which 50 per cent of girls had married did not deviate by more than two months from exact age 17 among birth cohorts spanning the same period. East Java showed similar stability. What appears to be visible, then, is a traditional pattern, 'fossilized', as it were, in a seemingly unchanging social and family structure. Then suddenly, with the 1951–5 birth cohort—the cohort marrying in the late 1960s and early to mid-1970s—the pattern begins to change. Data from the 1980 Census, of course, can only trace this change as far as the next (1956–60) birth cohort; the data for subsequent birth cohorts are distorted because some cohort members have not yet reached the relevant ages.

In West Sumatra, the trends were different. Age at marriage rose by almost a year between the 1926–30 and 1936–40 birth cohorts, then

82

MAP 3.1

Java: Proportion Single of Females Aged 20–24, by *Kabupaten*, 1980

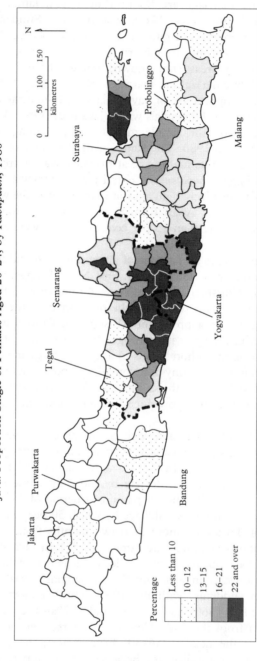

Source: Hatmadji (1990: Figure 3.5), based on calculations from *1980 Population Census.*

levelled off, then rose again (as in the other provinces) with the 1951–5 birth cohort. The traditional marriage ages were almost identical to those in Central Java, but from the 1936–40 cohort onwards, age at marriage in West Sumatra was one year higher than in Central Java. South Sumatra shared this higher age at marriage with West Sumatra from the 1936–40 cohorts onwards, but it differed from all the other provinces in its much higher ages at marriage in the pre-1936 birth cohorts. The reasons for these differences between the two Sumatra provinces and Java are not readily apparent.

The traditionally very early age at marriage in rural Java implies that many girls were married before reaching menarche. But child marriages, though legally registered, generally involved a delay in consummation, and sometimes also a delay in the social ritual of marriage (Hull and Hull, 1987). In a Yogyakarta community studied by Singarimbun and Manning (1974b), it was found that whereas about one-fourth of women were married before menarche, fewer than 1 per cent had intercourse before the first menstruation.

To avoid the need for presentation of detailed cohort data for every province of Indonesia, in Table 3.8 the summary period measure, SMAM, calculated from census and survey data, is shown for available years since 1964. Though caution is required in inferring time trends from comparisons of SMAM in different censuses and surveys, the data in Table 3.8 strongly suggest an accelerated rise in age at marriage in the 1980s, with a rise in the mean for Indonesia as a whole of more than one year in the five-year period following 1980. The series for Java is more complete than that for Indonesia as a whole, with the availability of estimates for 1964 and 1976. The series reads as follows:

1964	18.1
1971	18.7
1976	19.2 (Java–Bali)
1980	19.5
1985	20.7
1990	21.1

Again, an accelerated rise in the first half of the 1980s is strongly suggested.

Further examination of Table 3.8 indicates a tendency for inter-provincial differences to lessen between 1971 and 1985, as provinces with low initial ages at marriage (West and Central Java, Lampung, Jambi, and Aceh) experienced some of the highest increases and provinces with high initial ages (North Sulawesi and Maluku), the lowest increases. This narrowing of differences can be measured more precisely by comparing the average difference in SMAM from the Indonesian figure in the 25 provinces for which data are available in both 1971 and 1985. Disregarding the sign, the average difference fell from 1.15 in 1971 to 0.95 in 1985.

By far the largest provincial increase in mean age at marriage was registered by Jakarta, where special factors—heavy in-migration from all parts of Indonesia and rapid evolution into a metropolis of international stature—were operating. The only province to record a decline in mean age at marriage was North Sulawesi, where age at marriage in 1971 was one of the highest in Indonesia. With half its population Christian, and most marriages already self-arranged, the forces operating on age at marriage there (and in Maluku as well, where only a slight rise in age at marriage was registered) were no doubt very different from those in most of Indonesia.

Lowest Female Ages at Marriage in the Malay-Muslim World

Attention has already been drawn to the provinces or states where age at marriage was the lowest, and also the consistently lower age at marriage in rural areas. The lowest ages of marriage of all are therefore found in rural areas of these early-marriage regions, and these are presented in Table 3.9. Unfortunately, data for Kelantan are not available separately for urban and rural areas, and the rural ages at marriage were undoubtedly lower than the figures in Table 3.9. The urban proportion of the Malay population of Kelantan in 1980 was 26.3 per cent.

It would appear from the data in Table 3.9 that the youngest female ages at marriage among the birth cohorts of the 1920s and 1930s were found in rural areas of West Java and Kelantan. The data from the Southern Thai Muslim Survey suggest that this group also had a very low age at marriage, but the statistically representative data from the 1980 Census show rather higher ages at marriage. By the birth cohorts of the 1950s, rural West Java remained the lowest, but it had been joined by the Southern Thai Muslims, whose age at marriage had been declining. Unlike the other groups, the Kelantanese Malays had experienced a sharp increase in age at marriage by that time.

Although age at marriage in rural West Java was earlier than in rural East or Central Java, it must be borne in mind that these two provinces had larger non-Muslim populations in rural areas than did West Java (1.7 and 2.6 per cent in East and Central Java respectively, compared with 1.0 per cent in West Java). The age-at-marriage gap between West Java and these provinces would narrow slightly if their Muslim populations could be compared, but would certainly not be closed completely.

What were the age-at-marriage patterns in Southern Thailand and rural West Java? According to survey data, among Southern Thai Muslims in rural areas, one-quarter of female respondents were married before they were half-way through their fourteenth year (Rachapaetayakom, 1983: Table 5.5). In rural West Java, among cohorts born between the early part of the twentieth century and the end of the 1940s, one-quarter of girls were married by their fifteenth birthday, one-half by their sixteenth birthday, and three-quarters by their eighteenth birthday. These patterns were very stable over time. Small wonder, then, that in rural Sundanese society an unmarried girl in her later teenage years could be considered an old maid. By the late 1960s and early 1970s, a

TABLE 3.9

Islamic South-East Asia: Cumulative Percentages of Female Birth Cohorts Ever-married in Rural Areas of Regions with the Earliest Age at Marriage, 1980

Birth Cohort	Percentage Married by Exact Age										Age by Which		
	14	15	16	17	18	19	20	22	24	30	25% of Cohort Married	50% of Cohort Married	75% of Cohort Married
West Java: Rural													
1956–60	12	22	40	54	69	81	87	93	94		15.2	16.7	18.5
1951–5	14	25	46	60	74	83	88	94	98	99	15.0	16.3	18.2
1946–50	16	28	53	66	78	87	90	96	98	99	14.7	15.9	17.7
1941–5	15	26	53	66	79	87	90	96	98	99	14.9	15.9	17.7
1936–40	16	26	53	66	78	86	89	96	98	99	14.9	15.9	17.8
1931–5	15	25	54	67	79	86	89	95	97	99	15.0	15.9	17.7
1926–30	16	26	56	67	78	86	89	96	97	99	14.9	15.8	17.7
1921–5	13	23	53	65	77	85	87	95	96	98	15.1	15.9	17.8
1916–20	13	21	52	63	74	82	84	94	96	98	15.1	15.9	18.2

(continued)

TABLE 3.9 (continued)

Birth Cohort	Percentage Married by Exact Age										Age by Which		
	14	15	16	17	18	19	20	22	24	30	25% of Cohort Married	50% of Cohort Married	75% of Cohort Married
Central Java: Rural													
1956–60	6	11	21	34	50	63	72	82	84		16.3	18.0	20.3
1951–5	10	16	30	44	60	72	78	89	95	96	15.6	17.4	19.5
1946–50	13	21	37	52	66	77	82	92	96	98	15.2	16.9	18.8
1941–5	12	19	37	52	67	79	84	93	97	99	15.3	16.9	18.7
1936–40	12	20	37	51	65	76	82	93	96	99	15.3	16.9	18.9
1931–5	11	18	36	50	64	75	80	92	95	98	15.4	17.0	19.1
1926–30	13	20	38	50	63	74	78	92	95	98	15.3	17.0	19.3
1921–5	10	17	36	49	63	74	78	91	95	98	15.4	17.1	19.5
1916–20	10	17	36	49	61	71	76	92	95	98	15.4	17.1	19.8
East Java: Rural													
1956–60	8	15	28	42	56	70	77	85	87		15.8	17.6	19.7
1951–5	12	20	36	50	64	74	80	90	95	97	15.3	17.0	19.2
1946–50	13	23	42	57	70	79	84	92	96	98	15.1	16.5	18.6
1941–5	13	22	43	57	70	80	85	93	96	98	15.2	16.5	18.5
1936–40	14	23	43	57	69	80	84	94	96	98	15.1	16.5	18.5
1931–5	12	21	42	56	69	79	83	93	96	98	15.2	16.6	18.6
1926–30	14	23	43	56	68	78	81	93	96	98	15.1	16.5	18.7
1921–5	11	19	42	55	68	78	82	93	95	98	15.2	16.6	18.7
1916–20	12	20	41	53	65	75	79	93	96	98	15.2	16.7	19.1

Kelantan:
Urban and Rural

Year													
1956–60	2	6	12	21	31	42	51	61	65	91	17.4	19.9	n.a.
1951–5	4	10	19	31	43	56	65	77	84	96	16.5	18.5	21.6
1946–50	8	18	32	45	56	69	75	86	90	98	15.5	17.5	19.9
1941–5	12	24	40	54	65	79	84	92	95	98	15.1	16.7	18.7
1936–40	14	25	41	55	65	79	84	94	96	98	15.0	16.6	18.7
1931–5	13	25	43	57	66	80	85	94	96	99	15.0	16.5	18.6
1926–30	13	24	42	55	65	78	85	95	96	99	15.1	16.6	18.8
1921–5	12	24	44	57	67	79	84	94	96	99	15.1	16.5	18.7
1916–20	13	24	44	58	67	80	84	95	96	98	15.0	16.4	18.6
Before 1916	14	27	48	61	69	80	85	95	97	98	14.8	16.2	18.5

Sources: Indonesia: Computed from *1980 Population Census*, Provincial Reports: Tables 13 and 30.

Kelantan: Computed from *Population Census of Malaysia, 1980*, Kelantan State Report: Table 3.

(In all cases, a small group of 'not stated' age at first marriage was distributed pro rata.)

rise in marriage ages was detectable, but it was a very modest rise, adding less than a year to the earlier prevailing age at marriage. In rural Central and East Java, the rise was slightly greater.[10]

Still lower average ages at marriage could of course be found in subregions of these provinces and states. West Java, after all, had a population of 27 million in 1980, equivalent to the twenty-eighth largest country in the world at that time. Among the three major regions within West Java (Banten, or the westernmost region; the Priangan, or the highland region; and the northern coastal zone), Banten appears to have had the lowest ages at marriage and the Priangan the highest (Asari, 1985: 57).

Other population subgroups in Islamic South-East Asia for which data are lacking may well have had average ages at marriage as low as or lower than those in rural West Java and Kelantan. It has been noted that 16 per cent of Brunei brides and 20 per cent of Bajau brides in Kota Kinabalu (Sabah) were aged 14 or less in a study in 1968–70 (Robertson, 1971). In East Java, the Madurese speakers, concentrated in Madura and in parts of the main island, have a lower age at marriage than the Javanese (BPS, 1980: Table 14); in fact, data from the 1987 Demographic and Health Survey show a mean age at marriage below 14 for ever-married Madurese speakers aged 25–34 and 35–49. If these figures are correct, the Madurese speakers are the earliest-marrying group in the entire Malay-Muslim world.[11]

Ideal Age at Marriage

Are people's stated ideal ages at marriage consistent with the actual ages, and do differences in these stated ideal ages for different age-groups reveal anything about the preferences of older cohorts whose marriages were mostly arranged for them? Not very much information is available on ideal age at marriage, but data from the 1984–5 Malaysian Population and Family Survey (Hamid et al., 1988: Table 2.16) show a fair degree of consistency between stated ideals and the prevailing marriage ages around the time of the survey. The fact that Chinese women gave an ideal age at marriage for females (24.2) about two years higher than Malays (22.4) also reflects prevailing practice. Surprisingly, younger respondents gave lower stated ideal ages than other respondents, but as the survey was dealing only with married women, these younger respondents were unrepresentative of their age-group, especially at ages below 20. What is perhaps more interesting is the high stated ideal ages—above 22 on average—for women in their thirties and forties. On average, their own ages at marriage were very much younger than this. Different interpretations are possible. One is that with greater maturity, women come to favour an older age at marriage. But given the high proportion of these older women whose marriages were arranged, another interpretation is that if more of them had had any choice in the matter, they would have married at older ages than they did.

The 1981–Malaysian Marriage Survey questioned respondents about minimum and maximum ages by which they thought a girl should get married. For well over 80 per cent of Malay female respondents, both married and single, the maximum age at which a woman should marry was somewhere in her twenties. By contrast, more than half of Chinese women cited a maximum age of more than 30 (Tan et al., 1986: Table 11; Tan, 1986: Table 39). The minima and maxima cited by male and female respondents did not differ very much, nor did they differ much according to urban or rural residence (Tan, 1986: Table 40). The age range between mean maximum and minimum cited by Malay women— from 20 to 25.5 years—neatly encompasses the prevailing median age at marriage for Malay females at the time: a little over 22 years.

These single respondents were also asked whether they thought the age at marriage had changed since their parents were their age. Community awareness of changing ages at marriage is clearly reflected in the answers. Three-quarters stated that age at marriage had risen, and another 19 per cent thought that there had been no change. Very few (8 per cent of males and 5 per cent of females) thought that it had fallen. Among the reasons given for the rise, education predominated, followed by job insecurity and financial instability, 'value freedom', and the increased freedom to choose one's spouse.

V. J. Hull, in her village study in Yogyakarta in 1972, asked both married and unmarried women their ideal age at marriage. The unmarried women tended to give a higher ideal age (19–20 was the mode), but 35 per cent of them answered 'don't know'. Many unmarried girls claimed to have never thought about such questions, and lower-class girls were not accustomed to verbalizing any feelings they might have had (V. J. Hull, 1975: 198).

Socio-economic Differentials in Age at Marriage

Table 3.10 presents data on marriage timing in urban and rural areas of Peninsular Malaysia and Indonesia in 1980, and for Southern Thai Muslims in 1970. The results are much as one would expect: marriage is earlier in rural areas, and there is approximately a two-year difference between urban and rural areas in median age at marriage. In Indonesia, the urban–rural difference appears to be widening over time; the trend toward later age at marriage in urban areas has been relatively more pronounced and appears to have started five to ten years earlier in urban than in rural areas (Central Bureau of Statistics and World Fertility Survey, 1978: 32). In the Indonesian Fertility Survey of 1976, the percentage not married by the age of 25 in urban areas of Java–Bali had risen to 17 per cent in the 25–29 year age-group, whereas in rural areas it was only 5 per cent in the same age-group, virtually unchanged compared with older women.

Part of the urban–rural difference can be explained by differences in levels of education in rural and urban areas; in fact, 1980 Census data for Indonesia show that when education is controlled for, there is little difference between urban and rural ages at marriage (Kasto,

TABLE 3.10

Islamic South-East Asia: Indicators of Urban–Rural Differences in Marriage Timing
and Non-marriage among Females, 1970 and 1980

Indicator	Peninsular Malaysia Malays, 1980		Indonesia, 1980		Southern Thai Muslims, 1970	
	Urban	Rural	Urban	Rural	Urban	Rural
Percentage single at ages 15–19	93.0	88.1	82.2	65.4	63.9	44.7
Percentage single at ages 20–24	59.2	43.5	37.3	17.1	n.a.	n.a.
Percentage single at ages 25–29	22.7	14.8	14.5	5.2	n.a.	n.a.
Percentage never married[a]	2.7	1.4	1.9	1.0	0.9	0.8
Median age at marriage	23.6	21.7	21.0	19.0	20.2[b]	17.8[b]

[a]Percentage single at ages 45–49.
[b]Singulate mean age at marriage

Sources: Malaysia: Computed from *Population Census of Malaysia, 1980.*
Indonesia: Computed from *1980 Population Census.*
Thailand: Rachapaetayakom (1983: Table 1).

1988: Table 24). Consideration is given now to differences in age at marriage by level of education.

Table 3.11 summarizes data on the mean age at marriage for Malay females by educational level from various surveys in South-East Asia, imposing varying degrees of control for current age and for censoring bias. It shows a monotonic, and sharp, rise in mean age at marriage with education for Malay females in Peninsular Malaysia; the sharpest rise is associated with proceeding to some high school education. Comparison with data for Chinese and Indians (not shown in the table) indicates that in both of the Malaysian surveys, education makes far more difference to age at marriage for Malays than for Chinese, with the Indians in between. For example, in 1984–5, the mean age-at-marriage gap between the uneducated and those with more than twelve years' education was 5.9 years for Malays but only 3.6 years for Chinese. This appears to reflect the institutionalization of a later-marriage norm for Chinese, whereas the Malay age at marriage was in a state of flux, with sharp rises mediated mainly through increasing levels of education. Another important point is that in the 1981–2 survey, controlling for a range of other independent variables and covariates through multiple classification analysis leaves the educational differential largely intact, though somewhat reduced in spread, from 17.4 for the uneducated to 20.1 for those with secondary education or above (Tan and Jones, 1990: 184–7).[12]

Data for Muslims in Sabah in Table 3.11 show a positive association between education and age at marriage, though because of small numbers with high school education, the effect of reaching this level can only be shown for the Bajau, for whom high school education appears to have only a modest influence on age at marriage.

In Indonesia, according to both the 1973 Fertility–Mortality Survey, the 1976 Indonesian Fertility Survey, and the 1980 Population Census, every increase in education was associated with a higher age at marriage, though again the sharpest rise appeared to be associated with the transition from primary school to high school education. It is possible that this sharp dichotomy between primary school and at least some high school education is observed only because all levels of education beyond primary school are combined. The Asian Marriage Survey data for Central Java, which separate post-primary education into years of education equivalent to secondary schooling and post-secondary schooling, indicate that the sharpest impact on age at marriage comes with post-secondary education. Among Muslims in Southern Thailand, the transition from no school to some school led to a more pronounced rise in age at marriage than elsewhere (except Sulawesi), but because so few women had completed even upper primary education, the effect of higher levels of education remained indeterminate.

Table 3.12 shows, for Malays in Peninsular Malaysia, the persistence of educational differentials in age at marriage (as proxied by the percentage remaining single) across age-groups. As already mentioned, proceeding to some high school education is what appears to have the

TABLE 3.11

Islamic South-East Asia: Mean Age at First Marriage for Females, by Level of Education, from Various Surveys

	Years of Schooling				Total	No. of Cases
	0	1–6	7–12	>12		
Aged 25+ married before 25						
Pen. Malaysia Malays, 1981–2[a]	16.2	17.7	20.4	–	17.8	1,081
Pen. Malaysia Malays, 1984–5[b]	17.2	18.3	20.6	23.1	18.8	1,650
Sabah: Bajau, 1989[c]	17.3	18.0	18.7	–	17.8	n.a.
Sabah: Indonesian, 1989[c]	16.3	17.8	–[k]	–	17.5	n.a.
Sabah: Filipino, 1989[c]	17.3	18.6	–[k]	–	17.8	n.a.
Central Java						
(Asian Marriage Survey, 1980)[d]						
Rural (aged 19–45)	16.2	16.0	17.3[m]	19.8[m]	16.3	590
Urban lower class (aged 20–45)	16.5	16.8	18.0[m]	22.0[m]	17.2	459
Urban middle class (aged 22–45)	17.1	17.5	18.8[m]	20.9[m]	18.4	457

	No School	Some Primary	Completed Primary	Completed Lower Secondary and Above	Total	No. of Cases
West Java, women aged 25–34, 1973[e]						
Urban	16.5	16.6	17.4	20.6	n.a.	699
Rural	15.9	16.0	16.5	19.8	n.a.	2,569
Central Java, women aged 25–34, 1973[e]						
Urban	16.0	17.7	18.8	21.2	n.a.	469
Rural	16.7	16.9	17.5	20.1	n.a.	2,619
East Java, women aged 25–34, 1973[e]						
Urban	16.4	16.8	17.9	20.5	n.a.	741
Rural	16.0	16.2	17.1	19.0	n.a.	2,417
Sumatra, women aged 25–34, 1973[e]						
Urban	16.6	17.7	19.1	21.4	n.a.	973
Rural	16.2	16.9	18.0	21.4	n.a.	2,255
Sulawesi, women aged 25–34, 1973[e]						
Urban	17.3	17.8	18.2	20.9	n.a.	804
Rural	16.6	18.0	18.3	20.6	n.a.	2,363
Java–Bali, women aged 25–49, married before 25, 1976[f]	15.4	15.7	16.9	20.4	15.8	6,310
Indonesia, ever-married women aged 25–54, 1980[g]	16.9	17.0	17.7	20.3	n.a.	n.a.
Indonesia, ever-married women aged 25–34, 1987[h]	16.2	16.4	17.5	20.7	17.4	n.a.

(continued)

94

TABLE 3.11 *(continued)*

	No School	Lower Primary	Upper Primary	Some Secondary and Above	Total	No. of Cases
Southern Thai Muslims aged 25+ married before 30, 1976[i]						
Total	15.4	16.3	17.3	19.1	15.8	955
Urban	16.1	17.2	17.9	19.2	17.2	191
Rural	15.1	16.0	—[j]	—[l]	15.5	764

[a]Tan et al. (1986: Table 8).
[b]Hamid et al. (1988: Table 2.7).
[c]National Population and Family Development Board (1992: Table 4.5).
[d]Cherlin et al. (1985: Table 3).
[e]Muliakusuma (1976: Tables II.7a, II.7b, II.7c, II.7e, and II.7f).
[f]Central Bureau of Statistics and World Fertility Survey (1978: Vol. II, Table 1.1.3).
[g]Palmore and Singarimbun (1991: Tables 4 and 5).

[h]Kasto (1988: Table 24).
[i]Rachapaetayakom (1984: Table 5.6).
[j]Fewer than 10 cases.
[k]Fewer than 30 cases.
[l]Fewer than 5 cases.
[m]7–10 years, and > 10 years.

TABLE 3.12

Peninsular Malaysia: Percentage of Malays Never-married, by Age and Level of Education, 1980

Education	Age-group						
	20–24	25–29	30–34	35–39	40–44	45+
Females						
No schooling	25.4	10.4	6.5	3.1	2.1	1.5
1–6 years	31.6	13.1	6.7	3.8	2.0	2.3
7–11 years	61.4	24.9	15.3	9.9	6.0	4.3
12+ years	85.0	34.5	14.5	6.2	–[a]	–[a]
Males						
No schooling	63.8	30.5	7.4	9.7	4.4	3.5
1–6 years	69.3	29.3	9.1	3.9	2.7	2.0
7–11 years	85.7	40.0	10.3	4.4	1.6	0.9
12+ years	96.0	50.9	7.4	6.4	5.5	–[a]

Source: Unpublished tabulation computed from sample, 1980 Population Census.
[a]Numbers too small for reliable estimates.

greatest impact on age at marriage, and for females, this effect remains evident across age-groups. It is also clear for young males, though at ages above 30, the effect of education in delaying marriage for males is not at all clear.

In Thailand, age at marriage of Muslims has remained approximately two years below that of Buddhists throughout most of this century (Wayachut, 1993). To some extent, this is because of the low levels of education of Muslim women. However, the religious differences remain largely intact when level of education is controlled for. Figure 3.3 shows that among uneducated women, the Buddhist–Muslim differences are pronounced and, if anything, widening. For women with four years of education or more than four years, older Muslim women actually had higher ages at marriage than Buddhists. But these Muslim women were a tiny and unrepresentative group, mostly living in Bangkok (Wayachut, 1993). As these levels of education have spread more widely through the Muslim population in younger age-groups, age at marriage among these more educated Muslim women has fallen to levels below that of comparable Buddhists.

Detailed information on differentials in age at marriage by educational attainment in Indonesia are presented in Table 3.13, based on the Indonesian Fertility Survey of 1976. Again, the transition to secondary schooling represents a clear break point. Whereas mean age at first marriage rises gradually to 16.9 for those with completed primary education, it jumps to 19.5 for those with junior high school and rises sharply again to 21.4 for those with senior high school and above.

Further analysis of the Indonesian Fertility Survey data for 1976 has been conducted by Soeradji and Hatmadji (1982) and by BPS (1980), using both cross-tabulations and multivariate analysis. It might be noted that provincial differentials can to some extent be used as a proxy for differentials by ethnic–linguistic groups; for example, Central Java, Yogyakarta, and East Java are mainly Javanese, West Java is mainly Sundanese, West Sumatra is mainly Minangkabau. However, many provinces have very mixed populations, and the identification of age at marriage for certain linguistic groups in the BPS study (1980: Table 14) is particularly useful. It shows, for example, that Madurese speakers, most of whom are found on the island of Madura and elsewhere in East Java, have an earlier age of marriage than the Javanese, one that roughly matches that of the Sundanese as the lowest in Indonesia (but see n. 11).

Multivariate analysis of the Indonesian Fertility Survey data reveals that education is the most prominent determinant of age at marriage among the four factors studied, followed by work status before marriage. However, the four factors between them were only able to explain between 6 and 7 per cent of the total variance in age at marriage, except in DKI Jakarta, where the proportion of variance explained rose to 21 per cent (Soeradji and Hatmadji, 1982: 60).[13]

Table 3.14 shows the age by which 50 per cent of females were married, for Muslim women only, in Indonesia in 1985. Using data

FIGURE 3.3

Thailand: Age by Which 50 Per Cent of Female Birth Cohorts Were First
Married, by Religion and Level of Education, 1980

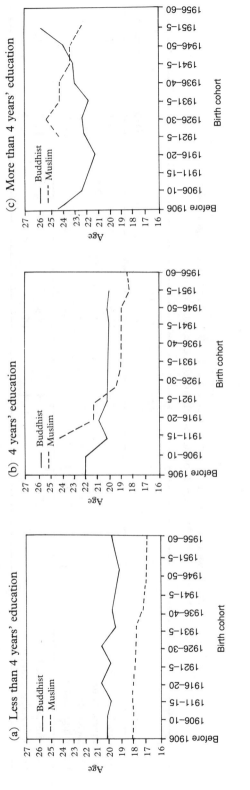

Source: Wayachut (1993).

TABLE 3.13

Java: Mean Age at Marriage for Women Aged 25–49 Who Married at Ages under 25, by Province and Level of Education, 1976

Education	Jakarta	West Java	Central Java	Yogyakarta	East Java	All Java–Bali
No schooling	15.6	14.8	15.6	17.2	15.3	15.4
Incomplete primary	16.2	15.1	15.9	17.8	15.8	15.7
Completed primary	18.1	16.3	16.7	18.6	17.0	16.9
Junior high and above	20.9	19.8	20.2	20.5	20.6	20.3
Total unstandardized	17.2	15.3	15.9	17.7	15.7	15.8
Standardized education	16.4	15.3	16.0	17.7	15.9	15.8

Source: Central Bureau of Statistics and World Fertility Survey (1978: Vol. 1, Table 4.3).

TABLE 3.14

Indonesia: Age by Which 50 Per Cent of Muslim Women Had Married,
by Level of Education, 1985

Education	Urban Areas	Rural Areas
No education	19.2	18.4
Some primary	19.6	18.4
Completed primary	19.9	18.6
Junior high	22.0	21.1
Senior high and above	24.9	23.7
All education levels	21.4	19.1

Source: Computed from tabulations of percentage ever-married by single year of age and
educational level, from data tapes, *1985 Intercensal Population Survey.*

tapes from the 1985 Intercensal Survey (Supas) it was possible to
extract current marital status for Muslim women alone: the only table
in this chapter where Indonesian Muslims are specifically identified.
The age at marriage may be slightly overstated for the highly educated
if some of those who married at younger ages were still pursuing their
education at the time of the survey and would later enter a higher
educational attainment group. But this is unlikely to be more than a
trivial proportion. The table supports the earlier finding of a very sharp
differential in age at marriage according to education, the impact of
education being substantial only with the transition to junior high
school. The transition from junior high school to senior high school and
above has an even more pronounced effect; half of those with senior
high and tertiary education in urban areas would have reached almost
25 before they married. The differences in age at marriage between
those with primary or no education and those with senior high and
above exceeded five years in both urban and rural areas.

Provincial differences in age at marriage in Java cannot be explained
to any great extent by interprovincial differences in education levels, as
Table 3.13 shows. Standardizing provincial mean ages at marriage by
education makes only a trivial difference except in the case of Jakarta,
where this standardization lowers the mean by 0.8 year. In other words,
for Jakarta the above-average age at marriage is in part associated with
women being somewhat better educated; after standardization, the
Jakarta figure is not much higher than those for Central and East Java.

Education is also a key determinant of non-marriage. Among
Peninsular Malaysian Malays, the percentage of women never married
at ages 30–34 to 40–44 rises sharply with education. The key break
point is the beginning of secondary schooling. For example, among
women aged 30–34, fewer than 7 per cent of those with six or fewer
years of education remained unmarried, compared with 15 per cent of
those with seven years or more of education. This factor alone could
lead to sharp increases in non-marriage among younger cohorts when

they reach their thirties, as the average level of education has been rising steeply in these cohorts.

Analysis of the 1976 Indonesian Fertility Survey data shows that women's age at marriage differs much more sharply with differences in their own occupation before marriage than with their husband's occupation. Women who worked in professional and clerical occupations, a highly educated group, have much higher age at marriage than do wives of men in the same group of occupations (Central Bureau of Statistics and World Fertility Survey, 1978: Vol. 1, Table 4.2). This is no doubt because of the wide range of education among women who marry professional and clerical men, as there has not traditionally been any stigma attached to men who 'marry down' in terms of educational level.[14]

Table 3.15 presents some findings from the Indonesian Marriage Survey, showing that women in all the locations surveyed were more likely to have married at the age of 17 or over if they had completed primary school. The more interesting finding is that religiosity appeared to make little difference, and that arrangement of marriage made less difference than might have been expected.

Two other Malaysian studies should be briefly summarized. On the basis of the 1966–7 West Malaysian Family Survey, Von Elm and Hirschman (1979) studied differences in age at marriage between different ethnic and socio-economic groups. The authors admit some problems with this survey for the study of marriage. The sample of married women aged 15–44 excluded young women who had postponed marriage, and for this reason the analysis was restricted to married women aged 25 and over. Nevertheless, the sample was under-representative of those who married late. Currently divorced or widowed women were also excluded from the sample. The analytical models used were only able to explain 7–15 per cent of the variance.

Despite these limitations, the study was important because it was conducted in the early stages of the sharp rise in Malay age at marriage. A key finding was that ethnic differences remained at almost their original level, even when holding background constant, thus revealing different cultural orientations about the appropriate timing of marriage. However, post-primary education was shown to be a powerful force in delaying marriage and in narrowing ethnic differentials in age at marriage. It was much more important than various indicators of socio-economic origins.

Data from both the 1980 Population Census and the 1984–5 Malaysian Population and Family Survey showed early marriage among Malays to characterize the less educated and rural dwellers. Further analysis of the Malaysian Population and Family Survey was carried out, confined to ever-married respondents aged 25–34 who married before the age of 25. This reduced truncation and selection bias, though it had the disadvantage of excluding from the analysis approximately 23 per cent of respondents, some of whom had married by the time of the survey but beyond the age of 25, and the rest of whom had not married by

TABLE 3.15

Indonesia: Proportion of Respondents Who Married at Age 17 and Over, by Region and Various Background Characteristics, 1978

Background Characteristics	Jakarta (Betawi)		South Kalimantan (Banjar)		South Sumatra		Java	
	Aged <36	Aged 36+	Aged <36	Aged 36+	Aged <36	Aged 36+	Aged <36	Aged 36+
Schooling								
None or incomplete primary	36	29	59	42	51	46	72	71
Completed primary and above	45	40	73	83	71	72	96	81
Work before marriage								
Did not work	40	26	–	–	–	–	–	–
Worked	49	41	–	–	–	–	–	–
Religion								
Devout	–	–	63	47	54	–	–	–
Not very devout	–	–	60	33	53	–	–	–
Choice of spouse								
Own choice	–	–	74	68	56	–	87	81
Not own choice	–	–	66	34	44	–	86[a](77)	70[a](78)

Sources: Muliakusuma (1982: Table 7.2); Mahfudz (1982: Table 7.2); Kasto (1982: Tables 7.3); Mahmud (1983: Tables 7.2 and 7.3).

[a] Actually 'parents' choice'. Numbers in brackets are for those whose spouse was 'chosen by others' (i.e. not parents).

the time of the survey: some of these would marry late and others would not marry at all.[15] Cross-tabulation analysis confirmed the relationship between age at marriage and education, rural background, and current rural residence. In addition, early marriage was shown to be associated with parental choice of spouse, wider age differences between husband and wife, and non-working status before marriage (Tan et al., 1988). Logit regression analysis indicated that education and freedom in choice of marriage partner are significant in the timing of Malay marriage. So are work status before marriage and age difference between husband and wife (Tan et al., 1988: Tables 15 and 16; see also Tan and Chak, 1988: Appendix Table 2). However, childhood residence and current residence lose their significance in this model, indicating that rural–urban differences result from differences between the rural and urban sample in some of the significant factors.

Male Age at Marriage and Age Differences between Spouses

To give some perspective before presenting the data for South-East Asian Muslims, the findings of an international comparative study of age differences between spouses in developing countries (Casterline, Williams, and McDonald, 1986: Table 1) will be briefly summarized. This study shows that South-East Asian populations, including Java and the Malaysian Malays, resemble those of Latin America much more than they do those of Africa and the Islamic world of North Africa, the Middle East, and South Asia, in a number of respects. The first is the relatively high proportion of women who marry men who are actually younger than they are: more than 10 per cent in parts of South-East Asia; less than 3 per cent in most of Africa and the Islamic world. The second is the relatively low average age difference between spouses. Whereas in Africa and the Islamic world, median age differences of six or seven years are normal, in South-East Asia, this falls to four years, though it is closer to five years in Indonesia and among Malaysian Malays.

The international study concluded that in most societies the age difference is largely determined by the age at marriage of the husband, reflecting the much greater variability within societies in the timing of marriage for men than for women. It also concluded that patriarchal societies and those characterized by patrilineal kinship organization, and (a not unrelated factor) societies in which women's status is low, tend to be characterized by relatively large age differences (Casterline, Williams, and McDonald, 1986: 374). The differences already alluded to in Chapter 1 between Muslim populations of South-East Asia and those elsewhere in the Muslim world no doubt help to explain the relatively small age differences between spouses in Islamic South-East Asia.

A recent study examining trends in female and male ages at marriage in a large number of Asian countries found that male ages at marriage have generally been rising, but the rise has been slower than that for females, resulting in a gradual convergence in male and female ages at marriage (Xenos and Gultiano, 1992: 14–20). Males have shown reduced dispersions in marriage ages, females increased dispersions, suggesting a diversification of role models for females and in the case of males, a reduction or disappearance of formerly important impediments to marriage near the modal age.

For the male populations of Islamic South-East Asia, too, ages at marriage have tended to rise over recent decades, though more slowly than female. Rather than present detailed cohort trends, the top segment of Table 3.16 shows trends in singulate mean age at marriage for males. Apart from a fall between 1947 and 1957 for Singapore Malays, which appeared to result from a trend towards a more balanced sex ratio in the marriageable age-groups, male ages at marriage rose steadily up to 1980 in Singapore and Peninsular Malaysia and more tentatively in Indonesia and Southern Thailand. Over the 1980s, the rise in Indonesia and Southern Thailand was more pronounced.

Age differences between spouses will now be examined. There are two main ways to do this. Where only census or survey estimates of average age at marriage for men and women are available, derived from distributions of marital status by age, differences in the average age at marriage for each sex can be taken as a proxy for the average age difference between spouses. While giving a useful summary indication of differences, this measure can be very inadequate if the distribution of age differences between spouses is skewed, for example if most couples are quite close in age but there is a group with very wide differences. The second measure is a direct comparison of husbands' and wives' ages where these are collected in surveys. The advantage of this measure is that the frequency of various age differences can be tabulated, as well as the average difference (median or mean).

Table 3.16 contains data of the first kind just mentioned, that is, differences in mean age at marriage of men and women based on the indirect estimates from marital status data in censuses and surveys, for Indonesia, for the Malaysian and Singaporean Malays, and for Muslims in Southern Thailand. There has been a clear tendency for the age difference to narrow over time. For Malaysian Malays, this narrowing took place mainly over the 1950s and 1960s, and was due entirely to the very sharp rise in female age at marriage over this period, which narrowed the age difference despite a rise of one-and-a-half years in the male age at marriage over the same period. For Singapore Malays, the narrowing also took place over the 1950s and 1960s and continued into the 1970s; again, it was due entirely to the very sharp rise in female age at marriage, which narrowed the age difference despite a slow rise (broken by a fall in 1957) in the male age at marriage over the same period. For Southern Thai Muslims, the narrowing of the age difference occurred later, in the 1970s, and widened again slightly in the 1980s. In Indonesia, data for the early periods are not available, but there has been a steady narrowing of the male–female marriage age differential since 1970, and by 1980 the differential had narrowed to roughly the value it had reached in Singapore in 1970.

The second category of estimates, those based on actual data on age

TABLE 3.16

Islamic South-East Asia: Trends in the Singulate Mean Age at Marriage for Males, and Male–Female Differences, 1947–1990

	1947	1960	1970	1980	1990
Singulate mean age at marriage for males					
Indonesia	n.a.	n.a.	23.8[a]	24.1	25.4
Pen. Malaysia Malays	23.4	22.7[b]	24.7	26.2	n.a.
Singapore Malays	26.0	24.8[b]	26.6	27.3	28.2
Southern Thai Muslims	n.a.	22.8	23.5	24.0	25.4
Male–female difference (years)					
Indonesia	n.a.	n.a.	4.5[a]	4.1	3.8
Pen. Malaysia Malays	6.2	4.8[b]	3.6	3.0	n.a.
Singapore Malays	9.3	7.7[b]	4.3	3.1	3.0
Southern Thai Muslims	n.a.	4.9	4.8	3.5	3.8

[a]1971. [b]1957.

Sources: Calculated from *Population Census* (Indonesia), 1971, 1980, and 1990; *Population Census of Malaya*, 1947 and 1957; *Population Census of Malaysia*, 1970 and 1980; *Census of Population, Singapore*, 1957, 1970, 1980, and 1990; Rachapaetayakom (1983: Table 5.2); unpublished data from *1990 Population and Housing Census* (Thailand).

differences between spouses, are available from a number of studies. In Indonesia, the 1973 Fertility–Mortality Survey tabulated such information,[16] and in Malaysia, tabulations are available from the 1981–2 Marriage Survey and the 1984–5 Population and Family Survey.

Table 3.17 presents data from Indonesia for 1973. Between 70 per cent and 80 per cent of women in both urban and rural areas married husbands between zero and nine years older than themselves. An alternative perspective on the data would emphasize that more than half of all women (and over 60 per cent in East Java) married husbands at least five years older than themselves. Bearing in mind that most women were still in their teens when they married, such age differences were very significant, implying that husbands were much more mature and experienced when they married, thus making it easier for them to impose their authority within the marital relationship. Really wide age differences between spouses were not uncommon. The proportion of first marriages in which the husband was at least ten years older than the wife ranged between 15 and 24 per cent in different regions and urban and rural areas. East Java had the highest proportion with wide age differences, followed by Sumatra.

No clear time trends towards wider or narrower age differences between spouses could be detected (Muliakusuma, 1976: Table II.10). What was very clear, however, was the inverse relationship between age of the woman at first marriage and the age difference between spouses (Muliakusuma, 1976: Table II.11). Women who married at 18 years or below (and they were the great majority) were much more likely than other women to be married to a husband at least ten years older than themselves. For example, in rural East Java, 24 per cent of girls who married by the age of 18 married a husband who was ten or more years older than them. The chances of this were particularly high for girls married at ages below 15, especially in Java and Sumatra.

For Malaysia, Malay respondents in the 1981–2 Marriage Survey recorded much the same distribution of age differences as those found in Indonesia: over half the husbands were five or more years older than their wives, and 19 per cent were ten or more years older (Table 3.18). Among the Chinese, differences were narrower; only 36 per cent of husbands were five or more years older than their wives. The widest average age differences between Malay spouses were recorded when wives were uneducated, were either not working or unpaid family workers, or where the marriage had been arranged (Table 3.18). In Kelantan, the reasons given in favour of an older husband were that he would be more mature and tolerant; also that a wife of the same age or older will appear to age more quickly, thus encouraging the husband's attention to stray to younger women (Kelantan focus groups, 1989).

Data for Malays from the 1984–5 Population and Family Survey show a distinctly narrower average age gap between husbands and wives than the 1981–2 Marriage Survey data (or the Indonesian data). While some of this may reflect a trend (see below), most of the difference is probably due to the different sample. Kelantanese, who tend to have

TABLE 3.17

Islamic South-East Asia: Age Difference between Husband and Wife at Time of First Marriage of Ever-married Women, from Various Surveys

	Husband Younger than Wife	Husband 0–4 Years Older	Husband 5–9 Years Older	Husband 10+ Years Older	Total	No. of Cases
Pen. Malaysia Malays						
1981–2	3.7	39.9	37.5	18.9	100	1,363
1984–5	6.6	44.0	35.9	13.5	100	1,999
Indonesia, 1973						
West Java: Urban	3.3	42.5[a]	35.5	18.8	100	1,838
Rural	2.4	45.0[a]	37.5	15.2	100	7,343
Central Java: Urban	3.1	43.1[a]	36.2	17.8	100	1,327
Rural	1.6	39.4[a]	42.0	16.8	100	7,287
East Java: Urban	2.7	31.9[a]	41.4	24.0	100	1,989
Rural	1.6	35.3[a]	40.4	22.7	100	6,150
Sumatra: Urban	3.2	39.9[a]	37.3	19.6	100	2,494
Rural	2.9	39.8[a]	35.4	21.9	100	5,992
Sulawesi: Urban	3.9	47.4[a]	31.0	17.7	100	2,065
Rural	4.7	48.4	31.5	15.4	100	5,730

Sources: 1981–2: Tan et al. (1986: Table 19).
1984–5: Hamid et al. (1988: Table 2.19).
1973: Muliakusuma (1976: Table II.9).
[a]Includes age the same.

TABLE 3.18

Peninsular Malaysia: Age Difference between Husband and Wife at Time of First Marriage of Malay Women Who Married before 25, by Freedom of Choice of Marriage Partner and Number of Years since First Married (percentage distribution)

Age Difference in Years between Husband and Wife	Choice of Marriage Partner				
	Own Choice with Parents' Blessing	Own Choice without Parents' Blessing	Arranged with Approval	Arranged without Approval	Total
<0	9	—a	6	8	8
0–4	43	—a	32	29	36
5–9	34	—a	41	40	37
10+	14	—a	21	23	19
Total	100	—a	100	100	100
N	571	9	334	307	1,221

Age Difference in Years between Husband and Wife	Years since First Married					
	1–4	5–9	10–14	15–19	20+	Total
<0	8	7	7	9	5	6
0–4	43	36	32	29	34	35
5–9	36	43	41	38	38	39
10+	13	14	20	24	23	20
Total	100	100	100	100	100	100
N	195	215	169	156	512	1,247

Sources: Malaysian Marriage Survey, 1981–2, reported in Tan et al. (1986: Tables 20 and 26); and unpublished tabulations from Malaysian Marriage Survey, 1981–2.

aNumbers too small to be meaningful.

wider age differences between husband and wife, were over-represented in the 1981–2 Marriage Survey, whereas the 1984–5 Population and Family Survey was representative of the Malay population of Peninsular Malaysia.

By contrast with Indonesia in the 1970s, Table 3.18 shows clear evidence of a trend over time toward narrower age differences between spouses among Malaysian Malays. The evidence is clearest in the declining proportion with an age difference of ten years or more: from well over 20 per cent among marriages contracted before 1966 to only 13 per cent among marriages contracted in the late 1970s. The proportion with an age difference of less than five years rose from less than 40 per cent among marriages contracted before 1966 to over 50 per cent among marriages contracted in the late 1970s.

Summary

It is now time to pull together the threads of the discussion in this chapter. In the 1950s, the Malay-Muslim world was characterized by what would nowadays be considered as child marriage. In both Malaysia and Indonesia, 50 per cent of women were married before their eighteenth birthday; in some quite large regions, 50 per cent were married before their seventeenth birthday.

Age at marriage for Malay females in Singapore and Malaysia, and possibly in Brunei as well, underwent a dramatic rise beginning in the 1950s and accelerating during the 1960s, a rise which continued into the 1970s and 1980s but at a slower pace. The rise was delayed by a decade in Kelantan and Trengganu. The key task in Chapter 4 will therefore be to explain the rise during the 1950s and 1960s. In Indonesia and Southern Thailand, by contrast, the 1960s saw only a modest rise in age at marriage from the prevailing very young ages, a rise concentrated in the urban areas. It was not until the 1970s that age at marriage rose more sharply, a rise which accelerated in the 1980s. This summary also holds true for Java and Sumatra, but in Kalimantan and Sulawesi, the rise in the 1960s was more pronounced.

By 1980, the median ages at marriage for Malay women in Singapore and Malaysia were 23.9 and 22.2 respectively, a level higher than the median in many Western countries (United Nations, 1990: Table 44). In Indonesia the median age was still well below this (19.5) and the level for Indonesian Muslims was somewhat lower still. An important issue is whether economic growth and educational development towards the levels reached in Malaysia will lead to further increases in age at marriage in Indonesia. The evidence of wide differences in age at marriage in Indonesia according to education suggests that they will. The rise in median age at marriage to 20.9, recorded by the 1990 Census, is consistent with this.

Finally, throughout the Malay-Muslim world, there has been a clear time trend towards narrower differences in ages between spouses, due to a sharper rise in female than in male age at marriage. Age differences have tended to be wider for women who married very young, who were uneducated, and whose marriages were arranged.

This chapter having established the levels, trends, and differentials in female age at marriage in the Malay world, the next chapter will move on to the more interesting, and more demanding, task of explanation.

1. There is very little information about the frequency of premarital sexual relations in earlier times, or about more recent trends, in Islamic South-East Asia. One extreme appears to be the high level of premarital chastity among the Maranao and Maguindanao Muslims in the Philippines, more than 98 per cent of whom reported that they did not experience premarital sexual relations with their present husband, compared with only about 75 per cent among Christians (Costello and Palabrica-Costello, 1988: 22). The situation in Java stands in sharp contrast to this. H. Geertz (1961: 70–1) reported that in her East Java study area, forced marriages of couples found illicitly sleeping together were common; fornication was cited as responsible for 3.6 per cent of the registered marriages in 1953. The Indonesian Fertility Survey of 1976 recorded that 7 per cent of women aged 20–24 had a premarital conception leading to a live birth during their teenage years (United Nations, 1989: Table 12). In the Indonesian segment of the Asian Marriage Survey, 11 per cent of the urban middle-class women aged 35–44 first married at the same age as, or after, the first birth. These percentages were much lower, 1 per cent and 2 per cent, respectively, in the urban lower-class study and the rural study. In more recent times, 'dating' practices have become more common in all these countries, and 'affairs between single people, which in former times usually culminated in marriage, now have less certain outcomes as village elders lose their ability to enforce social norms over an increasingly mobile and dispersed population' (Ong, 1987: 200). Of Malay female factory workers, Karim (1987: 52) writes that 'Malay and non-Malay men often formed liaisons with these girls, not so much for the purpose of marriage but merely to establish temporary sexual relationships'. These loose, irregular attachments 'rarely crystallize into marriages because of the negative sexual image they portray'. In villages near Semarang in Central Java, migrant female factory workers were blamed for increased sexual promiscuity and an increasing number of unwed mothers (Wolf, cited by Guinness, 1986: 147).

2. In Mindanao, average female age at marriage was just below 18 for Muslims and just below 20 for Christians (Costello and Palabrica-Costello, 1988: 22; see also Wong and Ng, 1985; Gastardo-Conaco and Ramos-Jimenez, 1986: 131).

3. The mean, particularly the measure 'singulate mean age at marriage' (Hajnal, 1953) is a more commonly used measure of central tendency in studies of marriage, but the median is used in preference in this book because it can be considered a more suitable measure where a distribution is skewed, as is the case with age at marriage. The median can be much more accurately measured where data on marital status are available by single year of age, provided that the quality of age reporting is good. This is unfortunately rarely the case, and most medians are therefore calculated by the indirect method, using marital status by five-year age-group and either linear or osculatory interpolation. This can easily lead to errors of up to about half a year in the calculations, if the actual median falls near the middle of a five-year age-group and therefore requires maximum interpolation. For details of calculation procedures, see Shryock and Siegel (1971: 292–4).

4. The main period measure used—the median age at marriage—uses stock (or prevalence) figures which cannot, strictly speaking, indicate trends in the incidence of marriage. Nevertheless, they do come fairly close to portraying the trends for birth cohorts whose current age approximates the median calculated for the particular year. The extent of discrepancy is shown in the following example for Indonesia. The median ages at marriage for females were calculated from 1971 and 1980 census data on marital status by five-year age-groups, while the cohort data were computed from 1980 census data for

cohorts whose ages in the two years were closest to the computed median age.

	1971	1980
Median age at marriage for females	18.9	19.5
SMAM for females	19.3	20.0
Age by which 50 per cent had married		
1946–50 birth cohort	18.0	
1951–5 birth cohort	18.2	
1956–60 birth cohort		18.5
1961–5 birth cohort		19.0

5. It is just possible that a comparable rise occurred among the Brunei Malays, whose median age at marriage in 1970 was not far below that in Singapore, but there are no trend data to prove it.

6. Age misstatement is a serious problem in Indonesia, although it has been improving and is less serious among younger women. Indices of improvement are as follows:

	1971 Census	1980 Census	1985 Supas	1990 Census
Myer's Index (females)	50.5	39.6	n.a.	20.6
Whipple's Index (females)	259.9	227.2	n.a.	166.3
UN Age Sex Accuracy Index	53.0	37.2	31.4	29.4

Aside from the general improvement over time, age statement is much better among younger women, most of whom have had at least primary schooling, than among older women.

People who do not know their age cannot be expected to know their age at marriage either, and this can introduce major problems in the data. For example, part of the rise in age at marriage shown for recent times in Table 3.3 and other tables could plausibly result from a more accurate knowledge of age and a systematic tendency for older women to understate the ages at which they married. However, this is probably not a major factor, for two reasons: the regional differentials in ages at marriage among older women are in line with what are known to be the case from other sources; and the rise in recent times has been too large to be accounted for by systematic understatement of age at marriage by older women.

7. Tan (1983: Table 5.5), applying the Coale-McNeil model to the 1974 Malaysian Fertility and Family Survey data, found an even sharper rise in Malay age at marriage between these cohorts. However, the result for the youngest birth cohort (1950–4) was suspect because of a large standard error.

8. On the whole, there is very close consistency between the estimates based on the 1980 and 1990 census data. The fairly wide differences shown for the 1956–60 birth cohort in urban areas (0.9 years) could be partly due to a change in the definition of urban areas between the two censuses. In rural areas, the 1990 census data tend to show a slightly higher age at marriage, the difference becoming greatest in the 1941–5 and 1946–50 birth cohorts (0.5 years).

9. The evidence appears to indicate that Chinese women in the region were marrying later than the Malays throughout the early twentieth century, despite the artificial inducement to early marriage provided by high sex ratios in an immigrant community (Freedman, 1957).

10. The Fertility–Mortality Survey data suggest a slightly earlier onset of the rise in age at marriage in rural Central and East Java. However, in general, the degree of consistency between the two sets of data is remarkable.

11. There must be some doubt about the 1987 figures, which show a lower age at marriage for Madurese speakers than did the 1976 Indonesian Fertility Survey data (BPS, 1980: Table 14). The 1976 data showed roughly identical median ages at marriage

for Sundanese and Madurese speakers; the 1987 data show Madurese age at marriage as two full years lower than Sundanese. Moreover, in Map 3.1, most of the island of Madura, which is the heartland of Madurese speakers, shows evidence of higher age at marriage than most of Java. The exception is the easternmost *kabupaten* of Sumenep. On the other hand, much of the 'east hook' area of East Java, where Madurese are prominent in the population, has low ages. The measure used in the map is percentage still single at 20–24; the data on percentage still single at 15–19 (not shown), while they still show above-average ages at marriage for the western part of the island of Madura, show it less prominently than do the data in Map 3.1. The balance of evidence does suggest very low mean or median ages at marriage for the Madurese as a whole (see also Hatmadji, 1990: 162), but just how low is clearly still at issue. For an ethnographic study in Madura which gives considerable attention to marriage, see Niehof (1985).

12. The independent variables besides education were childhood residence, premarital work experience, way of choosing marriage partner, and post-marriage living arrangements. The covariates were age of respondent and age of husband.

13. The sample population in these studies was restricted, respectively, to women aged 25 or over who were married before the age of 25 (BPS, 1980), and women aged 20 or over who were married before the age of 20 (Soeradji and Hatmadji, 1982).

14. The Southern Thai Muslim Survey, while it recorded clear differentials in age at marriage by education of either the husband or the wife, did not show any noteworthy difference according to work status of wife or occupation of wife or husband (agriculture or non-agriculture) (Rachapaetayakom, 1983: Table 5.8).

15. It would have been impossible to include women who had not married by the time of the survey in the analysis, because although some data were collected on these women in the household section of the 1984–5 Malaysian Population and Family Survey, some of the variables included in the multivariate analysis were not available for them (Tan et al., 1988: 29).

16. So too did Singarimbun and Manning (1974b: 13), V. J. Hull (1975: 201), and Chapon (1976: 14–15). Their findings, all of them for Java, were not very different from those reported here.

4
Influences on Age at Marriage

THE introduction to Chapter 2 noted that socio-economic change was a fundamental and multifaceted process throughout the region, and that it would therefore be futile to look for single-factor explanations of rising age at marriage. Nevertheless, it should be possible to identify aspects of the process that are of particular importance in understanding nuptiality change.

Before attempting to identify the determinants of change, it is necessary to understand the factors in the traditional setting which fostered early marriage. The very slight differences in Indonesian and Malaysian Malay marriage ages over four decades and probably much longer (up to the 1940 birth cohort in Malaysia and the 1950 birth cohort in Indonesia) attest to the acceptance of, and lack of challenge to, a set of norms governing age at marriage and arrangement of marriage.

One question to be kept in mind in this study of social change is whether and if so to what extent the process of social change was influenced by the Islamic setting in which it was taking place. Would trends towards a rising age at marriage have been any different (e.g. faster, slower) in a comparable rural but non-Islamic population? A related question is whether it is 'Malay culture' rather than Islam as such that was an important conditioning factor in social change.

Factors Traditionally Fostering Early Marriage

An explanation of traditional patterns of marriage requires an understanding of the cultural milieu of the times. Some insights will be provided here by focusing on the Malay world of the 1950s and 1960s, drawing on historical, sociological, and village studies.

Rural Setting

Whether in Malaysia, Indonesia, Brunei, Southern Thailand, or the Philippines, the Malay-Muslim world of the 1950s was a village world: villages without the distractions of electricity and the things it makes available, such as television and ready access to a range of consumer goods. Only in Singapore was there a substantial urbanized Malay population living with the modern amenities of life. Some of the cities of Indonesia were large enough, but they were decrepit and sadly lacking in infrastructure. Jakarta was often described as an overgrown kampong, with hardly a building over three storeys, no television, crowded and ramshackle buses, and almost no taxis, so that people had to move about mainly in *becak* (pedicabs), by bicycle, or on foot. Only a tiny proportion of its houses were supplied with electricity or sewerage systems.

Given the rapid urbanization taking place in recent times, it is worth stressing just how rural the Malay populations were in the 1950s and 1960s. In Peninsular Malaysia, 81 per cent of the Malays lived in rural areas in 1957, compared with only 27 per cent of the Chinese.[1] In Indonesia, 85 per cent of the population was rural in 1961, and in Southern Thailand, the proportion was even higher.

Village life followed the agricultural cycle, the steady pattern of life punctuated by the intensive activity of planting and harvesting, though in most of Malaysia and Southern Thailand it was rubber cultivation rather than paddy farming that dominated daily and annual activity patterns.[2] Women played an important economic role in fishing villages (Rosemary Firth, 1966: Chapter 2; Fraser, 1966: 12–13), in both smallholder and estate rubber-growing areas (Barlow, Jayasuriya, and Tan, forthcoming) and in paddy villages (R. O. Hill, 1977; Kuchiba, Tsubouchi, and Maeda, 1979). Very widely throughout the Malay world, they were the key market sellers, though the proportion of women among traders and market sellers differed greatly by region; for example, they were much more common in Kelantan than in the West Coast of Malaysia and much more prevalent in Central Java and Yogyakarta than in West Java or South Sulawesi.

Because of their access to sources of income, married women had a degree of economic autonomy in peasant society throughout much of the Malay world. This has been particularly stressed for Java, for the Minangkabau and Acehnese areas, and for the north-eastern states of Peninsular Malaysia—Kelantan and Trengganu. In Java, women typically sold food or garden products in the market, or worked as labourers during certain periods of the agricultural cycle. In Javanese towns, women dominated market selling, a feature also of Kelantan and Trengganu.

After marriage, the young couple typically lived for a period with or near one or the other set of parents. There was no particular preference for the bride's or groom's parents; the pattern was one of ambilocal residence, and the decision about where to live was normally based on practical issues. On the whole, residence with the girl's parents appears to have been more common, partly because it was thought that the young bride would feel more comfortable there and could be incorporated into her mother's mutual aid network.[3] It was usually a year or two— even up to five years, in the case of very young marriages—before the newly married couple could establish a nuclear family, but even then, their residence was normally not far from that of one or both sets of parents (Koentjaraningrat, 1985: 133–4; Williams, 1990b: 85–7; Tan and Jones, 1991: 178–84) and frequent contact with parents was maintained.[4]

Once a separate household was established, the wife gained a large sphere of authority. This was particularly in relation to finances and to the rearing of children, but it also overlapped into decisions such as planning the agricultural cycle. The following two statements, 'Women in general are convinced that men are chronically incompetent in the handling of money' (Jay, 1969: 92) and 'It is not unusual for a man to state that his wife is more clever than he about handling money' (Strange, 1981: 199), come from two areas widely separated geographically, East Java and Trengganu. Throughout the Malay-Muslim world, there seems to have been a large degree of acceptance by men that they were more likely to squander money than were their wives, and that household finances were therefore best left to women (H. Geertz, 1961: 122–8; Rosemary Firth, 1966: 27–8; Jay, 1969: 87–92; V. J. Hull, 1975: 113–15, 145–50). But the high regard in which women's capabilities were held went beyond finances: 'Nearly everyone in Java—male and female—would agree that women are more resourceful, more clever, than men at handling themselves in general.' (V. J. Hull, 1975: 113.) And their power within the Javanese household was legendary: 'Rarely is a Javanese wife completely under the shadow of her husband, but there are many husbands who have passively surrendered to their wives.' (H. Geertz, 1961: 125.)

Though the importance of women in handling the household's finances throughout the Malay-Muslim world has been established beyond a doubt, its significance in demonstrating women's independence, autonomy, and power may have sometimes been exaggerated. For example, holding the purse-strings did not necessarily indicate control over major financial decisions. Wolff (1992: 64) argues that the stress by H. Geertz and Jay on female dominance in the everyday affairs of the Javanese household, including financial management, obscured such issues as 'women's lack of control over sexuality and lack of power within and beyond the household, the constraints of poverty on women's lives, the miniscule amount of financial resources they might control, and the contradictions in expectations concerning women's economic behaviour and "feminine" behaviour'.

Marriage patterns in Europe have been greatly influenced by matters of land inheritance and primogeniture, which have tended to delay marriage and lead to relatively high levels of non-marriage (Laslett, 1972; Goody, 1976). By contrast, the Islamic law of inheritance which operates in much of the Malay world provides that the estate of a deceased Muslim shall be divided in specified proportions among all the immediate family of the deceased. This commonly leads to multiple ownership of plots, fragmentation and systems of tenancy, and sharecropping (Fisk, 1963: 183); sometimes these problems can be avoided by more pragmatic arrangements for the division of property, taking advantage of a provision of Muslim law that the distribution of estates can be settled by consent of the heirs (Winstedt, 1961: 48–9). *Adat*, or customary law, which operates quite widely, typically gives inheritance of the family home to the youngest daughter on the understanding that she will care for the parents in old age. In any case, these inheritance arrangements do not impose any particular constraints on the marriages of either males or females. With the important exception of Java and Bali, throughout the Malay world, land was not a severe constraint on people's economic opportunities in the 1950s and 1960s. If land 'shortage' developed in particular areas, migration to new land was always an option (Fisk, 1961; Lineton, 1975; Hugo, 1981; Hill, 1989: *passim*).

If evidence were needed of the minor importance of land in marriage decisions, it surely lies in the frequency of divorce in the very early stages of a marriage, to be discussed in Chapter 5; such divorces were of no great concern, because their implications for the division of property were minimal.

Religion was at the core of social and village life. It was a Malay Islam, unselfconsciously incorporating elements from an animist and a Hindu–Buddhist past. The *bersanding*, or sitting-in-state ceremony at Malay weddings; the *zikir*, or Sufi-like chanting; the *mak yong* dance-drama in Kelantan; the *wayang* with its Hindu epics of the *Ramayana* and the *Mahabharata*; the *selamatan* feast held in a wide range of circumstances—sacred, secular, or magical in character (Bachtiar, 1967; Koentjaraningrat, 1985: Chapter 5); and an assortment of agricultural and fishing rituals designed to appease malevolent spirits, not to mention some magical curing rites: all incorporated such non-Islamic elements. In Java, the syncretic elements of religion were taken furthest, and many followed a mystical set of beliefs and practices (termed *kebatinan*) which bore only a tenuous relationship with Islam; even though Islam itself possesses a mystical stream in Sufism, the *kebatinan* adherents did not appear to pay it any allegiance.

The *dakwah* movements of the 1970s in Malaysia, and the concomitant Middle Eastern form of dress, the stress on strict adherence to rules, and the hostility to traditional elements of Malay culture, had not yet taken root. Darul Islam, a full-fledged revolutionary movement seeking an Islamic state, was active in West Java, but this was an aberration, as the battle for a secular Indonesian state had already been won by Sukarno.

At the village level, Islam in the 1950s and 1960s was an integral part of Malay culture, lending force to traditional practices and beliefs. By and large, whether in Malaysia or Indonesia, these practices and beliefs were not under serious competition from alternative models, except perhaps from the irreligious Westernization of the popular movies.[5] Though many Malays were in close contact with Chinese and Indians, the residential and occupational segregation which was so marked at the time meant that they were thrown together with the other ethnic groups far less than they are today (Sidhu and Jones, 1981: Chapters 3 and 4). In Indonesia, alternative ideologies (nationalism, socialism, and communism) were vying for political loyalty but had little to say about family life and therefore provided no meaningful challenge to prevailing norms. In the area of marriage and divorce, cultural traditions with the sanction of religion held sway.

Patterns of Female Seclusion

Cultural traditions stressed the need for girls to be shielded from temptation and danger from the time they reached puberty and for them to be married at an early age. It was not only the girl's reputation and her chances of securing a good husband that were at stake but the family's honour. This honour was best preserved by marrying daughters shortly after they attained puberty, before they could do anything to disgrace the family. Some girls were married before their first menstruation (Ihromi et al., 1973: 18). In one Yogyakarta study (Singarimbun and Manning, 1974b), 23 per cent of respondents reported that they had married before their first menstruation, although only 1 per cent had intercourse prior to the first menstruation; in Peninsular Malaysia, if a Malay girl married before reaching the age of puberty, she was not allowed to consummate the marriage immediately and usually lived with her parents or in-laws (Swift, 1963: 289).

Norms adapted to the need to marry daughters early: throughout the Malay world, the pejorative term 'old maid' (*anak dara tua* in Malaysia and *perawan tua* in Indonesia) is ubiquitous. In Kelantan, people used to joke about girls who were not married by the age of 15, and referred to them as *anak dara tak laku* (maiden who is not 'saleable') (Kelantan focus-group discussions, 1989). In West Java, the comparable pejorative terms were *jomblo* for girls and *jajaka kolot* for boys (Tim Peneliti, 1988: 5).

The stress on premarital purity appears to have succeeded to a large degree in minimizing premarital conception in Malay societies. The 1984–5 Malaysian Population and Family Survey estimated that fewer than 2 per cent of Malay respondents had been premaritally pregnant, compared with almost 15 per cent of Chinese (Tey and Chak, 1988: Table 32), despite the fact that many of these marriages had been contracted recently, when Malay age at marriage was much later than before and mixing between the sexes much freer. While data from a number of surveys suggest that the 2 per cent figure for premarital pregnancy recorded more recently for Malaysian Malays may also have held among older respondents in Java (those marrying around the 1950s), premarital pregnancy is becoming more common among younger Javanese women, particularly those in self-arranged marriages, among whom the figure seems to exceed 10 per cent (Hull and Hull, 1987: 111–13).

These were times of restricted geographic mobility. As already discussed in Chapter 2, communications were also limited: movies were popular, but television was non-existent and radio, a luxury. The village was a close-knit community with great communal power to enforce adherence to behavioural norms. Families did not view with equanimity the social stigma that a daughter's wayward behaviour would inflict on them. Moreover, in Malaysia, particularly in the East Coast, *khalwat* (close proximity) laws were sometimes enforced with such strictness that an unattached boy and girl caught walking together on the beach could be forced to marry each other because they were seriously compromised by being seen together in this way.

The observations of those conducting anthropological studies in villages at this time may give the best 'feel' of sanctions governing the behaviour of girls and the choice of their spouse. In Kelantan, from the age of about 7 or 8, girls were encouraged to stay around the house and take minor responsibilities, while boys were allowed increasing freedom. 'Control over the girl's movements is intensified at the onset of puberty, not to be relaxed again until she is married for the first time.' (Rudie, 1983: 134.) These comments echoed those of Rosemary Firth (1966: 44–5) in her study of a Kelantanese fishing village. In a Malay fishing village in Southern Thailand, studied in the early 1960s, Fraser (1966: 27) reported that

as a girl approaches puberty she spends more and more time with her mother and any other mature female members of the family practising the domestic arts she will need for married life, and by the time she has become a young woman she will never be seen walking or playing in the village, being in virtual seclusion until marriage.

In Trengganu villages, 'women now in their late thirties or older were largely confined to their homes after menarche if not before, venturing beyond their immediate village neighbourhoods only when accompanied by a mother or other adult female chaperone' (Strange, 1981: 109). Kuchiba, writing of a rice-farming village in Kedah in 1979, stated:

... the social segregation of men and women other than spouses is remarkable. ... Segregation starts when boys and girls reach the age of about twelve ... if a boy of fifteen or sixteen should approach a girl of the same age he will be severely scolded by her father or older brother. ... The young men and women of the village can only eye each other from afar at wedding receptions (*kenduri kahwin*), festive occasions, farewell gatherings for villagers leaving to find work, and similar events. ... Young girls are extremely shy and bashful. (Kuchiba, Tsubouchi, and Maeda, 1979: 28.)

H. Geertz (1961) claimed that the major reason for young age at first marriage in her East Java town was the need to protect the girl from temptation and avoid her bringing shame to the family. A similar motivation seems to have applied in Serpong, West Java, which in the 1970s had one of the lowest average female ages at marriage in the Malay world: below 16 years, with no sign of rising. Parents worried if a child had grown up and did not yet have a marriage partner, because this could lead to prohibited behaviour: sexual intercourse outside marriage (Zuidberg, 1978: 80). Parent-arranged marriage remained the norm, but there appears to have been rather more freedom for girls to mix with the opposite sex than in some other places.

All youngsters go to the movies or to listen to the orchestra. Like the adults, they go in two groups, each sex separately, but they return in pairs. When a girl is brought home by a boy, dating (*pacaran*) may begin. The boy may meet his girl friend at night, but he has to stay on the outside verandah while she stays inside the house. (Zuidberg, 1978: 77–8.)

One study in the late 1950s of a village in the southern part of Central Java (Koentjaraningrat, 1967b: 255–6), while acknowledging a degree of segregation of the sexes and chaperonage of girls, also notes that boys and girls had the opportunity for contact at school, in planting and harvesting groups, and in particular at parties and festivals. It should perhaps be noted that this village had very few *santri* (devout Muslims who practised the five daily prayers, observed the fasting month, and other key Islamic practices).

Koentjaraningrat (1985: 252–4) notes that among the *priyayi* (the aristocratic or upper classes) in Java, although parents retained a good deal of control of their children's activities, even as early as the 1930s, formal dating patterns were already in existence. In many republican towns in Java in the late 1940s, mothers lost a degree of control over the comings and goings of their daughters who were involved in revolutionary activities.

Arrangement of Marriage and 'Family Honour'

Marriages among these Malay populations were traditionally arranged.[6] Writing of East Java in the 1950s, H. Geertz (1961: 55–6) noted that Javanese believed that younger people should acquiesce unquestioningly in the decisions of their parents on this matter:

> The choice of spouse, especially at the time of the first marriage, serves the interests of the parents primarily, by expanding the range of their social ties, or consolidating those already existing, and by validating their social rank in their community. Within the family, the fact that the child must surrender the choice of his spouse to his parents is a symbol of his social and psychological dependency on them, of his acceptance of his future responsibilities toward them in their old age, and of his lesser status in regard to them.

> The first marriage for a daughter is often arranged soon after her first menstruation. An early marriage is sought for her especially if she begins to show a marked interest in men, for her parents are concerned that she does not build a reputation for loose morals. . . . In a great many cases—perhaps most—the first meeting of husband and wife-to-be occurs at the wedding ceremony.

The following are some comments of older village women in Maguwoharjo (Yogyakarta) about the need for a young age at marriage (between about 15 and 18 years):

> Young age at marriage is the custom in the village. It may be different for city girls but the situation in the *desa* (village) is clear.

> Parents usually want their children to marry at that age and it's up to the parents to decide.

> That age is about when a man will notice a girl and decide to propose a marriage to her parents. The girl only waits for such a proposal.

> If you wait any longer than that, neighbours will gossip that you're getting old and no one wants to marry you.

> By that age your seeds are ripe and you can bear good children.

> (V. J. Hull, 1975: 200–1.)

Some (mainly older) respondents mentioned as a motive for early marriage the need to protect the girl from temptation and avoid the chance of her bringing shame to the family, but V. J. Hull thought this response was not as prevalent as in H. Geertz's study. Koentjaraningrat's (1967b: 256) study of a Central Javanese village in the late 1950s noted that village youth often did their own courting and might make their own choice of a mate with parental consent; even so, over the period of his study, 23 out of the 51 marriages that occurred were between 'very young people', all of which were arranged without the consent of either the girl or the boy.

Studies in Central and West Java showed that 67 and 70 per cent respectively of the marriages of female respondents had been arranged by parents (Chapon, 1976; Tim Peneliti, 1988: Table 13). In the West Java study, only 9 per cent of the respondents had chosen their own spouse. Unfortunately, the data were not controlled by age of respondent, but most of the marriages recorded in the Central Java survey, and about half of those in the West Java survey, would have occurred before the 1970s.

Arrangement of marriage in Madurese society is well described by Niehof (1985: Chapter 4), based on fieldwork in 1977–9. In many cases, the girl does not know what is going on until the engagement has been settled. Niehof (1985: 117) tells of asking an 11-year-old girl who was already engaged whether she knew her husband-to-be. 'I forgot his name,' she said. 'Do you know who he is?' 'Yes, I know him, I sometimes talk to him, but I have forgotten his name.' 'Do you like him?' 'I don't know.' The girl's grandmother only commented that in her time it was improper for an engaged boy and girl to speak to each other. Niehof also mentions a wedding she witnessed where the bride, aged about 13, expressed her disapproval of the marriage by violently throwing away the handkerchief offered to her as part of the ceremony and loudly bursting into tears. The ceremony continued, though with considerable uneasiness. In some cases, however, strong resistance on the part of the boy or girl could result in the breaking off of an engagement (Niehof, 1985: 122–3).

Describing the situation in Rusembilan, Southern Thailand, in the early 1960s, Fraser (1966: 29) noted that

with few exceptions, marriage in these communities is exogamous, the bride and groom belonging to different villages. Marriage arrangements are *always* [his emphasis] made by the parents of the prospective couple, and are usually initiated by the boy's father. . . . When the field has been narrowed to one or a few suitable girls, the boy's father seeks the assistance of an intermediary, a man who is known to both families. It is this man who either arranges for a surreptitious viewing of the girl by the boy and his father, or enters directly into negotiations with her family. When the negotiations have been completed, the girl is informed by her parents of her impending marriage, and must begin making preparations for the wedding.

In Rusila, Trengganu, patterns of mate selection were stable up to the mid-1960s. 'Choices were made by parents, and children were expected to accept them. Elopement was not unknown in the area, but it was unusual.' (Strange, 1981: 104.) Girls did not expect to be consulted: 'If they had opinions, they did not venture them, because even to hold one implied an unacceptable brazenness.' (Strange, 1981: 105.) Women— mothers, grandmothers, and matchmakers—were pivotal to the mate selection process because they were considered to be more astute at choosing and more clever at conducting preliminary negotiations.

The situation was not very different among the Malay population of Singapore. In 1949–50, among the two Malay villages (one urban and one fishing) studied by Djamour (1959: 72),

a firmly established principle was that an *anak dara*'s opinion, let alone consent, need not be sought when her marriage was contemplated ... even when the match was decided her parents did not inform her. Usually it was left to her sisters or young friends to give her the news. However reluctant the *anak dara* might be, either to the idea of marriage in general or to that of marriage with the particular man her parents had selected, she did not utter a word of protest. To do so was considered not only highly improper but plainly indecent. Her only resistance to the match could take place *after* the wedding ceremonies were over, and that was by refusing to consummate the marriage.

In his Kedah rice-farming village in the 1970s, Kuchiba (in Kuchiba, Tsubouchi, and Maeda, 1979: 29) noted that 'although the parents play a leading role in selection of a partner, the will of the young people is respected to a considerable degree. Since the couple barely associate before marriage, they can only judge their prospective partner by their parents' opinion and by outward appearances and reputation.' The apparently slightly more liberal approach in Kedah may have been due to the more recent period of the study, but it may also reflect a greater involvement of children in the choice of their own spouse on the West Coast of Peninsular Malaysia compared with the East Coast or Southern Thailand.

In general, young men had somewhat more say in the choice of their spouse than did young women. The Malay saying 'Untung si laki-laki ditanya-tanyakan, Untung si perempuan dinanti-nantikan', though difficult to translate into English in a way that captures its hidden meaning and intention, indicates that young men who wished to settle down could look about for a suitable bride, whereas marriageable girls would have to wait for an approach to be made to their parents on behalf of would-be husbands (Roose, 1963: 288). Data for Central Java from the Asian Marriage Survey, 1980, show that men had a great deal more say in choosing their spouses than did women: for example, in the 1944–52 birth cohort, 62 per cent of rural men selected their own spouses or did so with their parents' approval, compared with 23 per cent of rural women (Malhotra, 1991: Table 1; see also H. Geertz, 1961: 56; Jay, 1969: 39; Zuidberg, 1978: 82; Koentjaraningrat, 1985: 125; Williams, 1990a: 59).

Given the high levels of divorce and remarriage in areas such as Java, second and third marriages were relatively common. In such marriages, women were more likely to make their own choice (Zuidberg, 1978: 82; Williams, 1990a: 61). For example, in Sriharjo, Yogyakarta, a survey conducted in the early 1970s found that 17 per cent of first marriages were based on the young woman's choice, a proportion which rose to 37 per cent for second marriages, 49 per cent for third marriages, and 64 per cent for fourth marriages (Singarimbun and Manning, 1974b: 69). In Ngaglik, also in Yogyakarta, a survey in 1976 found that among first marriages, 28 per cent of young women made their own choice, rising to 55 per cent among higher-order marriages (Sudewa, 1980: Table 1.1). Important as it is to note the increasing self-choice for second and subsequent marriages, it is equally important to recognize that in second or third marriages, parents were still just as likely to choose the husband as was the woman herself. This evidence conflicts sharply with the sweeping generalization by Jay (1969: 39) that 'partners to later marriages exercise complete freedom in the selection of spouses'.

Low Education

Education beyond basic Koranic knowledge was not considered necessary for girls, so in most cases the problem of close association with boys in school did not arise. In Peninsular Malaysia, only 32 per cent of Malay girls aged 10–19 were in school in 1957—most of them, of course, in the younger ages within this range; the proportion of Malay males in school was almost double this (Sidhu and Jones, 1981: 227). In Indonesia, 33 per cent of girls aged 10–19 were in school in 1961, compared with 45 per cent of boys. A higher proportion of school-going girls than of boys attended religious schools, where the secular content was less and Islamic norms of appropriate female behaviour were reinforced (Oey-Gardiner, 1991: 65). Therefore a relatively low proportion of girls who were old enough for romantic attachments to develop were coming into contact with boys at school. Equally important, few girls were staying long enough in school for them to cultivate independent attitudes or for their parents to seriously contemplate continuing their education beyond the normal ages for girls to marry.

The Implications of Studies Showing Differentials in Age at Marriage

The above attempt to identify aspects of the traditional culture that fostered early marriage leads naturally into a discussion of factors making for change in marriage patterns. It is to be expected that it is the relaxation or modification of the forces traditionally fostering early marriage, or their replacement by entirely new forces, that has been responsible for the rising age at marriage among Muslim populations in South-East Asia.

As a background to this discussion, it is desirable to recall from Chapter 3 the key findings from studies conducted in the period before age at marriage had changed very much, showing differentials in age at marriage according to various socio-economic background characteristics.

Such differentials at a point in time could normally be expected to fore-shadow changes in behaviour as the proportion of the population with these characteristics changes. Unfortunately, the studies turned out to be rather a disappointment. The restricted number of variables available for analysis no doubt contributed to the small share of the variance that could be explained by these models. However, education, work experience before marriage, and freedom in the choice of spouse were all correlated with higher age at marriage. Therefore, to explain trends in age at marriage since the 1960s, it is necessary to investigate carefully trends in these three variables and interconnections between these trends.

The more important point to stress, though, is that too much emphasis on static studies of differentials can easily prevent a real understanding of social change. When major changes are taking place in something as important as marriage patterns, they tend to be the result of social change sweeping through a community 'across the board', rather than of changing proportions of the population who are educated, live in urban areas, or worked before marriage.

Factors Fostering Rising Age at Marriage

Before getting to grips with various 'volitional' aspects of rising age at marriage, there is one possible non-volitional factor whose role should be investigated. This is the relative availability of potential spouses, and the possibility that an imbalance between the sexes in the key marrying ages led to a 'marriage squeeze'. Earlier studies in Malaysia (J. C. Caldwell, 1962; Jones, 1980) showed that this factor was important for different ethnic groups at different times.

Non-volitional Factors: Marriage Squeeze

'Marriage squeeze' is clear enough as a concept, but difficult to measure because of the difficulty of drawing the boundaries of groups of potential marriage partners. In Malaysian studies, the usual assumption is that there is no inter-ethnic marriage. This is patently not true, though the extent of inter-ethnic marriage is quite limited.[7] Defining the age boundaries between potential spouses is also problematic, because although husbands are usually a few years older than their wives in Malaysia and Indonesia, there is no absolute barrier to wide age differences. Potential mates are certainly not confined to the single population, because of the frequency of divorce at quite young ages (Tan et al., 1988: 14–16). Social class and educational barriers to marriage may impose important, though again not absolute, restrictions on the pool of potential mates. The rapid rise in female educational levels in South-East Asia, allied to the convention that a man should marry 'down', may well have led to the emergence, in recent years, of a group of 'unmarriageable' (because they are over-educated) women.

Table 4.1 shows trends in the sex ratios in the main marrying age-groups in Islamic South-East Asia. The discussion will deal first with

TABLE 4.1
Islamic South-East Asia: Trends in Sex Ratios in 'Marrying' Age-groups[a]

	Males, 20–24	Males, 25–29	Males, 20–34
	Females, 15–19	Females, 20–24	Females, 15–29
Peninsular Malaysia Malays			
1947	81	85	81
1957	82	79	79
1970	74	76	76
1980	87	79	80
Singapore Malays			
1947	147	135	132
1957	117	96	105
1970	74	58	75
1980	101	82	88
Indonesia			
1971	63	90	75
1980	77	80	76
1990	82	87	83
Southern Thai Muslims			
1960	95	95	n.a.
1970	69	99	n.a.
1980	71	80	n.a.

Sources: Malaysia: *Population Census of Malaya*, 1947 and 1957 and *Population Census of Malaysia*, 1970 and 1980.
Singapore: *Population Census of Malaya, 1947* and *Census of Population, Singapore*, 1957, 1970, and 1980.
Indonesia: *Population Census*, 1971, 1980, and 1990.
Southern Thai Muslims: Rachapaetayakom (1983: Table 5.2).
[a]Sex ratio = Number of males per 100 females.

Peninsular Malaysia. The studies by J. C. Caldwell (1962) and Jones (1980) showed that marriage squeeze was of greater importance in earlier periods for the Chinese and Indians than for the Malays. In the Malay community, though, there was always a deficit of females compared to males aged 5 years older, and the deficit was even more marked if the comparison is restricted to the single population (Tan et al., 1988: 14–16). Thus 'the relative availability of marriage partners [after 1957] continued to be such that the Malay traditions of a wide age difference between spouses and young and universal marriage for women could be maintained only by perpetuation of the other Malay traditions of relatively widespread polygyny and easy divorce' (Jones, 1980: 283). But in fact there was a dramatic decline in divorce between 1957 and 1970, so the only remaining adjustments which could leave the tradition of universal female marriage intact were a narrowing of the age difference between the spouses and a rise in women's ages at marriage. Both these adjustments occurred, although the key mechanism was the rise in age. Not only did the median age at marriage for men not decline, it actually increased by more than 2 years between 1957 and 1970, and the narrowing of the age difference between husband and wife was due solely to the even more rapid rise in women's age at marriage.

By the early 1980s, sex ratios of potential marriage partners for young women in the Malay community were beginning to rise as a result of fertility decline; the 'marriage squeeze' had run its course. But the increased availability of potential spouses was to some extent offset, in its effect on age at first marriage, by the continuing decline in divorce and polygamy. The marriage market in some local areas could also have been disrupted by the heavy out-migration of single girls to the towns to seek factory work. In urban areas, the chances of female marriage may have been adversely affected by this heavy female in-migration, as well as the better job prospects for Malay women than for Malay men in the towns, further exacerbating their marriage chances because females with economic independence are less likely to marry low-status males (Jones, 1985: 158).

In Singapore, the marriage squeeze situation has shown dramatic fluctuations, although these may have been somewhat modified by the possibility of Singapore Malays drawing on the much larger pool of potential spouses in Malaysia. To the extent that spouses had to be sought in Singapore itself, however, there was a large surplus of males in the late 1940s, which was no doubt partly responsible for the wide gap between male and female ages at marriage in 1947 (see Table 3.16). By the 1960s though, the surplus had turned into a deficit and this no doubt contributed to the extraordinarily sharp rise of almost 5 years in the median age at marriage for females between 1957 and 1970, which substantially narrowed the gap between male and female ages at marriage. The sharp fertility decline in the late 1960s led to a rapid rise in ratios of males to females in the main marrying ages by 1980, thus releasing any upward pressure on female ages at marriage that there might have been from this source.

In Indonesia as in Malaysia, marriage squeeze was evident in the 1971 and 1980 figures. As in Malaysia, then, only in a high divorce situation could the young age at marriage for females and the wide age differences between spouses be sustained. In fact, though, divorce was declining over this period (see the discussion in Chapter 5). Female age at marriage did not rise very much, leaving as the only other possible adjustment the narrowing of the age difference between husbands and wives. Though the difference did not narrow very much over the 1970s (see Table 3.16), it is not known how much it narrowed over the 1960s. Data for Java alone show a narrowing from 5.2 years to 3.2 years between 1964 and 1971, strongly suggesting that for Indonesia as a whole, too, the narrowing of the age at marriage differential was one response to the relative availability of marriage partners over this period. By 1990, the effect of fertility declines in holding down the size of the marriageable female group relative to that of the (older) marriageable male group was raising the sex ratio in marriageable age-groups and therefore removing any upward pressure on female age at marriage from this source.

Among Southern Thai Muslims, too, a shortage of males in the 1970s and 1980s may have contributed to the upward movement in female age at marriage and the narrowing of the age differential in male and female ages at marriage. We know less about what happened to divorce in this population over this period.

It is very hard to reach clear conclusions about the importance of marriage squeeze in causing female age at marriage to rise, because of the difficulty of defining just who are the potential marriage partners, and because of the wide range of feasible adjustments to a notional shortage of men under prevailing marriage market conditions (Keyfitz, 1973; Casterline, Williams, and McDonald, 1986: 369–70). Studies in Europe throw doubt on changes in the age-difference distribution as a principal mechanism for coping with marriage squeeze constraints, because average age differences remained stable during periods when average ages at marriage changed (Hajnal, 1965). This has not entirely been the case, however, among the Malay populations of South-East Asia for which data have been presented, although the adjustment in age differences has certainly been less spectacular than the rise in female age at marriage. On the whole, there were no sharp discontinuities in trends in sex ratios among the 'marriageable population' in Islamic South-East Asia, and the main reasons for trends in both male and female ages at marriage in recent decades have to be sought elsewhere, in the major economic and social changes sweeping the region and their effects on the institution of marriage.

Volitional Factors

In this section, a range of volitional factors influencing rising age at marriage will be examined. Underlying these changes were the rapid economic development, urbanization, expansion of education, and improved transport and communications already discussed in Chapter 2. First, changes in the freedom of young people to mix with members of the opposite sex and to choose their own marriage partners will be examined; then possible reasons for these changes will be considered.

FREEDOM TO MIX WITH THE OPPOSITE SEX

A number of studies in Malaysia and Indonesia point to the gradual relaxation of controls over the freedom of young people to mix with members of the opposite sex. The Malaysian studies (see Table 4.2) indicate a social revolution in adolescent patterns of interaction over two to three decades. Note that the over-representation of Kelantanese in the Malaysian Marriage Survey of 1981–2 made for a more traditional than average group of Malay respondents in this survey. Among these respondents, the proportion who could not mix at all with the opposite sex fell from 74 per cent among those aged 45 and over to 16 per cent among those aged 15–24: that is, between those who were teenagers around the early 1950s and those who were teenagers around the late 1970s. The freeing of interaction was certainly not total; most of the decline was offset by a rise in the proportion who had limited freedom

126

TABLE 4.2

Peninsular Malaysia: Freedom to Mix with Members of the Opposite Sex during Teenage Years,
by Ethnic Group and Age-group of Women (percentage distribution)

| | Ethnic Group/Age-group | | | | | | | | | | | |
| | Malays | | | | Chinese | | | | Indians | | | |
Degree of Freedom	15–24	25–34	35–44	45+	15–24	25–34	35–44	45+	15–24	25–34	35–44	45+
Not at all	6	26	52	74	1	5	14	25	27	14	22	30
Limited	73	64	43	23	30	45	59	65	51	58	63	58
Freely	8	7	3	1	69	50	26	10	22	27	9	3
Festival	3	3	2	2	0	0	1	0	0	1	6	9
Total (%)	100	100	100	100	100	100	100	100	100	100	100	100
No. of cases	206	534	372	276	67	254	218	94	37	107	86	59

Source: Tan and Jones (1990: Table 3).

to mix. The proportion who could mix freely rose only to 8 per cent among the 15–24 age-group, compared with 69 per cent among the same age-group in the Chinese sample. Nevertheless, the trend towards freeing of interactions among Malays was a very important one.

McDonald (1984) presents information from different regions of Indonesia, drawn from the Indonesian Marriage Survey of 1978, to show changing practices and attitudes with regard to *pergaulan muda-mudi* or mixing with young people of the opposite sex. As he notes, this term was well understood in most cases and conveys the meaning of social interaction between young people more clearly than any equivalent term in English does in English-speaking societies.

Table 4.3 shows how young people got to know about potential marriage partners, in various regions of Indonesia, according to respondents in the Indonesian Marriage Survey. In Bali (Hindu) and the Christian sample in North Sulawesi (data not shown), mixing of the sexes before marriage had always been the norm, and was much more common than in most of these Muslim regions; nevertheless, South Sumatra stands out in contrast with the other Islamic regions; although it is a devout Islamic society, strict restrictions on the mixing of young people had clearly not been seen as part of Muslim life. Over time, *pergaulan* was clearly on the increase in various Islamic regions, most noticeably in Yogyakarta. This is confirmed by respondents' perceptions of the degree of difficulty of mixing with the opposite sex and the relative degree of freedom among youth today as compared with when they were young themselves (Table 4.4). Almost all of the oldest respondents as well as very sizeable proportions of the younger respondents said that young people were freer today than was the case in the respondent's own youth. Resistance to greater freedom of youth was stronger in the more fundamentalist Islamic societies such as those in South Sulawesi, South Kalimantan, Aceh, and to a lesser extent the Betawi in Jakarta, but the responses of single persons suggested that this resistance was being eroded. The responses of men and women reflect the greater restrictions placed on women than on men.

Table 4.5 reports on the personal experience of these respondents, not only with regard to *pergaulan* but also more precisely on such matters as whether each respondent was ever able to be alone with a person of the opposite sex before marriage and how many times each had met his or her spouse before engagement. The responses reveal a distinction in the respondents' minds between *bergaul* (mix or associate) and *bertemu* (to meet). In many cases, respondents who had met their husbands more than once before marriage had never had the chance to mix with them.

The data in Table 4.5 show remarkably rapid change in those areas where traditionally the sexes did not mix before marriage. The most striking change was in Aceh, where only 9 per cent of young, single women had never mixed socially with men compared with 95 per cent among ever-married women aged 45 and over. More typical, but still striking, was the contrast in South Kalimantan between the 23 per cent of young, single women who had never mixed socially with the opposite

TABLE 4.3

Indonesia: Percentage Distribution of Responses of Ever-married Respondents to the Question, 'When You Were Young, How Did Young People Get to Know about Potential Marriage Partners?', by Sex and Age, 1978

Region, Sex, and Age	Through Mixing or Steady Relationships	Through Formal Visits to the Girls' Homes	By Seeing in the Street, in the Market, at Work or on Public Occasions	By Being Told Beforehand by Parents	By Knowing Only on the Day of the Engagement or Wedding	Other	Total	N (Excludes Not Stated)
Aceh								
Men								
<30	25	0	0	67	3	5	100	36
30–44	9	1	3	78	3	6	100	199
45+	0	1	2	91	4	2	100	210
Women								
<30	15	2	2	64	10	7	100	122
30–44	8	2	1	68	15	6	100	215
45+	5	0	2	69	18	6	100	166
South Sumatra								
Men								
<30	83	0	0	6	1	10	100	95
30–44	70	0	2	6	2	20	100	158
45+	70	1	0	10	3	16	100	222
Women								
<30	79	0	0	9	3	9	100	146
30–44	72	2	0	6	4	16	100	208
45+	69	0	2	8	6	15	100	195

							Total	N
Jakarta								
Men	<30	7	66	11	1	5	10	100
	30–44	4	50	12	4	14	16	100
	45+	3	38	13	12	25	9	100
Women	<30	25	47	6	11	2	9	100
	30–44	5	59	4	24	2	6	100
	45+	6	50	5	31	2	6	100
Yogyakarta								
Men	<30	64	0	4	12	16	4	100
	30–44	43	0	2	28	25	2	100
	45+	24	1	3	40	31	1	100
Women	<30	52	0	2	26	20	0	100
	30–44	27	0	1	37	33	2	100
	45+	17	1	2	47	30	3	100
South Kalimantan								
Men	<30	24	13	43	1	12	17	100
	30–44	15	11	44	3	24	3	100
	45+	8	7	51	3	28	3	100
Women	<30	16	8	34	5	33	4	100
	30–44	12	6	28	6	48	0	100
	45+	14	4	27	2	53	0	100
South Sulawesi								
Men	<30	9	5	4	81	1	0	100
	30–44	9	4	3	79	3	2	100
	45+	13	1	3	81	0	2	100
Women	<30	5	1	0	85	7	0	100
	30–44	3	0	0	87	9	1	100
	45+	2	0	0	92	6	0	100

								N
Jakarta Men	<30							100
	30–44							182
	45+							135
Women	<30							224
	30–44							164
	45+							97
Yogyakarta Men	<30							25
	30–44							201
	45+							311
Women	<30							94
	30–44							254
	45+							249
South Kalimantan Men	<30							126
	30–44							198
	45+							152
Women	<30							248
	30–44							230
	45+							132
South Sulawesi Men	<30							110
	30–44							216
	45+							163
Women	<30							204
	30–44							261
	45+							119

Source: McDonald (1984: Table 4.1), based on the Indonesian Marriage Survey, 1978.

TABLE 4.4

Indonesia: Respondents' Perceptions of the Difficulty of Mixing in the Time of Their Youth and of the Relative Degree of Freedom of Youth Today, 1978

Measure	Sex and Marital Status	Age-group	Region					
			Aceh	South Sumatra	Jakarta	Yogyakarta	South Kalimantan	South Sulawesi
Percentage stating that in their youth, it was impossible or very difficult for young men and women to mix	Single males	17–35	65[a]	7[a]	7[a]	2	26	53
	Ever-married males	<30	50[b]	8[a]	25	0[b]	35	60
		30–44	75	31	63	16	67	79
		45+	89	45	83	33	88[a]	79
	Single females	15–29	63	9[a]	26	1[a]	28[a]	46
	Ever-married females	<30	73	16	34	14[a]	50	77
		30–44	90	40	84	44	77	91
		45+	99	49	91[a]	62	90	90
Percentage stating that mixing of young people is freer now than when they were in their youth	Ever-married males	<30	30[b]	51[a]	60	16[b]	49	35
		30–44	63	47	97	69	91	80
		45+	72	97	99	84	69	86
	Ever-married females	<30	66	53	68	51[a]	77	67
		30–44	78	93	95	86	95	78
		45+	83	96	97	94	100	81

[a]Indicates 50–99 cases.
[b]Indicates fewer than 50 cases.

Source: McDonald (1984: Table 4.2), based on the Indonesian Marriage Survey, 1978.

sex and the 86 per cent among ever-married women aged 45 and over. Similar massive changes in the space of little more than one generation were evident for women in Jakarta, Yogyakarta, and South Sulawesi. These changes appear to 'reflect a growing trend towards social activities for youth such as intervillage sporting competitions, or functions organized by the village or school' (McDonald, 1984: 5). When pressed, respondents typically attributed such changes to *perubahan zaman* (changing times), the *zaman moderen* (modern era), or something of the kind. McDonald asserts that what is being referred to is not so much Westernization as a national Indonesian process of modernization, a process in which the image of Indonesian youth of both sexes acting in relative freedom had been promoted by the independence movement, the Communist Party (before it was banned), and the ideology of post-independence governments.

If social mixing was restricted in Islamic parts of Indonesia, being alone with a person of the opposite sex was even more difficult. In all the regions included in Table 4.5 except South Sumatra and Jakarta, such an experience was virtually unknown among married men and women aged 45 and over, and still very rare among those aged 30–44. Among young men and women, it was becoming more common, though still rare, having been experienced by almost none of the young women in South Kalimantan and fewer than 10 per cent in Aceh, climbing to around 20 per cent in Yogyakarta and in the Betawi sample in Jakarta.

West Java was not included in the Indonesian Marriage Survey, but trends towards greater freedom to mix appear to be present there as well. A small study conducted in three regions of West Java in 1988 found that while one-third of married female respondents did not think there had been any change in the freedom of young people to mix with members of the opposite sex, 42 per cent thought mixing was freer these days whereas only 23 per cent thought it was less free (Tim Peneliti, 1988: Table 4).

SHIFT TO SELF-ARRANGEMENT OF MARRIAGE

For Malaysian Malays, the shift towards self-arrangement of marriage has been fairly well documented in two surveys: the Malaysian Marriage Survey of 1981–2 and the Malaysian Population and Family Survey of 1984–5. The relevant findings of the former are shown in Table 4.6, and a comparison between the two sources in Figure 4.1. According to the former source (which over-represented Kelantanese Malays), about 64 per cent of married Malay women aged 15–24 chose their own marriage partner compared with about 14 per cent in the age-group 45 and over. Arranged marriages, about half of them without the girl's consent, had been the lot of 85 per cent of Malay women aged 45 and over. Among those 20 years younger, the figure had fallen to 39 per cent. The Peninsular Malaysia representative Population and Family Survey of 1984–5 showed a rather lower proportion of older women whose marriages had been arranged, but it again showed a halving of the

TABLE 4.5

Indonesia: Respondents' Personal Experiences of Mixing with the Opposite Sex before Marriage, 1978

Measure	Sex and Marital Status	Age-group	Region					
			Aceh	South Sumatra	Jakarta	Yogyakarta	South Kalimantan	South Sulawesi
Percentage who never mixed socially with the opposite sex before marriage	Single males	17–35	20[a]	6[a]	8	6	12	45
	Ever-married males	<30	36[b]	0[a]	4	12[b]	21	62
		30–44	48	0	21	32	54	76
		45+	90	1	36	44	73	79
	Single females	15–29	9	1[a]	16	3[a]	23[a]	43
	Ever-married females	<30	47	0	26	14[a]	44	74
		30–44	76	1	60	46	76	89
		45+	95	3	74	59	86	94

Percentage who often mixed socially with the opposite sex before marriage

Single males	17–35	38ᵃ	50ᵃ	71	69	6	31
Ever-married males	<30	33ᵇ	88ᵃ	74	48ᵇ	9	18
	30–44	14	86	30	43	5	10
	45+	4	83	15	25	3	9
Single females	15–29	28	50ᵃ	44	54ᵃ	16ᵃ	21
Ever-married females	<30	10	65	29	44ᵃ	12	11
	30–44	2	54	10	22	3	4
	45+	1	51	4	10	2	3

Percentage who were able to be alone with a person of the opposite sex before marriage

Single males	17–35	20ᵃ	39ᵃ	49ᵃ	24	17	12ᵃ
Ever-married males	<30	26ᵇ	33ᵃ	57	32ᵇ	22	9
	30–44	14	27	27	13	12	4
	45+	3	22	14	4	3	5
Single females	15–29	9ᵃ	37ᵃ	25	17ᵃ	0ᵃ	18
Ever-married females	<30	8	25	23	21ᵃ	1	3
	30–44	1	17	9	7	0	2
	45+	0	16	7	1	0	1

ᵃIndicates 50–99 cases.
ᵇIndicates fewer than 50 cases.

Source: McDonald (1984: Table 4.3), based on the Indonesian Marriage Survey, 1978.

TABLE 4.6

Peninsular Malaysia: Percentage Distribution of Responses of Husband and Wife to Choice of Marriage Partner, by Ethnic Group and Current Age, 1981

Choice of Partner	Malays				Chinese				Indians			
	15–24	25–34	35–44	45+	15–24	25–34	35–44	45+	15–24	25–34	35–44	45+
Female												
Own choice with parents' blessing	64	61	24	14	88	76	59	41	29	19	6	12
Own choice without parents' blessing	1	–[a]	1	–[a]	7	7	3	7	18	11	6	0
Arranged with consent	17	22	39	44	3	11	30	38	7	11	12	15
Arranged without consent	18	17	36	41	2	6	8	14	46	59	76	73
Total (%)	100	100	100	100	100	100	100	100	100	100	100	100
No. of cases	167	442	289	239	58	218	180	76	72	152	109	57

Male

Own choice with parents' blessing	65	71	53	32	–[b]	77	68	52	–[b]	42	42	33
Own choice without parents' blessing	3	2	2	2	–[b]	9	6	6	–[b]	3	3	3
Arranged with consent	27	16	27	36	–[b]	11	20	28	–[b]	35	36	45
Arranged without consent	5	11	18	30	–[b]	3	6	14	–[b]	20	19	19
Total (%)	100	100	100	100	100	100	100	100	100	100	100	100
No. of cases	37	368	279	413	16	180	185	148	8	74	70	85

Source: Tan and Jones (1990: Table 5), based on the Malaysian Marriage Survey, 1981.

Note: Source of data for Indians is as follows: for females, a combination of data from the Malaysian Marriage Survey, 1981 and the Estate Survey; for males, only the Malaysian Marriage Survey, 1981, as the Estate Survey did not include men.

[a]Less than 0.5%.
[b]Fewer than 20 respondents.

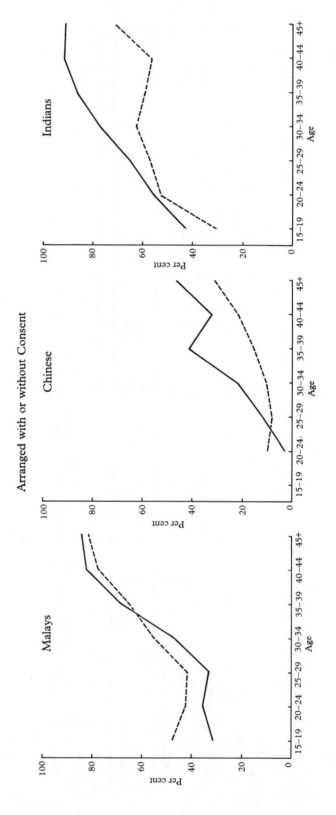

FIGURE 4.1
Malaysia: Choice of Marriage Partner, by Current Age and Ethnic Group

Arranged with or without Consent

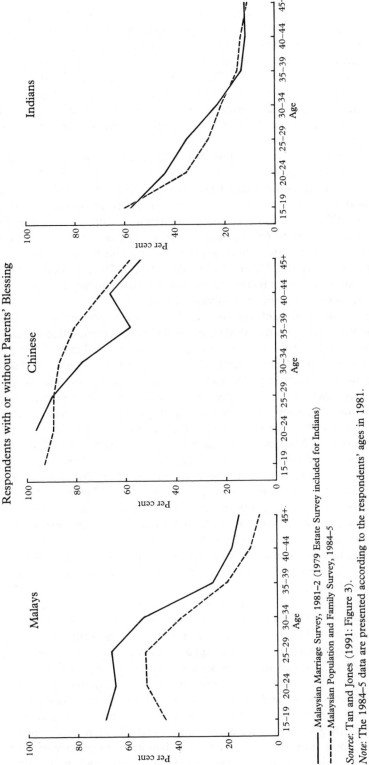

Respondents with or without Parents' Blessing

Malays

Chinese

Indians

——— Malaysian Marriage Survey, 1981–2 (1979 Estate Survey included for Indians)

------ Malaysian Population and Family Survey, 1984–5

Source: Tan and Jones (1991: Figure 3).

Note: The 1984–5 data are presented according to the respondents' ages in 1981.

proportion whose parents chose without their consent: from 62 per cent among those aged 45–49 to 31 per cent among those aged 20–24.[8] Among all age-groups, self-choice had been greater in urban than in rural areas, and choice by parents without consultation more frequent in rural areas (Table 4.7). The rise in parent-arranged marriages for the youngest age-group (15–19) does not reflect a trend, but rather is evidence that now that marriages at this age have become quite unusual, it is more likely that they will be of the traditional, parent-arranged variety.

Similar trends were also found in village case-studies carried out by University of Malaya students in 1978, two of them in Kelantan and one in Johore. Comparing males who married before 1960 with those who married between then and 1978, the two Kelantan studies showed a rise in self-choice of bride (the great majority with parents' blessing) from 31 per cent to 65 per cent and from 53 per cent to 75 per cent, respectively, while the Johore study showed a rise from 35 per cent to 74 per cent (Abdul Halim, 1979; Mustafar, 1979; Zalaluddin, 1979). Self-choice was much higher among males with secondary education than among those with primary education or less.

In Indonesia, available data on marriage arrangements are only available from the small community studies in different regions included in the Indonesian Marriage Survey, and from separate studies in West Java, Yogyakarta, and Central Java. Only one of these studies, the Jakarta (Betawi) case-study from the Indonesian Marriage Survey, was an urban one: here half the women aged 30 and over chose their own husband, as did three-quarters of the women aged less than 30. However, in the rural studies, the degree of arrangement, if anything, appears to be even higher than in Malaysia. For example, in Aceh and South Sulawesi (see Table 4.8) and in the West Java study (Tim Peneliti, 1988), fewer than 10 per cent of marriages had been self-arranged. In South Kalimantan, the figure was only slightly higher at 13 per cent (Mahfudz, 1982: 31). Much the same figure appears to apply to marriages contracted before 1960 in Yogyakarta. Only South Sumatra stands out as an area where the great majority of respondents, even older ones, chose their own spouses, and the figures seem to be so much out of line with other regions that some doubt must be entertained about whether the village chosen was typical of the region.

Parental choice of spouse did not always mean that a girl was married to somebody she had never met, although frequently it did.[9] The second segment of Table 4.8 indicates that in the Banjarese study, for example, half of both males and females aged 45 and over (i.e. marrying before the mid-1950s) had met their spouses, at most, once before their engagement. Even among those aged below 30 (i.e. marrying in the late 1960s and 1970s), around 40 per cent had met their spouses, at most, once. In South Sulawesi and Aceh, the proportions engaged without meeting their spouses were much higher, and although they were falling sharply over time, they remained above half among respondents younger than 30. Prior acquaintance with the spouse was much more common

TABLE 4.7

Peninsular Malaysia: Percentage Distribution of Ever-married Malay Women According to How Their First Marriage Partners Were Chosen, by Age-group, in Urban and Rural Areas, 1984

Age-group	Decision-maker					N
	Parents Alone	Parents with Consent of Respondent[a]	Respondent with Consent of Parents	Respondent Alone	Other	
Urban						
15–19	_b	_b	_b	_b	_b	14
20–24	22	13	43	21	1	83
25–29	28	10	42	19	1	151
30–34	27	9	39	20	5	122
35–39	31	17	32	15	4	93
40–44	31	27	26	7	9	55
45–49	61	19	7	0	14	43
All ages	31	14	35	16	4	561
Rural						
15–19	37	5	34	13	11	38
20–24	33	12	38	13	4	285
25–29	32	13	39	13	3	350
30–34	45	14	28	8	5	327
35–39	49	20	19	7	5	280
40–44	62	18	8	4	8	218
45–49	63	15	12	2	8	206
All ages	45	15	26	9	5	1,704

(continued)

TABLE 4.7 (continued)

	Decision-maker					
Age-group	Parents Alone	Parents with Consent of Respondent[a]	Respondent with Consent of Parents	Respondent Alone	Other	N
Total						
15–19	42	6	32	12	8	52
20–24	31	12	39	14	4	368
25–29	31	12	40	15	2	501
30–34	40	13	31	11	5	449
35–39	44	19	23	9	5	373
40–44	56	20	11	5	8	273
45–49	62	16	11	2	9	249
All ages	42	15	28	10	5	2,265

Source: Unpublished tabulations, Malaysian Population and Family Survey, 1984–5.

[a]Includes a small group who answered 'parents and respondent'.
[b]Only 14 respondents.

TABLE 4.8

Indonesia: Behaviour and Attitudes Regarding the Selection of a Spouse, 1978

Measure	Sex and Marital Status	Age-group	Region					
			Aceh	South Sumatra	Jakarta	Yogyakarta	South Kalimantan	South Sulawesi
Percentage who had informally agreed to marry in conversations (or letters) before engagement or marriage	Ever-married males	<30	44[b]	69[a]	51	44[b]	4	5
		30–44	15	81	47	32	3	5
		45+	5	73	31	12	1	4
	Ever-married females	<30	21	73	42	27	4	1
		30–44	7	74	30	16	0	2
		45+	3	73	19[a]	8	0	0
Percentage who had met more than once before they had become engaged (excludes persons married without being engaged)	Ever-married males	<30	44[b]	90[a]	97	83[b]	65	50
		30–44	32	92	90	68	56	46
		45+	13	85	88	51	49	37
	Ever-married females	<30	47	92	85	71[a]	58	42
		30–44	18	88	74	52	50	34
		45+	10	79	69	45	50	18

(continued)

TABLE 4.8 (continued)

Measure	Sex and Marital Status	Age-group	Region					
			Aceh	South Sumatra	Jakarta	Yogyakarta	South Kalimantan	South Sulawesi
Percentage who chose their own spouse (that is, the principal decision was theirs)	Ever-married males	<30	59[b]	97[a]	93	80[b]	43	16
		30–44	32	91	84	53	25	16
		45+	18	88	71	23	25	16
	Ever-married males	<30	11	94	78	44[a]	12	4
		30–44	2	89	57	22	13	3
		45+	0	88	54	10	11	0
Percentage saying that a young person should choose his or her own spouse	Single males	17–35	68[a]	94[a]	97	92[a]	52[a]	42
	Single females	12–29	45[a]	97[a]	86	92	13	36

Source: McDonald (1984: Table 4.4), based on the Indonesian Marriage Survey, 1978.

[a]Indicates 50–99 cases.
[b]Indicates fewer than 50 cases.

in Jakarta (the Betawi study), South Sumatra and, in recent times, Yogyakarta.

The trends according to the Indonesian studies are mostly consistent with the Malaysian data. As shown in Table 4.9, in various studies in Yogyakarta–Central Java, there has been a decline in parentally arranged marriage; parental selection is particularly low among young women in the cities, and was only nominal among the Yogyakartan urban élite. From studies that attempted to define the arrangement procedures more closely, forced marriage, in which the young woman has no say whatever, has declined rapidly. Of the 56 per cent of marriages contracted in 1970

TABLE 4.9

Yogyakarta–Central Java and Jakarta: Trends in
the Method of Arranging Marriages

Yogyakarta Rural Studies			
Percentage of Marriages Arranged by Parents According to Year of Marriage			
Before 1950	*1950–9*	*1960–9*	*1970+*
Sriharjo[a] 88	78	70	57
Maguwoharjo 89	70	42	20
Ngaglik 82	80	66	56

Urban Studies	
According to Current Age-group	
Semarang, 1980	Current age 30–49	Current age <30
Urban lower status	38	25
Urban middle status	30	12
Yogyakarta, 1975	Current age 35+	Current age <35
Urban élite	10	7

	Males		*Females*	
	<36	*36+*	*<36*	*36+*
Jakarta: Betawi				
Incomplete primary school	8	25	27	49
Completed primary school and above	9	28	25	50

Sources: Hull and Hull (1987: Table 2).
      Sriharjo: Chapon (1976: 19).
      Maguwoharjo: V. J. Hull (1975: 207).
      Ngaglik: Sudewa (1980: 11).
      Semarang: Adioetomo (1984: 5).
      Yogyakarta: Hull et al. (1976: Table 29).
      Jakarta: Muliakusuma (1982: Table 4.12).
[a]Before 1950 refers to 1940–9 in Sriharjo.

and later in Ngaglik, Yogyakarta, only 12 per cent were solely parental choice, without some form of conferring between parents and the young woman (Hull and Hull, 1987: 111). However, from the village studies included in the Indonesian Marriage Survey (Table 4.8), there is evidence of only a limited breakdown in the system of parentally arranged marriage in Aceh, and the traditional system appeared to be undisturbed according to the studies in South Sulawesi and South Kalimantan.

What is suggested by these data is that for some time, young women in urban areas of Peninsular Malaysia and Java have had a fair degree of freedom in the choice of a marriage partner, but that even in rural areas, in the space of just 30 or so years, the former system of arranged marriage was seriously undermined, though not yet to the point of total breakdown. In Indonesia outside Java, however, there may have been much less change in traditional ways of arranging marriages, and this also appears to be the case for the Maranao and Maguindanao in the Philippines, among whom two-thirds of female respondents aged 15–49 in the 1983 National Demographic Survey reported having had an arranged marriage (Costello and Palabrica-Costello, 1988: 19). Unfortunately, there are gaps in the information on quite major regions because no relevant studies have been conducted.

The shift to self-arranged marriage in Malaysia and Java was so intimately related to the shift to later age at marriage that it should perhaps be considered not so much a cause as a concomitant of delayed marriage. The task is not to use it as an explanation of delayed marriage but to find reasons why both self-arrangement of marriage and later marriage became so common.

There is no doubt that the expansion of female education and changing work opportunities played a crucial part in changing attitudes to women's roles, to the appropriate time to marry, and to arrangement of marriage. A general increase in girls' exposure to a range of ideas, due to education, greater geographic mobility, and exposure to the media (especially television) and movies was also undoubtedly crucial. These factors will be discussed in detail in the following section.

In Malaysia, the *dakwah* movement no doubt contributed to the swing to self-arrangement of marriages through the generational 'distance' it created. Some *dakwah* followers claim to be prepared to accept parental selection of spouses because parents have the best interests of their children at heart, and can therefore be trusted to find a mate sympathetic to *dakwah*. However, in practice the danger that parents will prove unsympathetic to the primacy of this criterion probably leads to more self-assertiveness concerning the choice of spouse on the part of the *dakwah* son or daughter (see Nagata, 1984: 144).

EDUCATION, WORK, INCOME OPPORTUNITIES, URBANIZATION,
AND CHANGING FEMALE ROLES

A detailed description and analysis of the expansion of education, particularly for girls, and the growth in modern sector employment in Islamic South-East Asia was given in Chapter 2. These trends, and all the concomitant changes in family relationships (J. C. Caldwell, 1980), were undoubtedly a major source of the modification in traditional patterns of arrangement of marriage and age at marriage. One can speculate about the profound implications of the shift in the modal level of education for Malay women in Peninsular Malaysia as revealed by the 1980 Population Census: from no education for women in their fifties to primary education for those in their thirties and secondary education for those in their teens. It is hardly necessary to speculate, though, about the direct influence on age at marriage of longer school attendance: in 1980, 73 per cent of 15-year-old, 59 per cent of 16-year-old, and 46 per cent of 17-year-old Malay girls were still in school in Peninsular Malaysia; yet back in the 1950s, more than half of Malay girls were already married at the age of 17.

As early as 1961, H. Geertz (1961: 56–7) had noted that in Java, 'with increasing higher education for both boys and girls, and the concomitant delay of marriage, young couples more and more meet in school, and marry on the basis of considerably longer acquaintance'. Though data on both educational enrolments and the extent of parent-arranged marriage at the time Geertz was writing suggest that she was exaggerating the frequency of marriages where the young couple knew each other well from school, her point is certainly valid when applied to more recent times. It became a major issue for parents. In Kelantan, 'parents who sent their daughters to secondary school in the sixties, when it was not yet very common to do so, worried a great deal lest they, the parents, should not be able to keep sufficient control' (Rudie, 1983: 134). Parents in Trengganu recognized that increased education was bringing their children into closer contact with members of the opposite sex, and that this might lead to formation of affective relationships and desire to participate in the mate selection process. This fear dissuaded some parents from allowing their daughters to pursue secondary education (Strange, 1981: 105). In the 1970s, it was the girls with secondary education, or with wage jobs, who were showing independence in mate selection (Strange, 1981: 104). In one conservative district of Probolinggo, a mainly Madurese area of East Java, as recently as 1987, people were expressing a preference for sending girls to the religious schools (*pesantren*) rather than the secondary school, because, as one commented, 'I do not want my daughter to become pregnant outside marriage, since I have heard some rumours that there were some students from high school who were pregnant.' (Hatmadji, 1990: 161.)

It is not only extended schooling, of course, which needs to be invoked to explain the growth of more independent attitudes among young women and the increasing influence of notions of romantic love. Indeed, the kinds of schools young women in Java were attending (Muslim schools and government schools which tend to reinforce respect for hierarchy, conformity, and acceptance of what is taught rather than independent thinking) were hardly designed to foster such attitudes. Popular culture, in the form of films, pop songs and, more recently, television, undoubtedly played a role in influencing even those girls who received little or no schooling, and who in earlier times would have had much more limited access to such influences.

One puzzle in explaining rising female age at marriage is how parents, who as recently as the 1950s and 1960s were cloistering young women until they were safely married off, could so quickly have relaxed these controls and permitted, even encouraged, their daughters to proceed further in school and to work outside the home before marriage, albeit with a strong preference for work to which they could commute from home rather than that to which they would have to migrate to the cities.[10] On education, of course, there was a strong official ideology in favour of both male and female education, and later introduction of compulsory education. With rising levels of education and changing attitudes among the young, parents may have realized that control was slipping from their hands, anyway, and they therefore bowed to the changing times and made a virtue of necessity. Strange (1981: 231) writes of the growing assertiveness about mate selection of young village women in Trengganu with increasing education and economic independence. Ong's study on Selangor revealed that parents were aware that with girls travelling about to go to high school and work in factories, it was not possible to control their contacts with the opposite sex (Ong, 1987: 199). Middle-aged focus group respondents in Kelantan spoke laughingly of young people's attitudes nowadays to the mate proposed by their parents as *kalau tok sir, tok sir sungguh* (if they don't want, they *really* don't want). Malay parents throughout Peninsular Malaysia, in the face of the growing economic independence and assertiveness of daughters, appear to have simply abdicated their former role in arranging their daughters' marriages.

But there has no doubt been more to it than this. Caldwell et al. (1989: 348) observed of Sri Lanka: 'The good marriage itself was no longer the completely dominant aim for the parents of daughters, as pride in their education and even their jobs became possible.' This statement from elsewhere in Asia was corroborated in rural areas of Malacca: 'Families are differentiated by the educational achievements and occupational status of their younger members. In rating the prestige of *kampung* families, informants always mention the educational attainments and earning capacity of the younger family members first; land ownership was cited as a secondary dimension of prestige.' (Ackerman, 1980: 128–9.)

It was not only a matter of prestige, but also the economic contribution daughters could make to the household. With the growing work opportunities for young women in factories and offices, the earning power of daughters was becoming crucial to the economic well-being of many rural households. Whereas before, daughters were considered liabilities in the family, they had now become assets. There is evidence that females migrating for work from the rural areas of Peninsular Malaysia tend to come from larger-than-average families, for whom their financial contribution can be very important (Lim, 1991: 24). In Java, increasing landlessness created the need for more off-farm work and therefore increased mobility of both men and women, while decreasing parental control over marriage and other decisions (Hüsken and White, 1989).

A number of studies of rural Malays from different parts of Peninsular Malaysia indicate the importance families place on the newly acquired income-earning capacity of young women. Various studies have indicated that two-thirds to over 80 per cent of unmarried female migrants sent regular remittances to their families (Hugo, Lim, and Narayan, 1989: 352). Daughters are more responsible and reliable contributors to the family budget than their brothers (Maude, 1981; Young and Salih, 1986; Ong, 1987: 99; Hugo, Lim, and Narayan, 1989: 352–3, 378; Li, 1989: 49–56). According to Young and Salih (1986: 48–9), 'female production workers will find ways and means to cut down on their expenditure in the urban context so that they can remit more money home. Male children often cannot find the extra money to send home with the excuse that the cost of urban living is very high. Instead, money is often remitted from the village to them.'

As one young working woman in Selangor observed: 'The males often do not want to listen to their parents' advice, and so parents do not have much hope in them. . . . Boys only know how to eat.' (Ong, 1987: 106.) In the same area, it has been argued that 'in a significant shift from past attitudes, village parents prefer their daughters not to marry straight out of school now that there are factory jobs close to home and daughters can be induced to earn an extra source of income' (Ong, 1987: 106–7). In Singapore, where Malay working daughters typically give their mothers a third of their pay, some women explicitly declare that this is the reason they do not want their daughters to marry too quickly (Li, 1989: 51). Once married, daughters can no longer be relied on for financial contributions.

The extent to which parents rely on daughters' financial contributions no doubt varies greatly by region and economic circumstance. But it is noteworthy that a number of studies show that females migrating for factory work came from families, many of them relatively poor, averaging more than six members (Hugo, Lim, and Narayan, 1989: 293). In such circumstances, remittances from a regular job are likely to play an important role in boosting family income, particularly in lean times.

In Alor Gajah, Malacca,

most of the (Malay) smallholders appear to derive their principal sources of income from the remittances of young wage earning members of the family who have migrated to urban areas or are working in factories and offices on the Alor Gajah Industrial Estate or in Malacca town. . . . The migrants have built new houses and purchased such consumer goods as television sets, refrigerators, and western style furniture for their parents. (Ackerman, 1980: 79–80.)

In her Malacca factory study and in another factory in Selangor, Ackerman (1980: 127, 220) found that factory girls' monthly contribution averaged between 13 and 16 per cent of total family income. Most of these families had additional income from other working children as well.[11] However, in her Selangor (urban) study, where over half the respondents were migrants, 40 per cent made no contribution to their parents.

Young female factory workers living at home are still expected to confine most of their activities to the house and to keep helping with housework. Ackerman (1980: 251) found that in rural Malacca, 'visiting their friends or going on excursions to town require special permission from their parents', although Ong's study in Selangor and Li's study in Singapore suggested less parental control. But a substantial proportion of young female factory workers are, in fact, migrants, who experience undreamed-of freedom compared to those who stay at home. The flaunting of this freedom by some, plus a great deal of sensationalizing by the press, earned female factory workers a reputation for loose morals which is well known to rural parents and places many of them in a quandary: they need the income that daughters who migrate for factory work can provide, but not the reputation that goes with it.

Interestingly, in a recent study on women's roles (Lim and Jones, 1989), 93 per cent of female respondents in Kelantan thought more jobs for women improved women's status. However, only about one-third agreed that rural–urban migration improved women's status, the same proportion as those who thought the *dakwah* movement improved their status. But in the case of rural–urban migration, half the respondents either thought it lowered women's status (13 per cent) or were unsure (37 per cent), whereas in the case of the *dakwah* movement, only 27 per cent either thought it lowered women's status (1 per cent) or were unsure (26 per cent).[12] Kelantanese focus group discussions revealed a real ambivalence about factory work that requires girls to leave home. Clearly, it was not women's work as such that caused concern, but work that required women to move away from traditional family and community controls.

Malay fathers tend to be embarrassed at the evidence that their daughters are helping to support the family, and try to distance themselves from financial transactions between daughter and mother (Li, 1989: 52–3). Two sisters in the Malacca study recounted that their father was deeply ashamed of his daughters working in factories and was always encouraging them to resign their jobs and stay at home, even though he was unemployed and needed his daughters' wages as well as those of his son to maintain the family. As Ackerman (1980: 132) noted, 'He often expresses to the family his humiliation at being unable to fulfil the traditional ideal of keeping daughters at home under close supervision, so that "they don't get spoiled", i.e. lose their virginity. . . . The daughters, however, insist on continuing to work.'

In a quite fundamental sense, gender relations have been transformed by the increasing importance of women in the wage economy. Male honour is 'undermined as the father's farm income steadily declines, unemployed brothers accept doles from working sisters, and the household budget derives increasingly from female wages. . . . In effect, the employment status of working daughters has loosened many from father–brother control.' (Ong, 1987: 107–8.)

The rural Malay world has become inextricably enmeshed with the world of the cities owing to rising levels of education, large numbers of scholarships for village children to university, burgeoning opportunities for government employment, and the growth of factory work. Improved roads have also cut travel times. No longer, then, is the village the sole frame of reference for village dwellers, and no longer do the social sanctions of the village maintain their former power over the behaviour of families and individuals.

In the 1970s, Indonesia did not see the same upsurge in female employment opportunities in factory or clerical work, or indeed in female education at the high school level, as did Malaysia. However, jobs in teaching and nursing did grow rapidly, and jobs as domestic servants and in trade and services in the urban areas were there for those young women who, for one reason or another (including contraction of female work opportunities in rural areas: see Hüsken and White, 1989), made the break from family control. In the 1980s, rapid industrialization brought more factory jobs for young women; in a study of female factory workers near Semarang, Central Java, Wolff (1990: 49; 1992: 214) found that girls employed in factory work were not pushed into early marriage by their parents because the parents recognized the economic benefits working daughters brought to their families.

Overall, the more rapid changes in female education and employment in Malaysia than in Indonesia are consistent with both the earlier and more rapid climb in female age at marriage there and the sharper break away from arranged marriage patterns.

STRICTER REGULATIONS ABOUT MARRYING

In Malaysia, concern about irresponsible marriage and easy divorce has led to stricter procedures about registering a marriage. For example, in Kuala Lumpur, it is now necessary for a Malay man contemplating marriage to have a letter from his employer stating that he is still a *bujang* (bachelor), a letter from a *kadi* supporting the marriage, and evidence that he and his prospective spouse have attended one of the many marriage courses currently on offer. Such regulations are stricter than those in Indonesia, where the prospective bridegroom simply has to apply for permission to marry at the Religious Affairs Office (KUA), bringing an official form from his local (*kelurahan*) official certifying that the personal details on his registration card are in order.

ATTITUDES TOWARDS FREEDOM TO MIX, AGE AT MARRIAGE,
AND MARRIAGE ARRANGEMENTS

There is very little survey information for this region on trends in ideal age at marriage; the ideal has certainly been rising along with the trend towards higher ages at marriage, but even the direction of causation is hard to determine. In one study in East Java (Gille and Pardoko, 1966: 512–13), ever-married female respondents tended to want a higher age at marriage for their daughters than they themselves experienced; the mean age at first marriage was 15.7 years but the mean desired age was 17.3 years. Sixty per cent of respondents wanted their daughters to marry at a higher age than they themselves had married, and of these, two-fifths wanted the daughter to marry at an age five or more years higher than their own age at marriage.

Earlier in the chapter, studies showing changes in the ease of mixing for young people and in the arrangement of marriage were reviewed. It is now time to examine the very limited data showing the changes in attitudes on these and related matters.

Table 4.10 is derived from the Indonesian Marriage Survey. In most areas, the vast majority of younger respondents and very substantial proportions of older respondents felt that a young couple should be given the chance to get to know each other if their families plan for them to get married. The major exception was South Kalimantan, where marriages were important in cementing alliances between families and these marriages were protected by very high bride-prices (McDonald, 1984: 5). Here women in particular considered that it is not necessary for the young couple to have mixed socially beforehand. On another question (not shown in the table), the vast majority in most areas considered that it was likely that a marriage not preceded by love would end in divorce.

The other attitudinal question reported on in Table 4.10 concerns further education for girls. The question was stated as follows:

Suppose a girl aged 16 who has just finished junior high school with good results receives a proposal of marriage from a man that both she and her parents like very much. With the strong likelihood that she will end her education if she marries, do you think that the girl's parents should advise her to reject the proposal so that she can continue at school or accept the proposal?

The proportions choosing further education are universally high among younger respondents, and even among older people (except for Betawi women in Jakarta), a majority chose further education. Older Betawi women had only attended religious schools which ignored academic subjects. In contrast, a high proportion of single Betawi women had attended Indonesian government schools and they were strongly in favour of further education for girls.

Respondents in the Indonesian Marriage Survey were asked what they considered to be the cause of the greater freedom of youth today. About 50 per cent of both male and female respondents attributed the change to *zaman moderen*. Only 1 per cent mentioned foreign or Western influences. 'Thus while if pressed, they may have said that the West was a major influence on the modern era, it is evident that they are talking about a modern era in Indonesia, a phenomenon with specifically Indonesian determinants.' (McDonald, 1984: 7–8.) Respondents also frequently mentioned the conventional channels of change: the mass media, the education system, and exposure to urban values. 'A new value system for youth behaviour has indeed been spread by the conventional channels of social change but ... this value system is not an unexpurgated Western model but rather a national, indeed nationalistic, Indonesian modification.' (McDonald, 1984: 8.)

Compared with many countries, there is in Indonesia an ideology of youth independence and activism. Indonesian youth had a very high profile in freedom and independence movements, exemplified by the

TABLE 4.10

Indonesia: Respondents' Personal Experiences of Mixing with the Opposite Sex before Marriage, 1978

Measure	Sex and Marital Status	Age-group	Region							
			Aceh	South Sumatra	Jakarta	Yogyakarta	Bali	South Kalimantan	South Sulawesi	North Sulawesi
Percentage agreeing that a young man and woman whose families want them to marry should be given an opportunity to get to know each other beforehand	Single males	17–35	82ᵃ	86ᵃ	97ᵃ	98	Not asked	37ᵃ	49	95
	Ever-married males	<30	85ᵇ	83ᵃ	0	96ᵇ		38	37	90
		30–44	65	93	0	92		36	41	90
		45+	44	86	0	96		33	39	90
	Single females	15–29	89ᵃ	90ᵃ	97	97ᵃ		12ᵃ	60	99ᵃ
	Ever-married females	<30	83	87	0	97ᵃ		13	42	90
		30–44	69	89	0	91		7	40	93
		45+	63	87	0	90		6	37	94
In a choice between education or marriage for a bright 16-year-old girl, the percentage who would choose further education	Single males	17–35	85ᵃ	91ᵃ	73ᵃ	98	93	71ᵃ	85	72
	Ever-married males	<30	87ᵇ	83ᵃ	84	42ᵇ	89	75	78	83
		30–44	87	72	68	58	84	68	73	87
		45+	84	72	60	57	89	70	72	90
	Single females	15–29	83ᵃ	80ᵃ	78	94ᵃ	93	89ᵃ	89	87ᵃ
	Ever-married females	<30	84	74	55	71ᵃ	96	74	84	88
		30–44	75	76	48	69	94	60	78	96
		45+	65	68	32ᵃ	63	90	56	73	95

Sources: McDonald (1984: Table 4.5), based on the Indonesian Marriage Survey, 1978.

ᵃIndicates 50–99 cases.
ᵇIndicates fewer than 50 cases.

national youth congresses of the 1920s and the heavy involvement of youth groups in the declaration of independence in 1945 and the ensuing war of independence. The Indonesian Communist Party put strong emphasis on its youth groups, while the present government has created several new youth movements and re-emphasized some older movements such as the scouting movement (Pramuka). It is in the context of such movements and such images of youth that the attitudes to arranged marriage, not only of the young but also the changing attitudes among older people, need to be interpreted.

Is it possible that increasing costs associated with transfer of bride-wealth at the time of the wedding or other costs associated with the wedding could have contributed to the delay in marriage? Apparently not. This is not a matter which ever seems to be raised in such a context. Although expensive weddings continue to be an important way of demonstrating the family's status, there is no evidence that a greater proportion of family income is spent in this way than it was traditionally, when age at marriage was much lower. However, as financial transfers and costs at the time of the wedding are a much neglected subject, Appendix 2 discusses it briefly.

NON-MARRIAGE AS AN OPTION

It was noted in Chapter 3 that the percentage of Malay women still single in their early thirties has been rising throughout the region. But this situation does not reflect widespread normative acceptance among the Malay community of greatly delayed marriage; rather, this is a cause for great concern. The revelation that in Malaysia there were 60,000 women aged 30–34 (10 per cent of the age-group) who were not yet married resulted in a spate of newspaper articles and letters to the editor in 1991. The overwhelming view was that the failure to marry by these ages is a serious problem; many assumed that the non-marriage was non-volitional, caused by a lack of potential partners or a lack of opportunity to meet potential partners in settings favouring the de-velopment of close attachments. These reactions reflect traditional Malay culture's difficulty in entertaining the idea of non-marriage or delayed marriage as a life option. Many articles and letters stressed that Islam requires its followers to marry and raise a family, and that Malay cul-ture is based on family life. It was left to the head of the Women's Advisory Group on the Integration of Women in Development (NACIWID), Datuk Hajah Zakiah Hanum, to stress that not all women unmarried at this age lacked suitors; half of them chose to live alone, she said, because they gave priority to their career (Shamsiah, 1991).

The more general response to the evidence of the non-married 30–34-year-olds was to seek ways to assist them to marry. An extreme reaction from the traditionalist side was that of Perlis's Islamic Religious De-partment director, who at a seminar in August 1991 urged women to allow their husbands to take second, third, or fourth wives as a way of tackling the problem and also of preventing extramarital affairs (*Far Eastern Economic Review*, 22 August 1991). Matchmaking bureaus were set up under various Islamic auspices, and religious officials were asked to comment on the propriety of women proposing marriage to men. The head of one Islamic marriage bureau, Hajah Ainun, commented that many of those who make use of the bureau are single because they cannot find suitable partners. They have many colleagues and friends but do not see any of them as potential marriage partners.

Some of them have been too busy studying in colleges and universities to mix around and find partners. And since they are now working, they find it difficult to find time to socialize. There are also those whose religious convictions discourage them from going out on a date with members of the opposite sex. Many of these single people know that the task of matchmaking was traditionally placed on parents' shoulders. However, many parents, due to changing times and attitudes, have discarded this practice, thinking that their offspring would want to find their own marriage partners. But, as Hajah Ainun notices, there are still those who need a little help. 'We are actually assuming the role of parents by choosing a wife or husband for the candidate who comes to us,' she says. (Simon, 1991.)

The 1981–2 Malaysian Marriage Survey also investigated community attitudes towards delayed marriage. Thirty-four per cent of Malay female respondents thought a woman could be considered an old maid if she remained unmarried in her twenties (mostly above the age of 25) and a further 54 per cent would consider her an old maid if she had still not married at ages 30–34 (Tan et al., 1986: 208). Respondents were also asked to give their reaction to the situation of a hypothetical woman aged 30 who is still single: 63 per cent of Malay female respondents said they pitied her as she might end up an old maid,[13] and a further 18 per cent said her family must be ashamed because they have not got her married off. Only 15 per cent of Malay female respondents (and 18 per cent of males) gave answers recognizing some advantages in her situation, compared with 29 per cent of Chinese females (Tan et al., 1986: 205). As for whether a person can live happily without marrying at all, only about 10 per cent of Malay respondents agreed, 40 per cent disagreed, and half were not sure (Tan et al., 1986: 211). The proportion disagreeing was considerably higher among Malay than among Chinese or Indian respondents. There is no evidence here that non-marriage is seen as an option except by a very small minority of married Malays. However, among single Malay respondents, although the proportion agreeing that a permanently non-marrying person can be happy was as low as it was for married respondents, the proportion saying that they cannot be happy was only half as high as for the married couples and the proportion undecided correspondingly larger (Tan, 1986: Table 26). This may be the harbinger of a more significant questioning of the traditional Malay position that marriage is the only credible state for both men and women.

THE INTERCONNECTEDNESS OF EXPLANATORY FACTORS

To sum up the discussion in this chapter, a basic issue raised earlier is recalled. Many changes were taking place simultaneously in Islamic South-East Asia over the period when female age at marriage rose sharply. Both analysis of cross-sectional survey data and village studies show that education, work experience before marriage, and freedom in the choice of spouse were all correlated with higher age at marriage. Both female education and wage-work opportunities for females were expanding rapidly, and the shift towards self-arranged marriages proceeding apace, over the period when age at marriage for females was rising rapidly. How closely were these trends interconnected?

A study by Cherlin, Fricke, and Smith (1985), based on the Indonesian segment of the Asian Marriage Survey of 1980 conducted among three groups in Central Java, throws some light on the issues, though several of their conclusions remain speculative. By constructing a scale of family influence over courtship and marriage, based on three different questions, it was possible to test the interaction between education and family influence, among other factors, in affecting age at marriage.

Older women in these samples reported higher levels of family influence over courtship and spouse choice than did younger women, suggesting that family influence had weakened somewhat in the decades before the Asian Marriage Survey, because of the acceptance and spread of new values stressing the greater autonomy of young people in the process of marriage. The authors argue that 'if one of the major effects of schooling on marriage and fertility is to impart new western-style values that weaken family-based authority ... then the Indonesian data should show that the effects of grades of school completed on marriage timing decline when the level of family influence is taken into account' (Cherlin, Fricke, and Smith, 1985: 20). Consequently, Table 4.11 presents two columns of adjusted means. The first controls for the other variables in the table, plus family background (a combination of father's occupation and family land ownership), birth cohort, and age at marriage. The second column adds to this list the family influence scale and another measure of family influence, whether or not the respondent was living with both parents before marriage.

Table 4.11 shows that a significant predictor of age at marriage in all three strata is grades of school completed, though the predictive power is greatest in the urban middle-class stratum and weakest in the rural stratum. The authors argue that this greater predictive power in urban areas is due to the greater variation in education in these areas. Grades of school completed, considered by itself, accounts for 24 per cent of the variance in marriage timing in the urban middle-class sample, 20 per cent in the urban lower-class sample, and 12 per cent in the rural sample.

Introduction of other explanatory variables—skills, occupation, wage work, family background, birth cohort, and age at menarche—greatly reduced the predictive power of education, as shown in the first column of adjusted means. But the effects of education were still substantial.

TABLE 4.11

Central Java: Unadjusted and Adjusted Mean Ages of Marriage, by Indicators of Education and Training for Women, 1980

Education and Training	Unadjusted Mean	Adjusted Mean (1)	Adjusted Mean (2)	N
Rural				
Grades of school completed				
0	16.1	16.2	16.2	110
1–3	16.2	16.4	16.4	114
4–5	16.2	16.2	16.2	106
6	16.3	16.3	16.3	110
7–9	18.1	17.2	17.0	27
10+	20.4	19.4	19.2	18
(Increment in R^2)	(0.125[a])	(0.033[a])	(0.028[a])	
Skills acquired prior to marriage				
None	16.1	16.3	16.3	369
One or more	17.5	16.9	16.8	116
(Increment in R^2)	(0.057[a])	(0.005)	(0.004)	
Worked for wages prior to marriage				
No	16.0	16.2	16.2	269
Yes	17.0	16.7	16.7	216
(Increment in R^2)	(0.038[a])	(0.004)	(0.003)	
Occupation prior to marriage				
None	15.7	15.1	15.1	15
Housework	16.0	16.1	16.2	194
Farm	16.7	16.9	16.9	108

(continued)

TABLE 4.11 (continued)

Education and Training	Unadjusted Mean	Adjusted Mean		N
		(1)	(2)	
Small trade	16.4	16.6	16.5	112
Unskilled labour	16.8	16.6	16.6	24
Skilled labour	17.6	16.6	16.6	12
White collar	19.7	17.3	17.3	20
(Increment in R^2)	(0.090[a])	(0.017)	(0.016)	
Urban Low				
Grades of school completed				
0	16.5	16.6	16.7	148
1–3	16.8	16.8	17.0	52
4–5	16.2	16.5	16.5	49
6	17.4	17.6	17.6	79
7–9	18.6	18.3	18.0	49
10+	22.1	21.3	20.8	24
(Increment in R^2)	(0.205[a])	(0.083[a])	(0.059[a])	
Skills acquired prior to marriage				
None	16.9	17.3	17.3	275
One or more	18.2	17.3	17.3	126
(Increment in R^2)	(0.038[a])	(0.000)	(0.000)	
Worked for wages prior to marriage				
No	16.8	16.7	16.7	252
Yes	18.3	18.4	18.3	149
(Increment in R^2)	(0.058[a])	(0.016[a])	(0.016[a])	

157

Occupation prior to marriage				
None	16.6	17.3	17.4	170
Housework	17.3	17.8	17.8	77
Small trade	17.6	17.0	16.8	27
Farm, unskilled labour	17.3	16.8	16.6	89
Skilled labour	18.4	16.9	16.8	20
White collar	21.3	17.7	17.7	18
(Increment in R^2)	(0.103[a])	(0.008)	(0.008)	
Urban Middle				
Grades of school completed				
0	17.0	17.4	17.6	72
1–3	17.8	17.9	18.0	32
4–5	17.4	17.6	17.7	52
6	18.0	17.9	17.9	70
7–9	19.1	18.8	18.8	85
10+	21.7	21.4	21.1	68
(Increment in R^2)	(0.239[a])	(0.123[a])	(0.092[a])	
Skills acquired prior to marriage				
None	18.2	18.6	18.6	242
One or more	19.4	18.6	18.7	137
(Increment in R^2)	(0.033[a])	(0.000)	(0.000)	
Worked for wages prior to marriage				
Yes	18.0	18.1	18.2	270
No	20.1	20.0	19.7	109
(Increment in R^2)	(0.083[a])	(0.021[a])	(0.012[a])	

(continued)

TABLE 4.11 (continued)

Education and Training	Unadjusted Mean	Adjusted Mean		N
		(1)	(2)	
Occupation prior to marriage				
None	17.9	18.5	18.4	185
Housework	18.8	19.2	19.1	73
Small trade	20.4	19.7	20.0	21
Farm, unskilled labour	19.2	18.4	18.6	44
Skilled labour	20.2	17.8	17.8	23
White collar	21.9	1.0	18.3	33
(Increment in R^2)	(0.087[a])	(0.018)	(0.021[b])	

(1) = Net of other education, occupation, and background variables.
(2) = Net of (1) and family influence variables.

Source: Cherlin, Fricke, and Smith (1985: Table 6).
[a]Significant at the 0.01 level.
[b]Significant at the 0.05 level.

Bullock carts in Malacca, 1964. Bus, taxi, railway, and air transport were already widespread at this time, but the bullock cart symbolized the slow pace of rural life.

2 Women harvesting paddy in Java. Women play a key role in planting and harvesting paddy throughout the Malay world.

3 Scene in the Gudang Garam *kretek* cigarette factory in Kediri, East Java. Some 6,000 young women work in this room alone. Altogether, the factory employs 36,000 workers, of whom about 80 per cent are women.

4 Scene in a Kelantanese market. Women are predominant as market sellers and prominent as customers.

During the 1970s and 1980s, job opportunities for women in teaching and nursing, and in clerical and service sector activities expanded rapidly, providing an incentive to continue education and delay marriage.

6   Office workers in Jakarta.

7 The end of another school day, Jakarta, 1993. There has been an enormous growth in enrolment of girls in secondary schools throughout the Malay-Muslim world.

8 These Muslim schoolgirls in Yala Province, Southern Thailand, attend the first school to observe Muslim dress codes. There has been poor attendance by Muslim girls in secondary schools in the region, partly because the school uniforms violate their religious beliefs but also because parents fear the influence of secondary schooling which does not highlight Islamic values. (*Bangkok Post*)

9 Young Malays sharing an intimate moment in a Kuala Lumpur shopping complex, 1993.

10 Middle-class Minangkabau wedding. (Courtesy of Sjafri Sairin)

11 Middle-class wedding in Bandung, 1990. The bridal couple and their parents are shown arriving for the wedding feast.

12 The bride and groom at a middle-class Javanese wedding reception in Yogyakarta in 1992, displaying the stylized make-up and ornamentation common to such weddings. (Courtesy of Sjafri Sairin)

13 Another Javanese wedding in Yogyakarta. The parents of the bride and groom pose with them. (Courtesy of Tri Manning)

14 In Malaysia, marriage courses have become very popular in recent times with young Malays about to marry.

15 The marriage registration office in Gabus Wetan, in the high divorce regency of Indramayu, West Java.

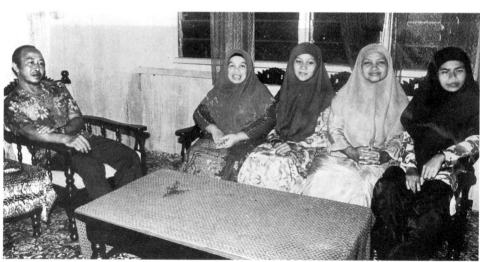

16 Syed Mohd. Zain, aged 50, of Kampung Patani, near Kota Bharu, Kelantan, with his four wives, whom he married in 1962, 1969, 1972, and 1987 respectively. (The first and fourth wives are seated next to each other on the left of the group.) He has 27 children. Syed Mohd. Zain's situation is hardly typical; fewer than five men in every thousand in Islamic South-East Asia have more than two wives. (*Berita Harian*)

Work for wages had significant net predictive power in both urban samples, and premarital occupation in the urban middle-class sample. Human capital variables and background factors, then, accounted for some of the effects of schooling.

In the second column of adjusted means, the level of family influence was also controlled. This reduced further the effects of schooling in the two urban strata. For example, in the urban middle-class sample, the unadjusted mean age at marriage for women with ten or more grades of school completed was 4.7 years greater than the mean for women with no schooling. The adjusted mean, controlling for everything except family influence, was 4.0 years greater; and the adjusted mean, including family influence, was 3.5 years greater. The introduction of family influence also reduced the effects of working for wages in the urban middle-class sample.

Though the causal chain of influence is uncertain, the positive correlation between more schooling and less family influence is 'consistent with the supposition that schooling and wage work transmit new values that lead to greater autonomy among young, urban Javanese women in courtship and spouse choice, values that, in turn, lead to a later age at marriage' (Cherlin, Fricke, and Smith, 1985: 22).

The fact that, in all three strata, the effects of schooling on marriage timing are substantial only at the secondary level and above suggests that schooling affects marriage timing in part by keeping women off the marriage market; it is when they are of secondary school age that women reach marriageable ages. Cherlin, Fricke, and Smith (1985: 22–3) conclude that their study provides evidence that 'schooling affects marriage timing by prolonging a stage of the life course that is incompatible with marriage for women, by providing the knowledge, skills, or credentials necessary to work for wages, and by promoting individual autonomy in courtship and marriage'.

Conclusions

The timing and extent of the rise in female ages at marriage and the shift to self-arranged marriages in Islamic South-East Asia reflected the basic structural changes taking place in the society, and were consistent with an explanation that emphasizes socio-economic development. Singapore experienced the earliest and sharpest rise, Peninsular Malaysia was next, followed by Indonesia and the Southern Thai Muslims. Except for the Southern Thai Muslims, where isolation from the mainstream was probably the main factor, this ordering of increases in marriage age is the same as the ordering of levels of socio-economic development. Within countries as well, there was a correlation; changes occurred earlier in the more economically developed parts of Malaysia, and age at marriage has risen more sharply in Indonesia's metropolis, Jakarta, than in other Indonesian provinces. Other factors, however, did play their part, notably the marriage squeeze in Singapore in the late 1940s and early 1950s.

Ideological impediments to such trends, rooted in fears of uncontrolled female sexuality, were clearly much less strongly grounded in South-East Asian Muslim society than they were in most of South Asia. This is not really surprising. South-East Asia lacks the severe patriarchal system of South Asia which requires that the young bride be cut off from her own family and moulded into the family of her husband, it lacks the caste system which increases the horror of wayward female decisions on marriage in South Asia, and it has always given women a more independent economic role, indeed one that is pivotal in the household economy.

Dixon's (1971) classification of factors into those relating to the 'feasibility' and to the 'desirability' of early marriage may be useful in summarizing the changes which have taken place. In traditional South-East Asian settings, early marriage was facilitated by bilateral kinship systems, flexibility in postmarital residence and in means of making a living, frequently on the landholding of one or the other set of parents, and lack of emphasis on the need for acquired characteristics such as education and childrearing abilities; these could be learned 'on the job', after marriage, in close association with the mother or mother-in-law. The desirability of early marriage hinged, first, on the inevitability of marriage itself, given a social organization based on the family which provided no acceptable role for an unmarried adult, and second, on the Islamic-based concern with sexual purity and family honour.

In more recent times, the feasibility of early marriage has been deeply altered by the society's emphasis on the need to acquire at least secondary education, and also by a changed perception of what resources, in terms of finance and knowledge-cum-experience, a couple needs before entering marriage. The latter perception relates to the much greater likelihood that the couple will live independent of either set of parents. The desirability of early marriage has been lessened in the eyes of many parents by the contribution a working daughter can make to the family finances, and an increased prestige accorded by the community to families whose children achieve success in education and in their careers.

Nowadays, with the choice about when to marry largely resting with young women themselves, factors influencing their decision must be considered seriously; and the decision is no longer only about when, but—for some women at least—about whether. Though the context in Japan is only partly comparable, the conclusions of a recent study on Japan are nevertheless relevant:

... educational and economic opportunities for young Japanese women have improved while the Japanese wife's subordinated and highly domesticated position in the family has changed little, a combination ... that has made young Japanese women reluctant to enter marriage before enjoying a period of relative autonomy and freedom from domestic burdens during which they can attend higher education and work for pay. Normative changes that have weakened the moral imperative for women to marry have simultaneously made such a postponement of marriage more socially acceptable. (Tsuya and Mason, 1992: 22.)

It is clearly impossible to identify just which aspects of socio-economic development have had the main effect on age at marriage. As B. Caldwell (1992: 278) put it in commenting on marriage change in Sri Lanka, 'Age at marriage has changed because society itself has changed and accordingly the nature of marriage within it. Because social processes are so complex, generally multidimensional, and often ambiguous, it is very hard to tie down the exact relationships involved.' The perceptions of so many ordinary people in the region that the changes in marriage arrangements and ages have been due to 'changing times' should probably not be too quickly discarded as excessively vague; rather, this perception emphasizes the profound truth that social change is a process not readily divisible into discrete component parts.

1. The percentage of Malays living in rural areas would rise to 89 per cent if the definition of 'urban' was changed from towns with a population above 10,000 to one of towns with a population above 1,000. In fact, in 1947, 93 per cent of Malays were rural according to the latter definition.

2. The 'rice-bowl' of Kedah and large areas in Kelantan and north coastal Selangor were the only really extensive paddy areas.

3. The tendency for postmarital residence to be with or near the bride's parents has been noted for the Javanese (Koentjaraningrat, 1967b: 257–8; Jay, 1969: 40; Hefner, 1990: 162–4; Williams, 1990b: 85), Trengganu Malays (Strange, 1981: 127–8), of course for the matrilineal Minangkabau (Bachtiar, 1967), for the Sundanese (Hugo, 1975: 427; Weekes, 1984: 729) and for the Acehnese, Buginese, Madurese, and the Taussug of the Philippines (Weekes, 1984: 6, 185, 459, 766). Jay (1969: 40) notes that 'economic considerations appear most important in the choice of residence: the financial advantages to be gained, the number of single children remaining in the two families, the parents' need for extra help, or the availability of land rights. Only one pair of parents may be willing and able to set the couple up in a separate house. If the bride is scarcely at or not yet past puberty, the first few years of the marriage are usually spent with her parents. In most cases the choice is left to the young couple.'

4. The strong influence of the mother over her young married daughter when the young couple still lived in her home is well described by two Malaysian grandmothers, relating their own experiences (Hamidah, 1979; my translation):

'If I was slow to serve my husband when he returned from the office, or didn't serve the food properly, she would chide me. In short, after I was married, it was my mother who gave me most of my guidance and instruction.... Mother always advised me: "Don't oppose or be disloyal to your husband. That is a big sin and displeasing to God. You must respect him and follow his instructions."

Only after we had been married ten years and had three children did we move from my parents' house and live alone. When I was pregnant with my first child, she forbade so many things. She said that whatever I did would have an effect on the baby I was carrying.

There follows a long list of dos and don'ts for pregnant women, some of them based on traditional Malay beliefs in the spirit world.'

5. In Kuala Lumpur in 1964, the author was struck by the incongruity of Malays flocking to see Elvis Presley in 'Fun in Acapulco' to celebrate the end of the fasting month.

6. This generalization holds not only for the Muslim populations of Indonesia, Malaysia, Singapore, and Southern Thailand, but also for the Islamic populations of the Philippines (Weekes, 1984: 766; Wong and Ng, 1985: 265 and Table 4.8; Lacar, 1992: 111–12).

7. In Singapore, between 1962 and 1970, 5.1 per cent of marriages were inter-ethnic, mostly between couples of the same religion (Hassan, 1974). The main groups inter-marrying were Indians with Malays, followed by Chinese with Europeans, then Chinese with Malays, and Chinese with Eurasians (see Jones, 1980: 282 n. 9). Inter-ethnic marriage is almost certainly less common in Malaysia than in Singapore.

8. Differences between the two surveys in the wording of questions preclude direct comparison of more disaggregated categories, for example, self-choice with approval of parents, self-choice without approval of parents (see Tan and Jones, 1991).

9. Data specifically on whether the respondent had ever met her husband before their engagement have been published for only three of the component studies of the Indonesian Marriage Survey (Arian, 1982: Table 4.6; Mahfudz, 1982: Table 4.4; Muliakusuma, 1982: Table 4.12). The percentages who had never met their husband are as follows:

	Aged < 36	Aged > 36
South Kalimantan (Banjarese)		
No school/incomplete primary	40	47
Completed primary or above	33	17
Jakarta (Betawi)	16	32
Aceh (Acehnese)	54	79

10. This strong preference for girls working in factories to do so from home was recorded by Ackerman (1980), as well as by the author in focus group research in Kelantan. However, a more sanguine view of an interstate move to find work was taken if there were relatives at the destination with whom the girl could stay.

11. In addition to the income working daughters directly bring in, a larger amount of *hantaran belanja* (the payment made by the bridegroom to the bride's parents as a con-tribution towards the wedding expenses) could also be required if the daughter was working in a factory, in the Malacca study. Large *hantaran belanja* payments (typically ranging from RM500 to RM1,000) were only asked if the bridegroom was from outside the local community. Although *hantaran belanja* is intended as a contribution towards the cost of the wedding and household goods for the young couple, some parents reserve a portion for themselves.

12. In two other Malay samples in the same study, one on a FELDA (Federal Land Development Authority) settlement scheme and the other in the capital city, Kuala Lumpur, there was also strong agreement that work opportunities improved women's status (though the percentages agreeing were not quite as high as in Kelantan). The rural FELDA women were also ambivalent about the role of rural–urban migration in raising women's status, though not as ambivalent as the Kelantanese; but well over half the Kuala Lumpur women thought rural–urban migration improved women's status.

13. The survey asked specifically people's opinion on the age at which an unmarried woman was considered an 'old maid'. About half the married Malay female respondents would use the term to describe an unmarried woman aged 30–34, and most of the rest would apply the term to a woman who had not yet reached 30 years of age (Tan et al., 1986: Table 19). On the maximum age at which a woman should be married, 8 per cent thought the maximum acceptable age was below 20, and a further one-third thought it lay in the 20–24 age-group. Fewer than 10 per cent thought that the maximum acceptable age lay above 30 (Tan et al., 1986: Table 11).

5
Marriage Dissolution: Widowhood, Divorce, and Remarriage

MARRIAGES officially entered can be officially broken in only two ways: through the death of one of the spouses or through divorce. Lengthy separation or desertion, even if it does not result in divorce, can also effectively terminate the marriage. The study of marriage dissolution can be approached in various ways. The various approaches are described and their strengths and weaknesses assessed in Appendix 3.

Incidence of Widowhood

Widowhood is not the main concern of this book, but a brief discussion of changing patterns of widowhood among the Malay populations studied is needed to provide the context in which divorce and remarriage take place.

Divorce is the major cause of marital dissolution at the young ages, but even in societies where divorce is common, widowhood progressively increases in importance at older ages. Table 5.1 shows the situation in Indonesia in 1980. At ages 35–39 and above, widowhood took over from divorce as the main reason why women were not in the married state. By their late forties, a very substantial proportion of women were widowed, and by ages 50–54, 29 per cent of females were widows. This proportion had been even higher in earlier times: 41 per cent only ten years earlier, in 1970 (Table 5.2).

There was a vast discrepancy between females and males in the proportion currently widowed. In Indonesia in 1980, compared to the 29 per cent of females aged 50–54 who were widowed, only 4 per cent of males in the same age-group were widowed. One reason is that, because of the wide disparity in average ages between husbands and wives and the slightly higher female expectation of life, women were much more likely to become widowed than were men. Another reason is that there is strong social pressure in Malay society for rapid remarriage of widowers. A widower or divorced man is considered incapable of doing even the most basic of domestic tasks, so he needs a wife or daughter to cook, clean, and take care of household finances (Hefner, 1990: 167–8). No such pressure exists for widowed women to marry if

TABLE 5.1

Indonesia: Percentage Distribution of Population Aged 10 Years and Over, by Age-group and Marital Status, 1980

Age-group	Males					Females				
	Single	Married	Widowed	Divorced	Total	Single	Married	Widowed	Divorced	Total
10–14	99.3	0.7	0.0	0.0	100	99.2	0.7	0.0	0.1	100
15–19	96.4	3.2	0.1	0.3	100	69.9	27.3	0.2	2.5	100
20–24	59.4	38.6	0.2	1.8	100	22.3	72.2	0.7	4.8	100
25–29	19.5	78.0	0.4	2.2	100	7.4	86.2	1.5	5.0	100
30–34	6.0	91.6	0.6	1.7	100	3.4	88.6	3.0	5.0	100
35–39	2.5	95.1	0.9	1.5	100	1.9	87.7	5.4	5.0	100
40–44	1.6	95.5	1.5	1.4	100	1.4	81.4	11.3	5.8	100
45–49	1.1	95.4	2.1	1.3	100	1.2	76.0	16.9	6.0	100
50–54	0.9	94.3	3.4	1.4	100	1.1	63.8	28.6	6.5	100
55–59	0.7	93.5	4.4	1.4	100	1.0	57.3	35.4	6.3	100
60–64	0.7	90.2	7.4	1.6	100	1.0	39.6	53.1	6.3	100
65+	0.9	81.7	15.5	1.9	100	1.0	25.5	68.3	5.1	100
All ages 15+	29.4	67.2	2.0	1.4	100	17.6	65.2	12.3	4.9	100

Source: 1980 Population Census, Series S, No. 2: Table 3.3.

they are past the age of menopause. (By the same token, though, there is not the strong resistance to remarriage of widows found in Hindu societies.)

Table 5.2 shows the proportion of the population currently widowed, by age, for Indonesia and for Malays in Peninsular Malaysia, according to different censuses and surveys. The general downward trend in widowhood over time reflects the improving health conditions and rising longevity over the period. For example, in Peninsular Malaysia, expectation of life at the age of 20 (i.e. the remaining number of years expected to be lived, on average, by persons surviving to the age of 20, according to the prevailing mortality rates), rose by more than four years for Malay males and by six years for Malay females between 1957 and 1971: from 44.7 to 49.1 years for males and from 44.3 to 50.3 years for females (Sidhu and Jones, 1981: 171). In Indonesia, although reliable life tables are not available, expectation of life at the age of 20 should have risen by roughly comparable amounts; certainly, other indicators of mortality indicate great improvement, such as the estimate that mortality up to the age of 5 fell from around 210 per 1,000 in the 1960s to around 160 per 1,000 in the early to mid-1970s (Committee on Population and Demography, 1987: 35).

The drop in the proportion widowed among females was caused not only by increasing longevity of their spouses, but also by the narrowing of the average age gap between husbands and wives. In Malaysia, however, the proportion widowed fell less sharply among Malays than among the other ethnic groups, because the alternative form of marital dissolution—divorce—was decreasing rapidly among the Malays, thus leaving a higher proportion of couples at risk of having their marriages broken by widowhood. Similar trends were occurring in Indonesia.

Even though divorce rates were very high in the Malay world in the 1950s, widowhood was much more important than divorce in raising the proportion of children who failed to reach adulthood living with both their natural parents. This is because (as will be discussed later in the chapter) over 40 per cent of couples who divorced appear to have been childless, whereas the high proportion of women who were widowed in their late forties implies that in a high-fertility society many children experienced the death of their father before they reached adulthood.

Incidence of Divorce

Of the three kinds of measures of marital dissolution mentioned in Appendix 3—measures based on the current marital status of the population, on divorce registration, and on the outcome of marriages contracted by members of different birth or marriage cohorts—data are most readily available on the first. Therefore, although in many respects these data are less satisfactory in revealing the incidence of divorce, they are presented first to show something of the regional differences between Muslim populations in South-East Asia.

166

TABLE 5.2

Peninsular Malaysia (Malays) and Indonesia: Proportion Widowed, by Sex and Age-group, 1947–1985

Age-group	Males					Females				
	1947	1957[a]	1970	1980	1985[b]	1947	1957[a]	1970	1980	1985[b]
Pen. Malaysia										
Malays										
15–19	0.1	0.1	0.2	0.0	0.0	0.9	0.3	0.7	0.1	0.0
20–24	0.6	0.3	0.7	0.2	0.0	2.4	1.0	2.1	0.6	0.1
25–29	1.1	0.6	1.4	0.4	0.2	3.6	2.0	3.3	1.1	0.5
30–34	1.6	0.9	1.7	0.6	0.6	6.2	4.0	4.6	2.2	1.0
35–39	2.0	1.2	2.0	0.8	0.8	10.2	7.6	6.9	3.8	1.5
40–44	3.0	1.7	2.5	1.2	0.6	17.7	14.7	11.6	7.0	7.8
45–49	3.9	2.4	3.2	1.7	1.2	24.9	23.4	17.4	12.3	14.2
50–54	5.4	3.5	4.2	2.7	3.2	36.5	33.6	28.7	21.4	15.6
55–59	6.2	4.8	5.2	3.7	4.7	41.6	44.6	37.7	29.9	21.0
60–64	8.5	6.7	7.6	6.0 }		56.3	54.9	51.5	43.0 }	
65+	14.8	13.2	13.6	12.8 }	10.0	69.0	70.8	68.8	62.2 }	47.9
All ages 15+	3.0	2.0	2.6	1.3	1.6	14.9	12.7	12.4	7.7	8.0

Indonesia								
15–19	0.5	0.3	0.1	0.0	2.2	1.4	0.2	0.2
20–24	1.8	1.4	0.2	0.1	3.5	3.0	0.7	0.5
25–29	2.2	2.0	0.4	0.3	3.6	3.8	1.5	1.1
30–34	1.7	1.9	0.6	0.5	5.6	6.2	3.0	2.4
35–39	1.5	1.9	0.9	0.8	10.5	10.2	5.4	4.5
40–44	2.2	2.7	1.5	1.4	19.4	18.7	11.3	9.6
45–49	2.8	3.3	2.1	2.1	28.1	25.6	16.9	16.1
50–54	4.2	5.5	3.4	3.6	43.9	41.1	28.6	26.1
55–59	6.0	6.6	4.4	5.0	53.1	47.1	35.4	37.8
60–64	9.6	11.1	7.4	8.0	65.5	63.4	53.1	56.5
65+	16.2	18.7	15.5	16.3	78.1	73.0	68.3	74.9
All ages 15+	2.5	2.6	1.7	2.1	14.9	13.2	10.3	12.7

Sources: Sidhu and Jones (1981: Table 8).
Indonesia: *Population Census*, 1971 and 1980; *1985 Intercensal Population Survey*; and National Sample Survey, 1964, reported in Nugroho (1967: Tables II.46 and II.47).

Malaysia: Unpublished tables from the Malaysian Population and Family Survey, 1984–5.
[a] For Indonesia, data are for 1964 and refer only to Java–Madura.
[b] 1984 in the case of Malaysia.

Percentages Currently Divorced

Table 5.3 shows the proportion of the population currently divorced, by age, for Indonesia and for Malays in Peninsular Malaysia, according to different censuses and surveys. A number of aspects of the table deserve comment. First of all, the proportion currently divorced rises steadily with age. Secondly, the proportions currently divorced are much higher for females than for males. Thirdly, there have been clear declines over time in the proportion divorced, with the notable exception of females in both Peninsular Malaysia and Indonesia in the period since 1970. Between 1970 and 1980, the proportions divorced turned up in all but the youngest two age-groups. Between 1980 and 1985, this rise continued in Peninsular Malaysia in all age-groups except 30–34, but it continued in Indonesia only among women aged 55 and over.

The decline in the proportion of women currently divorced in age-groups 15–24 in Indonesia, and its near-constancy in Peninsular Malaysia over the 1970–85 period, were clearly related to delayed marriage over this period, which was lowering the proportion of females 'at risk' of entering the divorced state. The rise in proportions of females divorced in other age-groups, and among adult females as a whole, occurred, as will be seen later, in a period of steadily declining divorce. Different explanations are possible. One is that, because of declining widowhood (see Table 5.2) the pool of married women 'at risk' of entering the divorced state was larger. Another could be that divorced women are having greater difficulty than before in finding a suitable partner to remarry. But it is more likely that in a period of rapid social change and expanding work opportunities for women, divorced Malay women saw less need than before to remarry quickly, if at all.

In Indonesia, the percentages currently divorced have changed much less sharply over time than have those for the Malays. Since 1970, the proportion currently divorced among Indonesian females has been well above that for the Malays, especially at the younger age-groups. This is mainly due to the higher proportions divorced in Java, but the remainder of Indonesia also has somewhat higher proportions currently divorced than do the Malays.

Table 5.4 shows regional differences in percentages currently divorced, where available, at the same dates as for Table 5.3. These data will have greater meaning once divorce rates for the different regions have been examined in the following section. It is clear that the percentages currently divorced have been, and still are, highest in the north-eastern Peninsular Malaysian states of Kelantan and Trengganu, and in the Indonesian provinces of West Nusa Tenggara, West Sumatra, West and East Java, and South Kalimantan. As in Peninsular Malaysia and Indonesia as a whole, the proportions divorced at the state or provincial level fell universally over time, with the exception of the already noted rise for females over the 1970–80 period, which occurred in all states of Peninsular Malaysia and all provinces of Indonesia.

The proportion of ever-married Malays in Peninsular Malaysia who

TABLE 5.3

Indonesia and Peninsular Malaysia (Malays): Proportion of Divorced Persons, by Sex and Age-group, 1947–1985

Age-group	Males				Females			
	1964[a]	1971	1980	1985	1964[a]	1971	1980	1985
Indonesia								
15–19	1.3	0.6	0.3	0.2	7.8	3.8	2.5	1.4
20–24	4.6	2.4	1.8	1.3	8.6	5.4	4.8	3.8
25–29	4.7	2.8	2.2	1.7	6.3	4.6	5.0	4.2
30–34	2.9	1.9	1.7	1.7	6.3	4.3	5.0	4.3
35–39	1.5	1.4	1.5	1.3	5.7	4.4	5.0	4.8
40–44	1.5	1.2	1.4	1.4	4.5	4.7	5.8	5.1
45–49	1.1	1.0	1.3	1.3	5.0	4.6	6.0	5.7
50–54	1.4	1.3	1.4	1.5	4.5	4.2	6.5	6.5
55–59	1.8	1.2	1.4	1.3	5.1	3.8	6.3	7.7
60–64	1.3	1.4	1.6	1.5	4.1	3.7	6.3	7.0
65+	2.2	1.6	1.9	1.6	2.4	3.0	5.1	5.8
All ages 15+	2.1	1.6	1.4	1.3	5.4	4.3	4.9	4.4

(*continued*)

TABLE 5.3 (continued)

Age-group	Males					Females				
	1947	1957	1970	1980	1984	1947	1957	1970	1980	1984
Peninsular Malaysia										
Malays										
15–19	1.1	0.6	0.1	0.0	0.0	7.5	3.7	0.4	0.3	0.4
20–24	5.7	2.6	0.5	0.2	0.2	9.5	5.2	1.1	1.0	1.1
25–29	6.7	2.7	1.0	0.5	0.0	7.6	4.7	1.5	1.7	2.1
30–34	5.4	2.5	1.1	0.7	0.0	7.1	5.0	1.5	2.3	2.2
35–39	4.3	2.3	1.1	0.7	0.0	6.7	5.7	1.7	2.8	3.5
40–44	4.1	2.3	1.1	0.9	0.3	8.2	7.0	2.2	3.5	5.0
45–49	3.7	2.5	1.2	1.1	0.8	8.7	8.2	2.8	4.2	6.7
50–54	4.1	2.9	1.6	1.4	0.5	9.7	10.3	3.6	5.7	6.6
55–59	3.9	3.3	1.9	1.6	0.0	9.3	10.5	4.4	7.3	10.8
60–64	4.9	3.8	2.5	2.3 ⎫	1.8	10.7	11.7	5.6	9.7 ⎫	16.2
65+	5.7	5.0	3.7	3.9 ⎭		9.6	10.7	6.8	12.5 ⎭	
All ages 15+	4.5	2.5	1.1	0.8		8.2	6.2	2.1	3.0	

Sources: Indonesia: 1964 figures are from the National Sample Survey, 1964, reported in Nugroho (1967); *Population Census*, 1971 and 1980; and *1985 Intercensal Population Survey.*
Malaysia: *Population Census of Malaya*, 1947 and 1957; *Population Census of Malaysia*, 1970 and 1980; and the Malaysian Population and Family Survey, 1984–5.
ᵃJava–Madura.

TABLE 5.4

Singapore and Peninsular Malaysia (Malays) and Indonesia:
Percentages Currently Divorced of the Population Aged 15 and Over, by State or Province, Various Years

	Males				Females			
	1947	1957	1970ᵃ	1980ᵇ	1947	1957	1970ᵃ·ᵇ	1980ᵇ
Singapore Malays	0.9	0.9	0.4	0.8	1.5	1.3	0.6	1.4
Peninsular Malaysia								
Malays	4.5	2.5	1.1	0.8	8.2	6.2	2.1	3.0
Kelantan	8.1	4.3	2.1	1.6	14.3	10.7	4.5	6.4
Trengganu	7.3	3.4	1.6	1.2	12.0	8.8	3.9	5.0
Pahang	3.3	2.6	1.1	0.8	5.3	6.1	1.6	2.8
Perlis	6.6	3.5	1.3	1.5	8.8	6.5	1.9	4.3
Kedah	4.5	2.6	1.0	1.2	7.7	5.6	1.5	3.7
Penang	2.8	2.0	1.0	0.7	5.8	4.4	1.7	2.4
Perak	2.7	1.6	0.9	0.6	5.9	4.6	1.4	2.0
Selangor	2.8	1.6	0.7	0.3ᶜ	5.1	4.6	1.2	1.5ᵈ
Negri Sembilan	3.9	2.2	1.1	0.7	7.9	7.0	2.1	2.8
Malacca	1.8	1.2	0.5	0.4	5.6	4.6	1.3	1.9
Johore	2.4	1.5	0.7	0.4	4.8	3.7	1.2	1.6
Indonesiaᵈ	–	–	1.6	1.2	–	–	4.3	4.9
Aceh	–	–	0.6	0.7	–	–	2.1	3.0
North Sumatra	–	–	0.6	0.8	–	–	1.3	1.8
West Sumatra	–	–	2.7	2.0	–	–	6.3	6.5
Riau	–	–	1.6	1.2	–	–	3.3	3.4
Jambi	–	–	2.0	1.3	–	–	3.9	3.9
South Sumatra	–	–	1.1	0.9	–	–	2.0	2.3

(continued)

172

TABLE 5.4 (continued)

	Males				Females			
	1947	1957	1970[a]	1980[b]	1947	1957	1970[a,b]	1980[b]
Bengkulu	—	—	1.1	1.1	—	—	2.5	2.7
Lampung	—	—	1.2	1.3	—	—	2.0	3.1
DKI Jakarta	—	—	0.9	0.7	—	—	4.3	4.3
Yogyakarta	—	—	1.0	1.0	—	—	3.6	4.1
West Java	—	—	1.8	1.7	—	—	5.7	6.4
Central Java	—	—	1.6	1.4	—	—	4.5	5.1
East Java	—	—	1.8	1.7	—	—	5.3	6.2
West Nusa Tenggara	—	—	3.2	2.5	—	—	6.4	6.5
West Kalimantan	—	—	1.0	1.1	—	—	1.7	2.1
Central Kalimantan	—	—	1.3	1.3	—	—	2.0	2.8
South Kalimantan	—	—	2.8	2.3	—	—	5.5	6.0
East Kalimantan	—	—	2.3	1.6	—	—	2.6	3.8
Central Sulawesi	—	—	1.9	1.5	—	—	2.5	3.1
South Sulawesi	—	—	1.7	1.5	—	—	4.0	4.4
South-east Sulawesi	—	—	0.9	1.0	—	—	3.0	3.6

Sources: Singapore: *Population Census of Malaya, 1947:* Tables 20 and 21; *Census of Population, Singapore, 1957:* Table 17; *Census of Population, Singapore, 1970:* Table 12; *Census of Population, Singapore, 1980,* Release No. 2, Demographic Characteristics: Table 40.
Malaysia: *Population Census of Malaya, 1947:* Tables 20 and 21; *Population Census of Malaya, 1957,* State Reports: Table 8A; *Population Census of Malaysia, 1970,* State Reports: Table 2.27; and *Population Census of Malaysia, 1980,* State Reports: Table 3.1.
Indonesia: *1971 Population Census,* Provincial Reports: Table 7; *1980 Population Census,* Provincial Reports, Table 3.

[a] 1971 in the case of Indonesia.
[b] The Malaysian data in both 1970 and 1980 combine the divorced with the permanently separated.
[c] Includes Federal Territory.
[d] Indonesian provinces with a minority of Muslims are not included, except in the total Indonesia figure.

have been married two, three, or four or more times is shown in Table 5.5. Precise interpretation of these data is impossible, because three different factors could have caused multiple marriages: remarriage after divorce, remarriage after widowhood, and polygamy. However, the main factor is almost certainly remarriage after divorce, for the following reasons: divorce more commonly breaks first marriages than does widowhood and is more commonly followed by remarriage;[1] and polygamy is much less common than are second marriages following divorce. Therefore the data in Table 5.5 are to a large extent an indirect reflection of the divorce situation. Certainly, the states with the greatest proportion of multiple marriages—Kelantan and Trengganu—are the states with the highest divorce rates, though they have the most polygamy and the highest rates of widowhood as well.

In Table 5.5, there are no major changes between 1970 and 1980, merely a general decline in the proportion with multiple marriages. Major changes would hardly have been expected, because most of those included in the two years were the same people, ten years older, plus people newly marrying since 1970, minus those who died since 1970. As expected, the substitution in the 1980 segment of the table of the cohort married since 1970 for those who died since 1970 lowers the proportion with multiple marriages, because this cohort reflects the much lower divorce, polygamy, and widowhood of more recent times.

Data on frequency of multiple marriages from the 1980 Population Census of Indonesia, specifically referring to Muslim women, are shown in Table 5.6. The advantage of these data is that they are disaggregated by interval since first marriage and education; they show, not surprisingly, a positive correlation between interval since first marriage and incidence of multiple marriage; so, too, do data from the 1973 Fertility–Mortality Survey, though they use age rather than interval since first marriage (Muliakusuma, 1976: Table V.1). Data for Malays in Peninsular Malaysia from the 1980 Population Census (not presented) also show a positive correlation between interval since first marriage and incidence of multiple marriage, though at every interval, multiple marriage is less than for Indonesian Muslims: for example, 5–9 years after marriage, 7 per cent of Malay females in Peninsular Malaysia have had two or more marriages, compared with 13 per cent among Indonesian Muslims; and 20–24 years after first marriage, 19 per cent have had two or more marriages in Peninsular Malaysia compared with 32 per cent in Indonesia.

What is not clear is the extent to which the relationship between interval since marriage and multiple marriage reflects the normal tendency for more multiple marriage among older people who have been 'at risk' of multiple marriage for longer, and the extent to which it is partly the result of a temporal trend towards less frequent multiple marriage. Such a trend would leave the younger age-groups with less multiple marriage once they reach the older ages.

Multiple marriage, which, as noted above, is mainly a result of divorce and remarriage, falls off markedly with rising education. For Indonesian Muslim women as a whole, 32 per cent of the uneducated have had

TABLE 5.5

Peninsular Malaysia: Proportion of Ever-married Malays Who Married More than Once, by State, 1970 and 1980

	Two or More Times		Three or More Times		Four or More Times	
	Males	Females	Males	Females	Males	Females
1970						
Kelantan	44.7	41.6	23.9	21.3	12.7	10.5
Trengganu	38.5	35.4	19.3	16.8	9.9	7.6
Kedah	28.4	23.1	11.5	8.3	5.1	3.1
Perlis	36.0	32.3	16.5	13.8	7.9	6.2
Pahang	27.4	22.9	10.9	8.5	5.0	3.4
Penang	19.1	15.4	6.3	4.2	2.4	1.2
Perak	20.1	14.2	6.9	3.9	2.8	1.3
Negri Sembilan	27.4	25.2	11.4	10.5	5.4	4.4
Selangor	15.1	12.0	4.7	3.1	1.8	0.9
Johore	17.0	12.2	4.9	2.7	1.8	0.7
Malacca	19.1	15.0	5.8	3.6	2.2	1.0
Towns >10,000	18.9	17.4	7.5	6.6	3.5	2.7
Small towns and rural areas	28.2	23.7	12.0	9.4	5.7	4.0
All Peninsular Malaysia	26.9	22.8	11.4	9.0	5.4	3.8

1980

Kelantan	34.3	30.8	n.a.	n.a.	n.a.
Trengganu	31.2	28.2	n.a.	n.a.	n.a.
Kedah	21.5	17.3	n.a.	n.a.	n.a.
Perlis	27.3	23.8	n.a.	n.a.	n.a.
Pahang	19.2	16.6	n.a.	n.a.	n.a.
Penang	13.2	10.8	n.a.	n.a.	n.a.
Perak	15.9	11.7	n.a.	n.a.	n.a.
Negri Sembilan	18.8	16.7	n.a.	n.a.	n.a.
Selangor	10.5	8.5	n.a.	n.a.	n.a.
Johore	12.6	9.7	n.a.	n.a.	n.a.
Malacca	13.8	10.0	n.a.	n.a.	n.a.
All Peninsular Malaysia	19.5	16.8	n.a.	n.a.	n.a.

Sources: Population Census of Malaysia, 1970, State Reports: Table 2.28; *Population Census of Malaysia, 1970,* General Report: Vol. 2, Table 4.27; and *Population Census of Malaysia, 1980,* State Reports: Table 3.2.

TABLE 5.6

Indonesia: Percentage Distribution of Number of Times Ever-married Muslim Females Had Married, by Interval since First Marriage and Level of Education, 1980

Interval since First Marriage and Education	No. of Marriages					Total
	1	2	3	4	5+	
0–4 years						
No education	93.1	5.7	0.8	0.2	0.2	100
Some primary	94.7	4.6	0.5	0.1	0.1	100
Primary	96.3	3.3	0.3	0.0	0.1	100
Secondary and above	98.5	1.4	0.1	0.0	0.1	100
All levels of education	95.3	4.1	0.4	0.1	0.1	100
5–9 years						
No education	83.3	13.1	2.6	0.6	0.4	100
Some primary	84.8	12.5	2.1	0.4	0.2	100
Primary	88.9	9.5	1.2	0.2	0.1	100
Secondary and above	95.2	4.3	0.3	0.1	0.1	100
All levels of education	86.6	11.1	1.8	0.4	0.2	100
10–14 years						
No education	74.5	18.2	5.0	1.5	0.9	100
Some primary	75.8	17.9	4.5	1.2	0.6	100
Primary	82.4	13.7	2.9	0.6	0.3	100
Secondary and above	92.2	6.8	0.8	0.2	0.2	100
All levels of education	78.3	16.1	4.0	1.1	0.6	100

15–19 years					
No education	69.0	20.8	6.6	2.1	1.5	100
Some primary	69.6	20.8	6.5	1.9	1.1	100
Primary	77.8	16.4	4.1	1.2	0.6	100
Secondary and above	89.2	9.0	1.4	0.3	0.1	100
All levels of education	72.1	19.3	5.8	1.7	1.1	100
20–24 years					
No education	66.3	22.0	7.6	2.4	1.7	100
Some primary	66.1	22.6	7.4	2.4	1.5	100
Primary	75.4	17.2	5.2	1.4	0.8	100
Secondary and above	87.0	10.0	2.1	0.5	0.3	100
All levels of education	68.2	21.1	7.0	2.2	1.4	100
25+ years					
No education	62.8	22.7	8.8	3.2	2.5	100
Some primary	60.9	22.9	9.6	3.7	2.9	100
Primary	73.7	17.2	5.8	1.9	1.4	100
Secondary and above	83.9	11.8	3.0	0.8	0.5	100
All levels of education	63.2	22.4	8.8	3.2	2.5	100
All intervals					
No education	67.8	20.5	7.3	2.5	1.9	100
Some primary	76.7	16.0	4.8	1.5	1.0	100
Primary	85.6	10.9	2.4	0.6	0.4	100
Secondary and above	93.4	5.5	0.8	0.2	0.1	100
All levels of education	74.9	16.7	5.4	1.8	1.3	100

Source: 1980 Population Census, data tapes.

more than one marriage, compared with less than 7 per cent of those with at least secondary education. With rapidly rising education over time, such a comparison is rather misleading, as the educated women will be concentrated in the shorter duration-since-first-marriage group. However, even when women in the same duration group are compared, substantial differences in multiple marriage according to education remain. For example, at a duration of 10–14 years since first marriage, almost 26 per cent of uneducated women have had more than one marriage, compared with 8 per cent of those with secondary education and above.

Table 5.7 shows the incidence of multiple marriage for Muslim women in Indonesia by province. Two provinces, West Java and West Sumatra, exceed the proportions of women with multiple marriages in Kelantan and Trengganu, and three others—Central Java, East Java, and West Nusa Tenggara—come close. Although it is not shown in

TABLE 5.7

Indonesia: Percentage of Ever-married Muslim Women Married
More than Once, by Province, 1980

	Married Two or More Times	Married Three or More Times
North Sulawesi	10.4	1.8
South Sulawesi	12.6	2.2
Central Sulawesi	14.9	3.4
South-east Sulawesi	14.0	2.7
East Kalimantan	13.6	3.2
South Kalimantan	22.1	6.7
West Kalimantan	9.6	1.9
Central Kalimantan	12.2	2.4
Jakarta	15.1	4.1
West Java	35.2	15.4
Central Java	27.0	8.1
Yogyakarta	17.6	3.7
East Java	26.1	7.9
Bali	15.8	4.4
West Nusa Tenggara	25.2	8.1
East Nusa Tenggara	10.0	1.4
Maluku	14.3	2.7
Aceh	12.5	2.8
North Sumatra	14.7	3.3
West Sumatra	34.5	15.2
Riau	18.1	5.5
Jambi	16.3	4.0
South Sumatra	12.4	2.6
Bengkulu	13.4	3.5
Lampung	19.7	5.3

Source: 1980 Population Census, data tapes.

Table 5.7, in almost every province, Christians are less likely to have had multiple marriages than are Muslims.

Divorce Rates

For the provinces of Indonesia, the states of Malaysia, and Singapore, data are available on divorces registered annually among the Muslim population.[2] Though there are some problems with the data, they are reliable enough to yield a picture of regional differences in divorce and trends in divorce over time provided that care is taken. This section will examine whether similar trends in divorce have characterized regions with traditionally high or low divorce rates, and compare divorce rates in different parts of the Malay world with those elsewhere in the Islamic world and in the West.

To set the scene, Table 5.8 shows general divorce rates (divorces per 1,000 population aged 15 and over) in various countries and regions since 1950. Three particularly striking aspects emerge: the very high divorce levels among some of the Malaysian states and in Java in the 1950s; the wide differences in divorce rates between different parts of the Islamic world; and the steady decline in divorce rates in the Malay world from the late 1950s onwards, in contrast with a steady rise throughout the Western world. These points require more detailed comment.

Because statistics on Muslim divorce in Malaysia are not available in summary form through any national statistical agency, they are not shown in the United Nations *Demographic Yearbook*, and therefore neither the exceptionally high divorce rates in earlier years nor the sharp decline in these rates in recent years is widely known internationally.[3] The traditional pattern of high divorce rates in parts of the Malay world is a complex one, and clearly something other than Islam must be invoked to explain it, because very wide differences in divorce rates characterized not only different parts of the Malay world but also different parts of the Islamic world as a whole. These differences were not explicable in terms of adherence or non-adherence to Islam or of degree of religiosity, however measured (see also Farid, 1987: 347). The highest divorce rates in Peninsular Malaysia were found in those states which were most backward economically and educationally, and where the influence of Islam was generally held to be strongest, but this correlation between the influence of Islam and the level of divorce rates did not hold more generally throughout the Malay world. Brunei, strongly Islamic and ruled by a Sultan in the tradition of the Malay states, had very low divorce rates: only one divorce for every ten marriages as far back as the 1960s, when divorce rates in many other parts of the Malay world were very high.[4] In Indonesia, Central and East Java are two of the provinces with the highest divorce rates, but the hold of Islam on much of their population was very weak. Divorce rates were obviously much higher in Kelantan, Trengganu, and Java than they are in Arab countries of the Middle East such as Iraq, Libya, Syria, Tunisia, and Egypt, with their varying degrees of Islamic orthodoxy and differing patterns of

TABLE 5.8

Various Countries and Regions: General Divorce Rates, 1950–1990

(Number of divorces per 1,000 population aged 15 and over)

	1950	1955	1960	1965	1970	1975	1980	1985	1990
Developed countries									
Australia	1.2	1.0	0.9	1.1	1.4	2.5	3.6	3.3	3.2
France	1.1	1.0	0.9	1.0	1.0	1.5	2.0[a]	2.5	2.4[b]
Germany (Federal Republic)	2.0	1.0	1.1	1.3	1.6	2.2	1.9	2.5	2.4[c]
England and Wales	0.9	0.8	0.7	1.0	1.5	3.2	3.8	4.0	3.7
United States	3.5	3.2	3.2	3.5	4.8	6.3	6.7	6.3	6.0
USSR	–	–	1.8[d]	2.2	3.7	4.2	4.7	4.5	–
19 developed countries[e]	–	–	1.8	2.1	3.1	4.0	4.4[f]	4.3	4.2
Muslim countries									
Egypt	4.8	4.1	4.3	3.9	3.6	3.6	2.7	2.8	–
Iran	2.8	2.5	2.1	1.8	1.1	0.9	1.0	1.4[g]	1.2[h]
Iraq	0.9	0.6	0.6	0.6	0.7	1.2	–	–	–
Libya	–	–	–	2.8	3.6	3.6	2.2	–	1.4[b]
Tunisia	–	–	1.7[i]	1.9	1.5	1.7	1.9	1.4	2.6[j]
Syria	1.2	1.1	1.4	1.2	1.1	1.2	1.1	1.2	1.3
Turkey	0.6	0.7	0.7	0.7	0.5	0.5	0.6	0.6	0.8[j]
Malay population									
Brunei	–	–	0.7	0.8	0.7	0.9	0.8[k]	1.2	–

Peninsular Malaysia									
Malay population	20.3	14.9	10.0[l]	7.4	6.1	5.6[m]	3.9	2.8	—
Kelantan	43.1	28.4	18.5	15.8	12.4	11.6	8.6	2.9	—
Trengganu	30.6	30.4	18.1	13.0	9.5	8.3	6.5	5.8	—
Kedah	21.7	14.0	–	7.0	5.6	6.7	5.1	3.4	—
Selangor	9.8	6.9	5.3	3.6	–	–	1.9	2.6	—
Malacca	10.7	8.9	7.1	2.8	–	–	1.7	1.7	—
Johore	8.4	6.0	4.1	3.3	2.7	2.6	2.1	2.2	—
Singapore									
Malays	18.2	12.5	5.5	2.6	1.3	1.5	2.2	2.7	3.6
Indonesia									
Muslim population	15.1	16.7	13.5	11.0	5.2	4.6	2.6	1.5	1.1
Java	—	20.9[n]	—	13.7	6.8	6.0	3.3	1.9	1.4
West Java	—	24.4[n]	—	17.7	7.1	7.8	3.0	1.7	1.1
East Java	—	21.7[n]	—	14.8	8.0	4.8	3.4	2.7	1.7
Central Java–Yogyakarta	—	18.5[n]	—	12.5	6.6	5.8	3.9	1.7	1.7
Jakarta	—	—	—	7.1	2.4	1.1	1.2	0.7	0.6
South Kalimantan	—	—	—	6.9	2.5	3.6	2.9	1.6	1.2
Aceh	—	—	—	5.2	1.5	1.6	0.8	0.9	0.6

Sources: Jones (1981: 262); United Nations (1991); United Nations *Demographic Yearbook*, various years; BPS, *Statistik Indonesia, 1984–85*; Department of Statistics, Singapore (1988); and unpublished Muslim marriage data for Malaysia from Pusat Penyelidikan Islam.

[a] 1979.
[b] 1988.
[c] 1989.
[d] 1961.
[e] United States, USSR, Hungary, Denmark, Czechoslovakia, East Germany, West Germany, England, Wales, Australia, Sweden, Austria, Poland, Nether-lands, Belgium, Portugal, Switzerland, France, and Canada.
[f] Excluding Portugal.
[g] 1984.
[h] 1987.
[i] 1961.
[j] 1989.
[k] 1981.
[l] Excludes Kedah and Perlis.
[m] 1973.
[n] 1953.

government. In other Middle Eastern countries such as Saudi Arabia and the Gulf states, no statistics are available. Morocco appears to have the highest divorce rate among Arab countries: 20 per cent of marriages are broken within 20 years (Farid, 1987); but even this is well below the rate traditionally found in many parts of the Malay world.[5]

The general divorce rate for the Malay population of Peninsular Malaysia began the 1950s above that for the Muslim population in Indonesia, but declines were faster in Malaysia, with the result that by the early 1960s the Indonesian rate was higher. Between 1965 and 1970, however, the Indonesian rate fell precipitously, and from 1970 until the present, Indonesian divorce rates have remained below those of the Malays, although both have declined steadily. In the 1950s and 1960s there was little to pick between Kelantan, Trengganu, and West Java at the top end of the divorce rate spectrum, though by the 1970s Kelantan and Trengganu had a clear lead.

What is striking in Table 5.8 is the universality of the decline in divorce rates throughout the Malay world, in contrast to the recent sharp rise in divorce rates in the West. In the late 1970s, the trend lines crossed: divorce rates among European and European-derived populations had doubled since 1960, whereas divorce rates among Muslims in Indonesia and Malaysia had dropped to approximately one-third of their 1960 figure over the same period. Divorce rates among Peninsular Malaysian Malays and Indonesian Muslims were already lower than those in the United States, the USSR, or England and Wales. The rise in European divorce rates was slackening by this time, but continuing declines in divorce rates in the Malay world had lowered these rates to less than half the European figure by 1985. The general divorce rate in the United States by this time exceeded even that in Kelantan. Admittedly, general divorce rates overstate the rate of divorce among the 'eligible' (currently married) population in Western countries as compared with Malay populations, because a higher proportion of young adults remain unmarried in the West.[6] Even so, the trends are clear and reflect the rather curious fact that whereas 'Westernization' is widely held to lower the divorce rates among the Malays, in the 1960s and 1970s the divorce rates among the 'model' Western populations moved rapidly toward the levels from which the Malay populations had just descended.

It is noteworthy that by the early 1980s, not only were divorce rates among Malay populations of Indonesia and Malaysia below those of Western countries, but also they were no longer the highest rates in the Muslim world. They were exceeded by divorce rates in Egypt and Libya, countries whose divorce rates had already exceeded those of Singapore Malays since the mid-1960s and of Brunei Malays since much earlier still.

Although the Western experience of rising divorce rates in recent decades predisposes many Western demographers and commentators to expect that increasing urbanization and industrialization will raise divorce rates generally throughout the world, a more sophisticated approach to the issue was that of Goode (1963: Chapters 10–11; see also

Goode, 1993: Chapter 8). He drew attention to the fact that divorce rates were declining in some urban regions, and that rates were high in some rural areas. Whether such rates rose or fell under the impact of industrialization would depend on where they stood beforehand, under the traditional system. Where divorce rates were high under traditional systems, industrialization would be likely to lead to declining divorce rates because the modernizing forces would begin to undermine the traditional ones that generated high divorce rates, although eventually the rates were likely to rise again. The relevance of Goode's argument to Islamic South-East Asia, where the traditional system generated high divorce rates, is obvious.

The author has prepared tables on time trends in divorce in certain regions and provinces of Indonesia, and for Muslims in the states of Peninsular Malaysia. These are not presented here for reasons of space, although a long time series of such data has never before been available to researchers. Here some of the key findings from these detailed tables will be summarized, and maps presented which show clearly the geographical patterns of high divorce rates within Peninsular Malaysia and Indonesia.

Figure 5.1 shows the trends among Indonesian Muslims since 1950 in three measures: the general divorce rate; the general marriage rate; and the number of divorces per 100 marriages each year. In each case, divorces are net of reconciliations (*rujuk*) to ensure that they only include divorces which effectively terminate the marriage. First, a word about the strengths and weaknesses of different measures of divorce.

Ideally, divorce rates should relate the number of divorces to the

FIGURE 5.1

Indonesian Muslims: Trends in General Marriage and Divorce Rates and in Ratio of Divorces to Marriages, 1950–1985

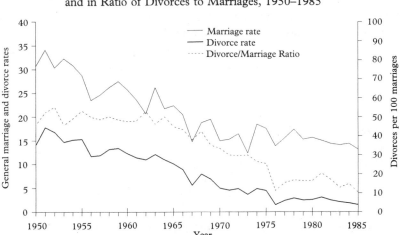

Source: Computed from data on Muslim marriages and divorces from *Statistik Indonesia*, various years; denominators for general divorce rates interpolated or extrapolated from data on Muslim population aged 15+ in population censuses.
Note: Divorces are *talak* net of *rujuk* (reconciliations).

population 'at risk' of divorcing, i.e. the currently married population. However, estimates of this population are hard to obtain, especially in earlier years. Instead, the General Divorce Rate is presented. This refines the Crude Divorce Rate (which relates divorces to the total population) by restricting the denominator to the population who in terms of age are roughly 'at risk' of divorcing (i.e. aged 15 and over). Actually, in Indonesia, particularly in earlier years, divorces frequently did occur below the age of 15, and a case could be made for setting the denominator of the General Divorce Rate as the population aged 13 and over.[7] If this were done, the General Divorce Rate in the 1980s would be slightly higher relative to earlier years, but not enough to make a major difference to the trends shown in Figure 5.1.[8] And the change in denominator would have the disadvantage of precluding direct international comparisons, since the age-group 15 and over is the accepted denominator for General Divorce Rates.

The ratio of divorces to marriages occurring in the same year is in some ways preferable to and in some ways inferior to the General Divorce Rate. It is preferable in that most divorces occur in the few years following the marriage, and therefore it is somewhat unrealistic to relate divorces to the total stock of adults, including the middle-aged and elderly. On the other hand, only something like one-fifth of divorces occur in the first year of marriage, and therefore the appropriate denominator is broader than the population marrying in the same year as the divorce took place. However, particularly for a time series, the ratio of divorces to marriages in the same year is quite a good indicator of the incidence of divorce; even better, perhaps, if smoothed by taking a three-year moving average or by relating divorces to marriages in the three previous years.

Both the general divorce rate and the ratio of divorces to marriages for Muslims in Indonesia show a steady downward trend, but the timing of this trend and the extent of the decline in different periods differ considerably. The trends may be summarized as follows:

	General Divorce Rate	Ratio of Divorces to Marriages
1950s	24 per cent decline	No change
1960s	59 per cent decline	21 per cent decline
1970s	51 per cent decline	60 per cent decline
1980s	Some further decline	Some further decline

The implications are very different. The ratio of divorces to marriages suggests that although a sizeable decline in divorce occurred in the 1960s, a really major decline did not occur until the 1970s, whereas the general divorce rate shows a substantial decline in the 1950s, accelerating in the 1960s and remaining very rapid in the 1970s. How can these differences be explained?

A clue is provided by the trend in the general marriage rate, which fell from over 30 per 1,000 in the early 1950s to much lower levels (between 25 and 15 per 1,000) in the 1960s, thus paralleling fairly closely the fall in the general divorce rate and causing the ratio of divorces to marriages to remain essentially unchanged until the mid-1960s. The fact that this happened while the general divorce rate was declining rapidly suggests that the decline in the marriage rate was intimately linked to the decline in the divorce rate, not only causally, that is, fewer marriages mean fewer divorces in the early years of those marriages, but also consequentially, that is, frequent divorce in the earlier years meant frequent remarriage, thus raising the overall marriage rate. Indeed, it is hard to imagine how such high marriage and divorce rates could have been observed in the 1950s unless some people were marrying, divorcing, subsequently marrying, and divorcing again within one year.

On this question, the 1980 Indonesian Population Census data on the number of times ever-married Muslim women married show that for those with long durations since their first marriage (those who would have been marrying around the late 1950s and early 1960s), around 32–36 per cent had married more than once and 11–14 per cent had married at least three times (Table 5.6). In Peninsular Malaysia, among Malay women of comparable durations in 1980, around 19–27 per cent had married more than once. These lower proportions no doubt reflect both the lower incidence of widowhood in Malaysia and the fact that the high-divorce provinces in Indonesia contain a high proportion of the population, whereas in Malaysia the high-divorce states contain a relatively small proportion of the population. In both countries, the incidence of multiple marriages was probably higher in earlier times. Occasional reports may be found in both countries of men who had married 100 or more times (*Kompas*, 16 September 1979, p. 7), but these are of curiosity value and the key question is whether many women were marrying four or more times. The answer is that not many were: even among the older Indonesian respondents, only 4–6 per cent.

Given that most second marriages occurred while women were still quite young, these percentages suggest that multiple marriages were frequent enough to raise the number of marriages occurring in any given year about 40 per cent above the number that would have occurred had no divorces been taking place; and these additional marriages would have resulted in some additional divorces as well. However, it appears unlikely that very many people would have married and divorced twice within the one year.

Figure 5.2 shows the trends in general divorce rates amongst Muslims in a number of states of Peninsular Malaysia for which statistics are available.[9] Divorces are net of *rujuk*, which are reconciliations between husband and wife after one *talak* divorce has been officially registered; so the figure reflects only those divorces which effectively and permanently terminate the marriage.[10] To smooth annual fluctuations and highlight the trend the figures are presented in the form of a three-year moving average.

FIGURE 5.2

Malaysia and Singapore (Muslims): General Divorce Rates, 1951–1987

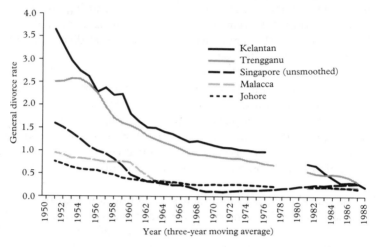

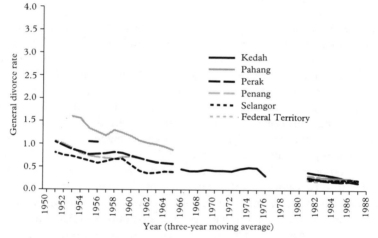

Sources: As for Table 5.8.

Note: Number of divorces per 1,000 population aged 15 and above (divorces are *talak* net of *rujuk*).

The sharpest decline in divorce rates in Kelantan appears to have occurred between the end of World War II and the mid-1950s, but there was another period of sharp decline during the early 1960s. In Trengganu, by contrast, the decline did not begin until the late 1950s. In Malacca and Johore, the decline (starting from much lower initial divorce levels) was a steady one, with an acceleration in Malacca during the early 1960s. In Singapore, a sharp decline occurred between 1959 and 1961, as a result of new legislation.[11] Historically, divorce rates among Singapore Muslims had been much higher than in Malacca or Johore, but by 1961 they had fallen below them and have remained lower ever since.

Historical Trends before the 1950s

It has already been noted (in Chapter 1) that high divorce rates have apparently characterized the Malay world for many centuries. But coming to more recent times, had the very high (though regionally variable) divorce rates in the Malay world in the 1950s previously been higher still, or did the 1950s represent merely the continuation of decades or centuries of high divorce rates? This question cannot be answered definitively, as data are not available before the 1950s for most areas.[12] However, it is reasonable to assume that divorce rates recorded for the 1950s did not differ very much from those earlier in the century. For one thing, they were so high in the 1950s that it would be hard to imagine much higher rates. For another, the changes believed to have played a major role in the decline in divorce rates after the 1950s— increasing female education, rising age at marriage, and increasing self-arrangement of marriage—had not got under way before the 1950s.

For Java, some important data on divorce are available back to the early part of the eighteenth century, though they come from a restricted number of residencies, most of them located in western and southern Central Java (Boomgaard, 1989: 145–6). These data show a consistently high ratio of divorces to marriages in the Priangan between 1830 and 1880, ranging from 60 to 114 per cent. Based on these non-representative data, the rate of divorces per 100 marriages in Java before 1860 ranged between 40 and 45 per cent (25 and 30 per cent if the Priangan is disregarded) and between 50 and 55 per cent after 1860 (40–45 per cent without the Priangan).

Around 1930, the ratio of divorces to marriages (*talak–nikah*) in Java–Madura was over 50 per cent: 53 per cent in 1929, 55 per cent in 1930, and 53 per cent in 1931 (Vreede-de Stuers, 1960: 129). This had not altered much by the early 1950s. For the highest-divorce area of Sumatra, West Sumatra, there is qualitative evidence that this had been the situation as far back as the 1920s at least: 'Among ... the Minangkabau, there is no bride-price and divorce is very frequent and can be obtained at will by either party.' (Loeb, 1972: 68.)

In Singapore, the ratio of Muslim divorces to marriages in the 1920s, 1930s, and 1940s did not differ very much from the ratio in the first half of the 1950s—around 55 divorces per 100 marriages (Saw, 1989: Table 2). Data for Malacca for the 1930s and 1940s (Tsubouchi, 1976: Table 1) similarly show a ratio of divorces to marriages, 35.4 per 100 marriages, which differs only slightly from the figure of 31.5 for the first half of the 1950s. However, in view of the earlier-noted possibility of divorce rates declining while divorce–marriage ratios remain constant, it is necessary to calculate general divorce rates for Singapore and Malacca in these earlier periods. When this is done, it is clear that the general divorce rate in Singapore had declined substantially between 1931 and 1952, from 28 to 18 per 1,000 population aged 15 and over, whereas in Malacca the rate, which had always been much lower than in Singapore, was unchanged at 10.[13] In both Singapore and Malacca there was a brief upsurge in divorces at the end of World War II, but by 1947 the pattern had settled back to its longer-term trend.

To sum up the evidence of the last two pages, the high levels of divorce prevailing in Islamic South-East Asia in the early 1950s were a continuation of a situation which in Java at least can be traced back to the early nineteenth century. On the whole, divorce rates do not appear to have changed much between the 1920s–1930s and the 1950s, although the general divorce rate among Muslims in Singapore did register a substantial decline over this period.

Geographic Differences in Frequency of Divorce

Maps 5.1 and 5.2 show detailed geographic differences in frequency of divorce among Malays in Peninsular Malaysia and in Java in periods for which data are available. The measure used is the number of divorces (net of *rujuk*) per 100 marriages, not because this is the ideal measure, but because data are more readily available for this measure. Although imperfect, the measure should give a reasonable picture of regional differentials; divorces and marriages are averaged over a number of years, and given that most divorces occur in the first few years of marriage, this goes some way towards relating divorces to the appropriate denominator.

Map 5.1 shows this divorce rate among Malays in Peninsular Malaysia in two periods, 1950–7 and 1972–6. Data are shown at the district level in Kelantan, Trengganu, Johore, Kedah, and Negri Sembilan, and for the state as a whole in cases where district-level data were not available. It should be noted that the data for certain districts bordering Thailand may be distorted by the practice of registering marriages over the border, presumably mainly in cases of polygamy involving irregularities that might be picked up by the local Malaysian officials.[14] There is simply no evidence of how frequent this practice is or has been in the past, but it seems unlikely to be a major factor in distorting the evidence summarized in the map. Except in cases where the marriage had been registered over the border, there was little incentive to register divorces over the border, as they were so readily obtained in the Malaysian states bordering Thailand.

The incidence of divorce differed widely by region. The north-east, Kelantan and Trengganu, was a high-divorce region, and Pahang's divorce rates were not much lower. Perlis and Kedah were also relatively high-divorce areas. Moving south into Malacca and Johore, rates were far lower, though in Singapore they were again somewhat higher. Interdistrict variation within states tended to be less marked than inter-state variation, probably reflecting to some extent state differences in divorce registration procedures.

Indonesia in the mid-1960s was characterized by very high Muslim divorce rates throughout Java, and by lower rates everywhere else. West Java had the highest rate of all, 59.5 divorces for every 100 marriages, but East and Central Java were also above 50. South Kalimantan led

Peninsular Malaysia: Ratio of Divorces (Net of Revocations) to Marriages, by States and
(in Some Cases) Districts, 1950–1957 and 1972–1976

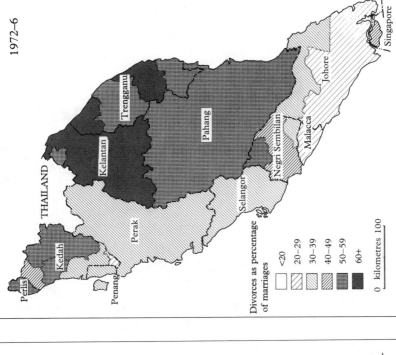

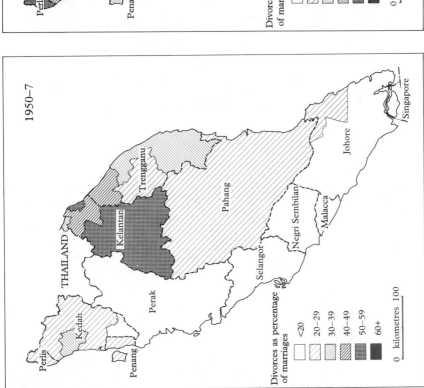

Sources: Computed from data in Gordon (1964), Jones (1981), and a variety of other sources.

MAP 5.2

Java: Ratio of Divorces (Net of Revocations) to Marriages, by *Kabupaten* and *Kotamadya*, 1969–1971, 1977–1979, and 1985–1987

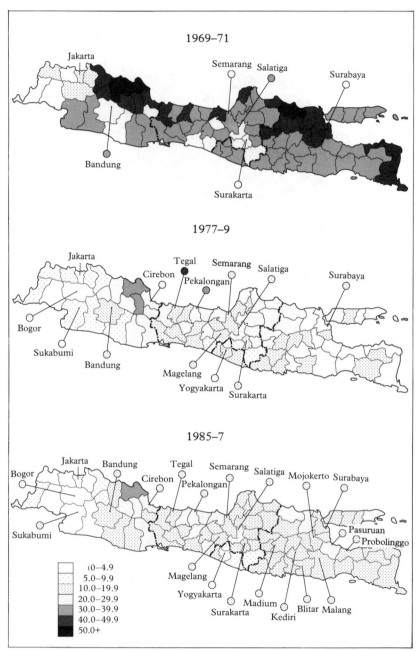

Sources: Calculated from data in *Jawa Barat dalam Angka*, *Jawa Tengah dalam Angka*, *Jawa Timur dalam Angka*, *DKI Jakarta dalam Angka*, and *DKI Yogyakarta dalam Angka*, various years.

the outer island provinces with 47.5 divorces per 100 marriages, followed by West Sumatra, Aceh, and West Nusa Tenggara, all just below 40. Sulawesi had the lowest Muslim divorce rates of major outer island regions.

By the early 1980s, divorce rates had fallen everywhere in Malaysia and Indonesia, but the regional differentials remained almost unchanged. In Indonesia, Central and East Java were now slightly ahead of West Java, South Kalimantan remained in fourth position, and West Sumatra in fifth. However, Aceh and West Nusa Tenggara had slipped in the divorce rankings. By 1985–6, Central and East Java maintained their slight lead over West Java and South Kalimantan maintained its fourth-place ranking. Bengkulu was now slightly ahead of West Sumatra. Indonesian divorce rates appeared to have fallen more sharply than for the Malaysian Malays: Malay divorce rates in a number of Malaysian states were higher than those in the highest-divorce provinces of Indonesia.

In Peninsular Malaysia, in the early 1980s, Kelantan and Trengganu still maintained the highest divorce rates, but they had been joined by the Federal Territory. By the years 1986–8 (using average figures), some surprising changes in ranking had occurred. The Federal Territory had run ahead of Kelantan, as had Pahang, Penang, and Perlis. Divorce rates overall, of course, were much lower than in the 1950s, but they were on the rise again. In this situation of relatively low divorce rates, there was no longer a clear-cut excess of divorce in the poorer, Malay-dominated states, and the dynamics of change had altered. The rise in both Malay and non-Malay divorce rates in Singapore, Kuala Lumpur, and Penang suggest that some of the same pressures toward divorce observable in Western societies were also affecting Malays in these booming cities.[15] This will be discussed in Chapter 6.

For Java, Map 5.2 shows frequency of divorce at the *kabupaten* level, for 1969–71, 1977–9, and 1985–7. Unfortunately the data are not available for as early a period as they are for Peninsular Malaysia. The divorce rates differed very sharply indeed by region. In the late 1960s, the rates were very high in the north coastal strip of West Java east of Krawang, and in the eastern parts of the Priangan region. With a few exceptions, high divorce rates continued along the entire northern coastal strip of Java to Surabaya in the east, with a substantial region of high divorce in East Java from Ngawi through Tuban to Sidarjo and Jombang. By contrast, divorce was much less frequent in the Banten region in the far west, through to Jakarta and its environs. It is not easy to find explanations based on differences in religiosity, educational or economic differences. By the late 1970s, the decline in divorce rates had been very pronounced, and there was a further decline by the late 1980s. However, regional differentials in divorce rates remained essentially intact during this period of rapid decline; the highest divorce rates were still centred on Indramayu and neighbouring *kabupaten* just west of the Central Java border, and on much of the northern coastal areas of Central and East Java. The low-divorce areas grew to encompass most of West Java west of a line from Bandung to Krawang, and parts of Central Java–Yogyakarta around Yogyakarta, Solo, and Salatiga.

Cohort Trends in Divorce Rates

From the Indonesian Fertility–Mortality Survey of 1973, there is excellent information on cohort trends in divorce. This has been thoroughly reported on by Muliakusuma (1976), but as this monograph, published in Indonesian, was not widely distributed, the data presented there are not well known. Some of the information is therefore reproduced here.

Table 5.9 shows the cumulative percentage of women from three marriage cohorts whose marriages ended in divorce within given time intervals. The information is presented separately for the main provinces and regions covered in the survey. The patterns of divorce following marriage, the interregional differences, urban–rural differences, and time trends revealed by these data will be discussed in turn.

The pattern of divorce was clearly one in which the relative risk of divorce was greatest in the early period of the marriage, the highest risk being in the first three years of marriage. Given the frequency of non-consummation of marriage reported in Java (see Chapter 3), it is surprising that in the provinces of Java there is no clear evidence in Table 5.9 of more frequent divorce during the first year of marriage than during the second and third years. In fact, in urban West and Central Java and rural Central Java, in the 1940–9 marriage cohort, divorce was apparently more common in the second and third years of marriage than in the first year, and in some subsequent cohorts the same pattern prevailed. However, in all cases except urban Sumatra, the divorce rate was clearly less in years beyond the third year of marriage than in the first three years, and the rate tended to decline progressively the longer couples had been married.

West Java clearly had the highest divorce rates, with little between Central and East Java in second place. Divorce rates for the younger cohorts in Sumatra were well below those in Central and East Java, although they roughly equalled them in the 1940–9 marriage cohort. Given that Sumatra has a substantial Christian population with lower divorce rates, and that there are wide interprovincial differences, this implies that divorce rates were very high in some Sumatran provinces at that time. Indeed, a provincial breakdown for Sumatra (which suffers from a degree of unreliability because the sampling design of the Fertility–Mortality Survey only aimed at representativeness at the island, not the provincial level)[16] shows that the proportion of marriages broken by divorce within 15 years was higher in West Sumatra (66 per cent in rural areas) than in any province of Java (Al Hadar, 1977: 65). Unfortunately, there are no divorce registration data from the 1940s and early 1950s to use as a cross-check on these findings.

Within each region, divorce rates in rural areas exceeded those in urban areas, though not always by very much. The one exception was the 1940–9 marriage cohort in West Java, where after a slower start,

TABLE 5.9

Indonesia: Cumulative Percentage of First Marriages Ending in Divorce of Various Marriage Cohorts, by Years since Marriage, 1973

Years since Marriage	Cumulative Percentages Divorced among Marriage Cohorts					
	1940–9		1950–9		1960–9	
	Urban	Rural	Urban	Rural	Urban	Rural
West Java						
<1	7	13	4	10	3	8
<3	28	28	16	23	10	20
<5	36	34	20	28	—[a]	—[a]
<10	41	39	22	33	—[a]	—[a]
<20	46	43	—[a]	—[a]	—[a]	—[a]
Central Java						
<1	3	6	5	6	2	5
<3	14	19	12	17	9	13
<5	17	23	16	21	—[a]	—[a]
<10	20	26	21	25	—[a]	—[a]
<20	25	29	—[a]	—[a]	—[a]	—[a]

(continued)

TABLE 5.9 *(continued)*

Cumulative Percentages Divorced among Marriage Cohorts

Years since Marriage	1940–9		1950–9		1960–9	
	Urban	Rural	Urban	Rural	Urban	Rural
East Java						
<1	5	6	3	7	4	6
<3	11	17	10	17	8	15
<5	13	21	14	20	—[a]	—[a]
<10	18	25	19	24	—[a]	—[a]
<20	21	28	—[a]	—[a]	—[a]	—[a]
Sumatra						
<1	2	7	1	4	1	4
<3	7	19	5	12	4	10
<5	13	22	9	15	—[a]	—[a]
<10	18	28	11	18	—[a]	—[a]
<20	20	32	—[a]	—[a]	—[a]	—[a]
Sulawesi						
<1	2	1	1	2	1	2
<3	6	7	5	7	3	5
<5	9	10	8	10	—[a]	—[a]
<10	12	13	12	13	—[a]	—[a]
<20	14	15	—[a]	—[a]	—[a]	—[a]

Source: Muliakusuma (1976: Table IV.2).

[a]Biased because not all women from this marriage cohort had reached this duration since marriage at the time of the survey.

the cumulative percentages divorced in urban areas within 5 years of marriage exceeded those in rural areas. Divorce rates for this cohort in urban West Java were much above urban rates in the other regions, a differential which, however, largely disappeared among marriage cohorts of the 1950s and 1960s.

The ranking of provinces by divorce rates and the tendency for the rates to be higher in rural than in urban areas suggests an association between very young ages at marriage and divorce. It is in rural areas and in West, Central, and East Java that the ages at marriage are lowest and the divorce rates highest.

As far as trends are concerned, the steady decline in divorce over time is seen in Table 5.9 as well as in Figures 5.3–5.6. With few exceptions, in all these regions, and in both rural and urban areas, there was a steady decline in the proportions divorced within different intervals since first marriage from earlier to more recent marriage cohorts. In most regions, however, the decline was sharper in urban than in rural areas; for example, the proportion divorced within three years of marriage in urban West Java fell from 28 per cent to 10 per cent between the 1940–9 and 1960–9 birth cohorts, whereas the corresponding decline in rural areas was only from 28 to 20 per cent. In East Java, the corresponding declines were from 11 to 8 per cent in urban areas and from 17 to 15 per cent in rural areas.

The 1976 Indonesian Fertility Survey also lends itself to cohort analysis of divorce in Java. Guest (1991) has produced life table estimates of the length of time (in months) which elapsed before certain percentages of marriages were broken by divorce. This study showed that divorce was more frequent and more rapid in West Java than elsewhere in Java and (a closely related point) more frequent and more rapid among the Sundanese than among the Javanese (see Table 5.10). Thus in West Java, it took only 26 months for 25 per cent of marriages to have been broken by divorce, whereas in Central Java it took 36 months, in East Java 48 months, in Jakarta 104 months, and in Yogyakarta, 120 months—10 years.

Guest's analysis also shows clearly the much higher divorce rates of young marriages and the effect of education in lowering divorce. A temporal decline in divorce is also apparent, but perhaps not as pronounced as would have been expected on the basis of trends in General Divorce Rates discussed earlier. Moreover, hazard model analysis introducing different variables sequentially shows that the temporal effect is largely captured by changing ages at marriage and altered educational composition. Of course, this does not mean that the passage of time was not of crucial importance in allowing changes in attitudes and perceptions that led to older marriage and more education of females.

It is worth mentioning here the limited information for Sabah on dissolution of marriage by divorce within given durations of marriage, from the Population and Family Survey in Sabah, 1989. Of the three predominantly Muslim groups in Sabah, the Bajau, Indonesians, and Filipinos, the Bajau had relatively low divorce (6.5 per cent of all first

FIGURE 5.3

West Java: Cumulative Percentages of First Marriages Ending in Divorce by Duration of Marriage of Marriage Cohorts, 1940–1969

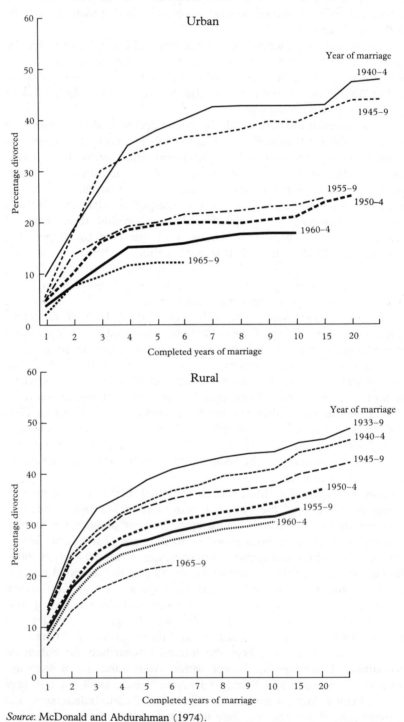

Source: McDonald and Abdurahman (1974).

FIGURE 5.4

Central Java: Cumulative Percentages of First Marriages Ending in Divorce
within Various Intervals since Marriage of Marriage Cohorts, 1933–1973

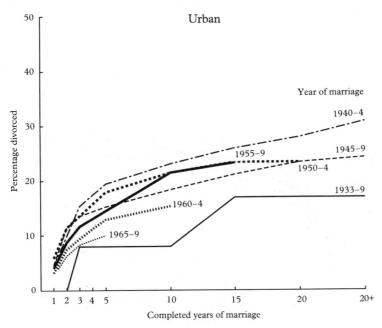

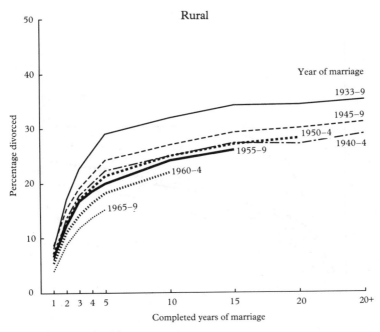

Source: Muliakusuma (1976).

FIGURE 5.5

East Java: Cumulative Percentages of First Marriages Ending in Divorce within Various Intervals since Marriage of Marriage Cohorts, 1933–1973

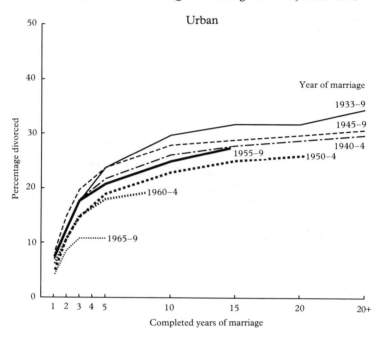

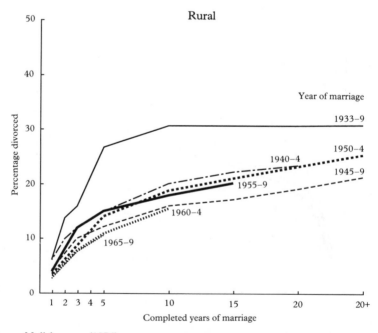

Source: Muliakusuma (1976).

FIGURE 5.6

Sumatra: Cumulative Percentages of First Marriages Ending in Divorce within
Various Intervals since Marriage of Marriage Cohorts, 1933–1973

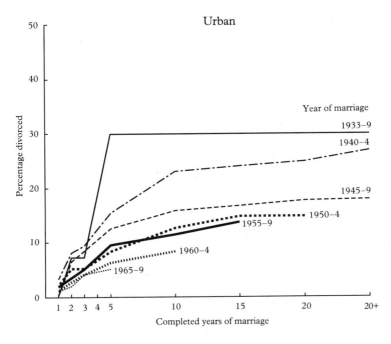

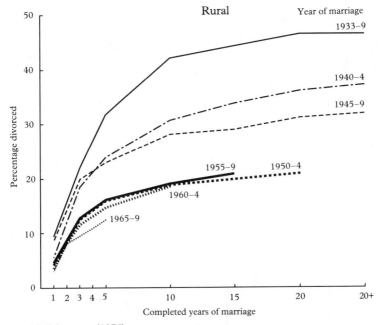

Source: Muliakusuma (1976).

TABLE 5.10

Java–Bali: Life Table Estimates of Length of Marriages (in Months) of Women Aged Less than 50, at the Point Where 5, 10, 15, 25, and 40 Per Cent of Marriages Had Ended through Divorce or Separation, by Demographic and Socio-economic Variables, First and Higher-order Marriages Shown Separately

	Percentage of Marriages Ended									
	First Marriages					Second and Higher-order Marriages				
Variables	5	10	15	25	40	5	10	15	25	40
Age at marriage										
Less than 15	4	8	12	23	80	2	4	6	10	28
15–16	5	10	17	36	300	2	4	7	16	84
17–18	7	15	30	100	—[a]	3	7	10	23	144
19–20	17	30	48	248	—[a]	4	8	15	33	284
21 or more	7	23	60	248	—[a]	5	10	16	44	204
Year of marriage										
1950 or before	5	10	15	31	192	2	4	7	15	44
1951–5	5	10	16	36	268	4	7	10	20	96
1956–60	6	11	17	36	—[a]	3	6	9	25	188
1961–5	6	11	17	36	—[a]	4	8	11	30	120
1966–70	5	12	21	60	—[a]	3	8	12	36	—[a]
1971–6	5	10	19	40	—[a]	3	6	11	29	—[a]
Birth in marriage										
Yes	44	76	156	—[a]	—[a]	26	60	112	—[a]	—[a]
No	2	4	5	8	14	2	3	4	8	14

Province of current residence									
Jakarta	9	19	36	104	—[a]	5	10	15	30	128
West Java	4	8	12	26	112	3	5	7	14	48
Central Java	6	11	17	36	—[a]	4	8	13	36	—[a]
Yogyakarta	10	18	30	120	—[a]	—[b]	—[b]	—[b]	—[b]	—[b]
East Java	6	12	18	48	—[a]	3	8	13	40	192
Bali	68	—[a]	—[a]	—[a]	—[a]	—[b]	—[b]	—[b]	—[b]	—[b]
Type of area of residence									
Urban	8	16	30	80	—[a]	5	10	16	40	192
Rural	5	10	16	36	268	3	6	10	23	136
Ethnicity									
Indonesian	12	26	48	160	—[a]	5	11	15	30	184
Sundanese	4	8	12	25	100	3	5	8	17	52
Javanese	5	11	17	36	—[a]	3	7	11	30	204
Madurese	7	13	19	60	—[a]	4	9	11	33	224
Balinese	76	—[a]	—[a]	—[a]	—[a]	—[b]	—[b]	—[b]	—[b]	—[b]
Other	13	28	48	200	—[a]	—[b]	—[b]	—[b]	—[b]	—[b]
Education									
None	5	10	16	35	268	3	7	10	23	144
Incomplete primary	4	8	14	31	164	3	6	9	24	84
Complete primary	6	18	27	92	—[a]	3	9	13	44	308
High school or above	18	56	116	—[a]	—[a]	—[b]	—[b]	—[b]	—[b]	—[b]
Work status before marriage									
Family employed	5	10	17	36	—[a]	3	8	14	52	—[a]
Self-employed	7	12	22	64	—[a]	6	10	17	44	—[a]
Employed other	4	9	16	36	268	3	6	9	22	176
Not in labour force	5	11	17	40	300	3	6	10	21	80

Source: Guest (1991: Table 2).

Note: Life Tables constructed with one-month intervals for first 36 months and four-month intervals thereafter.

[a] Percentage experiencing event not reached at the end of 30 years.
[b] Less than 100 observations.

marriages of sampled women broken by divorce, a figure slightly below that for the Kadazan and the Dusun), but Indonesians (16.4 per cent) and Filipinos (11.3 per cent) were much higher. On the whole, these differences persisted when controlled by years since first marriage.

Characteristics of Couples Who Divorced

The attempt to understand the reasons for the very high divorce rates in the 1950s and 1960s in Java, South Kalimantan, and the East Coast states of Peninsular Malaysia, and the lower rates among some of the other Malay populations (to be discussed in Chapter 6) requires a base of information about the characteristics of couples who divorced. Some useful data on characteristics of couples registering their divorce were collected in West Java, and will be presented here. But for most regions, the information was not available in systematic form, and had to be gleaned from a variety of sources.

Anthropological studies in the high-divorce areas have something to say about a number of aspects of divorce, and information is also available from divorce registration and from surveys. Some of the key information required is:

(a) Who initiated the divorce?
(b) How soon after marriage did divorce occur?
(c) Had children normally been born to the marriage before divorce occurred?
(d) Were second and higher-order marriages less or more likely to end in divorce?
(e) Was divorce more common among the poorer and less educated?
(f) Did divorce more commonly occur to polygamous or to non-polygamous marriages?

Other aspects of a more attitudinal kind, such as the stated reason for divorce, will be left for consideration in the next chapter.

Initiation of Divorce

The husband's unfettered right to dispose of his wife through a *talak* divorce is a major target of criticism of Islamic marriage laws, and a major focus of reform in many Muslim countries. Yet comment in the West on Islamic divorce frequently reveals ignorance both of the various avenues open to a wife who wants a divorce (see Chapter 2) and of the frequency of female instigation of a *talak* divorce. The reason for this ignorance is certainly not that female instigation of divorce is something new in the region. Raffles, writing on Java in the early nineteenth century, observed that 'a woman may at any time, when dissatisfied with her husband, demand a dissolution of the marriage contract, by paying him a sum established by custom' (cited in Reid, 1988: 152).

Concerning the avenues open to a wife who wants a divorce, in Peninsular Malaysia in the 1969–73 period, 93 per cent of all Muslim divorces were by *talak* (Jones, 1981: 259),[17] and in 1974, 91 per cent

(*Wanita*, June 1978, pp. 38–9), and this is consistent with the corresponding figure of 95 per cent for West Java between 1977 and 1989. The remaining 7 per cent (Peninsular Malaysia) and 5 per cent (West Java) of divorces were in the wife-initiated categories of *ta'lik talak*, *fasakh*, and *khula* (termed *syiqoq* in West Java). Although these categories of divorce are evidently not frequently invoked, the *ta'lik talak*, in particular, is of considerable significance. The *ta'lik talak* is a provision attached to the marriage contract whereby the husband agrees to a number of conditions whose violation permits his wife to demand divorce.[18] It has become fairly standard in Indonesian and Singapore Muslim marriages, though less so in Malaysia and elsewhere in the Muslim world (Ibrahim, 1965: 208–10; Djamour, 1966: Chapter 2; Lev, 1972a: 138–45).

As for *talak*, the circumstances of its use are not the same everywhere. In the Malay world, although *talak* has been very common indeed, and used by husbands with varying degrees of responsibility or irresponsibility, one unusual aspect has attracted frequent comment from researchers. Though *talak* divorces are registered by the husband, they are frequently, some researchers say mostly, instigated by the wife (H. Geertz, 1961: 72; Siegel, 1969: 174–5; Kuchiba, Tsubouchi, and Maeda, 1979: 162; Strange, 1981: 160). It is important to know whether these findings can be generalized, because the question of who initiates the divorce has important implications for the welfare of the parties concerned and the appropriate policies to adopt.

Muslim divorces registered in Trengganu between 1972 and 1976 (which numbered almost 10,000) included information about which spouse wanted the divorce. There was 'no response' in about a quarter of cases, but among those who did respond, information given by the husbands and wives was fairly consistent. Divorce was initiated by the husband in about 43–50 per cent of cases, by the wife in about 25–31 per cent of cases, and by both in about a quarter of cases. In the Malaysian Marriage Survey, which collected information on over 200 divorces (mostly in Kelantan and mostly occurring in the 1960s and earlier), there was again close consistency between replies of ex-husbands and wives: the proportion of *talak* divorces initiated solely by the husband was only 35 per cent, the wife initiated 17 per cent of them, and in the remaining cases (almost half), both husband and wife were inclined towards divorce (unpublished data, Malaysian Marriage Survey, 1981–2).

In Singapore, official statistics on Muslim divorces state who was the petitioner. Over the two years 1986 and 1987, the husband was the petitioner in 29 per cent of cases, the wife in 49 per cent of cases, and they petitioned jointly in the remaining 22 per cent of cases (Department of Statistics, Singapore, 1988: Table 2.22).

In Indonesia, data are available from Central Java for the single year of 1954 which show that, of 79,750 *talak* divorces in fourteen Central Java *kabupaten*, 29 per cent originated in the husband's disaffection, 22 per cent in the wife's, and the remaining 49 per cent were by mutual

consent. In the same year in Yogyakarta, the husband took the initiative in 39 per cent of cases, the wife in 28 per cent, and both in
33 per cent (Thaha, cited in Lev, 1972a: 147). In a 1988 survey in
West Java (Tim Peneliti, 1988), it was found that the husband desired
the divorce in 30 per cent of cases, the wife in 34 per cent of cases,
and both in 28 per cent of cases.

Nakamura (1983: 67–9) presents data on divorces in Kotagede,
Yogyakarta, which indicate both who petitions for the divorce and who
is responsible for causing the divorce. Divorce can be petitioned for by
both husband and wife, by the husband alone or by the wife alone.
The ratio of the three categories of petitioner is almost equally one-
third for each, implying that the husband and the wife claim divorce
with almost equal frequency. According to reasons reported in the
Divorce Registration Book, it is also possible to determine who is the
responsible party: for example when the wife petitions for divorce because
the husband has failed to maintain her, the husband is responsible for
the divorce. In 82 per cent of cases there was a clear description of the
reason for the divorce, and among these divorces, the husband was
responsible in 55 per cent of cases and the wife in 45 per cent of cases.

Enough evidence has been presented to justify the confident conclusion that throughout the Malay-Muslim world since the 1950s, in
only a quarter to a half of all *talak* cases has divorce been a unilateral
decision by the husband. More commonly, both husband and wife
wished the divorce, and in a substantial proportion of cases, frequently
as many as a quarter to a third, the wife was the prime mover.

Interval from Marriage to Divorce

This question has already been discussed above in the analysis of cohort
trends in divorce, which showed that the highest risk of divorce occurred
in the first three years of marriage, and declined progressively thereafter. For the 1940–9 marriage cohort in rural Indonesia, we find that
of all divorces occurring within twenty years of marriage, 20–30 per cent
occurred within the first year of marriage and 60–66 per cent within
the first three years of marriage (see Table 5.9). The exception is
Sulawesi, where the figures are lower, probably influenced by different
divorce patterns among the quite large Christian population, 18.8 per cent
of the total in 1971.

These findings are consistent with the anthropological literature, which
suggests that divorce frequently occurred very soon after marriage;
indeed, that it frequently occurred without the marriage being consummated (H. Geertz, 1961; Singarimbun and Manning, 1974b; V. J. Hull,
1975; Chapon, 1976: Chapter 3; Hull and Hull, 1987). Much of the
Indonesian evidence comes from the small Javanese province of
Yogyakarta, where non-consummation of marriage appears to be particularly high. Three studies can be mentioned. In Kotagede in the late
1960s, 10 per cent of divorces registered were from non-consummated
marriages (Nakamura, 1983: 74). In Sriharjo, 36 per cent of divorces

recorded were from non-consummated marriages (calculated from Chapon, 1976: Tables 25 and 30). In Mojolama, Yogyakarta, over 40 per cent of divorces recorded were from non-consummated marriages, one-third of which had been contracted by girls aged below 15. However, not all these divorces took place immediately; though they were not consummated, 36 per cent of the marriages lasted for 2 years or more (Singarimbun and Manning, 1974b). In Maguwoharjo, 24 per cent of divorces were from non-consummated marriages (V. J. Hull, 1975: 220). Apart from this Yogyakarta evidence, it is known that in Indramayu, West Java, *kawin gantung* or 'hanging marriages' in which the marriage ceremony was held for below-age children but they did not yet live together as husband and wife, were frequently followed quickly by divorce, often without the marriage having been consummated. The local term for such cases was *kawin elik*. Clearly more needs to be known about the incidence of divorce from unconsummated marriages in other regions, and more generally about the prevalence of divorce after various time intervals. Two alternative approaches to the latter question are to calculate the cumulative percentages divorced within different intervals after marriage, using survey data; and to tabulate the intervals since marriage from divorce registration data.

For Peninsular Malaysia Malays, unpublished data from the 1984–5 Malaysian Population and Family Survey are available for women aged 35 and over who divorced from their first marriage within fifteen years of the marriage. Among this group, 24 per cent divorced in the first year of marriage, 52 per cent within three years of marriage, and 69 per cent within five years of marriage. These proportions are slightly overstated owing to censoring effects;[19] nevertheless, there is clearly a 'decay curve' of divorce, with highest probability of divorce in the first three years and especially in the first year of marriage. Data for women aged 25–34, though affected more by truncation of the data, show comparable patterns, the one difference being that in this group divorce is more prevalent in the second than in the first year of marriage.

From divorces registered in the states of Perlis and Negri Sembilan between 1972 and 1976, it is also found that at least one-quarter of divorces occurred within one year of the date of marriage, and at least half within five years of the date of marriage. No information was given for 11 per cent of cases, some of which would have occurred within these early intervals. These two fairly small states are not necessarily representative of Peninsular Malaysia, but their data show extraordinary consistency with the Peninsular Malaysia data reported above. It is therefore clear that among Malaysian Malays, divorce has been heavily concentrated in the period soon after marriage, although viewed differently, almost half of all divorces do occur five or more years after marriage, in other words after an interval in which the spouses have had ample time to learn to adjust to each other, if this is possible.

As in Indonesia, it appears that many divorces in Malaysia were from non-consummated marriages. In the Malaysian Marriage Survey, one-fifth of divorces (56 per cent of which took place in Kelantan and most of them before 1960), occurred to marriages which had never been consummated, most of them involving young girls married by their parents to a man they did not find acceptable (Tan and Jones, 1991: 92–3). Kelantanese focus groups of middle-aged women (in 1989) indicated unanimous agreement that non-consummation of marriage followed by divorce had been a common pattern, and this was confirmed by discussions with officials who had served over long periods in registering divorces in the state; they attributed it to parent-arranged marriage at young ages which did not work out.[20] Similarly, divorce from non-consummated marriages appears to have been common among Southern Thai Muslims (Fraser, 1966: 73).

Three micro studies, by Wilder (1970) in a high-divorce village in Pahang in the 1960s, and by Tsubouchi (1976) in villages in Kelantan and Kedah around 1970, add additional insights. Of Wilder's sample of village marriages, 48 per cent had ended in divorce, and 69 per cent of all divorces had occurred after less than three years of marriage. Similarly, in Tsubouchi's villages, about 60 per cent of all divorces occurred in the first two years of marriage, with the heaviest concentration in the first year of marriage. These three villages probably reflect a more general tendency, when the divorce rate is high, for an especially high proportion of divorces to occur early in the marriage. Wilder, indeed, noted that when the early divorces are excluded, divorce in the remaining years of marriage in his village was not particularly high.

Finally, in Singapore, examination of records from the Singapore Muslim Matrimonial Court reveals that of divorces registered in the period 1969–80, only 40 per cent took place within five years of marriage. Over the 1981–90 period, this proportion remained at about 41 per cent, the average duration of marriage for divorcing couples was 8.8 years and the average age of women at the time of divorce was over 31 years (Department of Statistics, Singapore, 1990: Tables A2.24, A2.25). The divorce rate was already low in the period covered by these figures, and the pattern had clearly diverged quite markedly from the traditional one of quick divorce from parent-arranged youthful marriages, with its high concentration of divorce in the first three years of marriage.

It needs to be stressed that the Malay world was unique in the world setting in the high proportion of divorces occurring in the very early years of marriage. Of all twenty-seven countries included in the World Fertility Survey, the ratio of the probability that marriages would be broken in the first five years to the probability that they would be broken in the second five years was higher in Indonesia and Malaysia than in any other country (Guest, 1991: Table 1).

Children in Marriages Ending in Divorce

Data on this subject are not widely available. In the Malaysian Marriage Survey, 40 per cent of Malay couples who divorced were childless

(Tan and Jones, 1990: 103). Among divorces registered in Trengganu, Perlis, and Negri Sembilan between 1972 and 1976, well over 40 per cent of the couples were childless, and at least another 21 per cent had only one child.[21] Probably fewer than one-third, then, had more than one child at the time of divorce. Given the relatively high Malay fertility in Peninsular Malaysia, this indicates a very high concentration of divorces among the childless and one-child couples. Rather than interpreting this as suggesting infertility as a cause of divorce, however, stress should probably be laid on the typically short intervals from marriage to divorce, and the fact that many of these divorces occurred after too short an interval for fecundity to have been proven.

McDonald and Abdurahman (1974) were able to examine indirect evidence from the Indonesian Fertility–Mortality Survey 1973 on the relationship of infertility and subfecundity to divorce. Women who had married more than once were more likely to have had no children or only a small number of children. The authors concluded that infertility and subfecundity are both important among the causes of divorce in West Java.

Guest's analysis of the Java data from the 1976 Indonesian Fertility Survey showed that divorce was dramatically less frequent in marriages where a birth had occurred than in childless marriages. At durations of marriage exceeding 48 months, a woman who had not had a birth in her marriage was 84 per cent more likely to experience a divorce than a woman who had had a birth. The effect at shorter durations, where the influence of non-consummation could be a confounding factor, was even stronger (Guest, 1991: 17).

The finding that divorce rates among couples who had been married long enough to test their fecundity were much higher among childless couples is normally interpreted to demonstrate that infecundity was an important motivation for divorce. And no doubt it was. But an alternative explanation is that infecundity facilitated, rather than caused, divorce; in other words, the presence of children complicates the issue and may hold a couple together who would otherwise have divorced. Both explanations are no doubt valid, but it is impossible to know which is the more important. In general, people in the region (e.g. Kelantanese focus groups conducted by the writer and colleagues) argue that the presence of children in the marriage is a significant deterrent to divorce: there is an old Malay saying in the region which means 'When you have a child, think twice before you divorce'. The majority of people also argue that childlessness is not an acceptable reason for divorce: in both the Malaysian and Indonesian Marriage Surveys, only about a quarter of male respondents (but interestingly, a more variable proportion of female respondents, ranging from 28 to 79 per cent) agreed that the wife's barrenness is a justifiable ground for divorce, compared with, for example, over 90 per cent who agreed that a wife's adultery is adequate ground for divorce (see Table 6.7). These normative statements, however, do not necessarily reflect practice.

Frequency of Divorce by Marriage Order

The 1976 Indonesian Fertility Survey (Table 5.10) shows clearly that second and higher-order marriages in Java were even more likely to end in divorce within various intervals than were first marriages. For example, in East Java, a quarter of first marriages had ended within 48 months, but this took only 40 months in the case of second and higher-order marriages. This association held for each of the different ethnic groups and for each educational group. At first glance, this appears to show that people become ever more likely to divorce as they enter second or third marriages, and this is surprising, because they were likely to have more say in the choice of spouse in these higher-order marriages. But in fact, the data do *not* show that people are ever more likely to divorce as they enter higher-order marriages. The denominator for calculating divorce rates for second and higher-order marriages is restricted to those whose first marriage was terminated, mainly by divorce or much less commonly by widowhood. Therefore although second and higher-order marriages were less stable than first marriages, the second and higher-order marriages of those undertaking these marriages were certainly more stable than their first marriages, all of which had been broken.

Frequency of Divorce by Socio-economic Status

Divorce in Islamic South-East Asia is more common among the poorer and less educated. This is confirmed by both large-scale surveys and by village studies (H. Geertz, 1961: 137–9; V. J. Hull, 1975: Chapter 4; Peletz, 1988: 255–6; Hefner, 1990: 171). Muliakusuma's (1976) analysis of the 1973 Fertility–Mortality Survey data for Indonesia shows a strong negative relationship between schooling and incidence of divorce for Muslim respondents, and also a strong negative association between socio-economic status and divorce (see Table 5.11).[22] The data are age standardized, thus going a long way towards controlling the average length of time 'at risk' of divorce. The lack of control for duration since first marriage, however, remains a problem because in any given age-group, the better educated would tend to marry later and thus not be exposed so long to the risk of divorce. Of course, since most divorce takes place within the first three years of marriage, the duration effect should not be too important, certainly not important enough to greatly modify the very strong inverse relationship observed between education and divorce. The inverse relationship between socio-economic status and divorce was also very strong, and this relationship should be less affected by differing lengths of time 'at risk' of divorce.[23]

Guest's analysis of the 1976 Indonesian Fertility Survey data confirms the strong effect of completing primary school or going on to high school in lowering the probability of divorce (though incomplete primary schooling has no such effect). In compositional terms, divorce was higher among the poor because they were less likely to have any or much

TABLE 5.11

Indonesia: Proportion Ever Divorced among Ever-married Women Aged 15–49, According to Level of Education and Economic Status, by Province and Region, 1973

	West Java		Central Java		East Java		Sumatra		Sulawesi	
	Urban	Rural	Urban	Rural	Urban	Rural	Urban	Rural	Urban	Rural
Education (Muslim women)										
None or incomplete primary	45.8	56.8	31.3	33.4	35.5	35.2	25.1	35.0[a]	11.9	12.9
Completed primary and above	23.6	37.8	10.1	21.9	8.7	31.9	8.0	23.7	8.6	7.7
Economic Status[b] (women of all religions)										
0–5	50.1	58.4	31.2	42.0	35.3	37.5	22.1	32.7	11.6	15.2
6–9	34.2	52.0	28.0	28.4	29.2	31.7	15.8	25.3	14.0	12.5
10–14	26.3	50.2	20.5	25.3	21.9	28.1	14.3	20.3	7.4	9.5
15+	15.5	21.9	4.7	14.3	9.8	46.7[c]	3.9	8.7	4.6	2.2

Source: Muliakusuma (1976: Tables IV.6 and IV.7).
[a]This is only an approximate figure, derived from consistency checks with other data. The figure in this cell in the source table (60.2) was clearly incorrect.
[b]The economic status score was derived from questions on housing and owner-ship of various consumer durables. A higher score indicates a higher economic status.
[c]This figure was given in the original source, but it may have been a typograph-ical error.

education, also because they were more likely to marry at very young ages, where the chances of divorce were greater.

The Malaysian Marriage Survey findings were that rural areas have more divorce than urban areas, and that there was a negative relationship between education and divorce. The survey did not use an index of economic status, but it seems clear that divorce was more common among the poorer groups than among the wealthier groups.

In the Kelantan segment of the Malaysian Marriage Survey, the inverse correlation between education and prevalence of divorce held. But because low education tends to be correlated with early age at marriage as well as with marriages contracted in an earlier rather than later period, hazard rate analysis was employed, and it demonstrated that the independent influence of these three factors held (Hashim, 1984: 79–86).

Frequency of Divorce in Polygamous and Monogamous Marriages

Data are not available in a form which enables the incidence of divorce to polygamous marriages to be compared with its incidence in monogamous marriages. The form used in Indonesia to classify causes of divorce includes the category 'unhealthy polygamy' to indicate cases where 'unjustified' resort to polygamy by the husband was the reason for the wife to seek divorce. But this category would be indicated as the cause of divorce only if it was given priority over other possible causes of divorce, and if the official agreed with the wife that the resort to polygamy by the husband was 'unhealthy'.

In any case, the threat of polygamy rather than the event itself was frequently the precipitator of divorce. Sexual jealousy, the suspicion or evidence of a husband's (or, less frequently, wife's) adultery, was a very common reason for divorce (H. Geertz, 1961; Niehof, 1985: 175; Guinness, 1986), and a husband's intention to take a second wife frequently resulted in the first wife seeking a divorce. In V. J. Hull's (1975: 220) village study in Yogyakarta, the stated cause of 18 per cent of divorces was that the husband had taken or, less frequently, was going to take a second wife. In another 8 per cent of cases, the husband's unfaithfulness was given as the cause, and some of these cases as well may have reflected intended polygamy. The saying 'lebih baik dicerai daripada dimadu' (better to be divorced than to share your husband) finds overwhelming agreement from women in surveys and focus group discussions throughout the Malay world: for example, in the Malaysian Marriage Survey, over 70 per cent of Malay women agreed with the statement (Tan and Jones, 1991); in one Kelantanese village study, 74 per cent agreed (Zalaluddin, 1979: 143); in the Indonesian Marriage Survey, 90 per cent of women in the Java segment agreed, as did 64 per cent in the Aceh segment, 86 per cent in the Jakarta segment, 54 per cent in South Sumatra, and about 58 per cent among the Banjarese[24] (Arian, 1982: 58; Kasto, 1982: 61; Mahfudz, 1982: 58; Muliakusuma, 1982: 61; Mahmud, 1983: 57).

Rujuk (Reconciliation)

Rujuk (reconciliation) is, according to Islamic law, possible after *talak* by a simple procedure of registration.[25] But if the divorce (*talak*) is twice followed by *rujuk*, the third *talak* is irreversible; the couple cannot then be reunited as husband and wife unless the wife first marries, and consummates the marriage with, somebody else and is subsequently divorced. In earlier times when divorce was commonplace, some husbands, after rashly invoking the three *talak* simultaneously, would arrange for the ex-wife to marry another man on the understanding that he would quickly divorce her so that she could remarry the first husband. Such a situation, the source of much ribald humour, was not rare in the days when divorce regulations and their implementation were very loose; the term for the co-operative 'stand-in' husband, a *Cina buta* (colloquially translated as 'blind Chinaman'), is well-known Malaysian slang. For a fascinating case-study of such an event, see Strange (1981: 162–4).

In Malaysia, there has always been considerable interstate variation in the extent of reconciliation of husband and wife after *talak*, ranging in the 1950s from lows of 4.7 per cent of divorces in Pahang and 5.8 per cent in Negri Sembilan to highs of 24.6 per cent in Kedah and 19.9 per cent in Penang. Singapore was toward the low side of this range. There was little evidence of an association between the level of divorce rates and the rate of reconciliation; the highest divorce states (Kelantan and Trengganu) had an intermediate level of *rujuk*.

On the whole, these differentials have remained stable over time, though with some notable exceptions (see Table 5.12). Penang had the highest levels of reconciliation in the 1980s, followed closely by Kedah–Perlis and then a group including Perak, Selangor, and the Federal Territory. Johore and Negri Sembilan joined this group in the late 1980s. The reason why Kedah and Penang had the highest levels of reconciliation needs to be investigated. It may have to do with more systematic attempts by religious officials there to bring about a reconciliation following the registration of a *talak*. This may also account for the sharp rise in registration of *rujuk* in Singapore in the 1970s.

The lowest levels of *rujuk* have at various times characterized Malacca, Negri Sembilan, Pahang, and Kelantan. In recent times *rujuk* has been lowest in Pahang, Kelantan, and Malacca, strange bedfellows indeed considering the wide range in their divorce rates.

Indonesia, by contrast, has much lower levels of *rujuk*; it was only 7 or 8 per cent as frequent as divorce during the 1950s and 1960s (see Table 5.13). It has also become much less frequent in recent times, a big drop occurring after 1969 and another sharp decline after 1975, probably related to the enactment of the marriage law and its effect of discouraging hasty divorces. These declines are again in contrast to the prevailing trends in Malaysia. As for regional differentials in Indonesia, Sumatra has above-average incidence of *rujuk* (perhaps reflecting cultural similarities between Sumatra and Peninsular Malaysia), and South

TABLE 5.12

Peninsular Malaysia and Singapore: *Rujuk* (Reconciliations) as a Percentage of *Cerai* (Divorces), Various States and Time Periods

State	1950–7	1960–7	1970–7	1980–4	1985–8
Kelantan	8.5	13.3	13.0	13.9	7.2
Trengganu	16.6	14.8	14.3	14.7	14.3
Kedah	24.6	26.6[a]	27.2	26.7	27.3
Perlis	14.3	11.4[a]	17.8	24.0	25.1
Pahang	n.a.	n.a.	n.a.	12.1	6.8
Penang	19.9	n.a.	n.a.	24.1	30.2
Perak	16.9	n.a.	n.a.	25.2[b]	26.3
Negri Sembilan	6.1	n.a.	n.a.	18.8	25.3
Johore	15.9	16.3	19.0	17.8	23.5
Malacca	11.1	8.1	n.a.	9.5	12.6
Selangor	12.4	n.a.	n.a.	23.8	25.4
Kuala Lumpur (Federal Territory)	–	–	–	23.7	21.5
Singapore	12.4	11.9	24.2[c]	n.a.	n.a.

Sources: Calculated by the author from unpublished data from a variety of sources, prior to 1970; after 1970, from data supplied by the Pusat Pengajian Islam, Prime Minister's Department, Malaysia.

[a] 1965–7.
[b] 1983–4.
[c] 1970–5.

TABLE 5.13

Indonesia and Selected Provinces: Reconciliations as Percentage of Divorces,
1950s–1980s

	(Rujuk ÷ Divorces) × 100			
	1950s	1960s[a]	1970s[b]	1980s[c]
Indonesia	7.8	7.4	2.9	1.6
Java–Madura	n.a.	7.2	2.8	1.6
West Java	n.a.	8.2	3.5	3.4
Central Java	n.a.	5.8	2.3	0.8
East Java	n.a.	7.3	2.5	1.0
Jakarta	n.a.	10.2	3.8	2.1
Yogyakarta	n.a.	3.8	1.9	1.1
Aceh	n.a.	10.3	5.8	4.4
North Sumatra	n.a.	15.2	5.2	1.7
West Sumatra	n.a.	11.6	4.7	2.3
South Sumatra	n.a.	11.5	5.6	2.8
South Kalimantan	n.a.	8.4	2.6	1.9
South Sulawesi	n.a.	2.8	1.2	0.6

Source: Data published annually in BPS, Statistik Indonesia.
[a]For Indonesia, the data are available for each year of the 1960s; for the provinces, data
are available only for 1963–7 inclusive.
[b]Excluding 1971, for which no data are available, except for Indonesia as a whole.
[c]1980–6, excluding 1982 as the rujuk figures for that year are obviously incorrect.

Sulawesi has distinctly lower rates than average. Java is close to the
average; but higher rates prevail in West Java and Jakarta. As in Malaysia,
there is little evidence of an association between the level of divorce
rates and the rate of reconciliation in different regions.

Remarriage

In Malay–Indonesian society, although age at marriage for men has
been considerably higher than for women, once they have been married
men seem to be considered much less capable of living in a non-
married state than women, and there is stronger pressure on them to
remarry following divorce or widowhood. The results of this are clearly
evident in the lower proportions of men currently widowed and
divorced, shown in Tables 5.1–5.4. Another minor factor raising the
proportion of women who are currently divorced or widowed at any
given time is the requirement that the woman wait until the 100-day
period of eddah is over before remarrying.

The normal pattern, however, was for women to remarry quickly after
divorce. In the 1950s, when divorce rates were still very high and widowhood also prevalent, remarriage was a very frequent event indeed. It was
even more frequent if one includes rujuk (reconciliations), which were

not strictly speaking remarriages and required no ceremony, but resembled them in some respects. Second marriages had lesser financial implications than first marriages; in Galok, Kelantan, they were not accompanied by a grand feast, and the bride-wealth paid was half that for a first marriage (Kuchiba, Tsubouchi, and Maeda, 1979: 168).

Data from the Indonesian Fertility–Mortality Survey of 1973 show that remarriage after divorce is rather quick; for example, in rural East Java, after a first divorce, 19 per cent of women have remarried within 1 year, 54 per cent within 2 years, and 83 per cent within 5 years (Table 5.14). Remarriage occurs more quickly in rural than in urban areas. There is no consistent difference in the length of time taken to remarry following the dissolution of a second or subsequent marriage compared with the dissolution of a first marriage. Some of the implications of the speed of remarriage in modifying the effect of high divorce rates on fertility will be discussed in Chapter 8.

TABLE 5.14

Indonesia: Cumulative Percentage of Divorced Women (Whose Divorces Occurred at Least 5 Years before the Date of the Survey) Who Had Remarried within Various Intervals of Time since Occurrence of Divorce, 1973

Region and Marriage Order	Percentage Remarried within				
	1 year	2 years	3 years	5 years	N^a
West Java					
Urban					
First marriage	20	49	67	80	435
Second marriage	19	53	66	74	167
Third marriage	20	59	69	81	70
Rural					
First marriage	28	65	79	86	2,319
Second marriage	31	70	80	88	964
Third marriage	30	70	77	84	429
Fourth marriage	28	65	73	81	205
Central Java					
Urban					
First marriage	15	42	58	73	254
Second marriage	20	48	63	72	54
Third marriage	27	59	68	77	22
Rural					
First marriage	17	51	67	79	1,691
Second marriage	17	52	66	77	512
Third marriage	16	48	63	73	161
Fourth marriage	22	63	74	87	46

TABLE 5.14 (*continued*)

Region and Marriage Order	Percentage Remarried within				
	1 year	2 years	3 years	5 years	N^a
East Java					
Urban					
First marriage	14	45	59	71	333
Second marriage	13	43	57	68	122
Third marriage	17	50	60	71	48
Rural					
First marriage	19	54	70	83	1,426
Second marriage	24	60	73	83	478
Third marriage	26	57	67	77	159
Fourth marriage	19	40	57	64	58
Sumatra					
Urban					
First marriage	19	47	62	75	255
Second marriage	23	50	64	75	84
Third marriage	35	65	70	70	23
Rural					
First marriage	22	54	69	81	1,099
Second marriage	26	57	69	77	382
Third marriage	21	55	64	72	143
Fourth marriage	_b	_b	_b	_b	9
Sulawesi					
Urban					
First marriage	9	33	47	63	187
Second marriage	8	33	49	67	39
Third marriage	_b	_b	_b	_b	8
Rural					
First marriage	10	34	49	63	591
Second marriage	8	32	47	57	118
Third marriage	21	42	47	53	19
Fourth marriage	_b	_b	_b	_b	3

Source: Muliakusuma (1976: Tables V.2a–V.2f).
[a]Excludes 'not stated'.
[b]Fewer than 10 cases.

1. For example, in the Indonesian Fertility Survey, 1976, 33 per cent of first marriages had been broken by divorce or separation, compared with only 7 per cent broken by widowhood. Even among marriages contracted thirty or more years before the survey, the proportion broken by divorce or separation (44 per cent) was more than double the proportion broken by widowhood (20 per cent) (Central Bureau of Statistics and World Fertility Survey, 1978: Table 4.4).

2. In Malaysia, these data are collected state by state, by the Department of Religious Affairs, and are not available in summary form through any national statistical agency. They have instead to be painstakingly pieced together from various sources. The data

since 1970, however, were kindly made available by the Pusat Pengajian Islam in Kuala Lumpur. For further details about the data on Muslim divorces, see Appendix 1.

3. Among South-East Asian specialists, the high divorce rates were well known. After all, as long ago as 1817, Raffles stated that 'in no part of the world are divorces more frequent than on Java' (Raffles [1871] (1978): Vol. I, 80, 356) and almost all nineteenth century observers agreed with him (Boomgaard, 1989: 145). But myopia among the international demographic fraternity, induced by reliance on internationally accessible published statistics, was only relieved by published evidence of high divorce rates in Jones (1980). Before this, a well-known demographic text (Bogue, 1969: 316 fn. 18) stated that 'at the present time, the United States represents the upper limit in divorce, for divorce rates are higher in the United States than in almost any other nation'. In fact, at the time to which he was referring (around 1965), the divorce rate in Indonesia (even when the non-Muslim population is included) was approximately double that in the United States, and the rates in some of the states of Malaysia were even higher.

4. The Malays in neighbouring Sarawak also had low divorce rates in the 1960s, though divorce had been much more common in the 1940s and earlier (Harrisson, 1970: 193).

5. Divorce rates in the Arab Middle East appeared to be higher in the cities than in the rural areas, which was the opposite of the situation among Malays. In most of these countries, they appear to have declined since World War II (Prothero and Diab, 1974: Chapter 7). Turkey also had higher urban than rural divorce rates, and divorce rates declined between the mid-1950s and the mid-1970s (Levine, 1982). However, since the 1960s, no clear trends are discernible in the available data on divorce rates in the Arab world.

6. The relative overstatement of Western divorce patterns for this reason is lessening over time because of the sharp increases in female age at marriage in the Malay world. A refinement of general divorce rates to allow for the variable percentage of the population aged 15 and over who are currently married would lead to quite variable adjustment factors, due to wide differences in these proportions within Malay and European populations. These differences stem from different causes, including differences in age at marriage, proportions marrying, and incidence of divorce and widowhood.

7. The fact that in the 1950s, the median age at marriage for females in Java was only 17 meant that half of all marriages were occurring before this age. Since divorces were most frequent in the first three years of marriage, some divorces were clearly occurring at ages below 15. Such divorces would have become uncommon since the Marriage Law was promulgated in 1974. In order for the denominator of the General Divorce Rate to include all those 'at risk' of divorce in earlier years, it should probably include 13- and 14-year-olds.

8. Inclusion of 13- and 14-year-olds in the denominator would raise the denominator by a smaller percentage in the 1980s than in earlier years, because the number of 13- and 14-year-olds was a smaller proportion of the population in the 1980s than earlier as a result of the fertility decline during the late 1960s and 1970s. The inclusion of 13- and 14-year-olds in the denominator, then, would raise the General Divorce Rate in the 1980s slightly compared with rates for earlier years.

9. The adult Malay population (aged 15 and over) has been used as the denominator for these rates. All Malays are Muslims, but there are also a small number of non-Malay (mainly Indian) Muslims who are not included in the denominator for the estimates. They would number less than 2 per cent of the Malay Muslims in all the states included in Figure 5.2. Estimates of adult Malay population for most years are interpolations between the available census or projection data, and are therefore subject to a degree of error, but not large enough to invalidate the general trends shown.

10. A Muslim husband is allowed to change his mind and be reconciled with his wife after officially registering his divorce, provided that the reconciliation takes place within the 100-day period of *eddah* following the divorce. The frequency of such *rujuk* cases in Peninsular Malaysia (commonly 10 per cent and sometimes even 20 per cent of all registered divorces) attests to the frequency of hasty divorces which are later reconsidered.

11. A matrimonial court was established as part of the law reform of 1957, effective from December 1958; see Djamour (1966).

12. Moreover, there is sometimes disagreement about frequency of divorce. Writing in 1935 about Aceh, Loeb (1972: 238–9) states:
'While Kreemer writes that divorces are less frequent in Atjeh than in most Mohammedan countries, due to matrilocal residence and the independence of women, Jacobs claims that they are very frequent indeed, due to child marriages and the fact that the young couple scarcely know one another when engaged. The latter writes that Achenese who have married ten to fifteen times are no anomaly, and that he personally had met a young girl of thirteen who had just been cast aside by her third husband.'

13. A three-year moving average was employed in both cases to minimize the effect of year-to-year fluctuations.

14. For example, in Perlis in the late 1970s there was concern about 'runaway marriages' conducted in Southern Thailand. Most divorces from such marriages are probably registered in Southern Thailand as well (Kasimin, 1978: 111–13). Officials in Perlis believe that most 'runaway marriages' conducted in Southern Thailand occur when a bridegroom cannot produce a consent letter from his first wife to marry a second time, as required by Muslim law in Perlis (*New Straits Times*, 25 November 1978).

15. Muslim divorce rates in Singapore reached their low point in the 1970s. The annual number of Muslim divorces rose from 357 in 1978 to almost 800 in the 1985–7 period, 893 in 1988, and 907 in 1989. Non-Muslim divorces rose even more sharply. Two possible reasons are often mentioned: more liberal social attitudes, and the greater economic independence of married women (Tai, 1979; *Straits Times*, 27 February 1990). In Brunei, too, Muslim divorce rates were rising over the 1980s, but Brunei differed from Singapore and Malaysian cities in that the rise in divorce rates over the 1980s began from the very low rate which had prevailed since the mid-1960s or even earlier, at which time rates in most other parts of the Malay world were much higher.

16. Numbers were rather small for some provinces, and the cluster sampling design could yield misleading estimates at this level.

17. In the Malaysian Marriage Survey, with a smaller, non-representative sample over-representing Kelantan, the figure was much lower: 76 per cent (Tan and Jones, 1990).

18. These conditions (standard since 1955) are that he leaves her for 6 months or more consecutively, or fails to give her proper maintenance for 3 months consecutively, or physically abuses her, or neglects her for 6 months consecutively. A bride may insist on additional conditions, including the entitlement to divorce if the husband takes another wife without his first wife's permission. Such additional conditions are normally only invoked among well-educated, urban families (Lev, 1972a: 143–4).

19. Only 86 per cent of the respondents had been married for at least 14 years, though a further 10 per cent had been married for between 10 and 14 years. However, the incidence of divorce clearly falls off sharply beyond 10 years of marriage.

20. Registrars, for example, the *imam* of mosques, would learn of this because in cases where marriage was not consummated, the bride-wealth had to be returned.

21. The reason for the uncertainty over exact levels is the 21 per cent of cases where the number of children was not recorded.

22. The socio-economic status score was a composite index based on aspects of the dwelling and material possessions of the household.

23. It is interesting that in Java, the differences in divorce rates between those with completed primary school and those with incomplete primary school seem to be less pronounced in rural than in urban areas, although this is not the case in Sumatra and Sulawesi.

24. In the Indonesian Marriage Survey, the reason for the high proportion preferring to be divorced than to be in a polygamous marriage was not that the phrasing of the question encouraged such an answer; the question was whether the respondent agreed with the saying 'lebih baik dimadu daripada dicerai' (better to be in a polygamous marriage than to be divorced), requiring a negative answer to indicate that they would prefer to be divorced. In the Malaysian Marriage Survey, the question was asked the other way around.

25. *Rujuk* is not possible after a *khula* or *fasakh* divorce, although a man whose marriage has been dissolved in this way may remarry his ex-wife if she agrees (Djamour, 1966: 126).

6
Influences on Stability of First Marriage

THIS chapter will follow the same pattern as in Chapter 4, on change from the traditional pattern of early marriage. It will first summarize the factors which appear to have contributed to the traditional instability of marriage, and then seek to identify important areas of socio-economic and religious change which may have contributed to increasing stability.

It must be kept in mind that, as already shown in Chapter 5, divorce rates were not universally high among South-East Asian Muslims, nor were they high in many other parts of the Muslim world. The widespread belief in Western countries that divorce is common everywhere in the Muslim world is based on the ease with which a Muslim husband may divorce his wife. As already noted, however, some curbs have been placed on the ease of divorce in many Muslim countries, and the *hadith* (tradition of what the Prophet said or did) is often cited which states that 'of the things which are lawful the most hateful to God is divorce'. Both where divorce rates were traditionally high as well as where they were moderate, there appears to have been a declining trend everywhere among South-East Asian Muslims, a trend which continued into the 1980s except in Singapore, Brunei, and some of the larger cities of Malaysia. It is this trend which this chapter seeks to explain.

Factors Traditionally Fostering Divorce

Two factors are generally thought to facilitate divorce among Malays: the divorce procedure under Islamic law and the structure of Malay society. According to Kuchiba, Tsubouchi, and Maeda (1979: 33), Malays generally ascribe the high frequency of divorce to the simplicity of divorce procedures under Islamic law. 'This, however, seems to derive rather from the looseness of application of Islamic law than from the nature of the law itself.' This is an important point. The extremely wide range in divorce rates in Muslim societies throughout the world is sufficient proof that it is not Islamic law as such that causes high divorce; rather, it facilitates high divorce in societies which have a predilection towards divorce. This is the case in large sections of the Malay-Muslim world, and may predate the coming of Islam. Tsubouchi (1975: 28) notes that the kinship structure of Malay society readily allows divorce. In support, he cites the Jakun proto-Malays, 'whose kinship structure is almost identical to that of the Malays but who have not been influenced by Islam, [and among whom] divorce is quite common, though not as common as in Malay society'.

In Java in the nineteenth century, divorces were easily obtained and colonial observers noted that they took place 'on the slightest grounds' and that they were often caused by female whimsies (Boomgaard, 1989: 146). There appears to have been no explicitly formulated anti-divorce policy, though at some times and in some areas the fee for a divorce was very high, possibly as a revenue-earning measure rather than as an attempt to discourage divorce (Boomgaard, 1989: 147–8). Earl, commenting on the acceptance the Javanese gave to women aged 22 or 23 living with their fourth or fifth husband, attributed this attitude entirely to the freedom and economic independence enjoyed by women (Reid, 1988: 153). Some observers related divorce to young, parent-arranged marriage and others to the ability of women to initiate divorce proceedings. Most observers, however, offered little by way of explanation (Boomgaard, 1989: 146–8).

Divorce rates in Java remained high until the end of the 1960s, but the wide differences in divorce rates, even in closely contiguous areas, testify to the need to look more deeply into causes. The most striking example is the proximity of the highest divorce areas of Java (the Indramayu–Subang area west of Cirebon in West Java) with the lowest divorce areas (around Jakarta and west to the Banten region: see Map 5.2). Similarly, outside Java, Muslim divorce rates varied widely, from very high in West Sumatra, West Nusa Tenggara,[1] and South Kalimantan to low in North and South Sumatra and South Sulawesi.

Many aspects of family and social structure, institutions, socio-economic conditions, and beliefs, as well as administration of the law, can be expected to have influenced divorce levels in the Malay world. Djamour (1966: 139) listed several factors that she saw as congruent with the high frequency of divorce in the 1950s and earlier among Malays in Singapore: divorce is facilitated by law and tolerated by general morality; strong economic deterrents are lacking; remarriage is easy and inexpensive for both sexes; practical and moral support for a divorced woman is available from kin; access to children for both parents and their kin is possible; and adoption is possible if neither parent wants or is able to keep the children (see also H. Geertz, 1961: 144). Kuchiba, Tsubouchi, and Maeda (1979: 32–4) cite much the same factors as Djamour, though they also emphasize the social immaturity of young people when they marry, the effect of bilateral kinship systems, elements of individualism within the Malay family, and the widespread belief that fate plays a hand in divorce.

It would be wrong, however, to suggest that divorce was viewed without concern by Malay society. Even in earlier times of very high divorce rates, it was seen as a regrettable necessity. Downs (1967: 146) puts it well for Kelantan: 'Although divorce was not considered actually wrong, it was deplored for its effect on the children and was considered a reflection on the character of the people involved. It was thought much better not to divorce and it was said that "good people" did not do it.' Whether a divorced person was stigmatized depended on other people's (especially other women's) perception of that person. 'Most divorcees who are also outsiders, especially if they are young and attractive, are assumed to be threatening simply because they are an unknown quantity, potential rivals.' (Strange, 1981: 167.)

The probable influence of some of these factors will now be discussed more systematically. Kinship systems and inheritance as important underlying determinants of differences in incidence of divorce between different regions and groups in the Malay world, will be considered first. Then various socio-economic and attitudinal factors, both societal and individual, will be discussed.

Kinship and Inheritance Systems

In general, the Malay world is characterized by bilateral kinship systems, with no strong conventions about which parents' household the young couple should live in after marriage. It has been argued that such kinship systems foster divorce because of divided loyalties on the part of the partners to the marriage (Tsubouchi, 1975; Al Hadar, 1977: 67).[2] However, frequent divorce also characterizes Minangkabau society in West Sumatra, no doubt because of the weak position of the husband and the wife's strong rights over the children in the Minangkabau matrilineal family, which also practises matrilocal residence (Al Hadar, 1977: 66–70). In this system, which is characterized by long absences on the part of many males (the tradition of *merantau*), it is considered quite likely that the husband will leave the family, and such an event is not necessarily feared by the wife because her children's welfare is guaranteed by her wider family. By contrast, the patrilineal system in Bugis-Makassarese society, which also favours matrilocal residence after marriage, fosters lower levels of divorce, as does the substantial payment made to the bride's family at the time of the wedding (Al Hadar, 1977: 70–1).

Conventions regarding the disposition of the joint possessions of the couple on divorce can also influence the frequency of divorce. In Malay, Javanese, and Minangkabau society, each partner basically keeps the goods he or she brought into the marriage,[3] and there is therefore little deterrent to divorce on this score, whereas among the Bataks and the Bugis-Makassarese, the husband on divorce will lose the substantial payment made to the wife at the time of marriage. Batak and Bugis-Makassarese societies also give a strong role to marriage in cementing relations between wider clans or groups and according prestige, and divorce is therefore disfavoured (Al Hadar, 1977: 72–4).

Arranged Marriage at Young Ages

It has already been noted that traditionally among Malay populations a girl's first marriage was more in the interest of the family's honour and status than of the girl's welfare, though of course it was hoped that the two would coincide. It was important to get the girl married before shame came to the family, either through her 'getting into trouble' or reaching the status of 'old maid'. Should the marriage fail, a divorce could easily be arranged and a simpler wedding follow. Given this context, it is not surprising that T. E. Smith (1961: 304) believed that marriage at young ages increased the likelihood of a Malay marriage ending in divorce. H. Geertz, writing of East Java, was told by one informant:

Traditionally a man who had a daughter who was still a spinster at sixteen would be embarrassed to have such an old maid on his hands.... Some parents feel that the best solution in such a situation is to find a man who will agree to enter into a temporary marriage with the girl, the understanding being that after a week or so he will divorce her. Once the girl is a divorcee, she can easily get a husband, for a man who would have hesitated to ask for her before, when it would have involved an elaborate first wedding, will not be so afraid now; and she herself will, through her initiation into marriage, have lost her timidity and be eager to marry again. (H. Geertz, 1961: 70.)

The case just cited should not be taken as the norm for East Java. Fewer than 8 per cent of Muslim marriages in East Java at the time were terminating in divorce within one year of the marriage (see Figures 5.3 and 5.4; the East Java pattern was intermediate between the two). But the attitude it revealed was certainly widespread throughout Java. Singarimbun and Manning (1974b) report a grandfather's response to his granddaughter's refusal to marry the man chosen by her family: 'If you don't like him, you can always get divorced.'

The Malaysian Population and Family Survey of 1984–5 found a clear association between age at marriage and incidence of divorce. Among married Malay women aged 25–34, as many as 7 per cent of the marriages contracted at ages below 21 terminated in divorce within three years, compared to only 1.7 per cent of those contracted at ages 21–24 (Tan et al., 1988: Table 14). Of course, in earlier times, these probabilities of divorce would have been much higher, but it is highly likely that the association between later marriage and less frequent divorce held.

For Java–Bali, the Indonesian Fertility Survey of 1976 shows a much higher incidence of divorce among women who married very young. Within 5 years of the marriage, 28 per cent of those married below the age of 15 had divorced, compared with 14 per cent of those married at 15–19 and 11 per cent of those married at 20 or over. Even at much higher durations since first marriage, the effect of age at marriage on dissolution persists: for example, at durations of 20–29 years, the proportion broken by divorce is twice as high for women marrying below 15 as for those marrying at ages 20 and above (see Table 6.1). Age at marriage continues to have a strong influence on divorce when other factors are controlled in proportional hazard models (Guest, 1991).

Age at marriage is to some extent, of course, a proxy for many other things: parent-arranged marriage, low education, and poverty. But

TABLE 6.1

Java–Bali: Percentage of First Marriages Broken by Divorce or Separation within Specified Intervals, by Age at First Marriage of Wife, 1976[a]

	Age at First Marriage			All Ages at Marriage
Years since Marriage	<15	15–19	20+	
<5	32	18	15	20
5–9	36	25	14	27
10–14	39	33	18	34
15–19	45	36	22	38
20–24	49	34	21	39
25–29	43	34	23	37
30+	48	36	–[b]	44
All years since marriage	43	29	18	33

Source: Central Bureau of Statistics and World Fertility Survey (1978: Vol. II, Table 1.2.1).
[a]Of the 33% of marriages broken by divorce or separation, 30.2% were broken by divorce and 2.7% by separation.
[b]No cases.

Table 6.2 shows that within the background variable categories of wife's education and husband's occupation, pronounced differences by age at marriage remain. There is little direct information about incidence of divorce to parent-arranged as compared to self-arranged marriages. Guritno's (1964) study of a village in Central Java showed that 42 per cent of the arranged marriages ended in divorce, compared with only 20 per cent of self-arranged marriages. V. J. Hull's study in Yogyakarta showed that controlling for current age, there is a much higher frequency of divorce from parent-arranged than from self-arranged marriages: for example, 42 per cent compared with 12 per cent for women aged 30–34; 21 per cent compared with 1 per cent for women aged 20–24 (V. J. Hull, 1975: 213).

The 1987 Demographic and Health Survey in Indonesia measured the relationship between age at marriage and a crude indicator of divorce: the percentage of women married more than once. Controlling for current age, the relationship between early marriage and multiple marriage is very striking indeed. For example, among women aged 25–34, 31 per cent of those who married at ages below 15 married more than once, compared with 16 per cent of those married at 15–17, 6 per cent of those married at 18–20, and only 1 per cent of those married at 21 or more (Palmore and Singarimbun, 1991: Table 2).

It might be noted that the high divorce rate in West Sumatra, which has relatively high age at marriage by Indonesian standards, provides an exception to the generalization that divorce rates are higher among early-marrying populations. No doubt other factors mentioned earlier, related to the matrilineal and matrifocal society in West Sumatra, are more important than age at marriage in this case.

TABLE 6.2

Java–Bali: Percentage of First Marriages Dissolved for Any Reason, for All
Marriage Durations, by Age at First Marriage, Level of Education, and
Husband's Occupation, 1976

	Age at First Marriage			All Ages at Marriage
	<15	*15–19*	*20+*	
Level of education				
No schooling	53	45	32	47
Incomplete primary	52	33	27	40
Completed primary	36	25	19	27
Junior high	_a	19	7	16
Senior high	_a	13	6	8
Husband's occupation				
Professional/clerical	53	28	13	29
Sales and services	51	36	23	40
Manual	53	33	23	38
Farming	50	39	29	43
All	51	36	24	40

Source: Central Bureau of Statistics and World Fertility Survey (1978: Vol. II, Table 1.2.2).
Note: This table includes marriages broken by widowhood, but widowhood was responsible
  for only 7.5% of all dissolutions compared with 30.2% due to divorce and 2.7% to
  separation.
aOnly 12 cases with junior high and none with senior high.

Non-consummation

The statistics presented in the previous chapter demonstrate clearly
enough that non-consummation of marriage was very common, not
only in the areas of Yogyakarta–Central Java, in which a number of
studies have been done, but also much more widely throughout the Malay
world. The key point to make about divorce following non-consummation
is that it was inextricably bound up with the practice of very early,
parent-arranged marriages. Because of the tight control over the mixing
of young people, spouses could be strangers at marriage even when
they were from the same village. The difficulty faced by a young couple
(because the groom was normally quite young as well in such marriages)
in establishing any kind of relationship, let alone sexual relationship, in
such a situation was obviously very great, and in many cases, though
the bride was not permitted to assert her independence by refusing to
enter the marriage, she was able to (and frequently did) assert it
following the marriage ceremony by refusing to have anything to do
with the husband chosen for her.

Fate and 'Cocok' or 'Jodoh': Liberal Attitudes to Divorce

Rosemary Firth (1966: 46) made an important observation about differences in the views of Malay and European societies. Both societies 'apply some constraint and allow some freedom in regard to marriage and choice of partners. But whereas we allow the freedom before marriage in choice of partners and apply the restraint once the marriage tie is made, the Malay applies the constraint before marriage and allows freedom to break the tie and conclude another one afterwards.'

In the Malay world, there is a strong belief that people must be *cocok* (a word not used much in Malaysia) or *jodoh* in order to live together successfully. These words basically mean 'compatible', but they carry the connotation that fate is involved, that the compatibility is mystically bestowed, and that therefore the parties themselves are not necessarily to blame if they do not get along. What has been referred to as normative instability, or the recognition of a potential for divorce (Wilder, 1982), was thus a constant feature of Malay marriage. Based on this way of viewing the world, it was possible for a couple to divorce without bitter recrimination and assignment of blame, simply on the grounds that they were not compatible. This is not to say, of course, that anger and bitterness were not involved in many, perhaps most, cases.

Given the complexity of causes of most divorces (H. Geertz, 1961: 139–44; Rosemary Firth, 1966: 43), it is a rather artificial and potentially misleading procedure to collect data on 'the cause of divorce'. Nevertheless, this is frequently done, sometimes allowing multiple reasons to be given, sometimes not. The results are widely variable, and do little to allay concerns that classification of reasons for divorce is a not-very-illuminating and frequently quite misleading exercise. Nevertheless, some of the findings will be briefly presented.

Unpublished data made available on the stated causes of divorces registered in the Malaysian states of Trengganu, Perlis, and Negri Sembilan in the 1970s cited reasons which can be broadly classified under 'unsuitability or incompatibility' in the majority of cases for which reasons were given. Reasons so classified included such statements as 'unsuitable', not 'understanding', 'disagreeing with one another', 'unable to live peacefully together', 'behaviour differences', and 'lack of give-and-take attitudes'. Other less frequently cited reasons included the failure of the wife to serve or follow the advice or direction of her husband. Factors such as the husband's polygamy or interference from other family members were only cited in a few cases. The general impression from this listing of reasons is that a generalized incompatibility was indeed widely seen as sufficient reason for divorce.

The Malaysian women's magazine *Wanita* published a table showing the stated causes of Muslim divorces in the various states of Peninsular Malaysia in 1974. This is reproduced as Table 6.3. It reveals some obvious differences between states in the classification of reasons. For example, in the Federal Territory, only 4 per cent of causes are listed under the categories which account for all divorces in some of the other

TABLE 6.3

Peninsular Malaysia: Reasons for Muslim Divorces, by State, 1974 (per cent)

	Perlis	Kedah	Penang	Perak	Selangor	Federal Territory	Negri Sembilan	Malacca	Pahang	Trengganu	Kelantan
1. Ease of obtaining divorce in the villages	–	80	40	20	–	–	–	–	18	–	40
2. Interference of parents-in-law/other in-laws in the household	21	10	15	14	–	–	15	15	22	–	5
3. (a) Impatience of young husband	1	–	5	4	–	–	8	23	6	–	10
(b) Impatience of young wife	3	–	5	4	–	–	6	18	7	–	10
4. (a) Husband's irresponsibility in performing his duties	24	10	10	27	10	2	23	27	19	40	5
(b) Wife's irresponsibility in performing her duties	9	2	10	12	10	2	15	6	16	20	5
5. (a) Husband's wastefulness	–	5	–	11	–	–	5	–	5	–	5
(b) Wife's wastefulness	–	3	–	5	–	–	5	–	4	–	5
(c) Insufficient income	29	4	10	26	50	–	9	12	15	–	5
6. Wife has an independent source of income	–	–	5	4	–	–	8	8	5	–	5

(continued)

TABLE 6.3 (continued)

7. Other reasons	Perlis	Kedah	Penang	Perak	Selangor	Federal Territory	Negri Sembilan	Malacca	Pahang	Trengganu	Kelantan
(a) Jealousy	—	—	—	3	—	7	—	—	—	—	5
(b) Unwilling to stay in polygynous marriage	7	—	—	—	—	9	—	—	—	—	—
(c) Incompatibility	—	—	—	—	—	39	—	—	—	—	—
(d) Immorality	—	—	—	—	30	—	2	—	—	—	—
(e) Wife from another area/state	—	—	—	—	—	—	5	—	—	—	—
(f) Wife is disobedient	—	—	—	—	—	6	—	—	—	—	—
(g) Talak pronounced during a quarrel	—	—	—	—	—	—	—	—	—	—	—
(h) Talak pronounced idly	—	—	—	—	—	27	—	—	—	—	—
(i) Sickness	3	—	—	—	—	4	—	—	—	—	—
(j) Sterility	3	—	—	—	—	—	—	—	—	—	—

Source: Wanita, June 1978: 38–9 (author's translation).

states. In Johore, the data are missing altogether; in Perak and Kedah, the reasons add up to over 100 per cent; in Trengganu, they add up to well under 100 per cent. The reason 'ease of obtaining divorce in the villages' is not mentioned in some states but scores as high as 40 per cent in Penang and Kelantan and 80 per cent in Kedah. The problem is that this is simply an 'enabling' reason but does not explain the underlying causes of divorce.

In states where 'ease of obtaining divorce' is not cited in a high proportion of cases, the most commonly cited reasons tend to be irresponsibility of one or both partners (most frequently, the husband), interference by parents-in-law, and insufficient income. Overall, problems related to the immaturity of young couples, reflected in reasons such as irresponsibility and interference by parents-in-law, tend to be more prominent than incompatibility; however, in the Federal Territory, where a different system of recording reasons for divorce appears to have been used, incompatibility is cited in 39 per cent of cases and jealousy in a further 7 per cent. Without knowing more about the way in which information on causes of divorce was obtained and recorded in different states, further analysis of Table 6.4 is not warranted.[4]

Local studies in Malaysia also stress the role of incompatibility. In Kuala Langat, Selangor, it ran a very close second to 'non-maintenance by husband' as a cause of divorce over the 1970s (Ong, 1987: Table 15). Writing of a Kelantanese fishing village, Rosemary Firth (1966: 37) states that 'our general impression, gained from much discussion, is that incompatibility in one form or another is the basic reason for most divorces'. In Jeram, Kelantan, 'incompatibility would certainly seem to

TABLE 6.4
Singapore: Reasons for Muslim Divorces, 1984–1987 (per cent)

Reason for Divorce	1984	1985	1986	1987
Personality difference	40	38	37	28
Infidelity	15	13	11	12
Inadequate maintenance	14	14	22	17
Desertion	7	9	7	6
Neglect/indifference/ irresponsibility	4	3	n.a.	n.a.
Problems with in-laws	3	3	n.a.	n.a.
Assault	2	2	n.a.	n.a.
Nagging/complaining	2	n.a.	5	7
Mental illness	1	n.a.	n.a.	n.a.
Polygyny	1	n.a.	n.a.	n.a.
Other reasons	11	18	19	29
Total	100	100	100	100

Source: Department of Statistics, Singapore, *Statistics on Marriages and Divorces*, various years.

be the outstanding single factor and was usually present when other ones were involved' (Downs, 1967: 144).

Similarly, in Serpong, West Java, for both men and women, the dominant reasons given for divorce were 'disharmony', 'there is no blessing', or 'this has been no real match' (Zuidberg, 1978: 88). Two separate village studies in Yogyakarta recorded dislike of the partner, often associated with unconsummated marriages, as the major cause of divorce (Singarimbun and Manning, 1974b: 10; V. J. Hull, 1975: 219–20); H. Geertz (1961: 142) also found 'dislike' to be the major reason for divorce in her East Java community.

In Singapore, data on reasons for divorce have only been published for the very recent period 1984–7, when divorce rates were low, the average age of females at divorce was above 30 and the reasons for divorce were possibly rather different from the traditional ones. In any case, 'personality difference' was the outstanding reason for divorce, followed by inadequate maintenance and infidelity (Table 6.4). The primacy of incompatibility as a cause of divorce appears consistent with the traditional situation, when divorces occurred at a much younger age (see Djamour, 1959: 142).

The Department of Religion in Indonesia divides the causes of divorce into a number of categories and subcategories (Alfian, 1977: 157), and these are given on the forms used in the registration of divorce. The categories emphasize proximate determinants[5] and are not subtle enough to draw out the cultural differences between ethnolinguistic groups in Indonesia which have influenced the wide disparities in incidence of divorce among these groups (Al Hadar, 1977). Though there is a rather moralistic tone to many of the reasons, lack of harmony does not rank as the number one cause, at least in West Java; rather, economic factors were cited in 43 per cent of cases in West Java in 1988–9, followed by lack of harmony (21 per cent) and *krisis akhlak* or 'crisis of character' such as drunkenness, or gambling (19 per cent). Desertion and irresponsibility each scored well below 10 per cent (Jones, Asari, and Djuartika, forthcoming). Perhaps the greater incidence of poverty in Java makes economic crises a more potent factor than in Malaysia, but the fact that they so frequently lead to divorce indicates a widespread perception of divorce as a viable solution to any difficulties within a marriage.

The main reasons given for divorce in the Malaysian Marriage Survey (from a list of precoded reasons) were low family income (23 per cent), bad character of spouse (15 per cent), husband wants to marry another woman (12 per cent), wife wants to marry another man (8 per cent), jealousy (8 per cent), and 'other' (14 per cent) (Tan and Jones, 1991: Table 6). Of all reasons given, about 40 per cent reflect incompatibility, including no doubt some of the responses in the 'other' category.

The same respondents were also asked to check which of a list of possible causes of divorce applied in their own case, more than one reason being allowed per respondent. In this case, the importance of economic causes gained prominence; low income or unemployment of the spouse was cited by about half the respondents. In answer to a separate question, again about half the respondents agreed that economic difficulties had an influence on the divorce (Tan and Jones, 1991: Tables 5 and 7).

It is difficult to draw conclusions from the data on causes of divorce presented in the last few pages. Incompatibility clearly ranked high, and childlessness low, among causes of divorce (even though Koentjaraningrat (1985: 101) claims that in Java infertility, typically blamed on the wife, is often used by the husband as a reason to divorce her). Economic factors were important, but it is not always clear whether failure to pay maintenance reflects true economic difficulty or the husband's irresponsible attitude to the marriage. Interference by in-laws appears to be a major factor in some data (including a village study in Aceh by Baihaqi, 1977) but an unimportant one in others.

Perhaps more important than the specific reasons given for divorce is the confirmation of the impression that divorce was seen by many as the logical way out of a wide range of problems that might arise in a marriage. In areas where the incidence of divorce was highest, attitudes to divorce in the 1950s and 1960s were especially liberal. 'For a Sundanese woman there is no stigma attached to being a divorcee, nor to having married several times. On the contrary, this is an asset, because it indicates that she is a desirable woman.' (Than et al., 1970: 32, cited in Zuidberg, 1978: 88.) In Indramayu, West Java, 'there is often a pride among parents in a girl who is frequently married and divorced, because it means many men were interested in her. Materially, too, additional marriage ceremonies bring in gifts from the guests even when it is the girl's second or third marriage.' (Jones, Asari, and Djuartika, forthcoming.) 'A Kelantanese Malay woman might tell you with pride that she has had 2–3–4 or 5 husbands.' (Gordon, 1964: 24.)

Another aspect of the liberal attitudes to divorce prevailing at the time is that the woman could more readily obtain a divorce, should she want one, than in most Muslim countries. Rather than face the difficulty and expense of applying for one of the female-initiated forms of divorce, the most straightforward way for many women was to arrange for the husband to divorce her by *talak*. As Winstedt (1961: 48) put it, 'The average wife ... [prefers] ... to exasperate her husband till he divorces her.' Observers of the Kelantan and Trengganu scene since the 1950s seem agreed that this was commonly done, and that men had little choice but to accede to a wife's demands, if she played her cards right. She could spread malicious stories about him, refuse to obey him publicly, or do other things to enrage or embarrass him (Swift, 1963: 268–94; Rosemary Firth, 1966: 43; Zalaluddin, 1979: 113; Hashim, 1984; 67). In Negri Sembilan, 'tactics of shaming are both widespread and highly effective' (Peletz, 1988: 252). According to Strange (1981: 160), 'The villagers say that although it is not good, any smart woman can push her husband into divorcing her by embarrassing him publicly and making his life generally unpleasant in other ways. The other ways often involve food. ... In public he is made to feel *malu* ...

and at home he is at least subject to discomforts and annoyances.' Should the husband refuse, wives could and sometimes did file for divorce with the *kadi*, a situation very embarrassing for the husband, who would normally try to forestall this by pronouncing a divorce by *talak*. Hashim (1984: 67) notes several cases in which the wives requested divorce through the Shariah Court in Kota Bharu, but the husbands pronounced divorce by *talak* just before the Court sat in session.

Despite all the evidence of options open to women who wanted to divorce, though, the fact remains that the highly unequal access of men and women to divorce placed women at a considerable disadvantage, particularly if the husband would not co-operate in pronouncing the *talak*. A woman either had to go to great trouble or expense or both to obtain a divorce, or had to demean both herself and her husband by going through the ploys necessary to make him change his mind.

Economic Factors

At both community and individual levels, divorce was related to poverty and traditional occupations. The divorce rate was highest in rural areas of the poorest and most traditional states of Peninsular Malaysia; in Java, in the nineteenth century, divorce was more frequent in towns than in rural areas, but it was the lower classes in the towns that separated easily (Boomgaard, 1989: 146). By the mid-twentieth century, divorce was most frequent in rural areas of Java, which had some of the greatest poverty in Indonesia, and this remained the case in the 1960s and 1970s, although a casual examination of Map 5.3 does not suggest a correlation within Java between regions of widespread poverty and high divorce. Survey data for Indonesia show a strong inverse correlation between economic well-being and frequency of divorce (see Table 5.11). In Malaysian cities in more recent times, divorce, too, appears to have been more common among the poorer groups (Kassim, 1985: 136–41).

All this suggests that poverty may frequently have served as a cause of divorce. 'As villagers themselves acknowledged, a sound economic footing is essential for the stability of a marriage.' (Hefner, 1990: 171.) Conflicts over the allocation of income were likely to be sharper where that income was very limited, and claims of extravagance levelled at the wife or the husband more bitter (T. E. Smith, 1961; Hefner, 1990: 171). In many areas, low standard of living fostered out-migration of men in search of work and hence extended periods of separation of spouses, failure of the husband to provide adequately for his family's needs, and family quarrels. Generally, poverty was linked to low levels of women's education, early marriage, parent-arranged marriage, and other elements of the mutually reinforcing group of causes of high divorce rates. V. J. Hull (1975: 418) stated that in Java,

while marriage is emphasized as an economic partnership in the lower income groups, the husband and wife tend to live segregated lives, with the wife attaining a high degree of economic self-sufficiency. The segregated nature of the marriage relationship is found in an extreme form among couples who are physically separated for long periods of time while one partner seeks work in a distant area. In some of these cases the marriage bond is ultimately dissolved. . . .

Divorce among the more well-to-do was undoubtedly constrained by considerations of the division of property, and such considerations probably led to a more careful choice of spouse in the first place. Furthermore, in Java, ideology played a part. According to H. Geertz (1961: 137–9), the upper class (*priyayi*) viewed divorce as an action displaying lack of self-control, a trait which *priyayi* value highly and which they see as characterizing their class compared to the more impetuous lower classes. There was undoubtedly also a major difference between the upper and lower classes in Java in the perception (if not the reality) of a woman's ability to support herself. The upper-class woman had more to lose economically if she divorced, given the limited range of income-earning options considered appropriate for women in *priyayi* circles, whereas lower-class women were used to earning a living in trade, cottage industry, agriculture, or a combination of such activities (Vreede-de Stuers, 1960; V. J. Hull, 1975: Chapter 4).

Divorce as a Reaction to Polygyny

When asked whether they would prefer to be divorced or to be involved in a polygamous marriage, the great majority of Malay women surveyed opted for the former. In the Malaysian Marriage Survey, 71 per cent of Malay women said they would prefer to be divorced (Tan et al., 1986: 172); in one village survey in Kelantan, 78 per cent (Zalaluddin, 1979: 143). The great majority of the women in Kelantan focus groups said they would prefer to be divorced than to be in polygamous marriages, though a few said polygamy is acceptable provided the husband is really fair to his wives. In Indonesia, too, a majority of women surveyed said they would choose divorce rather than remain in a polygynous marriage (Arian, 1982: 64; Mahfudz, 1982: 58; Muliakusuma, 1982: 61; Mahmud, 1983: 57).

These attitudes suggest that the frequent recourse to polygamy by husbands, especially in the East Coast states of Malaysia and in West Sumatra and South Sulawesi (to be discussed in Chapter 7) would have contributed to high divorce rates, when first wives refused to continue living in a polygamous marriage. South Sulawesi may be an exception here, however, because although polygamy was very prevalent, divorce rates were not very high. As noted earlier, polygamy was not cited frequently as the reason for divorce in Malaysian states where data were available. Even so, data for Trengganu show that at least 18 per cent of husbands who divorced in the 1972–6 period had a second wife at the time (another 20 per cent gave no answer to this question). This was almost certainly above the proportion of all husbands who were polygamous at the time, thus suggesting strongly that, whatever reason may have been cited as the cause of the divorce, polygamy was a factor.

In any case, the importance of polygamy as a cause of divorce would be greatly understated by considering only the proportion of marriages that were polygamous when the divorce occurred, because it was frequently the husband's declared intention to take a second wife that triggered the divorce. This divorce would pre-empt the polygamous marriage, because the husband was then free to marry the second woman monogamously. In V. J. Hull's (1975: 220) study in Maguwohardjo, Yogyakarta, 15 per cent of divorces were attributed by wives to the husband's taking a second wife, while a further 3 per cent were attributed to his intention to take a second wife. Other studies are not available to determine whether these proportions were representative.

Loose Administration of Divorce Laws

MALAYSIA

Traditionally, in many of the states of Malaysia, the procedures for obtaining a divorce were very simple. As mentioned in Chapter 2, administrative provisions in the states did require that every effort at reconciliation should be made before a *talak* was registered. But in at least two states for which studies are available (Kelantan and Johore) these provisions were frequently not followed in practice (Maznah, 1975; Nik Ramlah, 1978). In Kelantan, Kedah, and Johore, it was not necessary to fill out an application form to obtain a divorce; a notification after the event was enough. In most other states, the forms were often filled out in a very perfunctory manner. In the 1960s and 1970s, divorces in Kelantan and Trengganu could be approved by the local Penulang Pendaftar Nikah dan Cerai (Assistant Registrar of Marriage and Divorce) or the *imam* of the local mosque. Before the mid-1970s, the *imam* were not salaried, and it has been argued (e.g. by Zalaluddin, 1979: 118; Hashim, 1984: 91) that the commissions they received[6] for registering marriages and divorces must in many cases have predisposed them against making efforts to reconcile couples seeking divorce. It was not necessary in Kelantan for the divorces to be approved by the *kadi*, *naib kadi*, or the Islamic religious courts, as in the other states.

It must be borne in mind that in the East Coast states, in particular, at the time, divorce rates were the highest in the world, polygamy was common, and religious teachers and officials were among the most prone to practise divorce and polygamy.[7] It is therefore not surprising if, in the administration of divorce laws, the interests of the males prevailed and the rights or welfare of the wife often received scant attention. 'A woman waiting in her kampong for the return of her husband may well receive her certificate of divorce through the mail, with no reasons stated, no evidence, no procedure, no appeal.' (Gordon, 1964: 25.) In Kelantan, should an *imam* not agree to a divorce application, there was nothing to stop the petitioner simply going to another district and registering the divorce there (Zalaluddin, 1979: 123).

The malaise in the administration of divorce in this period was certainly bound up with irresponsible male attitudes prevalent at the time. The tolerance of divorce in Islam (properly understood, a qualified tolerance, and certainly not an advocacy) was enthusiastically seized on by many men in a licentious way. Extreme cases may serve to illustrate the point. One middle-aged Kelantanese man who had married several times stated frankly that if he wants sex with a woman, it is a sin (*dosa*) to do so without marrying her—at least for a night. One well-off Trengganu man some decades ago, although he did not indulge in polygamy, married about 100 times, sequentially: this case was reported to the author by the man's granddaughter, a university lecturer. In Rusila, Trengganu, Strange (1981: 159) found two men who had undergone twenty-eight and seventeen irrevocable divorces, respectively, mostly with women who were already divorcees when they married them. In Jeram, Kelantan, one man had married twenty-nine times and another, twenty-eight. These were semi-itinerant men, who would take a new wife, for a few months or years, in each new place (Downs, 1967: 145).

Even these cases, however, could not match what is probably the Indonesian record: in Indramayu, West Java, one headman of Sindang was reported to have officially married 114 times, without ever having divorced his first wife, and one middle-aged woman had married fifty times, having only 'felt really married' when she tied the knot with her forty-eighth husband, whom she unfortunately felt constrained to divorce after five months because she found he was polygamously married (*Kompas*, 16 September 1979).

SINGAPORE

In Singapore, the Malay divorce rate remained very high before 1957; in fact, the ratio of 55 divorces per 100 marriages in the 1947–57 period was almost double the ratio in neighbouring Johore. Enforcement of divorce laws appears to have been lax, as in much of Malaysia. The introduction of the Muslim Law Act of 1957, however, enforced stricter controls on the registration of divorce. Although the power of the husband to repudiate his wife was not affected, it was provided that a *kadi* might only register such repudiations where the wife consented to it. In other cases the parties had to go before the Shariah Court, which would adjudicate the matter and was required to make every effort to effect a reconciliation before registering such a divorce. That the bureaucratic hurdles and financial costs placed in the way of quick and thoughtless divorce had an immediate effect seems to be indicated by the sharp decline in divorce rates after 1957, sharper than the decline in neighbouring Malaysian states where no such Act had been introduced.

INDONESIA

'In Indonesia, lack of government concern during the colonial period had permitted wide variation in Islamic marriage practices, corruption by unpaid registrars, and even a good deal of open avoidance of religious–legal obligations.' (Lev, 1972a: 143.) One of the first acts of the new Ministry of Religion in 1946 'was to try to bring some control, order, uniformity, and probity to registrars of marriage, divorce and re-conciliation' (Lev, 1972a: 142). Officials of the KUA (Kantor Urusan Agama, or Office of Religious Affairs) were subsequently encouraged to advise estranged couples against divorce and to try to reconcile them; the divorce registration form has long contained, in bold letters, the warning that divorce is an evil deeply repugnant to Allah. But the efforts of KUA officials in this direction appear to have been mostly rather perfunctory and rarely successful (Lev, 1972a: 146–7). On the whole, divorce seems to have been taken very much for granted, not only in the society but among most officials. Beginning in 1954, the establishment of the BP4 (Badan Penasehat Perkawinan dan Penyelesaian Perceraian, or Marriage Counselling and Divorce Settlement Bodies) within the KUA introduced a new element into the picture.

A major problem with studying the implementation of divorce laws in Indonesia is that very few studies exist for wide regions of this culturally complex archipelago. For example, for two of the provinces with very high divorce rates, West Java and South Kalimantan, dominated by the Sundanese and Banjarese respectively, no solid studies of the administration of divorce regulations and procedures appear to be available. For the Javanese, Lev's (1972a) and Nakamura's (1983) studies are invaluable and will be drawn on in the later discussion on legal and administrative changes affecting the incidence of divorce.

Nakamura shows the considerable efforts undertaken in Yogyakarta in the early 1970s, and presumably for some considerable time before that, to reconcile a couple petitioning for a divorce. The role of the BP4 is well portrayed. It is possible that these procedures may have been followed more closely in Yogyakarta than in some other parts of Java, although the author's fieldwork in West Java revealed that there, too, the role of the BP4 has been taken seriously for a long time. On the other hand, occasional reports of maladministration do appear (Jones, Asari, and Djuartika, forthcoming).

Effects of Divorce

Consideration must be given not only to the effects of divorce in particular cases, but also to the effect of the 'high divorce culture' prevailing in many parts of Islamic South-East Asia in the 1950s and 1960s. Every woman was aware of the possibility that her husband could easily repudiate her, or take another wife. According to Strange (1981: 139–40), 'This awareness can affect the way in which a married woman relates to her husband and to other women, and fosters her perception of young divorcees as dangerous competition.... Thus it is the possibilities, the potentials, as much as local instances of divorce and polygyny that affect a woman's thinking and behaviour.'

Women and children undoubtedly frequently suffered as a result of the high divorce rate. Islam specifies that the husband is responsible for his wife's support only for the *eddah* period (100 days) following divorce, and in many instances support for even this period was not forthcoming.

Therefore the wife needed a source of income or the support of her family to survive. Many Malay writers have portrayed the fate of Kelantanese divorcees driven to prostitution in other states in order to support themselves after divorce.

But it would not be accurate to portray the frequency of *talak* merely as evidence of women's subjugation to men's irresponsible whims. As already noted, *talak* was actually initiated by the wife in a substantial proportion of cases. The ability of a large proportion of Kelantanese or Trengganu women to sustain themselves economically enhanced their readiness to take this step, as did the ease of remarriage. Similarly, in Java, the fact that most occupations were open to them enabled most divorced women to achieve a degree of self-sufficiency after divorce, though as V. J. Hull (1975: 228) observes, H. Geertz's (1961: 46) claim that 'a woman has no difficulty supporting herself and her children' is excessively sanguine.

Compared with present-day divorce in Western countries, a higher proportion of divorces (around 40–50 per cent in a number of studies) were to childless couples, and in these cases the effect of divorce on children was not a concern. Even so, with divorce rates as high as they were, large numbers of children were affected by divorce, most of them very young when the divorce occurred. As a rough estimate, in the high divorce regions, about 60–85 per cent of Malay children in the 1950s would have reached adulthood (age 17) still living with both their natural parents. The lower probability pertained to children born to older mothers, for whom widowhood was more likely, and the higher probability pertained to children born a few years after marriage, after the risks of divorce had declined. Importantly, widowhood was a more frequent reason than divorce for children not to be living with both natural parents.

The effects of divorce on children involve a question not just of the financial circumstances in which these children were raised, but also of the psychological impact of divorce on children. Although there is evidence in the American studies of serious consequences of divorce for children and its effect on their own ability to sustain satisfactory marriages (Wallerstein and Blakeslee, 1989; Wallerstein, 1991), this is not supported by a recent Australian study (Dunlop and Burns, 1992). There is very little evidence on this matter in the Malay world. The ease of adoption within extended families and the common role of grandparents in raising children suggest that it would be inappropriate to expect Western studies of the effect of divorce on children to be fully relevant.

The Malaysian Marriage Survey questioned ever-divorced respondents (more than half of whom, it will be recalled, divorced before about 1960) about problems faced during the period between divorce and remarriage. One-quarter said they had faced no problems. Of the more important problems faced by the rest, financial difficulties headed the list for both sexes, followed by loneliness in the case of females and problems of managing the household and upbringing of children in the case of males (Tan and Jones, 1990: Table 13). Only a fairly small proportion mentioned that finding a place to stay had been a problem. In just over half of all cases, the husband was the one who left the house after divorce, and in over one-third of all cases, the wife moved. Irrespective of who moved, the move was typically back to the parents' house (68 per cent of males; 84 per cent of females), which was usually not far away. More than one-third of divorced females who moved did so within the same village or town, and over 30 per cent to a neighbouring village.

The finding that most women either remained in their parents' house, from which they had never moved, or moved back to their parents' house after divorce is in line with other evidence. For example, in Yogyakarta, V. J. Hull (1975: 227) found that 81 per cent of divorced women lived with their parents immediately following divorce. In West Java, Hugo (1975: 427) found that substantially more males moved as a result of divorce than females. Most migrations resulting from divorce were within the same village.

The division of property after divorce is based on the concepts of community property of husband and wife and their separately owned personal property. The goods they brought into the marriage or inherited during the marriage are returned to them and the communal property (called *gana gini* in Java) is divided in the ratio of two parts to the husband and one part to the wife, or equally divided between the husband and wife (H. Geertz, 1961: 50; Jay, 1969: 63–7; V. J. Hull, 1975: 224–6). In many cases (46 per cent in V. J. Hull's study), there is no *gana gini* to divide at all, because the couple had been married only a short time or had not been able to acquire any goods during the marriage.

Although the Shafi'ite code of Muslim law gives a mother custody of a daughter until puberty and a son until he is 7, whereupon custody of both reverts to the father, customary practice in Malaysia is for all children to stay with the mother following a divorce. This does not appear to be universal, however. In the Malaysian Marriage Survey, 19 per cent of children had stayed with the husband and a further 13 per cent with 'both husband and wife' (Tan and Jones, 1990: Table 15), presumably meaning that the children were divided between the two or that they spent time alternately with the mother and the father.

The economic burden of supporting the children normally falls on the mother and those of her kin who are able to help. Ideally, a father should contribute to his children's support, and in theory he can be required to do so if he is financially capable (Maznah, 1975), but 'I could not find one instance in which he did so in any regular manner either in 1965 or in 1979' (Strange, 1981: 165). Both Djamour (1966: 125) and Rosemary Firth (1966: 47–8) found similar patterns, as did V. J. Hull (1975: 228) in Yogyakarta.[8] The behaviour of husbands was not so universally irresponsible according to the Malaysian Marriage Survey, which found that, although 59 per cent of husbands paid no maintenance at all, at least 18 per cent (16 per cent according to the divorced wives' reports) paid it for more than seven years or until the children were adult (Tan and Jones, 1990: Table 16).

To some degree, it might be argued that in a context of young, parent-arranged marriages, women's welfare was protected by the ease of divorce. There was no place in Kelantan for 'the degrading spectacle of a man and woman tied together by law and religion for life, although they no longer wish to remain together'. Rather, 'freedom of divorce allows the first, early marriage to represent a probation, an experimental period. If the union works, then no more need be done; if it does not, then it is severed, and both parties can start again with the experience they have obtained.' (Rosemary Firth, 1966: 44.)

Factors Fostering Greater Stability

In the search for factors responsible for the increasing marital stability over time in the Malay world, it is necessary to keep in mind the time period over which the major changes in divorce rates occurred. For Peninsular Malaysian and Singapore Malays, the declines appear to have been going on ever since 1950 (see Table 5.8); no data are available on whether they began even earlier than 1950. In Indonesia, the decline apparently began a little later, around 1955. In Brunei, there was no decline, and the divorce trends for Southern Thai Muslims are unknown. What is to be sought, then, is divorce-lowering influences being felt during the 1950s, 1960s, and 1970s in Indonesia, Malaysia, and Singapore.

The discussion above has stressed the more benign aspects of the high divorce 'culture' in the traditional Malay world. Easy divorce avoided the need for incompatible couples to be locked into unsatisfactory marriages, and was frequently instigated by the woman (even in the case of *talak* divorces), as was shown in Chapter 5. Divorce was accommodated in Malay societies in ways that minimized hardship. For example, the divorcee and her children (if any) could normally find succour in her parents' home. A divorcee was not looked on as an inappropriate choice of marriage partner, at least in Java. Indeed, divorcees in many regions were considered particularly desirable.

From the 1960s on, however, there was growing and justifiable concern in Malay societies about the adverse social consequences of divorce. Opponents of divorce pointed to the social instability, the hardship caused to mothers and children, and the fundamental unfairness to women of the ease with which men could divorce. Economic hardship and recourse to prostitution were claimed to be the lot of many divorcees. This increasingly negative societal attitude to divorce provided the context in which other events played themselves out.

Rising Age at Marriage and Shift towards Self-Arrangement

If, as argued above, early, parent-arranged marriage and all that went with it (wide age differences between spouses, frequent non-consummation, immaturity of the couple) contributed importantly to the high divorce rate, then the rise in age at marriage since the late 1960s (dramatic in Malaysia, steady in Indonesia) and the almost wholesale shift to self-arrangement must have been a major factor in the subsequent decline in divorce. Certainly, the timing of these two trends was such as to suggest either that one caused the other or that the trends were closely related outcomes of major shifts in attitudes to the initiation and continuation of marriage.

The important aspect of self-arrangement of marriage as it relates to divorce is that the couple have a much greater stake in the success of the marriage.[9] Love marriages are unlikely to break down during the first year or two, the most vulnerable period in traditional arranged marriages. Accompanying the shift to love marriages was the rise in age at marriage and in the average educational level of those marrying, leading to greater maturity of the couple at the time of marriage. The rising frequency of non-marriage and the increasing acceptability of waiting until the mid to late twenties to marry mean that there has been a relaxation of the traditional pressure on young people, or their parents, to find a spouse before community ridicule and the taunt of 'old maid' befell them, and a decline presumably in the hasty choices of spouses to which such pressure led. One reason Singapore Malay parents give for their unwillingness to arrange their children's marriages is their fear of being blamed if the marriage fails (Li, 1989: 35).

Although the shift to later and self-arranged marriages was undoubtedly a major factor in the decline in divorce, it certainly could not provide the complete explanation. This is evident from the contrasting trends among Indonesian Muslims and Peninsular Malaysian Malays. In Peninsular Malaysia, age at marriage and the self-arranged proportion of marriages were rising more rapidly over the 1960s and 1970s than in Indonesia; yet divorce rates were falling more rapidly over this period in Indonesia than in Peninsular Malaysia.

Education and Women's Improving Economic Status

Since the 1950s, a progressively increasing proportion of girls have been staying longer in school and leaving with higher levels of educational attainment (see Chapter 2). Table 6.2 showed that in Java–Bali, even when age at marriage was controlled for, more education was associated with much less divorce (see also Guest, 1991). Increased schooling of girls, then, can be expected to have played a major role in the decline in divorce in Islamic South-East Asia.

Education has multiple effects on marriage, as on most other areas of social and family life. In the case of divorce, not only was it associated with the shift to older, self-arranged marriages just discussed, but education undoubtedly affected the expectations of young people about marriage. The traditional attitude that divorce was sometimes an unfortunate but not disastrous by-product of achieving the 'greater good' of preserving family honour was probably a casualty of education more than of anything else. Education contributed importantly to women's improving economic status and earning potential, giving them a greater sense of equality and dissatisfaction with the traditional role played by divorce. For men, education was also associated with greater acceptance of equality with women in various fields and a companionate concept of marriage. In general, the expansion of education probably served to inculcate middle-class values opposing divorce in a wider cross-section of the population than before.

As already discussed in Chapter 2, the economic condition of the Malays was constantly improving in Malaysia and Singapore throughout the 1960s and 1970s, though it was not until the late 1960s that Indonesia began to climb out of the economic morass of the Sukarno period, setting the stage for rapid, oil boom-fed development in the 1970s. Poverty by no means disappeared, but the proportion of the Indonesian population living in poverty, according to one measure (the Esmara measure), fell from 49 per cent in 1970 to 36 per cent in 1987 in rural areas, and from 38 to 30 per cent in urban areas. The 'official' Central Bureau of Statistics estimates show a more rapid decline (Booth, 1992: 342–5). To the extent that poverty contributed to divorce, this increased prosperity should have lessened the pressure on couples to divorce.

Changing Community Attitudes, Islamic Fundamentalism, and the Women's Movement

In Indonesia, the establishment of the Ministry of Religion in 1946 was followed in 1947 by instructions to civil servants to speak with both parties when a divorce was requested and to try to persuade the husband not to pronounce the *talak*. Following 'earnest requests continuously brought up by the women's associations and by all the female members of the provisional parliament', the government in 1950 appointed a commission to enquire into a new ruling on marriage (Vreede-de Stuers, 1960: 125). Demands for marriage-reform legislation were constantly at issue, to a greater or lesser extent, from then on.

The primary proponent of marriage-law reform has been a respectably powerful urban, intellectual, and upper-class women's movement, whose history begins almost simultaneously with that of the nationalist movement itself.... Their demands have grown out of the same kinds of social change that have produced similar reform movements elsewhere in the world: a growing intellectual liberation of upper- and upper-middle-class women, an easing control over women in urban society, the impact of egalitarian ideologies, and the influence of foreign examples. (Lev, 1972a: 137–8.)[10]

The influence of this women's movement, and the influence of individual women on their highly placed husbands, was no doubt a very important factor in the eventual passage of the marriage law in 1974, to be discussed below.

In Malaysia, too, sensitivity about the negative image of Malay culture occasioned by what was seen as an irresponsibly high level of divorce was an important factor making for change. As in Indonesia, opposition to easy polygamy and divorce among upper-class and upper middle-class women was an important element,[11] although the legitimacy lent to the Indonesian movement by its association with nationalism and the independence movement was lacking. An unease at high divorce rates may be evident in the roles of divorcees and much-divorced men in many Malay novels of the period (Banks, 1987). More recently, the Islamic resurgence in Malaysia, although it was not a unified movement, gave impetus to the attack on irresponsible divorce by emphasizing that Islam, properly understood, strongly opposes divorce. It is impossible to sort out the relative impacts of these movements, but what is clear is that a condemnatory attitude to easy divorce was being more commonly expressed in the 1970s, not only by women's leaders but by community leaders and indeed by the community at large. 'Divorce ... is now considered shameful and something to be avoided. ... In Kedah people have become noticeably more reticent about the subject.' (Kuchiba, Tsubouchi, and Maeda, 1979: xxi.)

Similarly in Singapore, early marriage and marital instability were increasingly seen as factors holding back the Malays in their competition with other ethnic groups, especially the Chinese. In the 1970s, Malay leaders were using the media 'to inculcate the virtues of late marriage and family stability' (Tham, 1979: 111).

Focus-group discussions with middle-aged women in Kelantan in 1989 drew out an almost universal attitude that it is sinful for a woman to ask her husband to divorce her. Whether these women had always felt this way was not clear.

In surveys conducted in Indonesia and Malaysia in the early 1980s, and in West Java in early 1988, respondents were asked what they believed their community's attitudes were to divorce, choosing between three precoded responses: 'biasa' (meaning common, or an everyday occurrence, the implication being that there is no particular moral judgement to make); 'kurang baik, tapi kadang-kadang perlu dilakukan' (not good, but sometimes necessary); and 'tercela' (disgraceful). The findings are presented in Table 6.5. Responses clearly varied widely between regions, with the strongest attitudes of condemnation being expressed in Aceh, known throughout Indonesia as a bastion of Islamic orthodoxy. However, only in South Sumatra and West Java did much fewer than three-quarters of respondents fail to adopt a generally negative attitude towards divorce. The most common reaction among Peninsular Malaysian Malays was that divorce is not good, but sometimes unavoidable; interestingly, Indian respondents adopted a far more condemnatory attitude to divorce than did Malays (see Table 6.6).

The Malaysian and Indonesian marriage surveys asked respondents whether they approved of divorce under a range of specified circumstances. The results are presented in Table 6.7. A number of points should be stressed. First, adultery, especially the wife's adultery, is considered a strong ground for divorce (except for the man's adultery in Aceh), and so is cruelty by the husband. Second, incompatibility evokes different responses: in most of the Indonesian regions, it was

TABLE 6.5

Percentage Distribution of Opinions about Divorce, Various Surveys of Malay Populations

Opinions	Malaysian Malays, 1981				Indonesian Marriage Survey, 1978							West Java Survey, 1988
	Married Sample		Single Sample		Aceh		Jakarta (Betawi)		South Sumatra	Java		
	Males	Females	Males	Females	Males	Females	Males	Females		Males	Females	
Common	5	3	7	6	5	3	27	26	47	22	29	38
Not good, but at times have to take such a step	78	80	67	68	2	13	21	40	{53	{78	{71	45
Disgraceful	14	15	19	20	93	84	52	34	–	–	–	11
Do not know	3	3	7	6	–	–	–	–	–	–	–	6
Total	100	100	100	100	100	100	100	100	100	100	100	100

Sources: Reports on the Malaysian Marriage Survey, 1981; Indonesian Marriage Survey, 1978; and Tim Peneliti (1988: Table 25).

TABLE 6.6

Peninsular Malaysia: Percentage Distribution of Opinions on Divorce,
by Ethnic Group, 1981–1982

Opinions	Ethnic Group		
	Malays	Chinese	Indians
Females			
Common	3	13	3
Not good, but at times have			
to take such a step	80	63	42
Disgraceful	15	21	53
Do not know	3	3	3
Total (%)	101	100	101
Male			
Common	5	16	4
Not good, but at times have			
to take such a step	78	61	42
Disgraceful	14	20	52
Do not know	3	2	2
Total (%)	100	99	100

Source: Tan and Jones (1990: Table 10).

considered strong grounds for divorce, but not so in Aceh or in Peninsular Malaysia. Third, a number of circumstances are not considered by most respondents to be appropriate grounds for divorce: for example, the husband's keeping a mistress or wanting to marry a second wife but not being able to afford it; interference by the family of one spouse; or the barrenness or impotence of one partner. On this last point, the ease with which children can be adopted in Malay society no doubt contributes to the relatively sanguine view of sterility (Djamour, 1959: 93; Banks, 1983: 99; Li, 1989: 36). Fourth, women are more inclined than men to approve divorce in a number of circumstances in which the fault lies with women: for example, where the wife is barren, or where she cannot carry out her duties because of illness, or where she frequently mismanages family finances. Fifth, there is quite wide variation in responses by region, probably highlighting cultural differences between different ethnolinguistic groups in some cases but in others perhaps the unrepresentativeness of the sample.

Indicators of recent official and community concern with the stability of marriage is the appointment of marriage counsellors (e.g. in Penang by the State Religious Department in 1986) and the popularity of marriage preparation courses conducted by various Islamic agencies in Malaysia and Singapore. Such courses were being conducted by the *kadi*'s office in the Federal Territory in 1986 (Shamsiah, 1986), by the Islamic Dakwah

TABLE 6.7

Malaysia and Indonesia: Percentage of Marriage Survey Respondents Who Agreed That under Particular Circumstances a Wife or Husband Can Ask for a Divorce

	Peninsular Malaysia (Malays)		Jakarta (Betawi)		South Kalimantan (Banjarese)		Aceh		South Sumatra		Java	
	Males	Females	Males	Females	Males	Females	Males	Females	Males	Females	Males	Females
Wife can ask for a divorce if:												
Husband is a drunkard, drug addict, gambler[a]	88	90	93	84	94	93	77	90	83	87	70	77
Husband often cruel to wife[a]	91	94	97	86	95	79	67	85	80	74	73	83
Husband in prison for more than 5 years[a]	58	61	46	15	50	40	21	24	35	23	41	46
Husband is a womanizer (committed adultery)[a]	87	91	78	81	92	93	35	46	66	63	75	82
Husband wants to take second wife but cannot afford two wives	61	78	62	71	31	36	26	51	39	52	72	86
Husband is impotent	81	64	34	57	45	36	24	30	77	62	53	76
Husband keeps a mistress/steady girl-friend	91	91	36	57	28	28	25	48	29	46	69	81
Husband left home for more than 3 months without consent of wife	66	68	89	73	65	66	20	34	62	56	67	69

(continued)

TABLE 6.7 (continued)

	Peninsular Malaysia (Malays)		Jakarta (Betawi)		South Kalimantan (Banjarese)		Aceh		South Sumatra		Java	
	Males	Females	Males	Females	Males	Females	Males	Females	Males	Females	Males	Females
Wife is in love with another man	90	90	36	39	26	41	35	46	n.a.	n.a.	48	40
Wife is not given maintenance	83	85	89	83	n.a.	n.a.	51	72	85	81	80	78
Interference from husband's family[b]	19	20	48	61	37	22	58	38	33	40	46	64
Husband can ask for a divorce if:												
Wife controls husband completely	91	93	75	68	66	60	36	48	80	60	46	63
Wife is barren	26	28	27	68	21	32	24	49	27	53	41	79
Husband wants to marry another woman but cannot afford two wives	38	44	21	67	10	27	28	32	19	25	30	41
Interference from wife's family[b]	11	11	56	71	27	22	21	31	31	31	34	57

Wife cannot carry out duties because of illness[a]	15	17	37	82	16	54	23	64	29	43	12	15
Husband and wife cannot get along[a]	46	50	96	93	75	90	53	57	80	65	79	86
Husband given a difficult time by step-children	29	29	n.a.	n.a.	27	22	n.a.	n.a.	n.a.	n.a.	n.a.	n.a.
Wife is in love with another man	95	92	67	64	62	68	35	34	85	46	77	90
Wife left home for more than 3 months without consent of husband	91	88	97	80	82	91	36	48	86	83	74	77
Wife often mismanages household finances	16	14	50	90	41	55	30	65	65	64	46	67
Wife committed adultery[a]	–	–	97	99	99	98	93	94	97	91	80	91

Sources: Tan and Jones (1990: Table 11); Muliakusuma (1982: Table 8.7); Mahfudz (1982: Table 8.5); Arian (1982: Tables 8.2 and 8.3); Mahmud (1983: Table 8.7); Kasto (1982: Tables 8.5 and 8.6).

[a] Permitted by the 1974 Marriage Law (Indonesia).

[b] In Peninsular Malaysia, question was worded 'Husband's family dislikes wife' or 'Wife's family dislikes husband'.

Institute of Malaysia in 1987 (Zainab, 1987), by the Selangor State Religious Department in 1990 (*Malay Mail*, 4 October 1990), by the *kadi*'s office in Penang in 1991, and by Muslim organizations, mosque committees, and even by the Shariah Court itself in Singapore (Li, 1989: 36). One such course in Penang was attended by 450 young people, mainly unmarried (Zainal, 1991). Malaysia's National Population and Family Development Board conducted the first Happy Family Campaign in 1990, and this has become an annual event.

Decline in Polygyny

The apparent decline in the practice of polygyny will be discussed in the next chapter. To the extent that polygyny contributed to divorce, this decline in polygyny must have contributed to lower divorce. The decline in the practice of polygamy, as well as a lessening of the perceived threat of polygamy and the irritant and source of suspicion this introduced in many marriages, must have contributed to more companionate and more stable marriage. On the other hand, the perceived threat of polygamy has certainly not been removed altogether, and controversy in the Malaysian press in the late 1980s and early 1990s has kept it in the public eye.

Legal and Institutional Changes

Singapore led the way in the Malay regions of South-East Asia in introducing legal changes directed towards closer regulation of divorce. The Muslims Ordinance of 1957, amended by the Muslims (Amendment) Ordinance of 1960 and the Administration of Muslim Law Act of 1968, made divorce rules stricter and their implementation more careful. The Act provided for the appointment of a Registrar of Muslim Marriages (*kadi*) and the appointment of Deputy Registrars of Marriage (*naib kadi*) in various districts of Singapore. The 1968 Act required that all divorces or revocations of divorces (*rujuk*) be allowed only after the *kadi* has been satisfied on enquiry that both parties have given their consent to the divorce. Not only does Section 96(4) of the Act expressly prohibit the *kadi* from registering a divorce arising from the husband merely pronouncing the three *talak*, a right traditionally given him, but in addition, the wife is permitted in certain circumstances to institute divorce proceedings against the husband. Should the *kadi* receive a divorce request from the husband, he must refer the application to the Shariah Court for adjudication. It may appoint arbitrators (*hakam*) and also provides marriage counselling to couples who are estranged. Such counselling is performed by the *kadi* and the Muslim Social Case Worker in the Shariah Court, who will initially interview the husband and wife separately, and after several such interviews, will talk with the couple together (Tai, 1979: 150). 'Every effort will be made to reconcile and to settle the differences of opinion between the parties.' (Singapore, 1973: 16.) The seriousness of this approach no doubt played a major role in the declining incidence of divorce among Singapore Malays:

from 49 per 100 marriages in 1958 to 20 per 100 marriages in 1967 and to 10 per 100 marriages in 1970.

Very important legal changes have also taken place in both Indonesia and Malaysia, following at some distance the administrative reforms introduced in Singapore. In Indonesia, the marriage law of 1974 immediately affected the whole population; in Malaysia, the Islamic Family Law Act of 1984 was gradually implemented in different states (see Chapter 2). In both cases, the main thrust of the legal changes and implementation procedures as they pertained to divorce was to lengthen the process of obtaining a divorce and institutionalize elements of counselling. The likely impact of all of these changes was to reduce divorce.

In Indonesia, before the 1974 marriage law was introduced, requests for *talak* were dealt with by the Kantor Urusan Agama (Religious Affairs Office). Only if there were legal complications did the case have to go before the Pengadilan Agama (Religious Court). Beginning in late 1954, marriage counselling boards (Badan Penasihat Perkawinan dan Penyelesaian Perceraian or BP4) began to be set up, attached to the Religious Affairs Offices, and couples contemplating divorce were supposed to be counselled by members of such boards (Lev, 1972a: 150–3).[12]

Since 1974, all requests for *talak* have had to be taken before a *sidang pengadilan* (court hearing) at the Pengadilan Agama. There normally have to be three court sittings to achieve such a divorce. The first sitting attempts to arrange reconciliation between the couple, and requires them to be counselled by BP4 (whose name had been changed to Badan Penyelenggara Penasihat Perkawinan Perselisihan dan Perceraian, or counselling body for marriage dispute and divorce settlements). The second hearing considers the results of the efforts to reconcile the couple,[13] and if the request for *talak* is not withdrawn, a third sitting is required to complete the arrangements for divorce. The charge for the court hearing, paid by the partner requesting divorce, has in recent years been set at Rp150,000 (about US$77). The cost of the court hearings, especially for poorer people, as well as the trouble and worry the procedure causes, undoubtedly make for lower divorce rates when compared with the previous procedures, where husbands could pronounce the *talak* at home and subsequently report this to the religious affairs office. Under current regulations, a husband who proceeds in this way faces a fine.

In the early 1980s, there was a further tightening of divorce procedures as they relate to members of the armed forces, police, and civil servants: about 7 per cent of the total workforce. In regulations enacted in 1980 (armed forces), 1981 (police), and 1983 (civil servants), a request for divorce could only be approved by the Pengadilan Agama if the permission of the applicant's superior was given. The regulation issued to those in supervisory positions required them to give careful attention to such cases and to counsel the applicant, where possible, to withdraw the application for divorce or polygamy (Indonesia, 1989). At the very least, these regulations led to considerable delays in the processing of divorce applications. More importantly, they were a clear indication of the government's negative attitude towards divorce, and its belief that government employees should show a good example to the people. The embarrassment of applying to superiors was undoubtedly, for many, a strong deterrent to initiating divorce proceedings in the first place.

In Malaysia, the Islamic Family Law Act of 1984, which was progressively enforced in most states by the late 1980s,[14] widened the grounds on which a wife could apply for a *fasakh* divorce and tightened up the regulations governing the *talak* divorce and the payment of maintenance. For any kind of divorce, an application has to be made to the court by the party desiring the divorce. The other party will have to appear in Court so as to enable it to enquire whether or not the other party consents to the divorce. If the Court is satisfied that the marriage is irretrievably broken down, it shall then advise the husband to pronounce one *talak* before the Court; or, in the case of *taliq* or *fasakh* applications, it will itself confirm the divorce.

However, if the other party does not consent to the divorce, and there is a reasonable possibility of a reconciliation between the parties, the Court will appoint a conciliatory committee consisting of a Religious Officer as chairman and three other persons, preferably close relatives of the parties, one of whom is to act for the husband and one for the wife. The committee is given three months to try to effect a reconciliation. If this fails, the Court will advise the husband to pronounce one *talak*.

This law obviously represents a considerable tightening up of procedures frequently followed in the past. Whereas in the past the wife frequently had no knowledge that her husband was divorcing her until after the event, according to the Islamic Family Law Act, any man who divorces his wife by pronouncement of the *talak* outside the Court and without the permission of the Court will have to pay a fine not exceeding RM1,000 and/or face six months' imprisonment.

The Act also spells out the requirements for maintenance of wife and children and for division of property following divorce. In addition to her right of maintenance during the *eddah* period, a woman who has been divorced without just cause may apply to the Court for *mut'ah* or a consolatory gift, and the Court may order the husband to pay a reasonable sum. The father also has a duty to maintain his children until the age of 18 years, instead of 15 years as before, or until the child has completed his or her higher education. The wife can also be required to contribute towards maintenance of the children if she is found to have the means.

As far as division of property is concerned, the Act safeguards the interests of the wife, even in cases where she has not contributed financially to the acquisition of assets during the marriage. The Act also empowers the Court to prevent a spouse from disposing of property so as to defeat the claim of the other spouse to maintenance, *mut'ah*, or division of property (Tan and Jones, 1990: 112–13).

The legal changes in Singapore and Indonesia were clearly important in lowering divorce rates; divorce rates fell faster in these countries following the enactment of the new laws than they did in Malaysia, where the laws had not changed. The more recent legal changes in Malaysia can also be expected to have had a similar effect. Only in Singapore, however, can the legal changes be said to have initiated the decline in divorce rates. In the other two countries, the legal changes served to accelerate a process already well under way, as can easily be observed from the timing of the decline in divorce rates in Table 5.8 and Figures 5.1 and 5.2. In Malaysia in particular, divorce rates were already quite low when the Islamic Family Law Act was introduced. It is possible that the debates leading up to the enactment of the new laws, and the increasingly negative official and community attitudes being expressed, had as great or greater influence on divorce trends as the laws themselves.

Case-studies of High-divorce Regions: Kelantan and West Java

In Chapter 5, the high divorce rates traditionally prevailing in Kelantan and West Java were noted, and some of the factors responsible for these high rates have already been discussed in this chapter. This section focuses in more detail on factors influencing recent divorce trends in these regions.

West Java

West Java is the most populous province of Indonesia. If it were a separate country, its 1990 population of 35 million would give it a ranking of twenty-seventh out of all the world's countries. It is inhabited mainly by Sundanese, though there is a substantial Javanese population (and those of mixed Sundanese–Javanese ancestry) in parts of the province which adjoin Central Java. Within the Sundanese ethnic group, there are substantial differences in culture, for example between the Banten area in the west and the upland areas of the Priangan. Given its historically high divorce rates, its varied geographical setting, and its ethnic and cultural diversity, West Java provides an appropriate focus for a study of trends in divorce. Although as mentioned earlier, West Java as a whole may no longer have the highest divorce rates in Indonesia, certain of its regions may.

This section will therefore discuss trends in divorce in West Java since the 1960s, concentrating on the effect of changes in marriage laws and their implementation on divorce rates. The analysis is based not only on survey data and statistics on divorce available from official sources, but also on fieldwork conducted in different parts of West Java in 1990 and 1991.[15]

DIVORCE TRENDS

Figure 5.3 showed a steady decline since the mid-1930s in the percentage of first marriages ending in divorce within a given duration of marriage. In urban areas, the big drop in divorce appears to have occurred between cohorts marrying in the 1940s and those marrying in the 1950s, whereas in rural areas there was a steadier downward sequence in incidence of divorce. The chances of marriages being broken by divorce were very high in the 1940s: in both urban and rural areas, about one-third of marriages had ended in divorce within three years of marriage. By the 1965–9 marriage cohorts, the proportion of marriages ending in divorce within 3 years had dropped to about 10 per cent in urban areas and slightly below 20 per cent in rural areas. In all cases, the likelihood declined after 3 years of marriage.

Trends in general divorce rates in West Java in an international context were shown in Table 5.8. The rate declined from a very high 2.3 per cent in 1953 to 1.8 per cent in the mid-1960s, but the biggest decline was between 1965 and 1970, when it reached 0.7 per cent. Figure 6.1 takes the story forward in more detail from the mid-1960s, presenting three indicators based on registered Islamic marriages and divorces.[16] None of the measures employed is perfect. Divorces per 100 married women is a better indicator than the general divorce rate, in that it relates divorces to the total population at risk of divorce. The pros and cons of the third indicator—the ratio of divorces to marriages occurring in any given year—were already discussed in Chapter 5. In one respect, it is preferable to the indicator 'divorces per 100 married women': most divorces occur in the few years following the marriage, and therefore it is somewhat unrealistic to relate all divorces to the total stock of married women. The ratio of divorces to marriages in a particular year is quite a good indicator of the incidence of divorce when a time series is available.

According to the measure 'divorces per 100 married women', the divorce rate in West Java by the mid-1980s was cut to a quarter of the 1972 rate, whereas according to the ratio of divorces to marriages, the figure was only cut to a half. The rise in 1975, the sharp fall in 1976, and the subsequent rise in 1977 and 1978 were no doubt short-term effects of the 1974 Marriage Law. The important point is that between 1978 (when short-term fluctuations had settled down at a level well below that of the early 1970s) and the late 1980s there was only a very gradual further decline.

REGIONAL DIFFERENTIALS

Map 5.2 showed sharp and persistent regional differences in the incidence of divorce. Divorce rates are low in the Banten area to the west, stretching through to the Jakarta region and Tangerang. The rates are high in the Priangan region around Bandung and to the east, and are especially high in the eastern Priangan and the north coastal strip from Cirebon to Subang. It is well recognized that there are ethnic,

FIGURE 6.1
West Java: Indicators of Trends in Divorce, 1965–1988

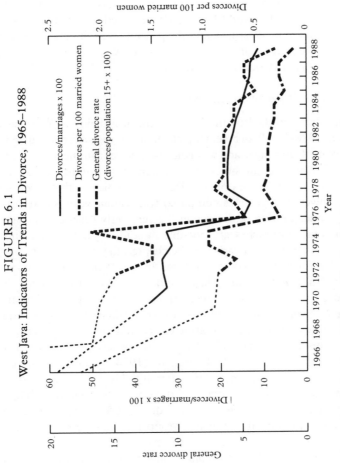

Source: Jones, Asari, and Djartika (forthcoming).

cultural, and religious differences between these regions; for example, the population of the Cirebon–Indramayu area contains a significant admixture of Javanese and has a higher proportion of *abangan* (people who mix Hindu–Javanese concepts, beliefs, and practices syncretically with Islamic ones) who rank low on the religiosity index, at least in relation to orthodox Islam. However, it is not easy to identify any particular explanatory factor for these wide differences in divorce rates. For example, both Banten and many areas of the Priangan devoutly follow orthodox Islamic beliefs, but their divorce rates differ very widely. Perhaps the key point about Banten is the very conservative nature of the religious and cultural beliefs. *Pesantren* education is stronger there than elsewhere in West Java and the general levels of education, especially for girls, are lower than elsewhere. For whatever reasons, divorce appears to be strongly discouraged in Banten.

GROUPS MOST PRONE TO DIVORCE

Recent data supplied by the Department of Religion in West Java show that in 1988–9, 19 per cent of all divorces registered occurred in the first year of marriage, and a further 44 per cent in the second to fourth year of marriage; in other words, almost two-thirds of all divorces occurred within 5 years of marriage. This indicates that, even with the much lower divorce rates compared with earlier years, there was still a heavy concentration of divorce in the very early years of marriage.

Different approaches are possible in studying the factors underlying divorce. As mentioned earlier in the chapter, the data on cause of divorce recorded for every divorce registered by the Pengadilan Agama are not very useful (see also Jones, Asari, and Djuartika, forthcoming). Another approach is to determine which subgroups in the population are more prone to divorce. Comparison of divorce incidence by income, education, place of residence, age at marriage, and number of children gives rise to some useful inferences about the causes of divorce. Figure 6.2, derived from McDonald and Abdurahman (1974), shows some of these differentials from the Indonesian Fertility–Mortality Survey data using the measure of average number of divorces to women in each age-group standardized for differences in age distribution. The number of ever-married women by five-year age-group in rural West Java was used as the standard population. Figure 6.2 shows that divorce is characterized by low education, Muslim religion, low socio-economic level, and early age at first marriage. Additionally, within each category, divorce was more prevalent among rural women than urban women. These findings are consistent with those of Guest (1991: Tables 2 and 3) for Java as a whole based on the 1976 Indonesian Fertility Survey, and with data from the 1980 Population Census on number of marriages of ever-married Muslim women by educational level, which show that divorce is far more common among the uneducated than the better-educated, even controlling for interval since first marriage to take account of a concentration of the better-educated among the more recently married (Jones, Asari, and Djuartika, forthcoming).

FIGURE 6.2

West Java: Standardized Average Number of Divorces by Socio-economic
Score, Religion, and Standardized Average Number of Marriages,
by Age at First Marriage, 1973

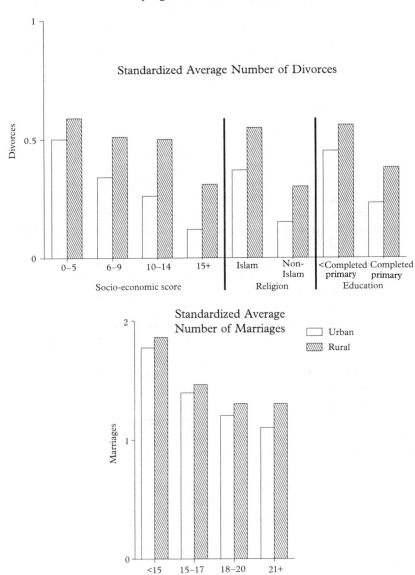

Source: McDonald and Abdurahman (1974: Table 14).

McDonald and Abdurahman (1974) raise the issue of whether divorces
in West Java can be divided into two discrete groups: those who divorce
from a parent-arranged and possibly non-consummated marriage but
enter a stable marriage the second time around; and the 'chronic
divorcers'. The answer seems to be that these two groups certainly do
exist; in the Indonesian Fertility–Mortality Survey, a little over 20 per cent

of West Java women aged 40–49 had been married twice, representing the first group, and in rural areas about 11 per cent had been married four or more times, presumably representing the second group. But another 11 per cent had been married three times, many of whom presumably were closer to the first group in that they may have simply run into unexpected difficulties in their second marriages (many of which were also parent-arranged) as well, rather than becoming 'chronic divorcers'. In other words, too sharp a dichotomy should not be made between 'victims of parent-arranged marriage' and 'chronic divorcers'.

EFFECT OF CHANGES IN DIVORCE LAWS ON DIVORCE RATES

The multiple causes of the decline in divorce rates in Indonesia have been discussed earlier in the chapter, and appear to have applied to West Java as well. This section concentrates on the effect of changes in divorce laws and regulations and their implementation.

In the past, an *amil* (a person appointed at the village level to register divorces and such matters) was frequently used to arrange the formalities of divorce. The procedure was simple. The *amil* could give agreement to the *talak* on the spot, or at the *kecamatan* (district) headquarters, and the wife was not required to be present. She could, for example, be informed by letter if she was living elsewhere. These days, the role of the *amil* varies; some regions insist that requests for divorce go through the *amil* but others do not. Another procedure sometimes used, a more costly one, is to make use of a *perantara*, a go-between or 'broker' who specializes in arranging divorce matters. The fee for such a broker can be quite substantial.

Before the 1974 marriage law was introduced, requests for *talak* were dealt with in the Religious Affairs Office, and were brought to the Pengadilan Agama only if there were legal complications. Since 1974, all requests for *talak* have had to be taken before a court hearing at the Pengadilan Agama, located in the *kabupaten* (regency) capital, an unfamiliar and apprehension-inducing environment for most rural people. The trouble and cost of the new procedures has undoubtedly been a factor in lowering the divorce rate, as has the further tightening, in the early 1980s, of divorce procedures as they relate to members of the armed forces, police, and civil servants. Their impact as a deterrent to divorce is enhanced by the requirements for maintenance of wife and children imposed on government servants who divorce, which can now be quite substantial.[17]

A key purpose of the 1974 marriage law and the more recent regulations was to reduce *talak* and polygamy, by tightening procedures and making divorce more time consuming and costly. On the other hand, not every official regulation since 1974 has been designed to make life more difficult for the party or parties seeking divorce. For example, a *sidang keliling* (travelling court) referred to also as a *safari perceraian* began operating around 1989 to serve the high-divorce *kabupaten* of Indramayu, Subang, and Cirebon. The purpose of this service is to enable divorce arrangements to be made without travelling to the *kabupaten* town, and to negate the common impression of the Pengadilan Agama as a kind of policeman rather than as an institution serving the needs of the people when divorce is necessary.

CASE-STUDY OF DIVORCE TRENDS IN INDRAMAYU

One *kabupaten* in West Java is famous for having Java's (and probably Indonesia's) highest levels of divorce and also as a major source of prostitutes to Jakarta. This is the *kabupaten* of Indramayu, located between Subang and Cirebon on the north coast, and traversed by the busy trunk road linking Jakarta, Semarang, and Surabaya. The northern coastal area of this *kabupaten* is dominated by sea-fishing and the operation of fish-ponds and salt-evaporation fields; the rest of the *kabupaten* is a predominantly rice-growing region. The people of Indramayu, though predominantly Muslim, are not noted for their religious devotion; an indicator is that there are no *pesantren* in Indramayu.

In a perceptive article in *Kompas* (16 September 1979), journalist Her Suganda described aspects of the divorce situation in Indramayu and attempted to link aspects of marriage arrangements, divorce, and prostitution. He recognized that Indramayu is a large *kabupaten* and that there are many variations within it. For example, the *kecamatan* (district) of Kandanghaur is noted for its *jaringan* activities (to be described shortly), Lelea is noted for its *ngarot* ceremonies, and Gabus Wetan in particular as a source of prostitutes to Jakarta.

Her Suganda portrayed a situation in which very early marriage[18] was frequently followed quickly by divorce, often without the marriage having been consummated. Indramayu at the time was characterized by low educational levels, and many of the girls concerned were illiterate. The reasons given for divorce were economic difficulties (cited by about 75 per cent), desertion by the husband, or the fact that the marriage was forced by the parents (*kawin paksa*).

The picture was one of very young marriage, at the behest of the parents; the dissolution of such marriages did not bring any great degree of censure or disapproval in the local community. There was believed to be a 'season' for marriage and a 'season' for divorce—divorces were relatively infrequent from December to February, but from March and April through the dry season, they were sharply higher, only to slacken off again in August. The harvest season was the time for marriages; the hungry season (*musim paceklik*) was the time for divorce. At this time, in the colourful language of Her Suganda, people were queuing to apply for divorce at the Pengadilan Agama like people queuing for trains at the time of Lebaran (the Muslim new year when the fasting month ends).

In general, the insights of Her Suganda were confirmed by the 1991 field visit. Officials believed that the high divorce rates, especially in the western part of Indramayu, were related to the very low levels of education and to parent-arranged marriage at early ages. Moreover, a daughter with a history of frequent marriage and divorce is frequently a source of pride both to herself and to her parents, because it means many men were interested in her. Materially, too, additional marriage ceremonies bring in gifts from the guests even when it is the girl's second or third marriage. This materialism amongst parents was also cited as facilitating prostitution. Parents are inclined to turn a blind eye because of the income or possessions the daughter can bring into the family. These days, the reputation of Gabus Wetan for sexually available young women is such that it attracts males from Jakarta, not only for short-term sexual adventures but also for longer-term liaisons.

Her Suganda noted the sharp drop in divorce rates following the enactment of the Marriage Law in 1974, due to the need to apply for divorce at the Pengadilan Agama and the provision that the couple had to be counselled at the *kabupaten*'s BP4 office. This office, however, was understaffed; the five officials on duty to counsel had to deal with an average of thirty to forty cases a day, preventing any very intensive counselling. Only about 5 per cent of those coming for counselling proved willing to change their minds and stay together.

By 1991, divorce rates, though still high compared with other areas, had fallen substantially since Her Suganda wrote. This is no doubt attributable to the factors already noted for West Java as a whole. Education and living standards had improved considerably; age at marriage was rising and self-arrangement increasing; and the marriage law was having some effect in limiting very early marriage. The establishment of BP4 was aimed at providing pre-marriage counselling as well as counselling to couples contemplating divorce. The thrust of the premarital advice was towards delaying marriage until the couple was more mature. But although such counselling was required, few couples were actually receiving it.[19]

If parent-arranged marriage at young ages was indeed a major factor in divorce, how can this be reconciled with the well-known customs in two *kecamatan*—the *jaringan* in Kandanghaur and the *ngarot* in Lelea? The former refers to the custom whereby on most nights but especially on Saturday nights and times of the full moon, young people from primary school age upwards gather in the evening in the centre of the small town to look each other over and pick out prospective partners. The latter refers to a once-a-year event in which young people gather for an evening of dancing and free intermixing which continues until morning. Clearly, in both these cases, the role of parents as initiators is absent, though they no doubt still played a role in approving what was initiated by the young people. In 1991, these customs were still being observed. Because of electricity, the *jaringan* ceremony can now take place every night (see also Wibowo et al., 1989: 24). Outsiders (i.e. people from outside the *kecamatan* itself) are ostracized if they try to participate. This is possible on the basis of variations in regional accents, which enable outsiders to be detected.

Perhaps the point to stress here, though, is that customs such as the *jaringan* and the *ngarot* were not present in most *kecamatan* of Indramayu; important as they may have been in particular *kecamatan*, in Indramayu as a whole, the role of parents in arranging very young marriages clearly contributed to the high divorce rate. But marriages do not appear to have been contracted very much earlier in Indramayu than elsewhere in Java; therefore the frequency of divorce must be attributed partly to other factors, presumably including an especially liberal attitude to divorce in Indramayu. It is in this context that the links between divorce and prostitution need to be examined.

Prostitution, again, is a phenomenon which differs greatly between different parts of Indramayu. In fact, it is one *kecamatan*—Gabus Wetan—which is famous as a source of prostitutes for Jakarta, Sukabumi, Tanjung Pinang, and elsewhere, although six other *kecamatan* along the main trunk road—Cikedung, Jatibarang, Karangampel, Losorang, Kandanghaur, and Anjatan—also supply large numbers of prostitutes (see Wibowo et al., 1989: 52). As described by Her Suganda, those who enter the trade are mostly young, divorced, uneducated girls. They typically return to Gabus Wetan before Lebaran or Lebaran Haji and return to the city a week or so after Lebaran. Enough of them do well enough, especially by local standards, to attract the envy of other young women. Their clothes and make-up are 'flashy', they adopt urban ways, and some of them can set up house back in Gabus Wetan complete with television and good furniture. Their skin is attractive as they no longer have to work in the rice fields. Sometimes, when they come back, they bring a man with them, occasionally a man with a car and other appurtenances of wealth. Many of them, indeed, continue to practise prostitution while back in Gabus Wetan over the holiday period, and men in cars with Jakarta number-plates are frequent visitors over this period. The demonstration effect on other young women is obvious, and the sex trade is an open secret in the area.

The above observations continued to hold true. Indeed, a common pattern was for younger women to work for three weeks or so in the city, then return to Indramayu at the time of their period and engage in prostitution there as well before returning to the city. Their clients in Indramayu may be local officials or traders or guests who have accompanied them back from the city. During these monthly visits, they bring back money for their parents and family, and gifts for their neighbours. There is considerable competition among these young women to build houses and acquire land to demonstrate their success. Divorced women continue to be those most likely to engage in prostitution.

The links between high divorce rates and prostitution, though, are complex. Although Gabus Wetan and the six other *kecamatan* with high rates of prostitution do lie in a belt of especially high divorce rates running through the middle of the *kabupaten* to Jatibarang in the east, interregional differences within Indramayu are not very great. In 1979–85, for example, the ratio of divorces to marriages ranged only from a little over 30 per cent to 57 per cent. If it is early divorce which pushes young women into prostitution, why does it not do so to the same extent elsewhere in the *kabupaten*? It is more reasonable to argue that this is a kind of regional occupational specialization that has developed over time, facilitated by a high degree of tolerance of such activities: a specialization comparable to the long-standing role of other localities in the supply of building labourers, or vendors of *jamu*, or *becak* (pedicab) drivers.

Seasonality of marriage and divorce is examined in Figure 6.3, based on data provided by the Religious Affairs Office in Indramayu on the monthly frequency of marriage and divorce during the years 1987–90. The availability of data for a period as long as four years permits some confidence that the seasonal patterns displayed reflect something more basic than random fluctuation. The data certainly support the dictum that people marry after the harvest; marriages are three times as frequent at this time as during the *paceklik* season. However, they do not support the generalization that the *paceklik* season is the time for divorce. Divorces do not vary much in number over the course of the year, although they tend to be least frequent in the December–March period, which is also the time when marriage is least frequent. The ratio of divorces to marriages is much lower in the May–August period, but this is because marriage is so frequent during this period, not because divorce is especially infrequent. What is not evident from the available data, of course, is whether the seasonal pattern of divorce in Indramayu has altered from earlier times when divorce was much more frequent and not subject to delays caused by divorce counselling procedures.

As for the decline in divorce rates that has occurred, as elsewhere in West Java, this appears to be explained by rising education and increasing

FIGURE 6.3

Kabupaten Indramayu: Monthly Pattern of Marriages and Divorces, Related to Seasonal Patterns of Rainfall, 1987–1990

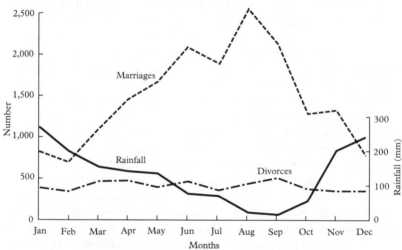

Sources: Calculated from data in *Jawa Barat dalam Angka*, various years, and in *Population Census*, 1971 and 1980 and *1985 Intercensal Population Survey*.

prosperity, by decline in parent-arranged marriages at very young ages, and by the tighter legal procedures than formerly. A new regulation of December 1989, whereby all divorce matters go to the Religious Court, whereas formerly the purely administrative process went to the Religious Affairs Office and only legal matters had to go to the religious court, can be expected to further discourage divorce, but a period of transition is being allowed in Indramayu while people get used to the new procedures.

SUMMARY AND CONCLUSION

The dramatic decline in divorce rates in West Java in the 1960s continued over the 1970s and 1980s, with a particularly sharp decline in 1976. A major cause of this decline appears to be rising age at marriage and greater self-arrangement of marriage, which in turn are related to socio-economic developments, including rising levels of education, more employment of young women away from the home, and widened influence of the media in changing traditional attitudes. Rising levels of living have lessened poverty-related causes of divorce. Finally, new laws and regulations affecting the ease of divorce from 1974 onwards have played an important role in strengthening a trend that was clearly already established. The Indonesian Marriage Law of 1974 and the subsequent regulations only served to codify an anti-divorce/polygamy attitude on the part of the Soeharto government that was actually clear for all to see.

It appears that the degree of enforcement of the current laws and regulations regarding divorce and counselling to those seeking divorce is sometimes inadequate owing to a shortage of staff in regency and district offices of the Department of Religion, especially in their marriage advice boards. There are also still some cases of failure to register marriages and divorces, including issuance of false certificates, although it is doubtful that this occurs on a very large scale.

Kelantan

Among Malaysian states, Kelantan is unique in many respects. The role of Islam is strong, but the earlier Hindu–Buddhist heritage is still visible in many elements of popular culture. Its isolation from the West Coast states and the almost complete absence of in-migration from other regions led to the preservation of a distinctive culture, little affected by the British imperialist impact.[20] Conversations conducted in the Kelantanese dialect are almost impossible for other Malays to understand. More than one observer has commented on 'the marked sensitivity of the Kelantanese to social affronts' (see Roff, 1974b: 228), which makes reconciliation between a husband and wife difficult once either has humiliated the other publicly.

Women's roles in Kelantan regularly attract comment; the paradox is that in this most conservatively Islamic of all states, even back in the 1950s women played a more powerful role in the economy and the family than they did in many parts of Malaysia. The major part of market trading and small village shops was in the hands of women. Women went on their own to public offices to have various kinds of business settled. As the Kelantanese economy gradually diversified, women, especially young women, also worked to some extent in banks, schools, offices, and factories. Women also played an active part in religious and ritual life, going to Koran lessons and prayers, participating in family and neighbourhood celebrations, and taking a key decision-making, planning, and implementing role in their families' special festivities (Raymond Firth, 1966; Rudie, 1983).

In 1946, Raymond Firth (1966: 80) commented on the freedom of women, especially in economic matters, in the fishing community he studied:

Not only do they exercise an important influence on the control of the family finances, commonly acting as bankers for their husbands, but they also engage in independent enterprises, which increase the family supply of cash. Petty trading in fish and vegetables, the preparation and sale of various forms of snacks and cooked fish, mat-making, spinning and net-making, harvesting rice, tile-making, the preparation of coconut oil, the selling of small groceries in shops are some of the occupations followed by women.... At least 25 per cent of the adult women of this community have some definite occupation that yields a regular income. And if casual or intermittent work is also taken into consideration— such as selling a husband's fish, fish-gutting, etc., probably some 50 per cent of the adult women are gainfully employed from time to time.

Markets were largely a female domain, coffee-shops a male domain. A wife's economic pursuits would take her to the market several times a week, where she mixed with other women sellers and 'middlewomen' who linked her to an extensive network of information concerning prices, politics, local scandals, and the availability of marriageable girls and boys.

Women, however, were more likely to have power in the domestic (family or household) than in the public domain. In the Kelantan survey in 1989, wives took care of the daily expenses of the household in most cases. Fifty-eight per cent of households surveyed had a bank account. Of these households, 15 per cent had accounts only in the wife's name, 5 per cent had joint accounts, and over half had separate accounts in the husband's and wife's names. Only 9 per cent had an account only in the husband's name. Focus-group discussions revealed that in many cases the wife held the passbook to the husband's account.

The independence of women was something which grew largely after marriage and with the bearing of children. As already noted, Kelantanese girls were carefully protected before marriage, which occurred at very young ages, and in the early years of marriage, they were likely to live with the parents or parents-in-law.

Between the 1950s and the early 1980s, Kelantan had divorce rates among the highest, probably *the* highest, in the entire Malay-Muslim world. The culture's tolerance of divorce as a way out of an unsatisfactory arranged marriage accounted for the frequent divorce in the first years of marriage; lax administration of divorce procedures facilitated easy divorce by men when another woman took their fancy or tensions arose in the household; and the independent economic role of women made for relatively high levels of female-initiated divorce beyond the first years of marriage. Some of the unique aspects of Kelantanese culture already alluded to no doubt contributed to the very high divorce rates.

Divorce rates in Kelantan appear to have declined sharply during the 1950s, from very high levels indeed, but from 1960 to the mid-1970s the decline was much slower than in most other parts of the Malay-Muslim world (see Table 5.8 and Figure 5.2). In 1975 and 1980, Kelantan clearly had the highest divorce rate in the region (Table 5.8). After 1978, though, the rate began to decline, as shown in Table 6.8. Between 1978 and 1983 the decline was a steady one, but in 1984 the number of divorces fell to little more than a third of their 1983 level and they then continued at this much lower level. Whereas the Kelantanese divorce rate was well above that in Trengganu in 1980, it was only half the Trengganu rate by 1985.

Many of the factors invoked in this chapter to explain declines in divorce rates throughout the region no doubt also applied in the case of Kelantan. However, changes came more slowly in Kelantan, which unlike other states of Malaysia was under the control of the key opposition party, Partai Islam Se Malaysia (Pan-Malaysian Islamic

TABLE 6.8
Kelantan: Trends in Divorce Rates, 1973–1991

	Divorces per Thousand Married Couples	Ratio of Divorces to Marriages (%)
1973	33.9	51.6
1974	30.4	50.8
1975	34.1	56.5
1976	31.9	52.5
1977	30.5	52.5
1978	n.a.	51.5
1979	n.a.	46.4
1980	26.6	41.0
1981	25.3	40.6
1982	23.4	37.7
1983	23.1	36.7
1984	9.1	17.9
1985	10.1	19.9
1986	n.a.	21.7
1987	n.a.	18.2
1988	n.a.	17.6
1989	n.a.	17.7
1990	n.a.	16.6
1991	n.a.	16.4

Sources: Abdullah (1986); data on Muslim marriages and divorces supplied by the Pusat Islam, Prime Minister's Department; author's calculations.

Party) or PAS from 1959 to 1977 and was starved of central government funds for development projects. The social and economic malaise in the state over this period is described in Husin Ali (1978). It may be significant that the slower decline in divorce rates in Kelantan than in other Malaysian states coincided rather neatly with the period of opposition rule.

The 'developmental' factors invoked to explain declines in divorce rates elsewhere in Malaysia had a less pronounced impact in Kelantan, which remained in last place among Peninsular Malaysian states on indicators such as per capita income, level of urbanization, and educational enrolment rates for girls. Kelantan remained far from the mainstream of Malaysian life in some ways, and this was reflected in the continued sway of traditional attitudes on many matters of marriage, childbearing, and family life. Most religious officials in Kelantan supported PAS, which opposed the setting of minimum ages at marriage for women and men, such as those established in Johore. Therefore, there was no minimum age established for women or men in the Shariah Courts or in the Muslim Matrimonial Causes Enactment, 1966 (Hashim, 1984: 47). Many religious leaders in Kelantan were actively opposed to family planning. Traditional attitudes in Kelantan were shared by the population of the neighbouring provinces of Southern Thailand. Kelantan held out against the declines in fertility recorded by Malays elsewhere in Malaysia, and in 1980, rates of contraceptive prevalence were lower in Kelantan and the neighbouring Muslim provinces of Southern Thailand than anywhere else in the ASEAN region (Jones, 1990b: 12–13).

The change to self-arrangement of marriage and rising ages at marriage, consequent largely on extended periods of education for girls, was certainly taking place in Kelantan but was somewhat muted compared to the changes in the West Coast states. This was undoubtedly one reason why the decline in divorce rates was slower in Kelantan than in many other parts of the Malay-Muslim world.

Yet from 1978 on, divorce rates in Kelantan recorded rapid declines, culminating in a spectacular decline in 1984. The remainder of this section will attempt to identify the main factors responsible for these declines. Although developmental factors were certainly important, the key role appears to have been played by the tightening up of the implementation of marriage regulations after the conservative Islamic party PAS lost control of the Kelantan state government in 1977, and the enactment in 1983 and enforcement in 1984 of the new marriage law.

With the defeat of PAS in 1977, greater financial assistance for development projects began to flow from the Federal government, which was anxious to demonstrate to the Kelantanese electorate the tangible benefits of having deserted the opposition. This probably led to some of the factors making for lower divorce rates increasing in salience over this period. Educational opportunities expanded more rapidly than before, and the infusion of central government development spending increased prosperity in the state and opened up many new jobs, including jobs for women. Transportation links with the West Coast improved with the opening of the East–West Highway in 1981, and large numbers of Kelantanese were studying in other states and migrating to the cities for work. Although this had the negative effect of removing some of the most dynamic Kelantanese from the local scene, their continued contact with their families opened up Kelantan to outside influences.

Religious and civil authorities under the new government appeared concerned about Kelantan's reputation for high divorce rates, and took steps to combat this. An Islamic Affairs Council (Majlis Hal Ehwal Agama Islam), established in 1980, took steps to tighten up administrative regulations governing the registration of divorce. In 1983, despite opposition from PAS, Kelantan became the first state to enact the Islamic Family Law Act, which had been formulated at the Federal level but had to be enacted by each state in order to be implemented.

What changes did the new Act bring about? Formerly, the husband could simply report that he had divorced his wife, and although the *imam* might chide him for being hasty, there was nothing much he could do about it. But under the new Act, couples could no longer divorce as they pleased: 'Enakment itu tidak membolehkan pasangan bercerai sesuka hati masing-masing.' (Abdullah, 1986.) The application form (*borang*) for a divorce had to be filled out in advance, and there was an interval of time during which counselling could be done if general causes such as incompatibility seemed to be the problem, rather than, say, the husband's desertion and failure to pay maintenance. All divorce cases now had to come before the *kadi*'s office. The *imam* could still be involved, but did not have to be. The *talak* had to be pronounced in front of the *kadi* with both husband and wife present. A man who pronounced the triple *talak* at home was now subject to a fine not exceeding RM300 or imprisonment not exceeding 3 months (Negeri Kelantan, 1983: 141).[21]

The traditionally high divorce rate in Kelantan certainly reflected tensions in the husband–wife relationship, but these were not the sort of tensions which arise, for example, in India when a girl is cut off from her own family on marriage and finds that her husband, in his own family house, is likely to be more influenced by his mother than by his wife. Frequent divorce, concentrated as it was in the early years of arranged marriages, reflected rather the adjustment difficulties of a young couple thrown together at the behest of their parents. Among older married couples, companionate marriage seems to be typical of Kelantan. One of the surprises in focus-group discussions was that focus-group respondents in their forties and fifties almost universally agreed that they still maintained a romantic (*bermanja*) relationship with their husbands. In the Kelantan survey, almost one-fifth of the respondents thought the husband's most important role was to be the wife's companion, and likewise for the wife in respect of her husband.

Although evidence of companionate marriage in a context of high divorce rates may seem paradoxical, a plausible explanation is that high divorce rates may actually have contributed to a companionate style in marital relationships by eliminating those marriages (almost all of them arranged marriages) where a degree of harmony and mutual affection did not develop.

Summary and Conclusion

An earlier study noted that historically high divorce rates among Malays in Peninsular Malaysia

reflected the application of Islamic marriage law in a social and cultural milieu very different from that in the Arab Islamic heartland in which it was first promulgated. The male freedoms inherent in the law had been enthusiastically accepted, with scant regard to the restrictive conditions attendant on them. Undoubtedly the rates would have been lower had those appointed to register Muslim marriages and divorces followed the administrative provision that they attempt to reconcile the partners to the marriage before registering a *talak*, and if they had strictly enforced the legal requirements for the payment of maintenance. But beyond this, aspects of Malay social and family structure facilitated high divorce rates: immaturity of the couple at the time of marriage, combined with a tolerant attitude to divorce as a natural solution if marriage does not work out; bilateral kinship system, focusing on the individual; lack of a tradition of a close husband–wife bond; flexible arrangements for residence of children after divorce; a tradition of equality of husband and wife in the conjugal union; women's important economic role and degree of 'self-sufficiency' (facilitating ... female-initiated divorce); and ease of remarriage. (Jones, 1981: 261–3.)

The dramatic decline in divorce rates in Islamic South-East Asia in the 1960s continued over the 1970s and 1980s. A major cause of this decline appears to have been rising age at marriage and greater self-arrangement of marriage, which in turn are related to socio-economic developments, including rising levels of education, more employment of young women away from the home, and widened influence of the media in changing traditional attitudes. Rising levels of living have lessened poverty-related causes of divorce. The Indonesian government has aligned itself with women's groups bringing pressure to bear to restrict the ease of *talak* divorce, though in Malaysia the situation has been a little more complex. Finally, new laws and regulations affecting the ease of divorce, from 1974 onwards in Indonesia and from 1984 onwards in Malaysia, have played an important role in strengthening a trend that was clearly already established.

One key mystery requiring further investigation is why divorce rates fell faster among Malaysian Malays than they did in Indonesia, where the rise in age at marriage was slower, where the erosion of the arranged marriage system also appears to have been less severe, and where education, urbanization, and economic development all lagged behind Malaysia's. This should indicate the complexity of factors influencing divorce, and perhaps lay additional stress on the legal and administrative changes introduced in Indonesia a decade before they were enacted (but in most states not enforced until much later) in Malaysia.

Does the decline in divorce in Islamic South-East Asia denote more stable and happy marriages? Unfortunately, this is by no means certain. The increased difficulty of obtaining a divorce could lead to more desertion, or simply tolerance of unhappy marriages. There could also be more cases of keeping a mistress (a fairly common practice among Chinese in Malaysia, for whom divorce is culturally unacceptable), as a way of getting around restrictions on polygamy and divorce. Nevertheless, the benefits to women and children in particular resulting from the climate of support for more stable marriages, of which the laws and regulations are only a reflection, should not be lightly discounted. More studies are needed of the extent to which the trend towards self-arranged and later marriage, and less frequent divorce and polygamy, has led to changes in spousal relationships within marriage.

1. The largest ethnic group in West Nusa Tenggara are the Sasak of Lombok. Cederroth (1983: 167) argues that the movement from a syncretic Islamic belief system, regulated by customary rules, to orthodox Islam, led to a relaxation of various social constraints which limited the number of divorces. One important change facilitating divorce was the replacement of high elopement fines in the traditional system with a simple wedding gift (*mas kahwin*).

2. Boomgaard (1989: 146) also notes the argument that the (often quite lengthy) temporary residence of the young couple with the parents of one of them, usually the bride's, must have been a source of much friction, but he is correct in his warning that to attribute high divorce rates to this factor reflects a twentieth-century West European prejudice against virilocal or uxorilocal residence of young couples. After all, lengthy residence in the household of the husband's parents characterizes many societies (e.g. in South Asia) where divorce rates are low.

3. In Java in the nineteenth century, all property obtained during marriage was divided on a two-to-one basis between man and woman, but this excluded the marriage portion and other goods obtained as a gift or inheritance by one of the parties (Boomgaard, 1989: 147). Much the same arrangements still hold, with either the two-to-one division or a fifty-fifty division of property acquired jointly since the marriage (V. J. Hull, 1975: 224–6).

4. Some much more recent information on causes of divorce in Trengganu and Kelantan has been summarized in the press. In Trengganu, the Chief Kadi stated that the three chief reasons for the relatively high divorce rate in the 1980s were dissatisfaction with sexual relationships, economic problems, and incompatibility of those married at very young ages (*Utusan Melayu*, 22 August 1987). The Religious Information Officer for Kelantan said that divorces in 1987 were mainly related to claims that the husband was a drug addict, that the wife was unfaithful, or that she did not want to be in a polygamous marriage. Formerly, claims that the husband was a gambler or a womanizer were more prominent. She noted the tendency for couples to be too much influenced by their emotions in dealing with household problems. Increasing strains on marriages in the town were due to educated wives' freedom in moving about, returning home late from the office or from visiting friends, thus arousing suspicion and jealousy in their husbands (*Utusan Melayu*, 14 November 1987).

5. The categories used are: (1) moral: unhealthy polygamy, crisis of character (drunkard, gambler, etc.), jealousy; (2) ignored responsibility: forced marriage, economic irresponsibility; (3) under-age marriage; (4) physical abuse; (5) conviction of crime; (6) physical abnormality; (7) continual disagreement: politics, interference by third party, lack of harmony.

6. The *imam* was entitled to keep certain percentages of the fees he received for

marriages and divorces and of the religious taxes he collected (50 per cent of the RM10 marriage fee, 20 per cent of the RM10 divorce fee, and 20 per cent of the *zakat*) (Downs, 1967: 172; Zalaluddin, 1979: 118). Such fees varied in other states. For example, the fee for registration of a divorce was RM5 in Trengganu, RM1 in Perlis, RM8 in Negri Sembilan, and RM50 in Johore. These were the same or lower than the fees for registering a marriage, except in Johore. The fees for registering a *rujuk* (reconciliation) were RM2, RM1, RM1, and RM4, respectively.

7. Many village parents considered it an honour to marry a daughter to a respected religious teacher, and a number of Malay novels written in the 1940s and 1950s were critical of resultant abuses. For example, some of Ahmad Lufti's novels, published between 1948 and 1951, 'were intended to criticize those members of the religious élite who had used Islamic marriage laws to construct a paradise for themselves consisting of a revolving series of wives, now married, now abandoned' (Banks, 1987: 25). The well-known novel *Tok Guru* deals with a situation in which a village father forces his daughter to marry an elderly religious teacher, only to discover after the marriage has taken place, that the teacher was already married. For a review of other novels touching on such themes, see Banks (1987).

8. H. Geertz (1961: 72) stated that usually the ex-husband, if able, gives over a piece of property—for instance, land—to the child at the time of divorce. Though she claimed to be talking of the reality, perhaps it was more the ideal that she was referring to.

9. The Indonesian Marriage Survey asked whether respondents agreed that a marriage not preceded by love is likely to end in divorce. Among respondents who were willing to give an opinion, the great majority of both male and female respondents agreed, except in Aceh, where the proportion of males agreeing was over half and of females about one-third, and in South Kalimantan, where only about one-third of both males and females agreed (McDonald, 1984: Table 4.5). It is interesting that Aceh and South Kalimantan are both characterized by relatively high proportions of parent-arranged marriages.

10. See also Vreede-de Stuers (1960) and Lev (1972a: 151–3, 1972b).

11. See, for example, the resolutions passed by the Conference of Islamic Women's Organizations in 1975. (Lapuran Muktamar Pertubuhan-Pertubuhan Perempuan Islam Malaysia, Dewan Bahasa dan Pustaka, Kuala Lumpur, March 1975.)

12. The BP4 established in Bandung in October 1954 was the first to be set up in Indonesia (Lev, 1972a: 151). As noted by Lev, although there was no reason to doubt the professional interest of those who first created these boards, in an important sense they represented an attempt to forestall the pressures towards reform of marriage laws by demonstrating a concern with marital stability and the protection of women.

13. As described by the head of the BP4 for Bandung municipality, the couple seeking divorce must come together to the BP4 for counselling. They must treat each other politely at this meeting, being asked to *salaam* (greet respectfully) each other, even if they do not want to. They are told they must wait one month to reconsider their request to divorce. If they still want a divorce then, they can proceed.

14. In many states, the date of enforcement was much later than the date of enactment. For individual states, the dates of enactment and enforcement, respectively, were as follows: Kelantan (1983, 1984), Malacca (1983, 1983), Negri Sembilan (1983, 1988), Federal Territory (1984), Kedah (1984, 1985), Perak (1984, 1989), Selangor (1984, 1989), Penang (1985, 1989), and Pahang (1987, 1988). By 1989, the Act had not yet been enacted in Trengganu, Johore, or Perlis.

15. For more details, see Jones, Asari, and Djuartika (forthcoming).

16. It can be assumed that the registration of Islamic marriages and divorces is nearly complete. Islam does not recognize the validity of a marriage or divorce that is not properly registered, and failure to register is therefore a serious shortcoming not only civilly but religiously. There must, of course, be a small amount of underregistration. One such case known to the author occurred in Ciamis around 1986. The official responsible for registering the marriage, the Pegawai Pencatatan Nikah, did not appear, for some reason, even though he had been informed in advance about the date and time of the wedding. Later, the couple divorced, but because their marriage had never been registered, they could not register the divorce either. Cases are also sometimes heard of 'syndicates'

arranging illegal marriages using false marriage papers. Presumably such marriages do not find their way into the official registration figures. For a report on such cases in Subang, see *Pikiran Rakyat* (19 October 1990).

17. In one case in Bandung, known to the author, the applicant was required to pay one-third of his salary to his wife and one-third to his children on a continuing basis, leaving only one-third for himself. Although other forms of income normally provide a substantial supplement to the basic salary and he was able to keep these in full, this applicant nevertheless felt that the maintenance requirement was punitive.

18. In some cases, *kawin gantung* or 'hanging marriages' in which the marriage ceremony is held for below-age children but they do not yet live together as husband and wife. The local name for *kawin gantung* is *kawin rasulan*; in Sliyeg, it is *pacangan*. The local term for marriages which end in divorce without the marriage having been consummated is *kawin elik*.

19. This was stated by the head of the Islamic Affairs section of the West Java office of the Department of Religion (*Pikiran Rakyat*, 12 November 1987). It was rather unrealistic of him to expect otherwise, not only because shortage of staff would have made such counselling on a large scale impossible, but also because it was hardly possible for the couple proposing to be married to appear at the BP4 for counselling in cases (still very frequent) where the parents arrange the marriage and the couple are not supposed to have anything to do with each other beforehand.

20. As recently as 1960, the road trip to Kelantan from the West Coast was long and arduous, with frequent ferry crossings of rivers. In the monsoon season, Kelantan was sometimes cut off for weeks. By the late 1970s, all ferries had been replaced by bridges, and the road trip from Kuala Lumpur took about eleven hours. There had been a slow train service since the railway was completed in 1931 and, more recently, air service.

21. These penalties were less than those in some other states of Malaysia. In practice, in Kelantan a fixed charge of RM300 appears to have been imposed, and the option of a jail sentence ignored.

7
Polygyny: Trends and Influences

Introduction

POLYGAMY refers to marriages in which a spouse of either sex has more than one mate at the same time. The two categories of polygamy are polyandry, where a woman has more than one husband at a time, and polygyny, where a man has more than one wife at a time. Since polyandry is not permitted in Islam, this chapter will deal only with polygyny. Polygyny has been touched upon at many places in this book, but only in the context of discussing the legal aspects of marriage in the Islamic world, and in the discussion of factors influencing divorce. It is now time to look more systematically at polygyny in Islamic South-East Asia, its incidence both past and present, the socio-economic groups among which it is more frequent, and the reasons for these trends and patterns.

In non-Muslim countries, there is widespread interest in polygamy in the Islamic world, often, it would appear, because the subject appears exotic, even titillating, in countries where polygamy is forbidden by law. In such countries, the popular understanding of polygamy in Islam is that 'Muslim men can have four wives'. Often enough, this translates into a belief that 'Muslim men often have four wives'. That this is a grave distortion of the situation is obvious to anyone with experience in Indonesian or Malaysian villages, or who is familiar with studies of village life in these countries. A more realistic picture is provided by Downs's study of a village in Pasir Puteh, Kelantan, in 1958:

Although Muslims are permitted as many as four wives at a time, polygyny is not common in the village. Only six current instances of it were found, each involving only two wives. In all cases separate houses were provided for the wives and in three instances the second wife lived in a separate village. While it is true that the economic burden of providing equal and separate establishments for two wives is too great for very poor people, in only one of the cases above could it be said that the husband was particularly wealthy by village standards. Aside from the economic disadvantage, however, the aversion of the women to such arrangements undoubtedly tends to keep their number to a minimum. There is also, of course, the fact that there is not a sufficient number of women to make widespread polygyny possible. (Downs, 1967: 140.)

This general picture, with slight variation, is painted by many village studies in the region.

Polygyny in Traditional Society

The Population Census of 1930 for the Netherlands East Indies (now Indonesia) collected information on the number of current wives of each husband. The findings are presented in Table 7.1, and show that polygyny was less than half as frequent in Java as in the Outer Islands; fewer than 2 per cent of husbands were polygynous in Java, compared with over 4 per cent in the Outer Islands. Data from the Population Census of 1920 were consistent with this, showing that 1.5 per cent of all married Javanese males had more than one wife (Boomgaard, 1989: 152). In 1930, the highest incidence of polygyny was in parts of Nusa Tenggara—Sumba and Flores—where 13 per cent and 12 per cent of men, respectively, were polygynous. These were areas where traditional beliefs had not been fully superseded by Islam (Sumba) or Catholicism (Flores). Among more mainline Islamic populations, the highest incidence of

TABLE 7.1

Indonesia: Percentage of Husbands Currently in Polygynous Marriages,
by Region, 1930

		Percentage of Polygynous Husbands with		
	Percentage in Polygynous Marriages	2 Wives	3 Wives	4 Wives and More
Java	1.9	94.7	4.7	0.6
West Java	1.9	94.5	4.8	0.8
Central Java–Yogyakarta	2.3	94.6	4.9	0.5
East Java	1.6	94.9	4.4	0.6
Sumatra	4.4	91.2	7.4	1.4
Aceh	4.2	94.2	4.9	0.9
North Sumatra	3.8	93.8	5.6	0.6
West Sumatra	9.0	88.9	9.3	1.8
Lampung	5.9	89.6	8.8	1.5
Palembang	2.3	93.6	5.3	1.1
Sulawesi	3.1	89.4	8.4	2.2
North Sulawesi	2.5	92.0	6.6	1.4
South Sulawesi	3.3	88.8	8.8	2.4
Maluku	4.2	91.0	7.5	1.5
Bali, Lombok	4.0	92.1	6.6	1.2
Timor and vicinity	8.1	86.6	10.5	2.8
Sumbawa	2.3	94.4	4.7	0.9
Sumba	13.5	83.4	12.3	4.2
Flores	12.0	86.0	11.2	2.8
Netherlands Indies	2.6	92.7	6.2	1.1

Sources: *Indisch Verslag, 1941*, Batavia: Table 10B; *Kantoor voor de Volkstelling* [Census, Netherlands Indies, 1930]: various tables.

polygyny was in West Sumatra, distantly followed by Lampung.[1] The frequency of polygamy in West Sumatra presumably reflects aspects of Minangkabau culture, including the marginal role of the husband in the household and the tradition of *merantau* which facilitates the keeping of a second wife in another place.

There is ample evidence that polygyny in traditional society was more frequently practised by the rulers than by their subjects (Koentjaraningrat, 1985: 259–62; Gullick, 1987: 52, 217; Boomgaard, 1989: 152–3) and by the well-to-do than by the common people. Crawfurd stated in 1820 that in the Malay Archipelago polygyny and concubinage existed only among a few of the higher ranks, and might be looked upon as a luxury of the great (Westermarck, 1922: Vol. 3, 13). In traditional Malay society, 'members of the upper class, especially the Sultan, always had an unremitting desire for beautiful women, whom they had the power to obtain. The queen usually had to share the ruler's love with his legal wives and numerous concubines.' (Husin Ali, 1981: 62.) Gullick (1987: 52) observed that 'royal wives submitted reluctantly to polygamous marriage as a price to be paid for their privileged position. To relieve the inevitable jealousy between wives, and because convention required it, a ruler usually accommodated his wives in different places. At the very least, he kept them apart by giving them separate wings of the *istana*.'

In Java, 'almost all nineteenth century Regents were polygamous' (Sutherland, 1978: 20). Raffles ([1817] 1978: Vol. 1, 81) states that the regents and lower nobility had only two wives and that only the sovereign had four but that the regents generally had three or four concubines, and the sovereign, eight or ten. Whatever the precise legal status of wives and concubines, some sultans and regents managed to produce offspring numbering in the dozens (Boomgaard, 1989: 153).

In more recent times, polygamy has continued to be associated with the aristocracy throughout the region. The Sultan of Yogyakarta has carried on a long tradition of polygamy in his family, as has the Sultan of Surakarta. The Sultan of Brunei took a second wife in 1981. The Tengku Mahkota of Pahang was following a much-trodden path among Malaysian royalty when he married a member of the Johore royal family in 1986 and subsequently took a movie actress as his second wife in 1992. Among the Maguindanao, one of the major Muslim groups in the Philippines, polygyny was rare among the common people but more frequent among the nobility (Weekes, 1984: 465).

Among commoners, men with power and prestige have been more able to attract the interest of other women, or rather of their parents; a striking, if extreme, example was President Sukarno. The power and prestige, of course, generally went along with relatively high income. It is widely believed by Malays (Strange, 1981: 147) that religious leaders generally had a higher rate of polygamy than the average villager, and there appears to be ample evidence to support this belief, whether in Indonesia, Malaysia, or Southern Thailand (for Kedah, see Nagata, 1982: 31; for Lombok, see Cederroth, 1983: 168; see also Kasimin, 1978: 75).[2] The proclivity towards polygyny among religious leaders was no doubt partly associated with the great respect and prestige accorded them in village communities, and partly with their tendency to be wealthier than the average villager (see also Jones, 1980: 288). One of the groups prominent in the *dakwah* (Islamic revivalist) movement in Malaysia, the Darul Arqam, encourages polygamy and its leaders typically practise it (Zainah, 1987: 76 fn. 42).

It may not only be that certain kinds of husbands were more likely to engage in polygamy, but that certain kinds of wives were more likely to remain in polygamous marriages. In Southern Thailand, villagers claimed that most men would prefer to divorce and remarry rather than take on the responsibilities of a polygamous household, unless their first wife was wealthy or was the religious leader's daughter (Rachapaetayakom, 1983: 152). Of course, there would still be the question of whether the woman herself would wish to remain in such a marriage.

In Islamic South-East Asia in general, there seems to be a correlation between economic status and polygamy. Among the Madurese in Java, the Sundanese in West Java, and the Tausug in the Philippines, although polygyny was rare, it was more common among village officials and the well-to-do than among the poorer folk (McDonald and Abdurahman, 1974; Weekes, 1984: 459, 769). This was probably the general situation throughout Islamic South-East Asia. Hugo (1975: 424) found that only 3.2 per cent of household heads he interviewed in fourteen villages in West Java had polygynous unions, but one-third of them were in the 'village leader' category in which more than 10 per cent were polygynous. Writing of Indonesia, Suprapto (1990: 146) claims that it is rare for successful traders and businessmen to have only one wife. In a village near Jakarta, not only is polygyny practised primarily by the wealthy villagers and the more well-to-do village officials but it is considered an important indication of a man's wealth. According to Boedhisantoso (1967: 339), 'Those who have succeeded in increasing their wealth try as well to gain status in the community by taking a new wife.'

Wealth clearly facilitates polygyny, but, as Rosemary Firth (1966: 49) observed of a Kelantanese village, 'the absence of it does not necessarily inhibit a man from becoming a polygynist'. In Rusila, Trengganu, Strange (1981: 147) found that only one of the polygynous men had higher-than-average income. However, although some poorer men engage in polygyny, they are generally considered rash to do so.

In the Islamic world as a whole, the evidence seems to be that polygyny is more frequently associated with relatively lower educational and socio-economic status (Huzayyin, 1979: 26). The positive association with educational and socio-economic status in Islamic South-East Asia resembles the pattern among sub-Saharan African populations, many of which, however, are comparable only in this respect as they have a much higher incidence of polygyny.

Trends in Polygyny

First of all, polygyny in the region should be set in its international context. In the Islamic world as a whole, polygyny is not particularly widespread.

Huzayyin (1979), who collected available studies, found that in most cases, the proportion of men with a polygamous background ranged between lows of 1 per cent (Damascus), 2 per cent (Cairo), and 7 per cent (Shibpur, Bangladesh). In North African and Middle Eastern Muslim countries, the proportion of married men in a polygynous union is typically around 3–6 per cent, though it was as high as 11.7 per cent among Muslim men in Kuwait in 1975 (Chamie, 1986; United Nations, 1990: 184–7). The rates were much higher in the Sudan (15.9 per cent in 1956 and as high as one-half of all ever-married males in some parts), but this appeared to represent an 'African' rather than a 'Muslim' pattern of polygyny (Huzayyin, 1979: 22; United Nations, 1990: 82). In sub-Saharan Africa, typically 20–30 per cent of married men are in a polygamous union (United Nations, 1990: 82–4).

As noted in Chapter 3, it is much harder to obtain reliable information on the practice of polygyny in South-East Asia than on the incidence of divorce. Nevertheless, most observers believe that the practice of polygyny has been decreasing. Winstedt (1961: 46) stated that 'few but Rajahs and wealthy men availed themselves of . . . [the latitude allowed in Islam to practise polygamy] . . . and nowadays monogamy is the common practice'. If indeed there has been a decline in polygyny paralleling the decline in divorce, it would hardly be surprising if some of the same factors were contributing to both declines.

In Indonesia, the 1973 Fertility–Mortality Survey collected information on the proportion of women whose current or most recent marriage was with a polygamous husband. The findings are presented in Table 7.2. Practice of polygyny was highest in Sulawesi (where 8–9 per cent of wives were in polygamous marriages) and Sumatra, with West Java the lowest. The same ranking held for the frequency of marriages where the husband had three wives. The consistency in regional differentials between the 1973 and the 1930 data is striking.[3] Not surprisingly, husbands with two wives were much more frequently encountered than those with three wives: between three and five times more frequently, depending on the province. Except in Sulawesi, taking a third wife was almost unheard of in urban areas; to the extent it happened at all, it was very much a rural phenomenon.

The relatively infrequent practice of polygyny in rural Java is confirmed in village studies. H. Geertz (1961: 131) reported that in 1953 only 2 per cent of the new marriage contracts in Modjokuto subdistricts were polygynous. Nitisastro (1956: 6) reported an incidence of 6–7 per cent in the village of Jabres in the Bagelen area. In the same general area of southern Central Java, Koentjaraningrat (1985: 139) observed that a little over 3 per cent of the households were polygynous.

The Indonesian Fertility–Mortality Survey showed a tendency for polygyny to decline over time. This is indicated in Table 7.2 by the tendency for a lower proportion of younger women than of older women to be in polygynous marriages.[4] This was true of all provinces. The decline in polygyny appears to have occurred at all levels of society. After World War II, 'the polygamous life-style . . . of high-ranking Javanese

TABLE 7.2

Indonesia: Percentage of Women Whose Most Recent Marriage Was to a Polygynous Husband, by Current Age of Wife, 1973

Region	Age-group	Percentage with 2 Wives		Percentage with 3 or More Wives		Percentage Polygamous	
		Urban	Rural	Urban	Rural	Urban	Rural
West Java	15–34	2.5	2.7	0.0	0.5		
	35–49	4.1	3.6	0.1	0.8		
	15–49	3.1	3.0	0.1	0.6	3.2	3.6
Central Java	15–34	3.1	3.3	0.1	0.7		
	35–40	4.8	4.8	0.2	0.8		
	15–49	4.0	4.0	0.1	0.8	4.1	4.8
East Java	15–34	2.1	3.3	0.3	1.2		
	35–49	4.1	4.5	0.3	1.3		
	15–49	3.0	3.8	0.3	1.2	3.3	5.0
Sumatra	15–34	2.8	5.1	0.3	1.0		
	35–49	6.0	8.4	1.0	3.0		
	15–49	4.1	6.4	0.6	1.8	4.7	8.2
Sulawesi	15–34	6.5	6.5	0.9	1.5		
	35–49	7.0	8.6	2.2	2.0		
	15–49	6.8	7.3	1.4	1.7	8.2	9.0

Source: Muliakusuma (1976: Tables III.3 and III.4).

priyayi administrative officials disappeared owing to more democratic ideas, and because in all social classes the number of better educated women who refused to become a *selir* or an inferior second wife of a *priyayi* gentleman has increased' (Koentjaraningrat, 1985: 262).

Village studies in Java show low but varying levels of polygamy in recent times. For example, in studies of two Madurese villages, Niehof (1985: 175–6) found that only about 0.5 per cent of reproductive-age wives were in polygamous marriages, although in one of the villages in her study, almost 9 per cent of women appear to have been deeply affected by the practice or threat of polygamy, in that 2 per cent of them had divorced because they did not like their position in a polygamous marriage and another 7 per cent divorced because the husband took another wife or planned to do so.[5] V. J. Hull (1975: 196–8) found in Maguwoharjo, Yogyakarta, that just over 3 per cent of wives entered a polygynous marriage and in another 6 per cent of marriages the husband took another wife at some point in the marriage. About 5 per cent of currently married women reported that they were currently living in polygynous unions. About 5 per cent of currently married men claimed to have ever been in polygynous unions. In the village of Djagakarsa, near Jakarta, not more than 5 per cent of the men were practising polygyny (Boedhisantoso, 1967: 338).

In Singapore, polygamy has been very infrequent, at least since the changes in the administration of Muslim laws beginning in 1957. Between 1970 and 1974, only 0.3 per cent of Muslim marriages solemnized in Singapore were polygamous (Tham, 1979: 112). Earlier, in a household survey conducted by the Social Welfare Department in 1947, only 0.4 per cent of Malay households were co-residential polygamous (Djamour, 1959: 60, 83); this was probably an understatement of the number of polygamous unions, because some males may have been maintaining wives in separate households, or in the case of Indonesian immigrants, still had a wife in Indonesia.

In Malaysia, only scattered information is available on the frequency of polygamy, still less on its trends. It appears to be still very common among the sultans and lesser royalty, though perhaps not as common as in the past. As far as the common people are concerned, there are a number of village studies from Kelantan, and a few elsewhere; the Kelantanese studies are first summarized. In the fishing community studied by Rosemary Firth, fewer than 3 per cent of the men had more than one wife, and almost all of these had only two wives (Rosemary Firth, 1966: 48). In Kampong Jeram, Pasir Puteh, fewer than 4 per cent of current marriages were polygamous in 1958, all of them involving only two wives living in separate houses (Downs, 1967: 140). In Galok, Kelantan, 5 per cent of men and 7 per cent of women have been in polygamous marriages, but most of these did not last very long as polygamous marriages, being broken by divorce of either the first or second wife (Kuchiba, Tsubouchi, and Maeda, 1979: 170–1).

Turning to other states, in Padang Lalang, Kedah, the proportion of ever-polygynous males appeared to be lower: less than 4 per cent (calculated from Kuchiba, Tsubouchi, and Maeda, 1979: 36 and Table 2). In Rusila, Trengganu, in 1965, 5 per cent of married men were polygynists; another 2 per cent admitted to prior polygynous unions. By 1979, the number of married men who were currently polygynous had fallen to a little over 2 per cent (Strange, 1981: 142). In one village study in Negri Sembilan, 11 per cent of the men and 8 per cent of the women had ever been partners to polygynous arrangements (Peletz, 1988: 235). Among Sarawak Malays, polygyny was rare (Harrisson, 1970: 192–3). In Singapore, Djamour (1966: 82–7) observed that active polygyny was rare, though there were also cases of formal polygyny, where immigrant Malays married without bothering to divorce the wives they had left behind in Malaysia or Indonesia.

Some recent incomplete official data show the number of polygamous marriages performed among Muslims in Peninsular Malaysia between 1984 and 1991. Excluding Pahang, for which there were no data, and excluding certain years for some of the other states because data were unavailable, there were 9,338 polygamous marriages registered out of a total of 331,434 marriages, or 2.8 per cent of all marriages. This figure cannot be taken as an accurate estimate of the proportion of Muslim marriages in Peninsular Malaysia that are polygamous, because different states have a different weighting in the figure as a result of the unavailability of data for a few states for some years. Nor do they allow conclusions to be drawn about the 'stock' of polygamous marriages, because as already observed, such marriages seem to be more frequently broken by divorce than marriages as a whole. But the data do at least hint at a figure well above 2 per cent for the proportion of marriages that are polygamous at any given time.

The proportions of polygamous marriages by state are shown in Table 7.3. Polygamy is relatively high in the high-divorce states of Kelantan and Trengganu, but fairly infrequent in Negri Sembilan, Perak, and Penang.

Data for recent years (1990 and 1991) give no clear evidence that polygamy decreased over the 1980s. With due allowance for missing states, it appears that altogether a total of slightly more than 1,000 polygamous marriages were performed in 1990 (see also Shamsiah, 1991). This amounted to about 1.6 per cent of all marriages performed, well below the average figure for the entire period since 1984. However, incomplete data for 1991 suggest higher rates. Caution is obviously required in generalizing from data for just one or two years.

It might be noted that the incidence of polygyny in some regions might be understated by official figures because they fail to catch 'cross-border polygyny'. For example, Malays from Perlis who marry Thai Muslims in Thailand are supposed to register their marriage with the Perlis Islamic Religious Department, but it has long been suspected that some fail to do so, particularly if they are entering polygynous marriages (*New Straits Times*, 8 February 1991). The same situation prevails in Kelantan. Similarly, it has recently been claimed that Singapore Malays are taking second wives in the neighbouring Indonesian island

TABLE 7.3

Peninsular Malaysia: Polygamous Marriages as a Percentage of All Muslim Marriages Contracted, 1984–1991

States	Years	Percentages
Johore	1984–90	1.9
Kedah	1987–90	1.3
Kelantan	1984–91	3.9
Malacca	1985–90	1.4
Negri Sembilan	1989–90	0.6
Penang	1984–90	1.1
Perak	1989–91	0.9
Perlis	1989–91	2.1
Selangor	1984–90[a]	1.6
Trengganu	1987–90	3.8
Federal Territory (Kuala Lumpur)	1987–90	1.5
All Peninsular Malaysia (excluding Pahang)	1984–91	2.8

Source: Data supplied by Pusat Islam, Prime Minister's Department.
[a]1989 is excluded owing to unavailability of data.

of Batam and keeping their first wives in Singapore. In Malaysia, particular problems have been encountered in determining whether Indonesian immigrants wanting to marry were married already, or indeed whether they were actually Muslims (*Berita Harian*, 9 April 1991). Cross-border polygamy is not a new phenomenon. After the tightening of regulations in Singapore in 1957, some Singapore men who were refused permission to contract a polygynous union went to one of the Malay states which did not frown on such unions, to register their marriage there (Djamour, 1966: 146).

Interviews were held with the Judge of Islamic Law of Pattani in Southern Thailand and with a member of the Pattani Islamic Committee,[6] the body entrusted with the registration of marriages and divorces in Pattani, in February 1992; they strongly disapproved of the recent regulations adopted in a number of Malaysian states, making polygynous marriage somewhat more difficult than before. They argued that there is nothing in the Koran requiring wives to be informed or in any way consulted about their husband's intention to take another wife, and they displayed some enthusiasm about their role in enabling husbands from states such as Kelantan to circumvent the regulations by registering their marriages in Pattani. Records are not readily available, however, about how many such marriages take place. Although in the nature of the case the number of cross-border polygynous marriages is unknown, it is unlikely that they would make a major difference to the figures on incidence of polygyny already cited.

Finally, in the Philippines, in 1983 only 2 per cent of Muslim household heads were living with two or more wives, although others undoubtedly kept second wives in a separate household (Costello and Palabrica-Costello, 1987: 29).

Correlation between Polygyny and Divorce

A close correlation might be expected between the practice of polygamy and frequency of divorce, because as noted in Chapter 5, polygyny was frequently a cause of divorce; moreover, in areas where divorce, which is really against the spirit of Islam, was frequent, polygamy, which is also against the spirit of Islam, might be high as well. It is therefore of considerable interest to find that, although such a correlation can be observed in Peninsular Malaysia, it does not exist universally. West Sumatra, where divorce rates were high, also had the highest rate of polygamy in Indonesia in 1930; but on the other hand, West Java, which also had high divorce rates, had much lower rates of polygamy.

Al Hadar (1977: 84–8) attempts to explain why this might be so, referring also to South Sulawesi, where levels of polygamy are intermediate between the high rates in West Sumatra and the low rates in West Java. She argues that one factor could be the greater distinction drawn between social classes in Bugis-Makassar and Minangkabau society, with an important group of *bangsawan* (nobility), who are more inclined to practise polygamy. Although the Minangkabau are matrilineal, the father's status influences the children's status, and this is one reason why many parents were willing to marry their daughters to a much older, polygamous man if he was of the right status. Another reason for the high incidence of polygamy among the Minangkabau was the matriarchal system, which left husbands relatively free from responsibilities to wife and children, and led to husbands and wives living separately and not developing close companionship; moreover, the wife's living pattern was not greatly affected by her marriage, so it mattered little if it was a polygamous marriage. In general, in Minangkabau society, polygamy was not seen as a bad thing.

Although the Javanese and Sundanese also acknowledged social strata, they practised strata endogamy whereas the Bugis-Makassarese and Minangkabau practised strata exogamy. The rise in children's status through the mother's marrying a man of higher status was not part of the Javanese–Sundanese world-view.

It is important to stress that divorce was much more frequent than polygamy throughout the Malay world, and therefore the occurrence of polygamy itself could not have been a major cause of divorce in more than a small percentage of cases. The overt threat of it, however, may have been a factor disrupting marriages in many more cases, and the implied threat of it based simply on its acceptance by religion and culture may have been a factor making for suspicion and 'distance' in the husband–wife relationship in many instances, thus providing a fertile breeding ground for divorce. In the village of Galok, Kelantan, Kuchiba, Tsubouchi, and Maeda (1979: 170–1) note that polygynous marriages are seldom sustained because divorce is readily available. Other village studies confirm this. When the first wife learns of her husband's *isteri muda* (young wife), she is likely to issue an ultimatum: either the young wife goes, or she goes. Frequently (perhaps in the majority of cases), it appears to be the second wife who goes (H. Geertz, 1961: 132–3).

Living Arrangements in Polygynous Marriages

Co-residential households appear to have been rare except among the nobility, whose wealth enabled wives to be kept in separate quarters, even though they were in the same house. Djamour (1966: 84–5) observed that in Singapore, it was considered to be not only humiliating for a woman to have a co-wife, but even more so if both wives were living under the one roof. This appeared to be the case more generally: in fact, co-wives frequently live in different villages and are sometimes unaware of each other's existence. Village studies in Indonesia and Malaysia indicate that it is rare for co-wives of a polygynous husband to be living under one roof (H. Geertz, 1961: 131–3; Boedhisantoso, 1967: 338; Chabot, 1967: 200; Downs, 1967: 140; Strange, 1981: 142–9).

The Malay-Islamic Context: Arguments for and against Polygyny

The Malaysian press, both English and Malay, has in recent years devoted considerable space to the place of polygamy in Islam. This debate helps to clarify the traditional situation and to understand changes taking place in more recent times.

The Koran is clear about the right of men to have up to four wives in certain circumstances provided that they can treat them equally (see Chapter 1). However, as argued by opponents of easy polygamy, the Koranic verses dealing with polygamy in fact represent a restriction on existing practice at the time of the Prophet according to which men could marry as many wives as they wanted.[7] The context of Verse 4: 3 in the Koran (many widows and orphans left without support after the Battle of Uhud) shows that polygamy was permitted to enable justice to be done to orphans; moreover, its practice was hedged around with many conditions (Sisters in Islam, 1990; Faisal, 1991).

Ranged on the other side in the debate in the Malaysian press was a variety of arguments. One was that men are adulterous by nature, or at least that a man's sexual desires are stronger than his wife's as they grow older. Therefore polygamy enabled Western vices such as widespread adultery and the keeping of mistresses to be avoided by enabling men's sexual desires to be met within marriage. Others argued that polygamy could be a solution to the problem of many unmarried Malay women in their thirties, or that it would ensure the expansion of the *ummah* (Muslim community). Some fundamentalists said that women should not oppose polygamy because that was tantamount to opposing the revealed will of Allah (Ramli, 1991). Women were sometimes told (apparently without Koranic basis) that if they agreed to their husband's taking another wife, this would ensure that they would get to heaven.

Some of the proponents of polygamy did recognize that the polygamy referred to in the Koran was in the interests of disadvantaged women and children, and that in this context the spirit of the contingent Koranic authorization to practise polygamy was hardly fulfilled when most Malay men who married a second wife seemed to choose young and attractive women.

In actual implementation of the law, emphasis has been given simply to the man's financial situation, and whether it enables him to provide materially for more than one wife. However, opponents of polygamy argue that as it is impossible to treat more than one wife equally, particularly in the matter of love and affection, the intention of the passage is actually to discourage polygamy.

Factors Underlying Decline in Polygamy

Reasons for Polygamy

Why do husbands take second wives? In some cases, it seems, because the first wife had not borne a child but the husband did not wish to divorce her. This is an acceptable reason for divorce, but it seems to have been rarely cited in available village studies; after all, fostering is an alternative solution in such cases. Another reason for a village man to take a second wife might be increased prestige in the eyes of his peers, but the fact that polygynists frequently try to keep second marriages secret does not suggest that they expect to gain prestige by the move (Strange, 1981: 147).

Probably it was more common to take a second wife in response to the desire for a further sex outlet (Rosemary Firth, 1966: 55). Itinerant men, particularly spirit doctors or *bomoh*, were especially prone to take second wives (Rosemary Firth, 1966: 55–6). It is also frequently believed in Malay village communities that magic is used either by the second wife to entrap the husband or by the husband to attract the second wife (Rosemary Firth, 1966: 55; Strange, 1981: 148–9), and such claims can still be frequently heard, even from educated Malays in the cities.

In very few instances are data available about stated reasons for entering a polygamous marriage, based on a large number of cases. The data presented in Table 7.4 for Johore over the years 1969–76, although they are undoubtedly affected by rationalization, are therefore of some interest. In roughly a quarter of cases, the first wife's sickness is mentioned, and in about another 10 per cent of cases, the wife's sterility or the desire to have children. The categories of responses—'no reason', 'they've fallen in love', or 'she's pregnant'—can probably be combined to indicate cases where love or sexual attraction was the main factor; such categories total about 39 per cent (1969–73) to 50 per cent (1974–6). The only other clearly defined category fairly frequently cited (8 per cent of cases) was 'to help his new wife' because she was from a different religion or poor,

TABLE 7.4
Johore: Reasons Given for Taking a Second Wife, 1969–1976

	1969–73		1974–76	
	Number	%	Number	%
Wife sick	92	24.9	53	22.4
Wife barren	33	8.9	14	5.9
Want children (male/female)	13	3.5	9	3.8
To help his new wife (from different religion, poor, etc.)	29	7.9	20	8.4
Husband more energetic	3	0.8	1	0.4
No credible reason	28	7.6	76	32.1
They've fallen in love	79	21.4	22	9.3
She's pregnant (adultery, rape, etc.)	35	9.5	20	8.4
New wife willing to move	4	1.1	7	3.0
Wants to remarry former wife after already married again	22	6.0	3	1.3
Other (forced by mother, far away, etc.)	31	8.4	12	5.1
Total	369	100	237	100

Source: Kasimin (1978: 119–20).

or something to that effect. As the Prophet Muhammad himself married additional wives in order to assist them, such a reason has a strong appeal to some Muslims.

The Changing Context

It appears that the extent of polygamy in the Malay world is tending to decrease, though the evidence is not clear-cut. That it is a practice frowned on by the great majority of Muslim women and by most men is clear. What are the factors responsible for its decline?

The increasing levels of education of both women and men and the growing influence of the ideas promoted by women's organizations appear to have led to growing doubt in the community as a whole that polygamy is just. Thus whereas in the past there was a degree of admiration for a polygamous man (at least on the part of other men) because he was wealthy enough or courageous enough to take on multiple wives, the reaction these days is more likely to be that he is holding very outdated attitudes.

The role of increasing economic prosperity is harder to fathom. It should, if anything, increase the proportion of men who are financially capable of supporting more than one wife. However, it should also (in combination with increased participation of women in the workforce) mean that fewer women need to accept a polygamous marriage for the financial support it will give them. In the past, many men who were not very well off did enter polygamous marriages, so the enabling factor of increasing incomes is probably more than offset by the changing community attitudes towards acceptability of divorce.

What role have legal changes played? Polygamy has been legal throughout Islamic South-East Asia, with the exception of Thailand, where it has been illegal under civil law since 1935 for men, including Muslim men, to have more than one wife. Even in Thailand, however, it is possible for Muslim men to engage in polygamy in the four southernmost provinces, because since 1946 Islamic laws have been acceptable there for certain matters, including family law.

Even though polygamy is legal, it is possible to make it more or less difficult to practise, and South-East Asian countries have varied in their approach to this issue. As noted above, the existence of national boundaries within the Malay world, facilitating the practice of 'cross-border' polygamy, complicates attempts to limit the practice of polygamy. In 1991, an agreement was reached between four ASEAN countries (Malaysia, Indonesia, Brunei, and Singapore) to synchronize the issuance of marriage documents, so that it would be easier for officials asked to perform marriage ceremonies involving a national from one of the other countries to determine whether they were already married.

The Indonesian Marriage Law of 1974 and the Islamic Family Law Act of 1984 in Malaysia, enacted in different states at different times thereafter, have tightened up the procedures for entering a polygamous marriage. Besides this, procedures adopted by institutions such as the armed forces, the police, and the government for their own employees in some cases go beyond the official requirements of the Acts, particularly in the matter of counselling for those requesting permission to enter a polygamous marriage.

In Malaysia, the Pusat Islam (Islamic Centre) under the Prime Minister's Department hoped that the Islamic Family Law Act would become a standardized legal model for the nation. However, as religion is a state matter, states enacted the Act at different times and with considerable modification of the provisions relating to polygamy in many cases. The Kuala Lumpur Federal Territory has the most comprehensive set of criteria, including the requirement for the first wife's permission in writing; in Selangor the Islamic Family Law Enactment requires evidence of some 'just and necessary' reason to take another wife, while in Perak a man's promise to treat his wives equally and fairly is sufficient (*Far Eastern Economic Review*, 22 August 1991). In most states, to the disappointment of Malay women's groups, a man does not need his first wife's consent to take a second wife, because religious hardliners have argued that the Koran does not require such consent.

Nevertheless, on the whole the new procedures in Malaysia do make it harder for a man to take a second wife. The man must apply formally to the *kadi*,[8] explaining his reasons for wanting to take another wife, attaching proof of income and other information. The *kadi* will then investigate. In many states, he will hold discussions with both the man and his wife before deciding; in Kelantan, he requires five people to come to his office for separate interviews: the husband-to-be, the wife-to-be, the father of the wife-to-be, and two witnesses from the husband's side.[9] Since early 1992 in Kelantan, he must at least inform the wife or wives of their husband's intention to take another wife, and give them fourteen days' notice to put in their objections. Many applications have failed. In the Federal Territory, only about 5 per cent of all recent applications have succeeded (Suhaini, 1991).[10] Fines or jail sentences can be imposed on men who enter a polygamous marriage without the permission of the *kadi*. In most states (as at 1988), the maximum fine was RM1,000 or 6 months jail; in Kedah and Sarawak, the maximum fine was RM500, while in Pahang and Malacca, there was no fine.

There have been changes in various states in recent years in the requirements for applying to take an additional wife. On the whole, these seem to be in the direction of weakening the process of consultation with the first wife. For example, in Selangor, from 1988, it was no longer necessary for the husband to obtain the first wife's signature on the application, indicating her approval (Shamsiah, 1991). In Johore, when the enactment finally took place in 1990, six years after the Act was introduced federally, there was no provision that the wife's permission had to be sought when a man applied to take another wife.

In any case, representatives of women's organizations argue that it is now possible for a man, refused permission to enter a polygamous marriage in one state, to 'shop around' and find another state where his application will succeed. Failing that (and the effort *could* fail, as residence in the state is supposed to be established before an application for polygamy can be approved), the option of going to Southern Thailand to marry in contravention of the Act is still available. The fine for reporting such marriages in Kelantan to legalize them is a maximum of RM1,000, but generally something like RM200. Even the figure of RM1,000 is no deterrent whatsoever to the wealthy men who are the most likely to engage in polygamy.

Community Attitudes to Polygamy

Although there are recorded cases of harmony between wives in polygamous marriages (Gullick, 1987: 224), the evidence is that nineteenth-century Malay women generally loathed the practice, and that this loathing continues to the present (Gullick, 1987: 52, 217, 223–5). Indonesian feminists have spoken out strongly against polygamy since the turn of the twentieth century. In a report on the improvement in the position of Indonesian women, which formed part of an official government enquiry in 1914, Dewi Sartika, founder of a girls' school, mentioned what she called the two scourges of family life, child marriage and polygamy. Like the well-known feminist Kartini before her, she advocated school education as a remedy for these excesses. Another contributor to the same report, the editor of a women's magazine, Siti Sundari, wrote that among the innumerable letters sent to her, complaints about polygamy and arbitrary repudiation appeared time after time. Some women from a *santri* (orthodox Muslim) background were also claiming that polygamy as practised at the time in Indonesia was against the spirit of Islam (Vreede-de Stuers, 1976: 82–3).

Malay writers have typically been critical of polygamous men, particularly those who use their wealth or religious influence to this end (Thani, 1979: 112). Certainly it was frequently on account of poverty that parents would consent to the union of their daughter with a man they knew to be already married. As Djamour (1966: 84) noted, '. . . the man usually bribed them with a large sum of money or [they] were already indebted to the suitor financially'. Many popular songs in Indonesia and Malaysia are critical of polygamy and hold up a faithful monogamous marriage as the ideal (Suprapto, 1990: 96–7).

It is argued by Suprapto (1990: 96) that women in certain strongly Islamic areas in Indonesia, notably the Bugis-Makassarese, Madurese, and Acehnese, are much more tolerant of polygamy than other Indonesian women, preferring their husbands to be polygamous rather than to commit adultery. Although it is true that the Bugis-Makassarese areas of South Sulawesi appear to have the highest levels of polygamy in Indonesia, and therefore it would not be surprising if wives there were more tolerant than elsewhere, it is not clear that the Madurese and Acehnese have particularly high rates of polygamy. Suprapto does not adduce any specific evidence for his view.

As a generalization about Islamic South-East Asia, it can be said that though not forbidden by Islamic law, polygyny certainly did not receive full social approval. The attitude was not the same as to divorce, which was regarded as a much more normal and socially acceptable behaviour than polygyny (Rosemary Firth, 1966: 203). Rosemary Firth (1966: 56) observed that 'the Malay of the [Kelantanese] villages regards it [polygyny] as a proper and in general desirable practice, to which people conform or not according to their resources, their inclination, and their chances of maintaining a harmonious domestic life', but this is not supported by other studies in the region. Djamour (1966: 86) 'met very few Malays in Singapore who publicly or privately praised polygamy. On the one hand, there were many who condemned the practice in no uncertain terms; the educated among them, on the grounds that it was "not really" permissible by Islam and in any case degrading to women; and many illiterate villagers on the practical grounds that it led to incessant and unbearable disputes in the household.'

In Rusila, Trengganu, Strange found only one woman who spoke positively about polygamy. Educated young people were almost un-animously negative about polygyny, viewing the practice as typical of the uneducated, but uneducated women and many men shared their attitudes (Strange, 1981: 146). In Maguwoharjo, Yogyakarta, V. J. Hull (1975: 198) found that 95 per cent of men and 98 per cent of women thought polygyny was bad. Polygyny appears frequently to be the subject of joking in Malay society, particularly if engaged in by a man who cannot really afford it, thus reflecting an unwise lack of control over sexual drives (Kuchiba, Tsubouchi, and Maeda, 1979: 36).

Case-studies in Indonesia show a range of attitudes to polygyny according to region. In Java, there are strongly negative attitudes to polygamy, both among men and among women (Table 7.5). In Aceh, the attitude of women is also strongly negative, but males are positive. In South Sumatra and South Kalimantan, both males and females are supportive of polygamy, although in the South Kalimantan study, females are less supportive than males (about 65 per cent of younger women support polygamy compared with about 96 per cent of younger men), and younger females are less supportive than older females. In Java, a range of controls does not seem to make much difference, although more

TABLE 7.5

Indonesia: Agreement That a Husband Can Engage in Polygamy without Any Particular Reason Provided His First Wife Agrees and the Husband is Economically Capable, 1978 (per cent)

	Males		Females	
	Aged <36	Aged 36+	Aged <36	Aged 36+
Java				
Education:[a] Low	37	34	34	41
High	27	28	37	19
Economic status:[b] Low	29	33	32	45
High	31	29	39	32
Religious activity				
Does not pray	34	32	37	42
Prays	26	28	33	32
Aceh				
Work before marriage				
Agricultural	80	70	32	33
Non-agricultural	70	72	35	34
South Sumatra				
Education:[a] Low	85	83		
High	83	77		
South Kalimantan				
Religious activity				
Does not pray	97	99	57	71
Prays	96	94	77	80
Education:[a] Low	97	96	70	77
High	95	93	63	83

Sources: Kasto (1982: Table 6.13); Arian (1982: Table 6.7); Mahmud (1983: Table 6.8); Mahfudz (1982: Table 6.15), from the Indonesian Marriage Survey, 1978.
[a]Low = None or incomplete primary.
 High = Completed primary and above.
[b]Low = Economic status score <30.
 High = Economic status score ≥30.

religious people seem to be less in favour of polygamy than the less religious.

Survey data cannot be expected to elicit the deeper feelings of respondents on a subject as sensitive as polygyny. The following report by an anthropologist on the strong feelings expressed in a conversation with a number of women in an Islamicized but still partly traditional Sasak village in Lombok in 1961 may therefore be more revealing.

One young woman who had been married for two years related the recurrent nightmares she had about her husband taking another wife, or having another wife and not telling her about it. She spoke of the difficulty women had in accepting polygyny. The older women of the group agreed with her, but they asked rhetorically, 'Certainly it's difficult, but what can one do?' The wife of a village official talked of fighting with her husband's second wife, stating that such conflicts between co-wives were frequent in Lenek. Another woman said that she dreamed of scratching her co-wife's eyes out. It must be noted that violence is strongly disapproved by the Sasak. She further stated that she felt 'betrayed' when her husband took another wife, and said that she could tolerate him only because she had his child. The woman spoke of other women who had committed suicide or become insane as a result of polygyny. (Krulfeld, 1986: 204.)

Data from the Malaysian Marriage Survey enable the opinions about polygamy of currently married Malay males and females to be compared, and in turn to be compared with the opinions of Chinese and Indians (Table 7.6). Malay males are much less likely than Malay females to consider that polygamy is bad (26 per cent compared with 45 per cent) and more likely to consider that it is good (11 per cent compared with 4 per cent). But half or more of both males and females answer either 'depends' or 'do not know'. Perhaps for many, this reflects a distaste for polygamy but also an awareness that polygamy is permitted in Islam in some circumstances and therefore cannot be adjudged outright as 'bad'.

Chinese are far more likely to condemn polygamy than are Malays; Indian males condemn it more than Malays, but condemnation by Indian

TABLE 7.6

Peninsular Malaysia: Opinion about the Practice of Polygamy in the Society, by Ethnic Group, 1981–1982 (per cent)

Responses	Husband			Wife		
	Malays	Chinese	Indians	Malays	Chinese	Indians
Good	11	6	2	4	–[a]	3
Bad	26	56	50	45	72	43
Depends	38	11	12	20	3	5
Do not know	25	27	36	31	25	49
Total	100	100	100	100	100	100

Source: Tan et al. (1986: Table 14), from the Malaysian Marriage Survey, 1981.
[a]Less than 0.5.

females is only in about the same proportion as by Malay females. Chinese and Indians are less likely to answer 'depends' than are Malays, probably because they do not have to worry about Islamic teachings which show polygamy to be acceptable in some circumstances.

Another question in this survey queried whether respondents thought marriages could be happy under certain specified circumstances. Whereas about half of Malay females thought that the marriage could be happy if the couple were living with the parents of one of them, or if the husband was older than the wife by 20 years or more, or if the wife was more educated than the husband, only 8 per cent thought it could be happy if the husband had a second wife. Among male respondents, the proportion who thought such a marriage could be happy rose to 18 per cent—still quite a low figure (Tan et al., 1986: 187).

Conclusions

Polygamy has important demographic functions in societies where it is widely practised. For example, Chojnacka (1980) argues that polygamy is associated with early marriage for females and late marriage for males, and promotes universal marriage among women. The incidence of polygamy in Islamic South-East Asia has not been high enough to have had a major demographic impact in these directions, with the possible exception of one or two areas such as South Sulawesi.

However, polygamy has undoubtedly had a major impact on husband–wife relationships in Islamic South-East Asia. The possibility, rather than the actuality, is the key factor; actual practice of polygamy is not as common as it might be because frequently the wife, learning of or suspecting the husband's intention to take another wife, seeks a divorce instead.

Polygamy remains a subject on which strong differences of opinion are expressed. It is a touchstone of gender relationships and a subject on which women feel very strongly. In the 1991 press debates in Malaysia, even many supporters of polygamy accepted that 90 per cent of Malay women opposed polygamy. Like divorce, polygamy was an area in which women felt disadvantaged in the past by a 'male conspiracy' whereby regulations were winked at by some religious officials (all of whom, of course, are men) in the male's favour. In Malaysia, there is the additional factor that non-Muslims are not permitted to practise polygamy, leaving Muslim wives feeling discriminated against compared with their non-Muslim friends or acquaintances.

There will undoubtedly be further attempts to restrict polygamy and to give the existing wife or wives a greater say in whether the husband can take another wife. Those who stress the rights of men in Islam will strenuously oppose any such attempts on the grounds that there is no requirement in the Koran for such a procedure.

1. The highest rates of polygyny within West Sumatra were in Agam (12.9 per cent), Padang (10.2 per cent), Tanah Datar (9.4 per cent), and Limapuluh Kota (8.9 per cent). Then followed Solok with 7.8 per cent and, much lower, Kerinci-Painan with 2.1 per cent. The high rates in West Sumatra were matched by those of the island of Buton in Sulawesi (9.3 per cent).

2. This observation is based not only on the references cited in the text, but on discussions with knowledgeable informants during fieldwork in Indonesia, Malaysia, and Southern Thailand.

3. Rates of polygyny could of course be higher in some other areas of Indonesia not covered by the 1973 Fertility–Mortality Survey or subsumed under wider geographic areas in the 1930 census report. For example, Krulfeld (1986: 202) found high rates of polygyny in two strongly Muslim Sasak villages she studied in Lombok in 1960–1. In one of them, a random sample of households recorded that 25 per cent of unions were polygynous and 63 per cent of household heads said that they had contracted polygynous unions at one time or another.

4. Such a finding would not necessarily indicate a decline in polygamy if there were a tendency for second or third wives in polygamous marriages to be chosen from among older women, thus raising the possibility that more of these younger women would enter polygamous marriages as they grew older. But the evidence is that second wives are usually chosen from among younger women.

5. This was calculated from Niehof's Table 5.12 and Table 8.1.

6. Islamic committees have been formed in the four southernmost provinces (Pattani, Narathivat, Yala, and Satun) and in Bangkok and, under a Special Act of 1946, Islamic laws are accepted in the four southernmost provinces, including the registration of marriages and divorces by the Islamic Committees. However, whereas Islamic law permits polygamy, Thai law does not. This has implications for the rights of the partners to the polygamous marriage. If there is a dispute over inheritance after the husband dies, the second wife has no way to prevent the full inheritance going to the first wife, because the first marriage is the only one recognized under Thai law.

7. Indeed, the Prophet Muhammad, after living monogamously with his wife Khadijah for 25 years, became polygamous after her death and left nine wives when he died. However, after receiving the revelation that the number of wives permitted by Allah did not exceed four, he did not marry any more wives (Ishak, 1988).

8. As stated in the Islamic Family Law Enactment in Kelantan in 1983, no male person shall marry another woman at any place while he is married unless he has obtained prior written consent of a Court of a Kadi.

9. Based on discussions with the Deputy Kadi of Kelantan, 5 November 1990.

10. A recent Malaysian case that received considerable publicity was the successful appeal by the wife of businessman Wan Mohamed Yusof Othman against the decision of a Shariah Court in Selangor to allow him to take well-known actress-singer Noorkumalasari as his second wife. The appeal succeeded on the grounds that, although Yusof said he wanted to remarry to legitimize his relationship with Noorkumalasari, he had not provided evidence of any 'just and necessary' reason to take another wife. Subsequently, however, Yusof and Noorkumalasari registered residence in Trengganu and applied successfully to the state Shariah Court for permission to marry.

8
The Effect of Changing Marriage Patterns on Fertility

CHANGING marriage patterns have many policy implications, related as they are to women's status, labour force participation, the stability of the family unit, and the welfare of children. But in view of the prominence given to population policy in the region, one of the most important policy aspects of changing marriage patterns could be their implications for fertility. If changing marriage patterns have an effect on fertility, whether intended or unintended, then a nation's fertility policy may do well to include policies to nudge marriage patterns in desired directions. Even if marriage changes do not alter patterns of completed fertility, they may nevertheless cause major modifications in the timing of childbearing over women's reproductive span. This is important because the annual rate of population growth is slowed if the mean length of each generation is extended by a shift in childbearing to later ages (Coale and Tye, 1961). It therefore appears likely that changes in age at marriage will affect population growth rates, and that age at marriage could represent an appropriate lever of population policy—one, moreover, more acceptable and effective in many settings than measures aimed directly at reducing fertility.

In China, late age at marriage (23 for women) was promoted by government regulations in the 1970s. Late marriage and, especially, late childbearing contributed significantly to controlling population growth in China over this period (Bongaarts and Greenhalgh, 1985; Zeng and Vaupel, 1989; Coale et al., 1991). However, a new Marriage Law, promulgated on 1 January 1981, legalized a minimum age at marriage of 20 for women, thus undercutting the locally administered restrictions on marriage before the officially designated desirable age. The resultant spate of younger marriages contributed substantially to the increase in Chinese birth rates in the 1980s (Coale et al., 1991; Zeng et al., 1991).

Marriage is certainly considered a target of fertility policy in some countries of South-East Asia. For example, a key aim of Indonesia's family planning programme is to raise the age at marriage as a means of reducing fertility. Roadside slogans posted by the BKKBN (Badan Koordinasi Keluarga Berencana Nasional or National Family Planning

Co-ordinating Board) therefore include one depicting a young man and woman, both in academic mortarboards, with the message 'Finish your studies before getting married'. By contrast, Singapore is now attempting to raise fertility and views with concern the high proportion of women, particularly the better-educated, who are not marrying at all or marrying very late. Therefore in the mid-1980s, Singapore embarked on policies to increase marriage, offering financial incentives to graduate women to marry, and using the Social Development Unit to bring together single graduates in various functions and social activities (Hull and Larson, 1987: 50–3). Though originally directed mainly at graduates, the focus of such policies was subsequently broadened to reach a greater proportion of the population, in line with a broadening of the pro-natalist focus from just the highly educated to the population as a whole.

At an individual level, decision-making about marriage is largely separate from considerations about fertility (Coale, 1979: 12). The lack of an adequate theory of marriage behaviour is therefore one of the biggest gaps in the explanation of fertility patterns (Easterlin, 1976; Coale, 1979; P. C. Smith, 1983). Policies to affect fertility through marriage patterns do not, of course, require changes in the marriage practices of individuals to be motivated by fertility considerations. What is important for policy is that at the macro level certain fertility consequences flow from certain changes in marriage patterns. The reasons for the changes are immaterial, though of course they must be understood if policies to influence the changes are to succeed.

Historical Analyses of Other Regions

In the European demographic transition, the role of nuptiality was very important. Fertility in Western Europe had been reduced to a moderate level by postponement and avoidance of marriage, well in advance of the modern decline in fertility. What Hajnal (1965) referred to as the typical European pattern of marriage, which characterized populations lying to the west of an imaginary line drawn between Trieste and St. Petersburg, entailed late marriage—an average age at first marriage for women of more than 23 years and sometimes as high as 28 years— and a substantial fraction of the population remaining unmarried even at the age of 50. The result was that at any given time, less than half of the potentially fertile women were cohabiting (Hajnal, 1965: 119).

Changes in age at marriage and in the proportion remaining permanently single accounted for a substantial part of the regional differences in fertility in Europe and in time-trends in fertility in the period before parity-related fertility control became important. In Europe as a whole, in 1870 these differences in marriage patterns appear to have been about twice as important as differences in natural fertility; in England, from the mid-sixteenth to the mid-nineteenth century, they were the dominant source of the variation in fertility (Wrigley and Schofield, 1981). Overall fertility in England varied substantially over this period, because of ups and downs in mean age at first marriage, and especially because of variation in the proportion remaining single, while marital fertility remained nearly constant.

Debate still centres on the extent to which the high marriage ages in parts of Europe were in intent, as well as in effect, designed to control fertility: Davis's (1963) idea of marriage postponement as part of a 'multiphasic demographic response' to pressures for lower fertility. In any case, in the twentieth century, early and more nearly universal patterns of marriage evolved in Europe. One factor contributing to this trend may well have been 'the dissociation of marriage from the previous more or less inevitable sequence of pregnancies and births as the practice of effective voluntary control of fertility within marriage became more or less universal' (Coale, 1979: 13).

Pre-modern patterns of nuptiality and fertility in Asia were much more varied than in Europe. For example, in China and in areas influenced by Chinese culture, age at marriage was lower than in Europe and marriage more universal, but marital fertility was relatively low. The period of strong fertility decline in these areas has been characterized by more ready access to improved means of birth control, and fairly strong family planning programmes, so that changes in nuptiality patterns did not need to play a major role in fertility transition. A tendency for age at marriage to rise has, however, reinforced the other factors tending to lower fertility. In Japan, the decline of almost half in fertility rates between 1950 and 1975, resulting in below-replacement fertility, was occasioned almost entirely by a decline in marital fertility. By contrast, the further decline in fertility in the 1975–89 period was due solely to postponement of marriage by young Japanese women (Tsuya and Mason, 1992: 10).

In Indonesia, analysis of regional differences in the Coale indices of marriage and fertility[1] for the period before much fertility decline had taken place showed that there was no clear association between regions with particularly early marriage patterns and those with high levels of fertility (Jones, 1977: 34–8; McNicoll and Singarimbun, 1982: 51–4). The generally later female age at marriage found outside Java, for example, coincided with higher fertility in these regions. International comparisons between Asian countries based on the fertility history of women building their families before the recent fertility declines had got under way also showed only weak evidence of an inverse association between age at marriage and completed fertility; for example, completed fertility was highest in Thailand even though its age at marriage was also among the highest, while completed fertility was lowest in Java–Bali where age at marriage was very low (Caldwell, McDonald, and Ruzicka, 1980: 21).

This lack of clear association between age at marriage and completed fertility reflects the relatively young female ages at marriage throughout the region at the time the comparisons were made; if average ages at marriage are everywhere below 20, a difference of two or three years can readily be compensated for through more frequent births over the course of a woman's reproductive period. But when marriage ages for women climb well into the twenties, there is less likelihood that such compensation will fully offset the later start to childbearing. As shown in Chapter 3,

average ages at marriage for Malay women in some parts of South-East
Asia have indeed advanced well into the twenties.

A Demographic Accounting Approach to Nuptiality–Fertility Relationships in Islamic South-East Asia

Fertility has fallen substantially among South-East Asian Muslim
populations since the 1960s. In fact, the Singapore Malays were the first
Muslim population in the world to reach replacement-level fertility when
they descended to a net reproduction rate of 1 in 1975. How much of
the fertility decline that has taken place was due to the dramatic changes
in marriage patterns? An answer can be given to this question in demographic accounting terms, although as will be seen later, it may be a
somewhat misleading answer.

If it is assumed that childbirth takes place only within marriage, there
are only three possible causes of lowered crude birth rates (i.e. the
number of births per 1,000 population in a given year). These are a rise
in the share of reproductive-age females in the total population, a reduction in the proportion of the fertile period spent in the married state,
or a reduction in the fertility of married women.

The first factor leading to change in birth rates, a change in the
proportion of reproductive-age women in the population, is the result
of demographic changes dating back decades and is thus not amenable
to manipulation through government policy. Among the Islamic populations being studied, the tendency over the 1970s and early 1980s was
for this proportion to rise, as a result of a declining proportion of children
in the population which in turn resulted from earlier declines in fertility
(see Table 8.1). This means that declines in fertility over this period

TABLE 8.1

Islamic South-East Asia: Trends in the Share of Reproductive-age Women
in the Total Population, 1970–2010

	Women Aged 15–49 as a Percentage of the Total Population		
	Indonesia	*Peninsular Malaysia Malays*	*Singapore Malays*
1970	23.6	22.5	22.7
1980	24.1	24.8	28.5
1985	24.8	25.0	n.a.
1990	25.7	24.8	28.2
1995	26.4	24.4	n.a.
2000	27.0	24.5	n.a.
2010	27.8	n.a.	n.a.

Sources: Indonesia: United Nations (1991).
Peninsular Malaysia: Department of Statistics, Malaysia (1987); Lim, Jones, and
Hirschman (1987: Table 3).
Singapore: *Census of Population, Singapore, 1990*: Table 5.

were not translated into equivalent declines in birth rates. In Indonesia, the rise in the share of reproductive-age females is continuing, though it will level off early in the twenty-first century as birth cohorts of roughly equal size, generated by declining fertility, enter the reproductive ages. For Peninsular Malaysian Malays, the share of reproductive-age women was already declining slightly by the late 1980s as a result of the earlier upturn in Malay fertility (Jones, 1990a: Figure 3), thus facilitating rather than hindering further declines in birth rates.

The second factor, the percentage of the reproductive period spent in the married state, has two components: the timing of entry into marriage and the durability of the marriage once contracted. The entry into the married state can be, and indeed is, addressed directly by policy, at least in Indonesia and Singapore. In Indonesia, the intent is to delay the entry into marriage and in Singapore, at least since 1984, to hasten it. The durability of marriages is influenced by mortality and by divorce and separation. Government attempts to lower these are always, in effect though not in intent, in pro-natalist directions, as they would increase the proportion of the reproductive period spent in the married state.

It should be stressed here that if a substantial proportion of marriages are occasioned by the pregnancy of an unmarried girl in a social context where either an extramarital birth or an abortion is unthinkable, then policy to delay marriage will be relatively ineffectual if it does not also address the problem of premarital conceptions. In Indonesia, as already discussed in Chapter 3, premarital sexual relations and premarital conceptions are not rare, and appear to be increasingly common among young people (Singarimbun, 1984; Hull and Hull, 1987). In Malaysia, data from the Malaysian Population and Family Survey of 1984–5 showed that only about 1.6 per cent of all Malay births were conceived premaritally (Hamid et al., 1988: Table 3.16),[2] and the incidence of premarital conceptions among Malays is only one-fifth as high as it is among the Chinese. But with still-rising ages at marriage, relaxation of social controls on mixing and dating among young people, and resistance to making contraceptive information and services available to young, unmarried people, it would not be surprising if premarital conceptions were on the rise quite generally throughout Islamic South-East Asia.

With regard to divorce and widowhood as factors reducing the proportion of a woman's potential reproductive period spent in the married state, it should be stressed that the effect of given divorce or widowhood rates on this measure will depend on the frequency and rapidity of remarriage after these events. In the Malay world, as already discussed in Chapter 5, rapid remarriage after divorce is the norm, and divorce therefore does little on average to shorten the potential reproductive period. On the other hand, remarriage after widowhood is less frequent and tends to occur at a longer interval after the event than in the case of divorce.

The third factor, a reduction in the age-specific fertility of married women, does not, in accounting terms, have anything directly to do with marriage patterns, although as will be shown, age at marriage can influence these rates in quite a number of ways. There could be many causes of lowered marital fertility, including longer breastfeeding, or poorer nutrition lowering women's capacity to reproduce, but the crucial factor causing lower fertility is normally an increase in the practice of contraception (thus preventing conception) or in some cases, in the practice of abortion (thus preventing conceptions from resulting in live births).

The main policy lever related to marital fertility, birth control practice within marriage, is tackled directly by family planning programmes. During the 1970s, the four countries of Singapore, Malaysia, Indonesia, and Thailand followed similar policies to lower fertility rates. More recently, policy has diverged. Thailand and Indonesia continue to foster lower fertility, but Malaysia follows a somewhat ambivalent policy[3] and Singapore is now actively pro-natalist.

A number of studies have disaggregated fertility declines into their component factors. In countries or regions that experienced substantial declines in crude birth rates during the 1960s and 1970s, postponement of marriage and falling proportions ever married at any given age played a considerable part. This was the case in the Republic of Korea, Taiwan, and Peninsular Malaysia between 1960 and 1970, in Java and Bali between 1967–71 and 1977, in Sri Lanka between 1963 and 1971, in Tunisia between 1966 and 1975, and in Turkey between 1960 and 1975 (see Caldwell, McDonald, and Ruzicka, 1980). Declines in proportions married had a clear role in the fertility declines in Malaysia, Thailand, and Indonesia between 1970 and 1980, though only in Malaysia did the contribution of the marriage component in any way rival that of the marital fertility component (Hirschman and Guest, 1990). In China, after playing a role in the sharp fertility declines of the 1970s and early 1980s, marriage again contributed to fertility change, this time a rise, between 1984 and 1987 (Zeng et al., 1991).

Proportion of Reproductive Span at Risk of Conception

Later in this chapter, the role of marriage change on fertility trends in Indonesia and among Malays in Peninsular Malaysia and Singapore will be analysed in more detail. Two things need to be done first by way of introduction. The first is to examine trends in the proportion of a 'representative' woman's reproductive span that is 'at risk' of contributing to fertility; this will be done in this section. The next section considers ways in which such accounting relationships may reveal less than the full truth.

Figure 8.1 shows a somewhat stylized version of the components of the reproductive period in Indonesia and among Malaysian Malays at different times. It is assumed that births do not take place outside the married state. This is fairly realistic in the Malay cultural setting, though it must be borne in mind that some—and probably a changing proportion over time—of the pregnancies resulting in births took place outside the married state and that this precipitated the marriage.

The proportion of the fertile period spent in the married state depends

FIGURE 8.1

Indonesia and Peninsular Malaysia (Malays): 'Average' Woman's Exposure
to Risk of Reproduction at Ages 15–44, 1950s and 1980s

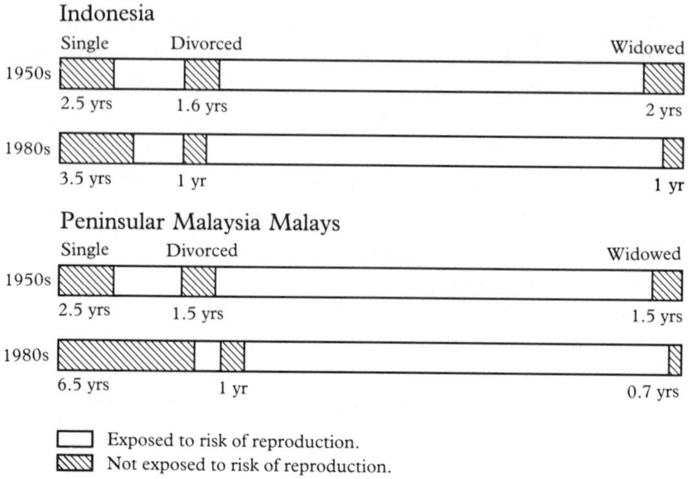

Indonesia

| | Single | Divorced | | Widowed |

1950s: 2.5 yrs / 1.6 yrs / 2 yrs

1980s: 3.5 yrs / 1 yr / 1 yr

Peninsular Malaysia Malays

| | Single | Divorced | | Widowed |

1950s: 2.5 yrs / 1.5 yrs / 1.5 yrs

1980s: 6.5 yrs / 1 yr / 0.7 yrs

☐ Exposed to risk of reproduction.
▨ Not exposed to risk of reproduction.

Source: Computed by the author.

Note: Composite of age at marriage situation of younger women, divorce situation of slightly older women, and widowhood situation of older women in the years concerned.

on two factors: age at marriage and the proportion of time lost from marriage before the age of 45 because of dissolution of marriage through divorce or widowhood without subsequent remarriage. In Java, age at marriage was traditionally very young and levels of divorce and widowhood relatively high. At ages below 45, divorce was far more important than widowhood as a cause of marital dissolution, despite the tendency for husbands to be five years or so older than their wives and for mortality rates to be high. There was considerable regional variation in these patterns throughout Indonesia. In Malaysia, a similar set of factors operated, except that levels of widowhood were lower than in Java because mortality rates were lower.

The effect of widowhood and divorce in disrupting a woman's reproductive life depends on the speed of remarriage. Both in Indonesia and among the Malays of Malaysia, remarriage tended to follow fairly hard on the heels of divorce, with the result that the average woman's potential reproductive period was only slightly shortened by divorce. For example, the Indonesian Fertility Survey of 1976 found that in Java–Bali, for women whose first marriage was dissolved under the age of 25 years (and most divorces did occur below this age), 60 per cent had remarried within 2 years, 85 per cent within five years, and 95 per cent within ten years (Caldwell, McDonald, and Ruzicka, 1980: 13; see also Muliakusuma, 1976: 86–93). On average, women in Java–Bali spent 90 per cent of their time since first marriage in the married state. This fraction was fairly uniform across age-groups and marriage cohorts. Women with completed primary or high school education spent even more of their time married: about 95 per cent (Central Bureau of Statistics and World Fertility Survey, 1978: Table 4.5). In Peninsular Malaysia, 1984 data show that the proportion of time spent in the married state since first marriage was even higher—almost 97 per cent—and differed little by ethnic group or socio-economic status (Hamid et al., 1988: 29–30). These high proportions of time spent in the married state resulted from the speed of remarriage after divorce, because divorce itself was very common: in Java–Bali, within five years after the first marriage, about a quarter of couples had divorced (Caldwell, McDonald, and Ruzicka, 1980: Table 5).

Figure 8.1 portrays the situation obtaining around the 1960s as well as in more recent times. A number of factors have changed:

1. Age at marriage has risen both in Indonesia and among the Malaysian Malays, though the rise has been much slower in Indonesia. There has also been a tendency for the age differences between spouses to narrow.
2. Mortality rates have declined markedly, and the joint risk of one of the partners to a marriage dying before the wife completes her reproductive period is further lowered by the narrowed age differences between spouses.
3. Divorce rates have fallen sharply in Malaysia and less sharply in Indonesia, thus lessening the likelihood that the marriage will be disrupted for this reason.

These trends are clearly working in opposite directions: the age-at-marriage trends have been lowering the proportion of reproductive life spent in the married state, while the mortality and divorce trends have been increasing it. The net effect, however, is towards a lowering of the proportion of reproductive life spent in the married state. This is because widowhood did not affect many women during their reproductive period (and mostly near the end of it anyway), and because the rapid remarriage after divorce which typified earlier times of high divorce meant that the subsequent lowering of divorce rates did not add greatly to the time women spent in the married state.

Marriage and Fertility: Aggregate and Individual-level Relationships

It is now time to introduce some complexity into the rather mechanistic relationships under examination, before reaching some conclusions about the effect of changes in marriage patterns on fertility in Islamic South-East Asia.

One important assumption about factors underlying relationships between marriage and fertility first needs to be noted and discussed. It is widely held that early marriage and high marriage prevalence go together. The implicit assumption is that similar causal influences operate on each. Dixon (1971, 1978) and P. C. Smith (1983) highlight some of these possible influences. First, where the economic feasibility of marriage is high, both the prevalence and timing of marriage will be affected. Secondly, where marriage is highly desirable—in part because of the absence of attractive social or economic alternatives, particularly for females—it will be not only earlier for females, but also more prevalent. Thirdly, shortage of potential partners over an extended period will not only raise age at marriage but also reduce prevalence. Fourthly, wherever marriage decisions are controlled by parents, marriage will be more prevalent.

The empirical evidence on the proposition that a shift towards later marriage is accompanied by a shift towards a lower prevalence of marriage is mixed (P. C. Smith, 1983: 509), with contrary evidence from Japan and Ireland. More important for the present study, though, is the lack of evidence that the widespread shift to later marriage in South-East Asia has resulted in a shift towards a lower prevalence of marriage. However, as noted in Chapter 3, the normal measure of non-marriage, the proportion single at ages 45–49, reflects the marital experience of cohorts a quarter of a century earlier than those currently postponing their marriages. Therefore the evidence is not yet in for the most recent cohorts, and there are certainly strong hints of an incipient fall in marriage prevalence in the rising proportions single in the 30–34 age-group.

It is often held that, when fertility control is widespread in a population, there need be no direct connection at all between marriage timing and fertility, only spurious correlations resulting from the association of both marriage timing and fertility with other variables. However, a marriage-timing–fertility association is sometimes found in populations practising fertility control (P. C. Smith, 1983: 482), and such an association will be confirmed in the analysis which follows.

Although there is only a weak association between age at marriage and completed fertility in regional or inter-country comparisons, in individual-level analysis, the relationship is usually quite strong. 'This indicates that country-specific factors affecting marital fertility are sufficient to cloud the underlying relationship between age at marriage and fertility in cross-national comparisons,' noted Caldwell, McDonald, and Ruzicka (1980: 23). They could have noted, with equal validity, that in Indonesia, region-specific factors are sufficiently strong to cloud the underlying relationship between age at marriage and fertility when regions are compared.

What is the evidence for the individual-level relationships? On the basis of data for various Asian countries from the World Fertility Survey, Caldwell and his colleagues showed that duration-specific fertility appears to be quite similar for women marrying at 18 years and over until the influence of older-age subfecundity commences, an influence which holds down the completed fertility of women marrying at ages 20 and above compared to earlier-marrying women, but which does not markedly hold down the completed fertility of, say, those marrying at age 19 compared to those marrying at age 16. Women who marry at particularly early ages, 15 and below, have significantly lower fertility in the first five years of marriage than other women, presumably because of factors such as adolescent subfecundity, delayed consummation, and

TABLE 8.2

Indonesia: Age-specific and Duration-specific Marital Fertility Rates for Women Continuously in the Married State, by Age at First Marriage, 1956–1976

| | Age-specific Marital Fertility Rates | | | |
| | Age at First Marriage | | | |
Age-group	<15	15–16	17–19	20+
10–14	0.076	–	–	–
15–19	0.304	0.260	0.108	–
20–24	0.300	0.321	0.355	0.199
25–29	0.267	0.294	0.299	0.293
30–34	0.217	0.222	0.251	0.245
35–39	0.146	0.167	0.184	0.194
40–44	0.057	0.087	0.091	0.114
45–49	0.014	0.021	0.018	0.033
Total marital fertility	6.9	6.9	6.5	5.4

| | Duration-specific Marital Fertility Rates | | | |
| | Age at First Marriage | | | |
Duration of Marriage	<15	15–16	17–19	20+
0–4	0.270	0.321	0.343.	0.354
5–9	0.305	0.314	0.318	0.294
10–14	0.275	0.282	0.264	0.210
15–19	0.247	0.212	0.205	0.176
20–24	0.179	0.156	0.146	0.086
25–29	0.092	0.073	0.041	0.045
30–34	0.042	0.012	0.000	0.000
Total marital fertility	7.1	6.9	6.6	5.8

Source: Caldwell, McDonald, and Ruzicka (1980: Table 19).

infrequent intercourse. However, this deficit is eventually made up and turned into a surplus by the end of the reproductive ages.

Table 8.2 summarizes the impact of age at marriage on subsequent fertility by showing age-specific and duration-specific marital fertility rates for Indonesia according to age at first marriage. The data refer only to once-married women who were still married at the time of the survey, and therefore are probably more representative of higher-fertility women, since marital disruption (which, as Chapter 5 showed, is more common among those marrying very young) has a dampening effect on fertility. Table 8.2 shows that fertility rates for a given age-group increase with age at marriage, except for the initial age-group in which the marriage occurs, implying that women marrying at an older age increase their fertility to compensate for their later marriage or women marrying early reduce their fertility at older ages. The duration-of-marriage section of the table, however, shows that except for the first five years of marriage, for any given duration group, the fertility rate tends to decrease as age at marriage increases. Caldwell, McDonald, and Ruzicka (1980) interpret this as reflecting the more rapidly declining fecundity of women marrying at older ages,[4] but it could also be due in large part to such women's reluctance to continue their childbearing into their late thirties and forties.

It appears, then, that only when age at marriage is pushed up from the teenage years to ages above 20 does age at marriage make much difference to completed fertility. Since this is precisely what happened to the Singapore and Malaysian Malays, however, one could expect their marriage trends to have had a strong impact on their fertility levels.

Though empirically the impact of rising age at marriage on fertility is demonstrated in Table 8.2, conceptually there are likely to be a variety of linkages, and their net outcome is not immediately apparent. For example, later marriage may be associated with relaxation of the cultural pressure for high fertility (McDonald, 1981); late marriage can lead to normatively fuelled 'catching up' behaviour through shorter birth intervals; very early marriage can reduce fecundity; early marriage may be associated with high early fertility if it is often precipitated by premarital pregnancy; early marriage may be (and certainly has been in Islamic South-East Asia) associated with high divorce rates.

A study for Indonesia based on the 1987 Contraceptive Prevalence Survey isolates the individual level effects of delayed marriage and multiple marriages on fertility (Palmore and Singarimbun, 1992). Among women aged 35–49, for example, being married more than once reduced cumulative fertility by more than one child. In the same age-group, those who had first married before age 15 had cumulative fertility almost three-fourths of a child higher than those married after age 18. Using multi-variate analysis and statistically controlling for eight socio-economic variables related to nuptiality and fertility, a five-year delay in age at first marriage was found to be associated with having approximately one less child, net of all the other variables. Being married more than once resulted in a woman's having about two fewer children—a strong negative effect on cumulative fertility. Part of this strong effect, of course, could be due to the effect of infecundity in triggering divorce.

The Palmore and Singarimbun study, like others, indicates that if past trends continue, rising age at marriage will lower fertility rates but lower divorce rates will tend to increase fertility. What does a careful examination of the empirical evidence about the relationship between marriage and fertility among the populations under consideration, both evidence based on 'accounting' relationships and evidence about the linkages discussed above, reveal?

Measures of the Net Impact of Marriage Change on Fertility

The changes in marriage patterns that can influence fertility have been systematically identified; how strong is their potential impact? As noted earlier, a woman's reproductive period stretches from puberty (about age 14) to menopause (around ages 45–49). This leaves a period of at least thirty years potentially available for procreation. Even if conventions restrict the 'acceptable' reproductive period from, say, 17 to 40, this 23-year period is not greatly shortened if the average age at marriage rises from 17 to 19. Analysis of a large number of countries covered by the World Fertility Survey showed that, despite wide differences in the typical age of entry into marriage, the range in average number of years of 'marital exposure' of women aged 40–49 was only 6.8 years (from 22.6 years among Fijians to 29.4 years in Bangladesh), partly because marital dissolution tended to occur more frequently the earlier the age at marriage. Even for women who did not marry until ages 20–24, and taking into account marital disruption, women aged 40–49 in all these countries still had an average of about twenty years (slightly less, nineteen years, in Indonesia) in the married state, ample time to have a considerable number of children (Caldwell, McDonald, and Ruzicka, 1980: 19).

What tends to happen during a fertility transition, however, is for the onset of reproduction to be more substantially delayed by a rise in average age at marriage into the twenties, and for women to become increasingly reluctant to bear children after about the age of 35, thus further constricting the available reproductive period. Even then, a period of ten or fifteen years is quite long enough for most women to bear four or five children, and it might therefore be argued that the rise in age at marriage would have to be very marked to have much effect on fertility. In strict accounting terms, this is true, but it entirely ignores the sociological implications of delaying marriage until into the twenties. Later marriage allows for an extended period of education, and then for a period in the workforce before marriage. The childbearing motivations of a woman marrying a spouse of her own choice at 23 or 24 are likely to be quite different from those of one marrying a spouse of her parents' choice at 16 or 17.

For the Malays of Malaysia, though, the desired number of children does not appear to have fallen despite a dramatic rise in age at marriage. Between 1970 and 1985, the median female age at marriage rose from 20.5 to 22.3, but desired family size, according to survey data, actually rose from 4.7 in 1974 to 5.6 in 1984 (Jones, 1990a: Table 2).[5] Although this rise was not accompanied by a rise in fertility between the same two points in time, it is significant that the total fertility rate for Malays did rise in the latter part of this period: from 4.3 in 1978 to 4.7 in 1984, suggesting that there may have been some reality in the rise in desired family size. On the other hand, changes in period fertility measures over a few years do not necessarily predict very well the changes in completed family size for the women involved, particularly in view of probable 'catch-up' fertility among those marrying at later ages. Moreover, there is some suggestion from renewed declines in Malay fertility since 1985 that the high desired family size recorded in 1984 had elements of response to perceived government pro-natalism at that time, rather than a personal goal, for many women (see also Govindasamy and DaVanzo, 1992).

Overall, in Peninsular Malaysia, the 'translation effect' noted by Ryder (1964), which can serve to prop up period fertility rates following rises in the average age at marriage without any tendency for completed fertility of cohorts of women to rise, and the fertility-enhancing effects of lowered divorce and widowhood rates, could have acted together to disguise to some extent the fertility-lowering effects of the substantial rises in age at marriage over the 1960s and 1970s.

Regional differences in fertility are also worth examining from this perspective. Falling divorce rates and declining mortality have undoubtedly played an important role in maintaining relatively high fertility levels in the high-divorce states in Malaysia.[6] Saw Swee Hock noted that the birth rate was low among Malays in these states in the 1940s and 1950s, and he attributed this partly to the influence of marital disruption and instability (Saw, 1967: 649; see also Hirschman and Fernandez, 1980). Since then, fertility has risen in these states, and it remains very high. The rise correlates with a substantial decline in the frequency of divorce, though disruption of marriage by widowhood has also decreased, and other factors may have been operating as well.

In accounting terms, what has been the effect of marriage trends on fertility? In the following discussion, the more refined fertility measure of total fertility rates is used; therefore the role of changing age structure, needed for an analysis of factors influencing crude birth rates, is eliminated, and only marriage patterns and marital fertility need to be considered.

First of all, what were the fertility trends that must be explained? Figure 8.2 shows the trend in the total fertility rates in Indonesia, and among Malay populations of Singapore and Peninsular Malaysia over the period since 1966. For the Singapore Malays, the entire fertility transition was squeezed into a twelve-year period, from 1964 to 1976 during which time fertility dropped by a remarkable 75 per cent. For the Malays of Peninsular Malaysia, the fertility decline set in at much the same time, but it was much more modest and fertility turned upwards from 1978 to 1985. In Indonesia, although the evidence is softer, fertility appears to have declined steadily from the early 1970s, the pace of decline picking up in the 1980s. After 1979, Indonesian fertility has been below that of the Malays of Peninsular Malaysia, the gap exceeding one child by the mid-1980s, despite the lower ranking of the Indonesians on socio-economic indicators (Jones, 1990a).

For the Singapore Malays, although age at marriage was rising rapidly during the period of fertility decline, changes in marital fertility accounted for most of the decline (Jones, 1990a: 512). In Indonesia, too, almost the entire decline was due to a decline in marital fertility. By contrast, among the Malays of Peninsular Malaysia, the fertility decline in the 1960s was fuelled almost entirely by a rising age at marriage. In

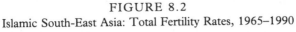

FIGURE 8.2

Islamic South-East Asia: Total Fertility Rates, 1965–1990

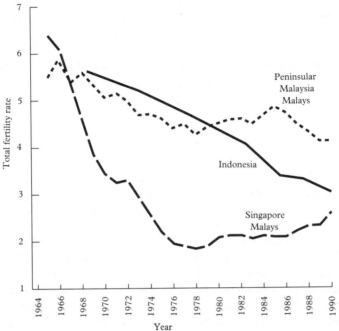

Sources: Jones (1990a: Figure 1), updated from recent Singapore and Malaysia vital statistics; Indonesia, Central Bureau of Statistics et al. (1992).

the 1970s, age at marriage continued to rise but marital fertility also fell at birth orders four or higher, rising again after 1978 across all birth orders except those sixth or higher. Part of the rise in Malay period fertility in the late 1970s and early 1980s resulted from the making up of postponed births among a population in which young adults, though marrying much later than before, showed little evidence of wanting fewer children than the previous generation (Tan, 1983; Hirschman, 1986; Lim, Jones, and Hirschman, 1987; Leete, 1989).

Even though no special efforts were made in Malaysia to raise age at marriage, over the period 1957–80, the median age at marriage for females rose more sharply there than in Indonesia: by five years in Malaysia but by only about two years in Indonesia. The rise was more than six years among Singapore Malays over the same period.

The patterns of marital fertility of Malays in Peninsular Malaysia support the argument that Malay women continue to want larger families than the other Malaysian ethnic groups and that they are simply rescheduling their births to older ages because they are marrying later. In the 1970–80 period, marital fertility did not change markedly at ages 25–34, but in both age-groups 25–29 and 30–34 there was an increase in first- to third-order births and a reduction in higher-order births. Even for age-groups 35 and above, there was an actual reduction in fifth- and higher-order births. In other words, there is evidence of a decline in the incidence of large families among Malays; the 'making up' that is being carried out after marriage at later ages is leading to only medium-sized families (Lim, Jones, and Hirschman, 1987: 422; see also Leete, 1989).

It should be noted that the Malays provide a perfect example of the effect of delayed marriage in slowing reproduction even where fertility is not falling. The mean length of a generation was stretched considerably by recent shifts in family-building patterns, and this resulted in slower rates of population increase than would have resulted from an earlier pattern of childbearing, even if completed family sizes were exactly the same.

Conclusions

After reviewing the evidence from a number of World Fertility Surveys in Asia, Caldwell, McDonald, and Ruzicka (1980) concluded that for all countries, whether or not practice of contraception is common, completed fertility declines with increase in age at first marriage. If contraceptive practice is limited, however, women marrying at 20–24 still have five to six children, partly because they tend to accelerate their childbearing to make up for lost time. Therefore, increased age at marriage, in itself, is unlikely to be very significant in the achievement of low fertility in a society. On the other hand, a society-wide increase in age at first marriage will have a short-term fertility-lowering 'translation effect' (Ryder, 1964) and the longer-run growth of the population will be slowed through a lengthening of each generation.

An important point is that early age at marriage is a prominent feature of traditional societies and a shift to later age at marriage is likely to reflect fundamental changes in the roles of women, education, family and economic structures, and parent–child relations. These changes in social structure are also likely to have implications for fertility. It is doubtful whether delayed marriage is often a strategy adopted specifically to lower fertility. Certainly, there is no evidence that postponement of marriage in Islamic South-East Asia was part of Davis's multiphasic response to pressures for fertility decline, a response frequently invoked to explain marriage delays historically in parts of Europe. For example, desired family size fell in Indonesia but not much among Peninsular Malaysia Malays; yet age at marriage has risen much less in Indonesia. The causes of changes in marriage appear to have been largely in-dependent of fertility motivations, a conclusion also drawn by Caldwell et al. (1989) in their study on Sri Lanka.

In the Malay world, changes in age at marriage and in divorce have been sufficiently dramatic to have had significant effects on fertility, though their net effect has been dampened by their mutually offsetting impacts. For Malaysian and Singaporean Malays, the fertility-dampening effect of rising age at marriage has clearly dominated the fertility-increasing effect of lowered divorce, though in Indonesia, where age at marriage has risen less and divorce has declined even more sharply than in Malaysia, this may not be the case. In any event, marital fertility declines have been the overwhelmingly important element in Indonesia's fertility decline. For Malaysian Malays, sharp increases in age at marriage reduced period fertility rates substantially in a situation where the desired number of children was not declining. Ryder's fertility translation effect was clearly important here, as evidenced by the rise in period fertility in the late 1970s and 1980s when the rise in age at marriage slowed and later-marrying women accelerated their childbearing to reach still-high fertility goals. There is evidence that Malay fertility norms may now at last be dropping to the kinds of levels expected among a late-marrying population, and that marital fertility is therefore falling. Even before this happened, however, the rising age at marriage had exerted a permanent downward influence on population growth rates by extending the mean length of a generation.

1. Coale uses three basic fertility indices: the overall fertility of women of childbearing age (If), the fertility of the currently married women (Ig), and the fertility of the non-married women (Ih); for a full definition, see Coale, 1967. Coale (1974: 55) argues that 'the advantage of these indices over direct calculations of general fertility, marital fertility, and the simple proportion married among women 15 to 50 is that the indexes incorporate an indirect standardization for age distribution within the childbearing span, and that the value of the fertility indexes has a direct intuitive meaning (i.e. fertility is stated relative to the maximum on record)'.

2. This estimate is only approximate, because about 12 per cent of women did not report month of marriage and/or month of first birth, and about 13 per cent of the dates given by the respondents were not verified with documents. Premaritally conceived live births were taken as those occurring less than seven months after the date of first marriage.

3. In 1982, the Prime Minister stated that Malaysia could support a population of up to 70 million, and such a long-term goal became enshrined in policy in the Mid-Term Review of the Fourth Malaysia Plan. This controversial policy was accompanied by pronatalist statements by the Prime Minister and various government ministers, a de-emphasizing of family planning, and some relatively minor taxation concessions for fourth and fifth children (Jones and Tan, 1985: 277–80). Marriage was targeted as well: the Wanita UMNO president, Datin Paduka Rafidah Aziz, stated that women should marry at a younger age so that they could start having children earlier. However, the policy never attracted much support from senior planners, and by the late 1980s there was evidence that the Prime Minister was no longer enthusiastic about it, and that it was being allowed to quietly die.

4. The patterns observed are consistent with the controlled fertility situation described by Henry (1976: 92), an interesting finding since fertility rates are quite high.

5. Actually, the 1974 figure referred to desired family size and the 1984 figure to ideal family size, so they are not strictly comparable. However, a survey in Johore–Perak in 1982–3, which had questions on both desired and ideal number of children, found that for respondents overall, the numbers on each were identical.

6. Theoretically, the effect of increased marital stability in raising fertility could be offset by the role of divorce in terminating sterile or subfecund marriages and giving the spouses a chance to find a more reproductively compatible partner. This is particularly so where divorce is followed by early remarriage, as it normally is among the Malays. Nevertheless, although sterility and subfecundity are no doubt sometimes cause for divorce amongst Malays, they do not appear to be major causes, and it is most unlikely that the net effect of more divorce would be to raise fertility.

9
Conclusions

THE South-East Asian Malay-Muslim world covers a very extensive region populated by numerous ethnic–linguistic groups characterized by striking differences in aspects of culture and family organization. In seeking to understand the broad patterns and trends in customs relating to choice of spouse, age at marriage, marriage arrangements, post-marital residence, divorce, and polygamy, this book has undoubtedly failed to do justice to all these differences and nuances. Nevertheless, there is something to be said for establishing broad patterns and trends, against which further, more specialized studies can test the differences noted for specific subgroups.

This book has chronicled a remarkable story of familial, social, and cultural change in the South-East Asian Malay-Muslim world. The changes have been studied through a focus on marriage and its dissolution—the central aspect of family and community life. The actual measurement of trends, though it leaves a great deal to be desired, nevertheless provides a clear and basically incontestable picture of what has been happening. The trends have been so pronounced that they must be accepted unless the grossest errors in data are assumed. It is in explaining why they have taken place that there is scope for a range of interpretations.

In the 1950s, although South-East Asia was generally characterized by early marriage, marriage was earliest of all in Islamic populations. Thus female age at marriage was considerably higher for Malaysian Chinese, for Thai Buddhists, and for Filipino and Indonesian Christians than it was for the Muslim populations in these countries. Only the Indian population of Malaysia could match the early marriage patterns of the Muslims. Given that there were only minor differences in family organization in different South-East Asian populations, McDonald (1985: 95) has observed that 'religion seems to be a better discriminator of age at marriage for women than the type of family organization'. This may have been the case in the past, but the differences are narrowing; over the past thirty years, female ages at marriage have moved up for all these populations, but they have moved up most sharply of all for the Muslims.

The other justification for focusing exclusively on Muslims in this book is that the extremely high divorce patterns prevailing among South-East Asian Muslims in the 1950s were distinctive to this group. Certainly, separation was common among the Thais and Filipinos (though surely not as common as was divorce among the Muslims), but legal divorce was not. Similarly, although the keeping of minor wives or mistresses was not uncommon among Thais and Chinese, legal polygyny was a feature only of Muslim populations.

The coming of Islam to the region had, by the 1950s, led to more fundamental changes in some aspects of marriage than in others, but it has been a constant theme in this book that the pre-existing marriage system and roles of females in society continued to influence events strongly. The greatest impact of Islam appears to have been in constraining the mobility and social interactions of young women before marriage and imposing a pattern of arranged marriage, probably at younger average ages than before. The impact of Islam on divorce appears to have been less, requiring adaptation but not basic change in the high divorce pattern. It is only in recent years that the orthodox Islamic opposition to easy divorce has come to the fore, buttressed by a tightening of divorce laws and regulations.

To a great extent, both the differentials in age at marriage and in divorce within the Malay-Muslim world in the 1950s, and the trends since then, are consistent with a 'modernization' or 'developmental' explanation of marriage change. By and large, in Malaya–Singapore in the 1950s, age at marriage was lower and divorce rates higher in the most traditional, least economically advanced regions. In Indonesia, regional variation was complicated by wide cultural differences between ethnic–linguistic groups, but within Java, age at marriage was lowest and divorce most prevalent among the poor and uneducated. The rise in age at marriage was earlier and sharper in more developed regions, as was the decline in divorce in Malaysia–Singapore.

The 'developmental' explanation does not rest so easily, though, with the faster decline in Indonesian than in Malaysian divorce rates from the mid-1960s to the mid-1970s, and indeed during the following decade as well. Other factors must clearly have been important, including stronger official discouragement of divorce in Indonesia and more serious efforts to counsel couples contemplating divorce.

One question raised early in the book concerned the extent to which the trends in age at marriage and divorce were driven by changes in Islamic laws and practices, and the extent to which they were the same kinds of changes that could be expected in any early-marrying population subjected to far-ranging social and economic change. What has emerged is that, except in Singapore, legal changes followed, rather than led, the changes in marriage practice. But this does not mean that the legal changes were unimportant: their role in accelerating declines in divorce rates is very clear in Kelantan and West Java. Nor should the distinction between Islamic and non-Islamic societies be relaxed in assessing what has been happening. The fact is that changes in marriage patterns have been more pronounced for the Islamic than for the non-Islamic populations of the region, and these changes presumably reflect (because they must have required) more fundamental changes in beliefs, perceptions, and customs.

It may be helpful to recapitulate here the changes which occurred between the 1950s and 1980s in the Malay-Muslim pattern of entering marriage and proceeding through married life. This is done by providing a thumbnail sketch of the life cycle of an 'average' young woman reaching marriageable age in the 1950s and the 1980s. But since marriage and divorce patterns differed so much between the high-divorce areas (Java, West Sumatra, Kelantan and Trengganu, and Southern Thailand) and the lower-divorce areas (the West Coast of Peninsular Malaysia; most of the Outer Islands of Indonesia), the sketch is provided separately for each set of regions.

Turning first, then, to the high-divorce regions, a young woman in the 1950s could expect to be married to a man of her parents' choosing before she reached her seventeenth birthday. She had about an even chance of being consulted or not by her parents about their choice. She then had a 20 per cent probability of being divorced before her twentieth birthday, and a 25–40 per cent probability of being divorced by her thirtieth birthday. If such a divorce occurred, her chances of remarriage were very high: a 70 per cent probability of being remarried within three years. She was likely to have more say in the choice of marriage partner the second time around, though it was still quite likely that this would also be an arranged marriage. There was about a 30 per cent probability that she would be widowed by her late forties, and remarriage after widowhood was not very likely.

By the 1980s, the average young woman in these regions was marrying at 19 or 20, choosing her own husband with her parents' consent. Her probability of divorcing by her thirtieth birthday was about 10 per cent. Not only was her first marriage more likely to remain intact than that of her mother's generation, but her chances of being widowed by her late forties were only about 15–20 per cent, much lower than in the 1950s. This was because of both higher life expectancy among males and the tendency for a smaller gap in ages of marriage partners.

In the lower-divorce regions (West Coast of Peninsular Malaysia; most of the Outer Islands of Indonesia) in the 1950s, the representative young woman could expect to be married to a man of her parents' choice at the age of 18. She then had about a 5 per cent probability of being divorced by her twentieth birthday and a 15 per cent probability of being divorced before her thirtieth birthday. Her chances of remarriage following divorce were very high: a 50–60 per cent probability of remarrying within three years, to a man in whose choice she probably had some say. Her chance of being widowed by her late forties was a little over 20 per cent, and remarriage after widowhood was not very likely.

By the 1980s, young women in these relatively low-divorce regions were marrying quite late—in West Coast Peninsular Malaysia at about 22 on average—and they were choosing their own husbands, normally with the blessing of their parents. Relatively few were divorcing—only about 5 per cent by their thirtieth birthday—and not very many of their marriages were broken by widowhood before the age of 50.

Though divorce rates were high in the 1950s, the proportion of children affected by divorce was lower than might have been expected, because almost half of divorces occurred to childless marriages. In the high-divorce regions, there appears to have been about a 60–85 per cent probability of children reaching adulthood (17 years) living with both their natural parents. By the 1980s, in the lower-divorce regions, about 80–85 per cent of children could be expected to reach the age of 17 living with both their natural parents. In both cases, but especially in the lower-divorce regions, widowhood was a much more frequent reason than divorce for children to be separated from at least one natural parent.

One paradoxical aspect of trends in divorce is the temporal juxtaposition of rapid declines in divorce in the Malay-Muslim world with a steady rise in divorce rates in the West. A major reason why divorce rates fell so fast in the Malay-Muslim world was that the traditional pattern of parent-arranged early marriage was fading away, and young people now had a greater stake in the success of their marriage. It is extraordinary that parents abdicated the hitherto strictly maintained right to control their daughters' sexuality, a right that parents (and indeed brothers) in other Islamic regions of the world appear to maintain with grim determination. What accounts for the change in parental attitudes in the space of just a few decades? The speed of economic and social change was clearly important, and distinguished this region from most other parts of the Muslim world. But some of the oil-rich countries experienced very rapid economic growth without much relaxation of control over daughters. Probably more important was the initially stronger and more independent role of women in Malay societies, and the more thoroughgoing social change in the Malay world.

Rapid expansion of female education was probably the nail in the coffin of traditional patterns of control over daughters. The very fact that secondary education for girls expanded so fast in Islamic South-East Asia indicates a weaker parental resolve to control daughters than was more commonly the case in the Islamic world, where such education, particularly in a mixed-sex setting, was often fiercely resisted. The effect of education was reinforced by the pattern of employment opportunities opening up for young women. The opportunity to enjoy income earned by daughters, who are generally considered more reliable in these matters than sons, was undoubtedly a strong incentive both to allow daughters to stay longer in school and to forsake the more extreme views about seclusion of unmarried daughters.

But central to the dramatic shift to a dominant pattern of self-arranged marriages and the freedom for girls to arrange other aspects of their lives was apparently the growing perception among Malay parents, most of them with little education themselves, that 'the modern world' was a world in which girls had to be permitted to do such things; that the world of strict control over daughters was a thing of the past. Government ideology and the increasingly-accessible mass media fostered this perception.

The shift to self-arranged marriages and away from the system whereby divorce was the 'escape valve' of an arranged marriage system, while important in understanding the dramatic decline in divorce rates in the Malay-Muslim world, is clearly inadequate to explain why divorce rates in this region had declined to less than half those in Western countries by the mid-1980s. After all, the marriage system in the West had long been one of self-choice. Rather, major differences in the evolution of societal perceptions of divorce must be invoked. In the West, divorce was gradually becoming accepted both for the reason it had long been prevalent in the Malay-Muslim world—its role in releasing the partners in an unsatisfactory marriage—and more broadly because the cult of individual self-fulfilment undercut many of the motives previously inhibiting partners from breaking a marriage except in extreme circumstances. Legal changes in the West appeared to follow rather than lead such attitudinal changes. By contrast, in the Malay-Muslim world, a sort of puritan reaction to previous very high divorce rates, fuelled by women's groups, by religious revivalism, and by a perception that high divorce strengthened negative images of the culture by foreigners and other local ethnic groups, was leading to a level of condemnation of divorce long since missing in the West. Again, legal changes reinforced this trend rather than led it.

Delayed marriage has brought with it new issues. In the context of early achievement of sexual maturity, it has produced prolonged periods of adolescence, defined as the period between the two events. In the past, adolescence was very brief or did not occur at all; by the 1980s, among the Malays of Singapore and Peninsular Malaysia, it had been extended by 5 years or more. Parental control during this formative stage of life has been weakened by its long duration, and further weakened by other changes, notably the extension of schooling into adolescence, the rise of work-related migration to cities, the ability of young Malay women to be economically independent, and the increasing legitimacy of Western notions of 'romantic love'. With increased mobility and the widening of young people's horizons, the social controls of the village have ceased to exert the dominant influence they formerly did.

Prolonged adolescence has brought with it problems barely evident in the 1950s. One is a much freer pattern of mixing between young men and women, and much more frequent premarital sexual relations. This need not necessarily be viewed as a problem, of course, but it certainly is being viewed as such in Indonesia and Malaysia, where premarital sexual relations and living together outside marriage are frequently deplored. It must be conceded that, in a society coming to terms with rapid change in so many aspects of life, prolonged adolescence does bring with it difficulties of a somewhat different kind, or at least of a different degree, from those in Western societies. One is that many of the young people thrown together in the cities are from a traditional rural background and are therefore inexperienced in handling relationships with strangers of the opposite sex. The negative image of partying, wearing of make-up and promiscuity among 'factory girls' in Malaysia in the 1970s, though it was a parody of the real-life circumstances and behaviour of most of these young women, reflected both a deep concern in the society about where change was leading and the reality that some of the factory workers engaged in behaviour that flouted community norms. Many men were only too willing to take advantage of the new-found independence of these young women and their inexperience in handling it.

In the past, the need for access to contraception among the unmarried was hardly an issue. Now it is, and the difficulty many Western countries have found in handling this issue does not bode well for a sensible approach to it in the South-East Asian Muslim world.

A whole range of other problems have emerged in relation to in-creasing age at marriage, rising education levels among women, and self-choice of spouse. In Muslim society, as in many other cultures, men typically 'marry down' in terms of educational level. Nowadays, with as many educated young women as young men being produced by the educational system and the continued tendency for men to marry women younger than themselves, there are not enough well-educated men to go around as potential partners for women with high school education and above. This problem is exacerbated by the female-dominant movement to the cities in recent times, causing even greater shortages of potential husbands in the cities and perhaps an 'over-supply' in some rural areas. These shortages are undoubtedly part of the explanation for the increasingly large numbers of Malay women remaining unmarried into their thirties.

But there are other causes as well of the much-debated problem of the unmarried 30-year-olds. One appears to be that women are increas-ingly interested in developing their own careers, and many see marriage and motherhood as interfering with this. Another is that many women feel anxious about making a bad choice of husband and are therefore very cautious in this matter. Another is undoubtedly a preference on the part of many males, even well-educated ones, for a wife with a lower level of education whom they can more readily control.

As for divorce, both the very high divorce rates in earlier times and the speed of recent change are remarkable, and leave many unanswered questions. In Java, and probably in many other places as well, divorce rates had been very high for centuries, but this did not seem to destroy the fabric of family and society. Some of the reasons for this have been given: the typically young age of divorcees, the speed of remarriage, and the societal acceptance of divorce as a way out of an unsatisfactory marriage. Divorce was concentrated in the first few years of marriage to a greater extent than anywhere else in the world, and this meant that children had been born to the marriage less frequently than in modern-day Western divorces.

But for all this, the ability of the society to cope with these very high divorce rates remains something of a puzzle. Children had been born to more than 50 per cent of all divorcing couples. In the light of evidence in the West of serious consequences of divorce for children and its effect on their own ability to sustain satisfactory marriages, the question must be raised: 'Did divorce have equally deleterious effects on children in the Malay-Muslim world?' Was high divorce a self-perpetuating process partly because of the effect of divorce on the expectations of children for their own marriages? Probably so, to some extent; but then, the decline in the proportion of each cohort of marrying couples who had experienced their own parents' divorce could hardly have been as rapid as the actual declines which occurred in divorce rates. The decline in divorce appeared to have much more to do with the radical changes in the marriage system (growing self-arrangement of marriages and rising age at marriage) and with increasingly negative official and community attitudes towards divorce than with the growing up into the marrying ages of children without experience of parents' divorce. Perhaps the key point to bear in mind about the children whose parents divorced in traditional society was that they were very young at the time of divorce and typically went with the mother.

Divorce rates are now well below those which prevail in the West, and much of this decline in divorce rates happened without the extra pressure more recently exerted by new marriage laws. The declines have been widely welcomed and have undoubtedly had beneficial effects on family stability and the welfare of women and children. A note of warning, however, should be sounded. The one advantage of the traditional, easy divorce system was that it enabled a couple to escape from an unsatisfactory marriage. There is a danger in hedging divorce around with so many restrictions that this flexibility is entirely lost.

Divorce has been on the rise again in the 1980s in Singapore, admittedly from a very low base, though apparently not in the other large cities of the region. Although divorce in Singapore remains well below Western levels, the rising trend bears watching, because the nature of the problem of divorce is almost entirely different for couples who chose their own spouses. As stressed in Chapter 6, traditional Malay society sanctioned early divorce for couples in arranged marriages who found each other to be incompatible. With self-choice of spouse, the couple are investing in the success of the marriage and are likely to be much more deeply affected by its dissolution. Moreover, the wife is likely to be considerably older at the time of divorce than was the case in her mother's or grandmother's generation, with much less chance of returning to the family home following an unsuccessful marriage. Although hard evidence on this is lacking, except for Singapore, the duration of the average marriage before divorce is likely to be considerably longer in modern-day divorces, and children are more likely to have been born to the marriage. Thus the problem of divorce for modern-day Malay urban dwellers resembles Western divorce problems much more closely than was the case twenty or thirty years ago.

This being said, it must be recognized that there is disturbingly little information on the consequences of divorce in Malay-Muslim society. Survey data reveal little about so intimate and sensitive a subject. Sociologists, psychologists, economists, demographers, and others need to conduct in-depth studies into aspects such as the effect of divorce on children, the economic consequences of divorce for both partners to the marriage, ways of coping with grief and anger about divorce, and the probability that second marriages will remain intact to a greater or lesser extent than first marriages.

On the whole, polygamy has not been very prevalent among ordinary people in the Malay-Muslim realm. Monogamy has been reinforced by the ease of divorce, which has been the preferred way to end an unsatisfactory marriage. Polygamy has been strongly opposed by women's groups and by men of liberal bent. In recent years, however, polygamy has become a rallying point of sorts for those in Malaysia who oppose the erosion of the men's rights they perceive as guaranteed in Islam. This is not likely to increase its incidence, given the practical difficulties of polygamy in modern urban society, but it has the potential to be a divisive issue between fundamentalists and liberal Muslims.

Finally, how important have changes in marriage patterns in Islamic South-East Asia been in the fertility declines that have occurred at varying speeds in the region? Rising female age at marriage and declining rates of divorce have had partly offsetting effects on fertility. For Singaporean and Malaysian Malays, the fertility-dampening effect of rising age at marriage has clearly dominated the fertility-increasing effect of lowered divorce, though for Indonesia, this might not be the case. Sharp increases in age at marriage reduced Malaysian Malay period fertility rates substantially in a situation where the desired number of children was not declining. In Indonesia, by contrast, declines in marital fertility were the dominant cause of fertility decline. That delayed marriage has affected fertility in Islamic South-East Asia is clear; that it has been a strategy adopted specifically by families, couples, or individuals to hold down family size appears most unlikely.

Appendices

APPENDIX 1
Data Sources

Censuses

THE population censuses drawn on in this study are listed in the Bibliography.

Surveys

1. West Malaysian Family Survey, 1966–7

This survey obtained a representative sample of all married couples of child-bearing age in Peninsular Malaysia. It featured a detailed interview about fertility and family planning with 5,457 currently married women in the child-bearing years, living in three major strata: metropolitan, other urban, and rural areas. The survey included a brief marriage history. For further details, see National Family Planning Board, Malaysia (n.d.).

2. Malaysian Fertility and Family Survey, 1974

This survey was conducted as part of the research programme of the World Fertility Survey. The survey covered a sample of 6,321 ever-married women aged 15–49 in Peninsular Malaysia. It provided a wide range of information on nuptiality and fertility trends, knowledge and use of contraception and family building intentions, by ethnic group and a number of socio-economic characteristics. For further details, see Chander et al. (1977).

3. Malaysian Population and Family Survey, 1984–5

This survey covered a representative sample of ever-married women aged 15–49 in Peninsular Malaysia. A total of 4,141 ever-married women were interviewed. Along with a wide range of fertility, family planning and attitudinal data, the survey collected marriage histories. Data were collected for a subsample of husbands. Basic information on single women living in the selected households was also collected.

This survey collected more detailed data on marriage than the earlier surveys, including information about how marriage partners were chosen and attitudinal data on ideal age at marriage (see Hamid et al., 1988).

4. Malaysian Marriage Survey, 1981–2

The Malaysian Marriage Survey was carried out between July 1981 and June 1982 in the states of Kelantan, Pahang, Penang, Negri Sembilan, Malacca, Selangor, and the Federal Territory of Kuala Lumpur. The preselected areas, chosen as case-studies rather than as being statistically representative of the ethnic group in the particular state, were stratified according to urban–rural residence and ethnic groups, and subsequently a random sample was selected from each of these areas. The sample included ever-married women in the age-group 15–59, out of which a total of 2,310 were currently married women, 1,388 of them Malay women. For these women, the same questionnaire was administered to the spouse, if present in the household. (For more details, see Tan et al., 1986). In interpreting the results, it should be noted that for Malays and Indians, two rather traditional groups (Kelantanese Malays and estate Indians) were over-represented compared with the Malay and Indian populations as a whole. Some results will also be reported from a survey of a subset of single men and women above 15 years of age in the selected households.

The questionnaire consisted of open- and closed-ended questions and covered the following areas: household composition, respondent's background information, marital history of respondent (enabling analysis of age at marriage, marital dissolution, and remarriage), social mixing and mate selection, courtship, background information on spouse, marriage ceremonies, life as a couple, attitude towards marriage and divorce, work history, and economic situation. Given the age range of respondents, trends in these aspects of marriage in the surveyed areas could be studied over a period of about 40 years preceding 1982.

Men and women in the ever-married sample who were ever divorced (108 Malay women and 121 Malay men) were also asked to answer a questionnaire on divorce and remarriage. Of these respondents, 56 per cent were from Kelantan and 31 per cent from Selangor. Two-thirds of them were aged over 40, reflecting the higher divorce rates in earlier times.

5. Malaysian Family Life Survey, 1976–7

This survey includes interview information from 1,262 ever-married females aged 50 and younger and, if available, their husbands. The sample was chosen through a multi-stage cluster sampling design. Detailed period information on current social, economic, and demographic characteristics was collected, along with information on changes in many of these characteristics since the age of 15. Detailed community characteristics for each of the sampled locations were also collected. See Butz and DaVanzo (1978).

6. Women's Roles and Contraception Study, 1988–9

The Malay component of this study covered case-study populations in Kuala Lumpur, in a Federal Land Development Authority (FELDA) scheme in Perak, and in the small towns of Pasir Mas and Pasir Puteh, Kelantan. These respondents were given a detailed questionnaire covering many matters related to women's status. Seven focus group discussions were also conducted in Pasir Mas and Pasir Puteh with female market traders and housewives (Lim and Jones, 1989). These focus group discussions are occasionally referred to in the book, using the citation 'Kelantanese focus groups, 1989'.

7. Indonesian Fertility–Mortality Survey, 1973

This was the first major demographic survey ever conducted in Indonesia: a massive survey, covering 54,214 households, drawn by random cluster sampling, stratified for rural and urban areas. The samples were drawn to represent West Java, Central Java–Yogyakarta, East Java, Sumatra, Sulawesi, and Bali. These areas contained 86 per cent of Indonesia's population. The survey covered the topics of marriage and marital dissolution, fertility, mortality, and knowledge, attitudes, and practice of contraception. The survey was unusual in that it was co-ordinated by the Demographic Institute, Faculty of Economics, University of Indonesia, drawing on the resources of regional universities for supervision in their own region. The Central Bureau of Statistics assisted with sampling (McDonald, Yasin, and Jones, 1976).

8. Indonesian Fertility Survey, 1976

This survey, conducted as part of the World Fertility Survey, covered the islands of Java and Bali (i.e. 67 per cent of Indonesia's population) and was conducted over a multi-stage probability sample of around 10,500 households. Within rural and urban sectors of each of the six provinces in Java and Bali, the sample was approximately self-weighting. The individual questionnaire included detailed maternity and marriage histories, knowledge and use of contraception, fertility regulation and preferences, and socio-economic background of ever-married women and their husbands. For further details, see Central Bureau of Statistics and World Fertility Survey (1978).

9. Indonesian Marriage Survey, 1978

The Indonesian Marriage Survey was conducted in eight case-study villages, located in the following provinces: Aceh, South Sumatra, Jakarta, Yogyakarta, South Kalimantan, Bali, South Sulawesi, and North Sulawesi. These provinces were chosen to give a wide range of cultural settings for study. The target number of respondents in each region was approximately 600 ever-married males, 600 ever-married females, and about 200 unmarried young people, roughly equally divided between males and females. Most ever-married respondents were husband and wife pairs; they had to be aged less than 60, except in the case where one spouse was currently aged below 60 but the other was older than 60. They answered a detailed questionnaire dealing with socio-economic background, freedom to mix when young, marriage history (including marriage arrangements), polygamy, and divorce and remarriage. Many attitudinal questions were included.

10. Asian Marriage Survey, 1980: Indonesian Component

This study was conducted in and near the city of Semarang in Central Java, where the population is overwhelmingly Javanese. Three community types were selected purposively: an urban lower-class area, an urban upper middle-class area, and a rural area. In each urban study site, 500 females and 300 males were selected for interview, and in the rural site, 600 females and 300 males. The questionnaire covered a wide range of questions on all aspects of marriage and divorce.

11. First National Survey on Family Planning in Singapore, 1973.

12. Second National Family Planning and Population Survey in Singapore, 1977.

13. Third National Family Planning and Population Survey in Singapore, 1982.

As these Singapore surveys did not present many findings separately for Malays, they have not been used very much in this book. Details can be found in Wan and Saw (1974) and Emmanuel et al. (1984).

14. Southern Thai Muslim Survey, 1976

This survey was conducted by the Population and Manpower Planning Division, National Economic and Social Development Board, Bangkok, with assistance from the Prince of Songkhla University. A total of 1,391 female and 691 male respondents were drawn from 2,082 households in Pattani, Narathivat, Yala, Satun, and those districts of Songkhla with a Muslim majority population, employing a stratified multi-stage sampling design. The survey was restricted to households with an ever-married woman aged between 15 and 49. The questionnaire included sections on background characteristics, marriage history, pregnancy history, contraception, and the position of Southern Thai women. For further details, see Rachapaetayakom (1983).

Marriage and Divorce Registration Data

Traditionally in Indonesia, Peninsular Malaysia, and Southern Thailand, Muslim marriages and divorces were registered by the *imam* of the local mosque, who was responsible for passing them on to the relevant authorities for central record keeping. In the case of Indonesia, the relevant authority was the Religious Affairs Office of the *kabupaten* (regency), which in turn passed the figures on to the provincial authorities. Even after the Marriage Law of 1974 was passed, requiring that petitions for divorce be lodged at the Pengadilan Agama (religious court), the Religious Affairs Office continued to keep the records on marriages and divorces. In Malaysia, the relevant authority was the *kadi*'s office at the state level. In Southern Thailand, the relevant authority was the Islamic Committee of the *changwat* (province).

For Indonesia, data on registered marriages and divorces among Muslims in recent years may be found in *Statistik Indonesia*, published by the Biro Pusat Statistik (BPS or Central Bureau of Statistics), for various years. For some earlier years, the data were provided in the *Statistical Pocketbook of Indonesia*, also published by the BPS, or in *Almanak Indonesia*. More detailed data for some provinces are available in statistical yearbooks for those provinces.

For the states of Peninsular Malaysia, Muslim marriage and divorce data are collected at the state level and formerly were not collected centrally. An early compilation of available data was carried out by Gordon (1964). The writer has compiled more recent data from a variety of sources, including *kadi*'s offices in some states. More recently, the Pusat Islam in the Prime Minister's Department has undertaken to compile Muslim marriage and divorce data for the period since 1980, and has kindly supplied recent data.

For Singapore, Muslim marriages and divorces are published in *Statistics on Marriages and Divorces*, published annually by the Department of Statistics.

In Southern Thailand, although records of marriages and divorces are kept by the Islamic Committees, these committees have never processed the data, so no tabulations are available on the number of marriages and divorces by year.

The author has prepared a database consisting of a time series of data on Muslim marriages, divorces, and reconciliations, processed to yield various rates and ratios, for Singapore, the states of Peninsular Malaysia, and the provinces of Indonesia, going back as far in time as possible. These data can be made available to interested researchers.

APPENDIX 2
Costs of the Wedding

IN the Malay world, the bride's family typically bears the cost of the wedding reception.[1] The bridegroom's family is expected to contribute, however, usually in kind (e.g. rice, coconut, bananas, sugar, and meat). Apart from this, the bridegroom or his family has to make two forms of payment to the bride: the wedding gifts (the *hantaran belanja*), and a form of bride-wealth, or *mas kahwin*, which has been identified in Malay custom with the Islamic *mahr* payment. The important questions for the purpose of this book are: to what extent does the bride herself benefit materially from the transfers of goods and money associated with the wedding? Which family (the bride's or the groom's) gains or loses more from the costs and financial transfers associated with the marriage? Which family contributes more in setting up the young couple for their independent life together? Has the burden of costs associated with a marriage risen over time?

In surveys and discussions about marriage, the burden of costs associated with a marriage is seldom mentioned, and certainly not as a reason why the marriage had to be delayed. The fact that traditional ages at marriage were very young indicates that, whatever the strain marriage payments or wedding costs may have imposed on the household's resources, they were not permitted to interfere with the timing of the marriage.

It is not easy to obtain a balanced picture of financial and resource transfers associated with marriage. The Malaysian Marriage Survey of 1981–2 attempted to do this, but it had limited success. Table A2.1 presents some information on the amount spent on the wedding and the feast. Quite a large proportion of respondents, particularly in rural areas, reported not knowing the amount involved. Of those who were able to provide information, urban respondents reported higher wedding expenses than rural respondents, and respondents married more recently than 1970 reported greater expenses than those married before 1970. These figures convey little unless they are related to family incomes for the groups concerned. The median family income for Malays in the mid 1970s was RM1,920 per annum (Malaysia, 1981: 56). Urban incomes were at least 50 per cent higher than rural incomes, so rural and urban incomes may have been of the order of RM1,700 and RM2,550 respectively. On the assumption that these income levels also held in the areas covered by the survey, and assuming as well that respondents who did not state their wedding expenses followed the distribution of the known cases, then about 55 per cent of urban dwellers and 75 per cent of rural dwellers incurred wedding expenses equivalent to at least one-third of the average annual household income for

[1]In the Malaysian Marriage Survey, the bride's family bore the wedding costs in 88 per cent of cases, the spouse's family in 7 per cent of cases, and both families in 5 per cent of cases; see also Wolff (1992: 212).

TABLE A2.1

Peninsular Malaysia: Percentage Distribution of Amount Spent for the
Wedding Including the Feast, by Place of Residence and Year First Married,
of Malay Female Respondents

Amount Spent (RM)	Married before 1970			Married at 1970 and after		
	Rural	Urban	Total	Rural	Urban	Total
<400	17	10	15	4	2	3
400–799	16	22	18	7	10	8
800–1,199	12	21	14	14	20	17
1,200–1,599	2	5	3	5	16	10
1,600–2,399	2	7	3	14	16	15
2,400+	1	1	1	11	13	12
Do not know	50	34	46	45	23	35
Total (%)	100	100	100	100	100	100
No. of cases	566	212	778	310	254	564

Source: Unpublished tabulation, Malaysian Marriage Survey, 1981–2.

their group. In other words, a substantial proportion of respondents appear to have incurred expenses large enough to cause economic difficulties for the family and perhaps to cause the marriage to be delayed. On the other hand, only a small proportion of the respondents or their families (3 per cent) either borrowed money, sold assets or pawned assets to meet the wedding expenses. This is probably because a substantial proportion of the costs of the wedding reception are recovered from the guests (in Galok, Kelantan, about 70–80 per cent of costs were recovered among wealthy classes and 50–60 per cent among poorer classes: Kuchiba, Tsubouchi, and Maeda, 1979: 158–9).

The Malaysian Marriage Survey also investigated other aspects of financial transactions associated with the marriage, including the property brought into the marriage, the exchange of gifts and the payment of *mas kahwin*. On the first of these, fewer than 20 per cent of Malay respondents stated that they brought family property into the marriage or gained rights to a house or land as a result of the marriage, although a large group failed to answer the question. More than 80 per cent of brides received wedding gifts (*hantaran belanja*); the uncertainty over the exact proportion is due to the fact that 7 per cent of respondents gave no answer to this question. The main forms of wedding gifts were jewellery (customarily in the form of a complete set of gold earrings, necklace, bracelets, and rings), clothing and money, most of them received by the respondents themselves, though sometimes they went to the parents (Table A2.2). The bride's side was more likely to receive gifts than the groom's side.[2]

The great majority of Malay respondents agreed that the amount of *hantaran belanja* depended on the social status of the family, if not for everybody, at least among the rich people. Other factors seen to influence the amount

[2]In Java as well, the engagement present for the bride was likely to consist of clothing and possibly jewellery (usually gold); see H. Geertz (1961: 64) and Wolff (1992: 212).

TABLE A2.2

Peninsular Malaysia: Percentage Distribution of Malay Respondents
by Whether They Received Any Gifts at the Time of Marriage and Whether
They Received Particular Types of Gifts, by Ethnic Group and Sex

	Male	*Female*
Received no gift	24	12
No answer	10	7
Received specific gift(s)[a]	66	81
Total	100	100
No. of cases	1,388	1,388
Percentage receiving specific kinds of gifts:[b]		
Jewellery	14	22
Clothing	36	30
Food and drinks	17	9
Money	10	18
Furniture	1	1
Property/land/house	_[c]	_[c]
Others	22	20
Total	100	100

Source: Unpublished tabulation, Malaysian Marriage Survey, 1981–2.

[a]The gifts referred to are those received by the respondents or received by their parents or others on their behalf.

[b]These are percentages of total gifts received; some respondents received more than one kind of gift, and they are double counted.

[c]Less than 0.5.

of *hantaran belanja* included inflation (as a general cause of the rising cost of *hantaran belanja* over time), the wealth and occupation of the couple and their families (obviously closely related to social status), and the education and beauty of the bride. With rising female participation in the workforce, a larger *hantaran* is likely to be requested for a young woman with a good job (Ong, 1987: 121–31).

With regard to *mas kahwin*, the convention among West Coast Malays is to fix it at a nominal figure of about RM23 (Maznah, 1975: 29), and this is reflected in a clustering of responses in the RM20–24 category, as seen in Table A2.3. However, in the East Coast states, much higher levels of *mas kahwin* have frequently been paid, depending on factors such as the social and economic standing of the bride's family. In the Malaysian Marriage Survey, 1981 (which over-represented Kelantanese), about two-thirds of respondents received more than RM25 in *mas kahwin*. On the whole, however, the level of *mas kahwin* could not be considered a significant burden on the prospective husband or his family; among respondents marrying in the 1970s, only 13 per cent paid a sum exceeding RM500 and only 5 per cent paid a sum exceeding RM1,000. The sum of RM1,000 was equivalent to more than one-third of the median annual household income level of Malays, although in Kelantan, where high levels of

TABLE A2.3

Peninsular Malaysia: Percentage Distribution of Malay Respondents
Receiving Different Amounts of *Mas Kahwin*, by Year First Married

Amount of Mas Kahwin (RM)	Total	Married before 1970	Married at 1970 and after
0–19	2	3	–[a]
20–24	33	35	30
25–49	22	33	6
50–99	20	9	34
100–199	6	5	8
200–299	5	6	3
300–399	3	3	3
400–499	2	1	3
500–999	5	4	8
1,000+	2	1	5
Total	100	100	100
No. of Cases	1,342	785	548

Source: Unpublished tabulation, Malaysian Marriage Survey, 1981–2.
Note: Unknown cases excluded from denominator.
[a]Less than 0.5.

mas kahwin tended to be concentrated, Malay income levels were significantly lower, and the *mas kahwin* payments may therefore have represented a greater burden.

Participants in Kelantanese focus groups in 1989 tended to combine the *hantaran belanja* and the *mas kahwin* into the concept of *belanja kahwin*, the total amount the groom's side had to pay. It was generally agreed that in the 1970s the lower classes had to pay around RM100–200, whereas the more well-to-do had to pay about RM300–500. By 1989 these payments had risen to about RM1,000–2,000 for poorer people and RM3,000–5,000 for wealthy people. If correct, these estimates indicate a rise in marriage payments over the space of about 15 years that is well in excess of inflation and also well in excess of the admittedly rapid rise in income levels. It was agreed that the level of the wedding payments depends partly on the education of the bride and whether she is working. Interestingly, the rapid rise in marriage payments was not seen to play a role in delaying marriage.

The balance of marriage payments appears to differ in Java. In Mojolama,

It costs even the poorest families ... approximately two months' subsistence wages and six months' work tapping coconut trees to marry their sons and much more to marry their daughters. It is not surprising, therefore, that marriage ceremonies are frequently only made possible by the sale or pawning of scarce capital goods and indebtedness. This cost is incurred despite the high probability that within a few months the marriage will have ended in divorce. (Singarimbun and Manning, 1974b: 24.)

H. Geertz (1961: 68) also writes of parents going deeply into debt to provide a suitable wedding feast for their daughter; which more than incidentally serves to reinforce their social standing in the community.

One other cost to the bride's parents should be noted: the contribution they typically make in giving the newly-weds shelter in the early months (and often the early years) of the marriage. Where the couple immediately move into a house of their own, the bride's parents are more likely than the groom's parents to supply most of the funds for construction—at least in the region of East Java studied by Hefner (1990: 163).

The answers to the questions raised at the beginning of this appendix, at least for Malaysian Malays, then, are as follows: the bride does benefit materially from the payments and gifts made at the time of the wedding, and she keeps these gifts if divorce occurs, unless she was the one to initiate the divorce; the bridegroom's family makes a greater net payment at the time of the wedding than the bride's family, because, although the cost of the reception may exceed the *belanja kahwin* made by the groom's side, much of this cost can often be recovered; the costs of the wedding have certainly risen substantially over time, and appear to have also risen in relation to average incomes, though this question requires much more careful investigation.

APPENDIX 3
Approaches to Measuring Widowhood and Divorce

ONE approach, which has the advantage of drawing on readily available data from censuses and surveys, is to take a 'snapshot' of the marital composition of the population at particular times, with emphasis on the proportions currently widowed or divorced in different age-groups. The difficulty with this measure is that it is influenced both by marital dissolution and by subsequent remarriage. Even if divorce and widowhood are common events, proportions currently widowed or divorced will be low if there is a tendency to remarry quickly after such events. On the other hand, the value of knowing how the dynamics of divorce/widowhood and subsequent remarriage work out in terms of the current marital status of the population cannot be denied.

A second approach is to obtain period measures of the incidence of widow-hood or divorce by dividing the number of cases of widowhood or of divorces registered during a particular time period (e.g. one year) by a denominator which may consist of the population exposed to the risk of widowhood or divorce (i.e. the total currently married) or, in the absence of such information, some other population such as the total population (thus giving the crude widowhood or divorce rate) or the total adult (usually 15 and over) population of marriageable age (thus giving the general widowhood or divorce rate). Another commonly used index of divorce is the ratio of divorces to marriages occurring during a particular time period (e.g. one year). This is clearly an inappropriate ratio to use in the sense that divorces can and do occur to marriages which took place ten or twenty years earlier; on the other hand, in Islamic South-East Asia, a high proportion of divorces do occur within the first five years of marriage, so the ratio of divorces to marriages should give a reasonably accurate reflection of trends, particularly if there is a time series extending for some years.

A third approach yields measures which can be interpreted more precisely. This is a cohort approach, in which the fate of individual marriages is traced and cumulated into an aggregate picture for the society. For example, the cumulative proportions of marriages intact after a certain number of years can be computed, or the inverse of this, the percentage broken by widowhood or divorce. These calculations can be carried out separately for different birth or marriage cohorts to indicate trends over time. Such birth or marriage cohorts can also be defined by characteristics such as educational attainment to test the prevalence of divorce according to such characteristics.

Bibliography

Censuses and National Surveys

Brunei

1971 Population Census
1981 Population Census
1991 Population Census

Indonesia

Kantoor voor de Volkstelling [Census, Netherlands Indies, 1930]
1961 Population Census
1971 Population Census
1976 Intercensal Population Survey
1980 Population Census
1985 Intercensal Population Survey
1990 Population Census

Peninsular Malaysia

Population Census of Malaya, 1947
Population Census of Malaya, 1957
Population Census of Malaysia, 1970
Population Census of Malaysia, 1980
Report of the Labour Force Survey, Malaysia, 1976
Report of the Labour Force Survey, Malaysia, 1985–1986

Singapore

Census of Population, Singapore, 1957
Census of Population, Singapore, 1970
Census of Population, Singapore, 1980
Census of Population, Singapore, 1990
Report of the Labour Force Survey of Singapore, 1988

Thailand

1980 Population and Housing Census
1990 Population and Housing Census

Books and Articles

Abdul Halim Haji Mohammed (1979), 'Sikap dan Amalan Masyarakat Melayu Terhadap Perkahwinan dan Perceraian—Satu Tinjauan di Kampung Pasir, Johor Baru', Graduation Exercise, Faculty of Economics and Administration, University of Malaya, Kuala Lumpur.

Abdullah Mohd. Amin (1986), 'Sistem Perkahwinan Muik Kurangkan Cerai di Kelantan', *Utusan Melayu*, 20 February.

Ackerman, S. E. (1980), 'Cultural Process in Malaysian Industrialization: A Study of Malay Women Factory Workers', Ph.D. thesis, University of California, San Diego.

Adelaar, K. A. (1985), *Proto-Malayic*, Alblasserdam: Offsetdrukkerij Kanters B.V.

Adioetomo, S. M. (1984), 'Marriage and Family Formation', Unpublished manuscript, Demographic Institute, University of Indonesia, Jakarta.

_____ (1993), 'Changes in Reproductive Behaviour in Java: Social, Economic and Cultural Influences', Ph.D. thesis, Australian National University, Canberra.

Alfian (1976), 'Some Observations on Television in Indonesia', Paper presented at Fair Communication Policy for International Exchange of Information Conference, East–West Center, Honolulu.

_____(ed.) (1977), *Segi-segi Sosial Budaya Masyarakat Aceh*, Jakarta: Lembaga Penelitian, Pendidikan dan Penerangan Ekonomi dan Sosial (LP3ES).

Al Hadar, Y. (1977), 'Perkawinan dan Perceraian di Indonesia' [Marriage and Divorce in Indonesia], Lembaga Demografi, Fakultas Ekonomi, Universitas Indonesia, Jakarta.

Ali, A. (1991), 'Women as Syariah Court Judges', *New Straits Times*, 10 October.

Arian, C. (1982), 'Perkawinan dan Perceraian pada Masyarakat Aceh' [Marriage and Divorce among the Acehnese], Pusat Penelitian dan Studi Kependudukan, Universitas Gadjah Mada, Yogyakarta.

Arif, M. S. (1992), 'Pegawai Wanita dan Faktor-faktor yang Mempengaruhi Kerjayanya dalam Birokrasi Kerajaan Indonesia', Ph.D. thesis, University of Malaya, Kuala Lumpur.

Asari, Y. (1985), 'Fertility Differentials by Ecological Zone in Rural West Java Province', MA thesis, Australian National University, Canberra.

Ashakul, T. (1990), *Regional and Provincial Urban and Rural Population Projections*, Background Report 2-2, National Urban Development Policy Framework, Bangkok: Thailand Development Research Institute.

Australian Bureau of Statistics (ABS) (1991), *Divorces Australia 1990*, Cat. No. 3307.0, Canberra.

_____ (1992), *Estimated Resident Population by Country of Birth, Age and Sex: Australia June 1990 and Preliminary June 1991*, Cat. No. 3221.0, Canberra.

Azizah Kassim (1982), *Wanita dan Perceraian dalam Masyarakat Melayu Randaran*, Kuala Lumpur: Nusantara.

_____ (1985), *Wanita dan Masyarakat*, Kuala Lumpur: Utusan Publishers and Distributors.

Bachtiar, H. (1967), 'Negeri Taram: A Minangkabau Village Community', in Koentjaraningrat (ed.), *Villages in Indonesia*, Ithaca: Cornell University Press.

Baihaqi, A. K. (1977), 'Masalah Perceraian di Aceh: Studi Kasus di Dua Kecamatan', in Alfian (ed.), *Segi-segi Sosial Budaya Masyarakat Aceh*, Jakarta: LP3ES, pp. 143–72.

Banks, D. J. (1983), *Malay Kinship*, Philadelphia: Institute for the Study of Human Issues.

—— (1987), *From Class to Culture: Social Conscience in Malay Novels since Independence*, Yale University Southeast Asia Studies, Monograph Series 29, New Haven.

Barlow, C. (1978), *The Natural Rubber Industry: Its Development, Technology, and Economy in Malaysia*, Kuala Lumpur: Oxford University Press.

—— (1982), *Smallholder Rubber in South Sumatra*, Kuala Lumpur: Oxford University Press.

Barlow, C.; Jayasuriya, S. K. W.; and Tan, C. S. (forthcoming), *The World Rubber Industry*, London: Routledge.

Barro, R. J. (1989), 'Economic Growth in a Cross-Section of Countries', Working Paper No. 3120, Cambridge, Mass.: National Bureau of Economic Research.

Beaujot, R. (1986), 'Libération de la Femme et Marché Matrimonial en Tunisie', *Population*, July–October: 853–7.

Beck, L. and Keddie, N. (eds.) (1978), *Women in the Moslem World*, Cambridge, Mass.: Harvard University Press.

Becker, G. S. (1981), *A Treatise on the Family*, Cambridge, Mass.: Harvard University Press.

—— (1991), *A Treatise on the Family*, enlarged edn., Cambridge, Mass.: Harvard University Press.

Bellah, R. N. (1970), *Beyond Belief: Essays on Religion in Post-Traditional World*, New York: Harper and Row.

Benda, H. J. (1970), 'South-East Asian Islam in the Twentieth Century', in P. M. Holt, A. K. S. Lambton, and B. Lewis (eds.), *The Cambridge History of Islam*, Cambridge: Cambridge University Press.

Boedhisantoso, S. (1967), 'Djagakarsa: A Fruit-producing Village in Djakarta', in Koentjaraningrat (ed.), *Villages in Indonesia*, Ithaca: Cornell University Press.

Bogue, D. J. (1969), *Principles of Demography*, New York: John Wiley.

Bongaarts, J. and Greenhalgh, S. (1985), 'An Alternative to the One-Child Policy in China', *Population and Development Review*, 11(4): 585–617.

Boomgaard, P. (1989), *Children of the Colonial State: Population Growth and Economic Development in Java, 1795–1880*, Amsterdam: Free University Press.

Booth, A. (ed.) (1992), *The Oil Boom and After: Indonesian Economic Policy and Performance in the Soeharto Era*, Singapore: Oxford University Press.

BPS (Biro Pusat Statistik) (1980), *Pola Umur Perkawinan*, Jakarta.

—— (annual), *Statistik Indonesia*, Jakarta.

Butz, W. P. and DaVanzo, J. (1978), *The Malaysian Family Life Survey: Summary Report*, Santa Monica: Rand.

Caldwell, B. (1992), 'Marriage in Sri Lanka: A Century of Change', Ph.D. thesis, Australian National University, Canberra.

Caldwell, J. C. (1962), 'The Population of Malaya', Ph.D. thesis, Australian National University, Canberra.

—— (1980), 'Mass Education as a Determinant of the Timing of Fertility Decline', *Population and Development Review*, 6(2): 225–55.

Caldwell, J. C.; McDonald, P. F.; and Ruzicka, L. T. (1980), 'Interrelations between Nuptiality and Fertility: The Evidence from the World Fertility Survey', Paper presented at the World Fertility Survey Conference, London, 7–11 July.

Caldwell, J. C.; Gajanayake, I.; Caldwell, B.; and Caldwell, P. (1989), 'Is Marriage

Delay a Multiphasic Response to Pressures for Fertility Decline? The Case of Sri Lanka', *Journal of Marriage and the Family*, 51: 337–51.

Casterline, J. B.; Williams, L.; and McDonald, P. F. (1986), 'The Age Difference between Spouses: Variations among Developing Countries', *Population Studies*, 40(3): 353–74.

Cederroth, S. (1983), 'Islam and Adat: Some Recent Changes in the Social Position of Women among Sasak in Lombok', in B. Utas (ed.), *Women in Islamic Societies: Social Attitudes and Historical Perspectives*, London: Curzon Press.

Central Bureau of Statistics and World Fertility Survey (1978), *Indonesia Fertility Survey, 1976: Principal Report*, Vol. 1, Central Bureau of Statistics, Jakarta.

Central Statistical Office (1992), *Annual Abstract of Statistics, 1992*, London: HMSO.

Chabot, H. T. (1967), 'Bontoramba: A Village of Goa, South Sulawesi', in Koentjaraningrat (ed.), *Villages in Indonesia*, Ithaca: Cornell University Press.

Chamie, J. (1986), 'Polygyny among Arabs', *Population Studies*, 40(1): 55–81.

Chander, R.; Palan, V. T.; Datin Nor Laily Aziz; and Tan, B. A. (1977), *Malaysian Fertility and Family Survey, 1974: First Country Report*, Kuala Lumpur: Department of Statistics and National Family Planning Board.

Chandra Muzaffar (1987), *Islamic Resurgence in Malaysia*, Petaling Jaya: Penerbit Fajar Bakti Sdn. Bhd.

Chapon, D. (1976), *Divorce and Fertility: A Study in Rural Java*, Population Institute, Report Series No. 40, University of Gadjah Mada.

Che Man, W. K. (1990), *Muslim Separatism: The Moros of Southern Philippines and the Malays of Southern Thailand*, Kuala Lumpur: Oxford University Press.

Cheng, S.-H. (1978), 'The Changing Female Labour Force in Singapore', *Asian Studies*, 16: 75–99.

Cherlin, A.; Fricke, T.; and Smith, P. C. (1985), 'Education and Age at Marriage: Evidence from Four Asian Societies', Report of the Asian Marriage Survey Research Team.

Cheung, P.; Cabigon, J.; Chamratrithirong, A.; McDonald, P. F.; Syed, S.; Cherlin, A.; and Smith, P. C. (1985), 'Cultural Variations in the Transition to Marriage in Four Asian Societies', in *International Population Conference, Florence, 1985*, Vol. 3, Liège: International Union for the Scientific Study of Population, pp. 293–308.

Chojnacka, H. (1980), 'Polygyny and the Rate of Population Growth', *Population Studies*, 34(1): 91–107.

Chua, B. H. and Wong, A. K. (1988), 'Catching Up with Development: The Singapore Experience', *Journal of Asiatic Studies*, 31(1): 209–22.

Chu, G.; Alfian; and Schramm, W. (1991), *Social Impact of Satellite Television in Rural Indonesia*, Singapore: Asian Mass Communication Research and Information Centre.

Coale, A. J. (1967), 'Factors Associated with the Development of Low Fertility: An Historic Summary', in *Proceedings of the World Population Conference, Belgrade, 1965*, Vol. 2, New York: United Nations, pp. 205–9.

———— (1974), 'The Demographic Transition', in *International Population Conference, Liège*, Vol. 1, Liège: International Union for the Scientific Study of Population, pp. 53–73.

———— (1979), 'The Demographic Transition: A Summary, Some Lessons, and Some Observations', in L.-J. Cho and K. Kobayashi (eds.), *Fertility Transition of the East Asian Populations*, Honolulu: University Press of Hawaii.

Coale, A. J. and Tye, C. Y. (1961), 'The Significance of Age-Patterns of Fertility in High-Fertility Populations', *Milbank Memorial Fund Quarterly*, 39: 631–46.

Coale, A. J.; Wang, F.; Riley, N. E.; and Lin, F. D. (1991), 'Present Trends in Fertility and Nuptiality in China', *Science*, 251(4992): 389–93.

Committee on Population and Demography, National Research Council (1987), *Recent Trends in Fertility and Mortality in Indonesia*, Papers of the East–West Population Institute, No. 105, Honolulu: East–West Center.

Costello, M. (1992), 'The Demography of Mindanao', in M. Turner, R. J. May, and L. R. Turner (eds.), *Mindanao: Land of Unfulfilled Promise*, Quezon City: New Day Publishers.

Costello, M. A. and Palabrica-Costello, M. (1987), *Religion, the Status of Women and Fertility: Findings from the Southern Philippines*, Status of Women and Fertility Project Report No. 1, Research Institute for Mindanao Culture, Cagayan de Oro City: Xavier University.

—— (1988), 'Religious Differences in Fertility in the Southern Philippines: How Fares the Status of Women and Fertility Model?', Paper prepared for the Rockefeller Foundation Workshop on the Status of Women and Fertility, Bellagio, 6–10 June.

Coulson, N. and Hinchcliffe, D. (1978), 'Women and Law Reform in Contemporary Islam', in L. Beck and N. Keddie (eds.), *Women in the Moslem World*, Cambridge, Mass.: Harvard University Press.

Crawfurd, J. (1820), *History of the Indian Archipelago Containing an Account of the Manners, Arts, Languages, Religions, Institutions and Commerce of Its Inhabitants*, Edinburgh: Constable.

Daly, P. (1987), *Hukum Perkawinan Islam*, Jakarta: Thinker's Library.

Davis, K. (1963), 'The Theory of Change and Response in Modern Demographic History', *Population Index*, 29: 345–66.

Davis, K. and Blake, J. (1956), 'Social Structure and Fertility: An Analytic Framework', *Economic Development and Cultural Change*, 4(3): 211–35.

De Graaf, H. J. (1970), 'South-East Asian Islam to the Eighteenth Century', in P. M. Holt, A. K. S. Lambton, and B. Lewis (eds.), *The Cambridge History of Islam*, Cambridge: Cambridge University Press.

De los Santos, R. (1974), 'Muslim Values: A Challenge to Education', in P. G. Gowing and R. D. McAmis (eds.), *The Muslim Filipinos: Their History, Society and Contemporary Problems*, Manila: Solidaridad Publishing House, pp. 235–41.

Denison, E. F. (1985), *Trends in American Economic Growth, 1929–1982*, Washington, DC: Brookings Institute.

Department of Statistics, Malaysia (1987), *Population Projections, Malaysia: 1980–2000*, Kuala Lumpur.

Department of Statistics, Singapore (various years), *Statistics on Marriages and Divorces*, Singapore.

Dhofier, Z. (1989), 'Pesantren and the Nahdatul Ulama in the New Order', Paper presented at the International Conference on Indonesia's New Order, Australian National University, Canberra, 4–8 December.

Dick, H. and Forbes, D. (1992), 'Transport and Communications: A Quiet Revolution', in A. Booth (ed.), *The Oil Boom and After: Indonesian Economic Policy and Performance in the Soeharto Era*, Singapore: Oxford University Press.

Dixon, R. B. (1971), 'Explaining Cross-cultural Variations in Age at Marriage and Proportions Never Marrying', *Population Studies*, 25(2): 215–33.

_____ (1978), 'Late Marriage and Non-marriage as Demographic Responses: Are They Similar?', *Population Studies*, 32(3): 449–66.

Djamour, J. (1959), *Malay Kinship and Marriage in Singapore*, Monographs on Social Anthropology No. 21, London: London School of Economics.

_____ (1966), *The Muslim Matrimonial Court in Singapore*, London: Athlone Press.

Downs, R. (1967), 'A Kelantanese Village of Malaya', in J. H. Steward (ed.), *Contemporary Change in Traditional Societies*, Vol. II, *Asian Rural Societies*, Urbana: University of Illinois Press.

Dunlop, R. and Burns, A. (1992), *'Don't Feel the World is Caving in': Adolescents in Divorcing Families*, Monograph No. 6, Melbourne: Australian Institute of Family Studies.

Easterlin, R. (1976), 'Population Change and Farm Settlement in the Northern United States', *Journal of Economic History*, 36: 45–75.

Edmundson, W. C. (1977), 'Two Villages in Contrast: 1971–1976', *Bulletin of Indonesian Economic Studies*, 18(1): 95–110.

Edmundson, W. and Edmundson, S. (1983), 'A Decade of Village Development in East Java', *Bulletin of Indonesian Economic Studies*, 19(2): 46–59.

Emmanuel, S. C.; Li, S. B.; Ng, T. P.; and Chen, A. J. (1984), *Third National Family Planning and Population Survey, 1982*, Singapore: Singapore Family Planning and Population Board.

ESCAP (Economic and Social Commission for Asia and the Pacific) (1982), *Migration, Urbanization and Development in Malaysia*, Comparative Study on Migration, Urbanization and Development in the ESCAP Region, 4, New York: United Nations.

Evers, H.-D. (1987), 'The Bureaucratization of Southeast Asia', *Comparative Studies in Society and History*, 29(4): 666–85.

Faisal Hj. Othman (1991), 'Poligami Tidak Boleh Dijadikan Dasar Negara', *Utusan Malaysia*, 5 December.

Farid, S. (1987), 'A Review of the Fertility Situation in the Arab Countries of Western Asia and North Africa', in *Fertility Behaviour in the Context of Development: Evidence from the World Fertility Survey*, Population Studies No. 100, Department of International Economic and Social Affairs, New York: United Nations.

Fawcett, J. T. (1973), *Psychological Perspectives on Population*, New York: Basic Books.

Fell, H. (1960), *1957 Population Census of the Federation of Malaya*, Report No. 14, Kuala Lumpur: Department of Statistics.

Firth, Raymond (1966), *Malay Fishermen: Their Peasant Economy*, 2nd edn., London: Routledge & Kegan Paul.

Firth, Rosemary (1966), *Housekeeping among Malay Peasants*, London: Athlone Press.

Fisk, E. K. (1961), 'The Mobility of Rural Labour and the Settlement of New Land in Underdeveloped Countries', *Journal of Farm Economics*, 43(4): Pt.1, 761–78.

_____ (1963), 'Rural Development Policy', in T. H. Silcock and E. K. Fisk (eds.), *The Political Economy of Independent Malaya*, Canberra: Australian National University Press.

Fraser, T. M. (1966), *Fishermen of South Thailand*, Prospect Heights, Ill.: Waveland Press.

Fox, James J. (ed.) (1980), *The Flow of Life: Essays on Eastern Indonesia*, Cambridge, Mass.: Harvard University Press.

Freedman, M. (1957), *Chinese Family and Marriage in Singapore*, London: HMSO.

Gastardo-Conaco, C.; Ramos-Jimenez, P.; and Barniego, R. N. (1986), *Ethnicity and Fertility in the Philippines*, Research Notes and Discussion Paper No. 54, Singapore: Institute of Southeast Asian Studies.

Geertz, C. (1960), *The Religion of Java*, Glencoe, Ill.: Free Press.

――― (1968), *Islam Observed: Religious Development in Morocco and Indonesia*, Chicago: University of Chicago Press.

――― (1972), 'Religious Change and Social Order in Suharto's Indonesia', *Asia*, 27: 68–70.

――― (1984), 'Culture and Social Change: The Indonesian Case', *Man*, 19: 511–32.

Geertz, H. (1961), *The Javanese Family: A Study of Kinship and Socialization*, Glencoe, Ill.: Free Press.

Gille, H. and Pardoko, R. H. (1966), 'A Family Life Study in East Java: Preliminary Findings', in B. Berelson et al. (eds.), *Family Planning and Population Programs*, Chicago: University of Chicago Press.

Glang, A. C. (1974), 'Modernizing the Muslims', in P. C. Gowing and R. D. McAmis (eds.), *The Muslim Filipinos*, Manila: Solidaridad Publishing House.

Goethals, P. R. (1967), 'Rarak: A Swidden Village of West Sumbawa', in Koentjaraningrat (ed.), *Villages in Indonesia*, Ithaca: Cornell University Press.

Goode, W. J. (1963), *World Revolution and Family Patterns*, Glencoe, Ill.: Free Press.

――― (1993), *World Changes in Divorce Patterns, 1950–1990*, New Haven: Yale University Press.

Goody, J. (1976), *Production and Reproduction: A Comparative Study of the Domestic Domain*, Cambridge: Cambridge University Press.

――― (1983), *The Development of the Family and Marriage in Europe*, Cambridge: Cambridge University Press.

Gordon, S. (1964), 'Marriage/Divorce in the Eleven States of Malaya and Singapore', *Intisari*, 2: 25.

Govindasamy, P. and DaVanzo, J. (1992), 'Policy Impact on Fertility Differentials in Malaysia', *Population and Development Review*, 18(2): 243–67.

Guest, P. (1991), *Marital Dissolution and Development in Indonesia*, Working Papers in Demography No. 24, Canberra: Australian National University.

Guinness, P. (1986), *Harmony and Hierarchy in a Javanese Kampung*, Singapore: Oxford University Press.

Gullick, J. M. (1987), *Malay Society in the Late Nineteenth Century: The Beginnings of Change*, Singapore: Oxford University Press.

Guritno, P. (1964), 'A Cross-Cultural Study of Divorce, with Special Reference to a Javanese Village in Jogjakarta, Indonesia', MA thesis, Cornell University, Ithaca.

Haemindra, N. (1977), 'The Problem of the Thai-Muslims in the Four Southern Provinces of Thailand (Part Two)', *Journal of Southeast Asian Studies*, 8(1): 85–105.

Haeri, S. (1989), *Law of Desire: Temporary Marriage in Shi'i Iran*, Syracuse: Syracuse University Press.

Hajnal, J. (1953), 'Age at Marriage and Proportions Marrying', *Population Studies*, 7(2): 111–36.

――― (1965), 'European Marriage Patterns in Perspective', in D. V. Glass and D. E. C. Eversley (eds.), *Population in History*, London: Edward Arnold.

Hamid Arshat; Tan, B. A.; Tey, N. P.; and Subbiah, M. (1988), *Marriage and*

Family Formation in Peninsular Malaysia: Analytic Report on the 1984/85 Malaysian Population and Family Survey, Kuala Lumpur: National Population and Family Development Board.

Hamidah Hassan (1979), 'Nona-nona Zaman Sekarang: Tiada Pantang, Tiada Larang', *Berita Minggu*, 18 February.

Handley, P. (1990), 'Wind from the South', *Far Eastern Economic Review*, 9 August.

Harrisson, T. (1970), *The Malays of South-West Sarawak before Malaysia: A Socio-Ecological Survey*, London: Macmillan.

Hashim Hassan, Che (1984), 'Marriage and Divorce in Kelantan, Malaysia', MA thesis, Australian National University, Canberra.

Hassan, R. (1974), *Interethnic Marriage in Singapore: A Study in Interethnic Relations*, Occasional Paper No. 21, Singapore: Institute of Southeast Asian Studies.

Hatmadji, S. H. (1990), 'The Impact of Family Planning on Fertility in Java', Ph.D. thesis, Australian National University, Canberra.

Hefner, R. W. (1990), *The Political Economy of Mountain Java: An Interpretive History*, Berkeley: University of California Press.

Henry, L. (1976), *Population, Analysis and Models*, London: Edward Arnold.

Hill, H. (1989), *Unity and Diversity: Regional Economic Development in Indonesia since 1970*, Singapore: Oxford University Press.

Hill, R. O. (1977), *Rice in Malaya: A Study in Historical Geography*, Kuala Lumpur: Oxford University Press.

Hirschman, C. (1976), 'Recent Urbanization Trends in Peninsular Malaysia', *Demography*, 13(4): 445–62.

—— (1985), 'Premarital Socioeconomic Roles and the Timing of Family Formation: A Comparative Study of Five Asian Societies', *Demography*, 22(1): 35–59.

—— (1986), 'The Recent Rise in Malay Fertility: A New Trend or a Temporary Fall in a Fertility Transition?', *Demography*, 23(2): 161–84.

Hirschman, C. and Fernandez, D. (1980), 'The Decline of Fertility in Peninsular Malaysia', *Genus*, 36(1–2): 93–127.

Hirschman, C. and Guest, P. (1990), 'The Emerging Demographic Transitions of Southeast Asia', *Population and Development Review*, 16(1): 121–52.

Hooker, M. B. (1978), *Adat Law in Modern Indonesia*, Kuala Lumpur: Oxford University Press.

Hugo, G. J. (1975), 'Population Mobility in West Java, Indonesia', Ph.D. thesis, Australian National University, Canberra.

—— (1981), 'Road Transport, Population Mobility and Development in Indonesia', in G. W. Jones and H. V. Richter (eds.), *Population Mobility and Development: Southeast Asia and the Pacific*, Development Studies Centre, Monograph No. 27, Canberra: Australian National University.

Hugo, G. J.; Lim, L. L.; and Narayan, S. (1989), *Malaysian Human Resources Development Planning Project, Module II: Labour Supply and Processes, Study No. 4: Labour Mobility*, Adelaide: Discipline of Geography, Flinders University.

Hugo, G. J.; Hull, T. H.; Hull, V. J.; and Jones, G. W. (1987), *The Demographic Dimension in Indonesian Development*, Singapore: Oxford University Press.

Hull, T. H. (1987), *The 1985 Intercensal Survey of Indonesia: 1. Changing Patterns of Marriage*, International Population Dynamics Program Research Note No. 74, Canberra: Australian National University.

—— (1988), *Marriage and Divorce Trends in Indonesia*, IPDP Research Note No. 87, Canberra: Australian National University.

Hull, T. H. and Hatmadji, Sri Harijati (1992), *Regional Fertility Differentials in*

Indonesia: Causes and Trends, Working Papers in Demography No. 22, Canberra: Australian National University.

Hull, T. H. and Hull, V. J. (1987), 'Changing Marriage Behavior in Java: The Role of Timing of Consummation', *Southeast Asian Journal of Social Sciences*, 15(1): 104–19.

Hull, T. H. and Larson, A. (1987), 'Dynamic Disequilibrium: Demographic Policies and Trends in Asia', *Asian–Pacific Economic Literature*, 1(1): 25–59.

Hull, V. J. (1975), 'Fertility, Socioeconomic Status, and the Position of Women in a Javanese Village', Ph.D. thesis, Australian National University, Canberra.

Hull, V. J.; Kodiran; and Singarimbun, I. (1976), *Family Formation in the University Community*, Population Institute, Report Series No. 9, Yogyakarta: Gadjah Mada University.

Husin Ali, S. (1978), *Kemiskinan dan Kelaparan Tanah di Kelantan*, Petaling Jaya: Karangkraf.

—— (1981), *The Malays: Their Problems and Future*, Petaling Jaya: Heinemann Educational Books (Asia).

Hüsken, F. and White, B. (1989), 'Java: Social Differentiation, Food Production, and Agrarian Control', in G. Hart, A. Turtan, and B. White (eds.), *Agrarian Transformations: Local Processes and the State in Southeast Asia*, Berkeley: University of California Press.

Huzayyin, S. A. (1979), 'Nuptiality and Fertility: Plural Marriage and Remarriage in Islam', Paper presented at the IUSSP Seminar on Nuptiality and Fertility: Plural Marriage and Illegitimate Fertility in Historical Demography, Kristiansand, Norway.

Ibrahim, A. (1965), *The Status of Muslim Women in Family Law in Malaysia, Singapore and Brunei*, Singapore: Malayan Law Journal.

—— (1978), *Family Law in Malaysia and Singapore*, Singapore: Malayan Law Journal.

Ibrahim, A.; Siddique, S.; and Hussain, Y. (1985), *Readings on Islam in Southeast Asia*, Singapore: Institute of Southeast Asian Studies.

Ihromi, T. O.; Tan, M. G.; Rahardjo, J.; Wahjudi, M.; Djuarini, S.; and Djahari, A. (1973), *The Status of Women and Family Planning in Indonesia*, Preliminary Report, Jakarta: Indonesian Planned Parenthood Association.

Indonesia (1989), *Undang-Undang Pokok Perkawinan*, Jakarta: Bumi Aksara.

Indonesia, Central Bureau of Statistics/National Family Planning Co-ordinating Board/Ministry of Health, and Macro International Inc. (1992), *Demographic and Health Survey, 1991: Final Report*, Jakarta and Columbia.

Inglis, C. (1979), 'Educational Policy and Occupational Structures in Peninsular Malaysia', in J. C. Jackson and M. Rudner (eds.), *Issues in Malaysian Development*, ASAA Southeast Asia Publications Series, Singapore: Heinemann.

Ishak, N. (1988), *Poligami (Mengapa Rasulullah Berbilang Isteri)*, Kuala Lumpur: Pustaka Al-Mizan.

Iskandar, N. (1970), 'Some Monographic Studies on the Population in Indonesia', Lembaga Demografi, Fakultas Ekonomi, Universitas Indonesia, Jakarta.

Jamilah Ariffin (1983), 'Malaysian Women's Labour Force Participation in the Manufacturing Sector: Changing Structural Patterns', in *Proceedings of the Seminar on Economic Activities of Women in Malaysia*, Kuala Lumpur: National Family Planning Board.

Jay, R. R. (1969), *Javanese Villages: Social Relations in Rural Modjokuto*, Cambridge, Mass.: MIT Press.

Johns, A. H. (1987), 'Islam: Islam in Southeast Asia', in M. Eliade (ed.), *The Encyclopedia of Religion*, Vol. 7, New York: Macmillan, pp. 404–22.

Jones, G. W. (1965), 'Female Participation in the Labour Force in a Plural

Economy: The Malayan Example', *Malayan Economic Review*, 10(2): 61–82.

—— (1966), 'The Growth of Malaysia's Labour Force', Ph.D. thesis, Australian National University, Canberra.

—— (1976), 'Religion and Education in Indonesia', *Indonesia*, 22: 19–56.

—— (1977), 'Fertility Levels and Trends in Indonesia', *Population Studies*, 31(1): 29–41.

—— (1980), 'Trends in Marriage and Divorce in Peninsular Malaysia', *Population Studies*, 34(2): 279–92.

—— (1981), 'Malay Marriage and Divorce in Peninsular Malaysia: Three Decades of Change', *Population and Development Review*, 7(2): 255–78.

—— (1984), *Women in the Urban and Industrial Workforce, Southeast and East Asia*, Development Studies Centre, Monograph No. 33, Canberra: Australian National University.

—— (1985), 'Further Research Areas on Migration and Development in ASEAN Countries', in P. M. Hauser, D. B. Suits, and N. Ogawa (eds.), *Urbanization and Migration in ASEAN Development*, Tokyo: National Institute for Research Advancement, pp. 147–66.

—— (1986), 'Differentials in Female Labour Force Participation Rates in Indonesia: Reflection of Economic Needs and Opportunities, Culture or Bad Data?', *Majalah Demografi Indonesia*, 13(26): 1–28.

—— (1990a), 'Fertility Transitions among Malay Populations of Southeast Asia: Puzzles of Interpretation', *Population and Development Review*, 16(3): 507–37.

—— (1990b), 'Family Planning Programs in ASEAN Countries', Paper presented at the Eighth Biennial Conference of the Asian Studies Association of Australia, Brisbane, 2–5 July.

Jones, G. W. and Manning, C. (1992), 'Labour Force and Employment during the 1980s', in A. Booth (ed.), *The Oil Boom and After: Indonesian Economic Policy and Performance in the Soeharto Era*, Singapore: Oxford University Press.

Jones, G. W. and Tan, P. C. (1985), 'Recent and Prospective Population Trends in Malaysia', *Journal of Southeast Asian Studies*, 16(3): 262–80.

Jones, G. W.; Asari, Y.; and Djuartika, T. (forthcoming), 'Divorce in West Java', *Journal of Comparative Family Studies*, 25(3).

Karim, Wazir-Jahan (1987), 'The Status of Malay Women in Malaysia: From Culture to Islam and Industrialization', *International Journal of Sociology of the Family*, 17(1): 41–55.

Kasimin, A. (1978), *Konflik Poligami di Malaysia*, Petaling Jaya: Karya Publishing House.

Kassim, A. (1985), *Wanita dan Masyarakat*, Kuala Lumpur: Utusan Publications and Distributors.

Kasto (1982), 'Perkawinan dan Perceraian pada Masyarakat Jawa', Pusat Penelitian dan Studi Kependudukan, Universitas Gadjah Mada, Yogyakarta.

—— (1988), 'Socio-Economic and Regional Variation in Age at First Marriage', Pusat Penelitian Kependudukan, Universitas Gadjah Mada, Yogyakarta.

Katz, J. S. and Katz, R. S. (1975), 'The New Indonesian Marriage Law: A Mirror of Indonesia's Political, Cultural, and Legal Systems', *American Journal of Comparative Law*, 23(4): 653–81.

—— (1978), 'Legislating Changes in a Developing Country: The New Indonesian Marriage Law Revisited', *American Journal of Comparative Law*, 26(2): 309–20.

Keyfitz, N. (1973), 'The Mathematics of Sex and Marriage', in *Proceedings of the Sixth Berkeley Symposium on Mathematical Statistics and Probability*,

Vol. 4, Berkeley: University of California Press.

_____ (1985), 'An East Javanese Village in 1953 and 1985: Observations on Development', *Population and Development Review*, 11(4): 695–719.

Khoo, S.-E. and McDonald, P. F. (1988), 'Ex-Nuptial Births and Unmarried Cohabitation in Australia', *Journal of the Australian Population Association*, 5(2): 164–77.

Koentjaraningrat (ed.) (1967a), *Villages in Indonesia*, Ithaca: Cornell University Press.

_____ (1967b), 'Tjelapar: A Village in South Central Java', in Koentjaraningrat (ed.), *Villages in Indonesia*, Ithaca: Cornell University Press.

_____ (1985), *Javanese Culture*, Singapore: Oxford University Press.

Krulfeld, R. (1986), 'Sasak Attitudes towards Polygyny and the Changing Position of Women in Sasak Peasant Villages', in L. Dube, E. Leacock, and S. Ardener (eds.), *Visibility and Power*, Delhi: Oxford University Press, pp. 194–208.

Kuchiba, M.; Tsubouchi, Y.; and Maeda, N. (1979), *Three Malay Villages: A Sociology of Paddy Growers in West Malaysia*, Honolulu: University Press of Hawaii.

Lacar, L. Q. (1992), 'Philippine Muslim Women': Their Emerging Role in a Rapidly Changing Society', in M. Turner, R. J. May, and L. R. Turner (eds.), *Mindanao: Land of Unfulfilled Promise*, Quezon City: New Day Publishers.

Laderman, C. (1983), *Wives and Midwives: Childbirth and Nutrition in Rural Malaysia*, Berkeley: University of California Press.

Lapidus, I. M. (1988), *A History of Islamic Societies*, Cambridge: Cambridge University Press.

Laslett, P. (ed.) (1972), *Household and Family in Past Time*, London: Cambridge University Press.

Lee Kok Huat; Tan, P. C.; and Siti Rohani Yahaya (1985), *Family Events and Marital Stability in Peninsular Malaysia*, Population Studies Unit Discussion Paper No. 6, Kuala Lumpur: University of Malaya.

Leete, R. (1989), 'Dual Fertility Trends in Malaysia's Multiethnic Society', *International Family Planning Perspectives*, 15(2): 58–65.

Leinbach, T. R. and Chia Lin Sien (1989), *South-East Asian Transport: Issues in Development*, Singapore: Oxford University Press.

Lesthaeghe, R. (1974), 'The Feasibility of Controlling Population Growth through Nuptiality and Nuptiality Policies', in IUSSP, *International Population Conference, Liège 1973*, Vol. 3, Liège, pp. 319–41.

Lev, D. S. (1972a), *Islamic Courts in Indonesia*, Berkeley: University of California Press.

_____ (1972b), 'Judicial Institutions and Legal Culture in Indonesia', in C. Holt (ed.), *Culture and Politics in Indonesia*, Ithaca: Cornell University Press.

Levine, N. (1982), 'Social Change and Family Crisis: The Nature of Turkish Divorce', in C. Kagitcibasi (ed.), *Sex Roles, Family and Community in Turkey*, Indiana University Turkish Studies 3, Bloomington.

Li, T. (1989), *Malays in Singapore: Culture, Economy, and Ideology*, Singapore: Oxford University Press.

Lim, L. L. (1986), *Impact of Immigration on Labour Markets in Peninsular Malaysia*, NUPRI Research Paper Series No. 31, Tokyo: Nihon University Population Research Institute.

_____ (1991), 'The Structural Determinants of Female Migration', Paper presented at the UN Expert Group Meeting on the Feminization of Internal Migration, Aguascalientes, Mexico, 22–25 October.

_____ (1993), 'The Feminization of Labour in the Asia–Pacific Rim Countries: From Contributing to Economic Dynamism to Bearing the Brunt of Structural Adjustments', in N. Ogawa, G. W. Jones, and J. G. Williamson (eds.), *Human Resources in Development along the Asia–Pacific Rim*, Singapore: Oxford University Press.

Lim, L. L. and Jones, G. W. (1989), Unpublished survey tabulations, Department of Demography, Australian National University, Canberra.

Lim, L. L.; Jones, G. W.; and Hirschman, C. (1987), 'Continuing Fertility Transitions in a Plural Society: Ethnic Trends and Differentials in Peninsular Malaysia', *Journal of Biosocial Science*, 19: 405–25.

Lineton, J. A. (1975), 'An Indonesian Society and its Universe: A Study of the Bugis of South Sulawesi (Celebes) and Their Role within a Wider Social and Economic System', Ph.D. thesis, University of London.

Loeb, E. M. (1972), *Sumatra: Its History and People*, Kuala Lumpur: Oxford University Press.

Logsdon, M. G. (1985), 'Women in Government Services in Indonesia', *Prisma*, 37: 57–67.

McCarthy, J. (1982), 'Differentials in Age at First Marriage', *Comparative Studies: Cross-National Summaries*, World Fertility Survey, No. 19, London.

McDonald, P. F. (1981), 'Social Change and Age at Marriage', in *International Population Conference, Manila 1981*, Liège: International Union for the Scientific Study of Population.

_____ (1984), 'Changing Courting Behaviour among Indonesian Youth: National Image versus Local Custom', Mimeograph, Department of Demography, Australian National University, Canberra.

_____ (1985), 'Social Organization and Nuptiality in Developing Societies', in J. Cleland and J. Hobcraft (eds.), *Reproductive Change in Developing Countries*, New York: Oxford University Press.

McDonald, P. F. and Abdurahman, E. H. (1974), 'Marriage and Divorce in West Java: An Example of Effective Use of Marital Histories', Lembaga Demografi, Fakultas Ekonomi, Universitas Indonesia, Jakarta.

McDonald, P. F.; Yasin, M.; and Jones, G. W. (1976), 'Levels and Trends in Fertility and Childhood Mortality in Indonesia', Lembaga Demografi, Fakultas Ekonomi, Universitas Indonesia, Jakarta.

McNicoll, G. and Mamas, S. G. M. (1973), *The Demographic Situation in Indonesia*, Papers of the East–West Population Institute, No. 28, Honolulu.

McNicoll, G. and Singarimbun, M. (1982), *Fertility Decline in Indonesia: I. Background and Proximate Determinants*, Center for Policy Study Working Papers No. 92, New York: Population Council.

Mahathir bin Mohamad (1970), *The Malay Dilemma*, Singapore: Donald Moore.

_____ (1991), 'Malaysia: The Way Forward. Vision 2020', Working Paper presented at the Inaugural Meeting of the Malaysian Business Council, Kuala Lumpur, 28 February.

Mahfudz, G. (1982), 'Perkawinan dan Perceraian pada Masyarakat Banjar', Pusat Penelitian dan Studi Kependudukan, Universitas Gadjah Mada, Yogyakarta.

Mahmud, S. (1983), 'Perkawinan dan Perceraian pada Masyarakat Ogan Ilir', Pusat Penelitian dan Kependudukan, Universitas Gadjah Mada, Yogyakarta.

Malaysia (1981), *Fourth Malaysia Plan, 1981–1985*, Kuala Lumpur: National Printing Department.

_____ (1991), *The Second Outline Perspective Plan, 1991–2000*, Kuala Lumpur: National Printing Department.

_____ (various years), *Vital Statistics, Peninsular Malaysia*, Kuala Lumpur: Department of Statistics.

Malhotra, A. (1991), 'Gender and Changing Generational Relations: Spouse Choice in Indonesia', *Demography*, 28(4): 549–70.

Mandelbaum, D. G. (1989), 'Women's Seclusion and Men's Honour: Sex Roles in North India, Bangladesh and Pakistan', *Journal of Asian Studies*, 48(3): 657–86.

Manderson, L. (1978), 'The Development and Direction of Female Education in Peninsular Malaysia', *Journal of the Malaysian Branch of the Royal Asiatic Society*, LI(2): 100–22.

_____ (1979), 'A Woman's Place: Malay Women and Development in Peninsular Malaysia', in J. C. Jackson and M. Rudner (eds.), *Issues in Malaysian Development*, ASAA Southeast Asia Publications Series, Singapore: Heinemann.

Marsden, W. (1811), *The History of Sumatra*, London: Published by the Author.

Mason, K. O. (1984), *The Status of Women: A Review of Its Relationships to Fertility and Mortality*, New York: Rockefeller Foundation.

Mather, C. (1983), 'Industrialization in the Tangerang Regency of West Java: Women Workers and the Islamic Patriarchy', *Bulletin of Concerned Asian Scholars*, 15(2): 2–17.

Maude, A. (1981), 'Population Mobility and Rural Households in North Kelantan, Malaysia', in G. W. Jones and H. V. Richter (eds.), *Population Mobility and Development: Southeast Asia and the Pacific*, Development Studies Centre, Monograph No. 27, Canberra: Australian National University.

Maznah bte. Hj. Haron (1975), 'Muslim Marriage and Divorce in the Federal Territory', Project paper, University of Malaya, Kuala Lumpur.

Mernissi, F. (1975), *Beyond the Veil: Male–Female Dynamics in a Modern Muslim Society*, New York: Schenkman Publishing Co.

Mirrian Sjofjan Arif (1992), 'Pegawai Wanita dan Faktor-Faktor yang Mempengaruhi Kerjayanya dalam Birokrasi Kerajaan Indonesia', Ph.D. thesis, University of Malaya, Kuala Lumpur.

Mohtar, Haji bin H. Md. Dom (1979), *Malay Wedding Customs*, Kuala Lumpur: Federal Publications.

Muliakusuma, S. (1976), 'Berbagai Aspek Perbedaan Pola Perkawinan di Indonesia Dewasa Ini', Lembaga Demografi, Fakultas Ekonomi, Universitas Indonesia, Jakarta.

_____ (1982), 'Perkawinan dan Perceraian pada Masyarakat Betawi', Pusat Penelitian dan Studi Kependudukan, Universitas Gadjah Mada, Yogyakarta.

Mustafar Che Mat (1979), 'Beberapa Aspek Perkahwinan dan Perceraian di Kampung Pengkalan Kubur, Tumpat, Kelantan [Some Aspects of Marriage and Divorce in Kampung Pengkalan Kubur, Tumpat, Kelantan]', Graduation Exercise, Faculty of Economics and Administration, University of Malaya, Kuala Lumpur.

Nagata, J. (1982), 'Islamic Revival and the Problem of Legitimacy among Rural Religious Elites in Malaysia', *Man* (NS), 17: 42–57.

_____ (1984), *The Reflowering of Malaysian Islam: Modern Religious Radicals and Their Roots*, Vancouver: University of British Columbia Press.

Nakamura, H. (1983), *Divorce in Java*, Yogyakarta: Gadjah Mada University Press.

National Family Planning Board, Malaysia (n.d.), *Report on West Malaysian Family Survey, 1966–1967*, Kuala Lumpur: KUM Printers.

National Population and Family Development Board, Malaysia (1992), *Report of the Population and Family Survey in Sabah, 1989*, Kuala Lumpur.

Nayer, S. (1987), 'Economic Performance and Growth Factors of the ASEAN Countries', in L. C. Martin (ed.), *The ASEAN Success Story: Social, Economic and Political Dimensions*, Honolulu: University of Hawaii Press.

Negeri Kelantan (1983), 'Islamic Family Law Enactment 1983', *Government of Kelantan Gazette*, 26 May.

Nicolaison, I. (1983), 'Introduction', in B. Utas (ed.), *Women in Islamic Societies: Social Attitudes and Historical Perspectives*, London: Curzon Press.

Niehof, A. (1985), 'Women and Fertility in Madura (Indonesia)', Ph.D. thesis, Leiden University, Leiden.

Nik Ramlah binti Nik Mahmud (1978), 'Muslim Divorces in Kelantan—A Socio-Legal Study', Project paper, University of Malaya, Kuala Lumpur.

Nitisastro, W. (1956), 'Some Data on the Population of Djabres, a Village in Central Java', *Ekonomi dan Keluarga Indonesia*, 9: 731–84.

Noor, K. (1992), '48,757 Cerai di Kelantan', *Berita Harian*, 20 February.

Nothofer, B. (1975), *The Reconstruction of Proto-Malayo-Javanic*, The Hague: Martinus Nijhoff.

NUDS (National Urban Development Strategy) (1985), *NUDS Final Report*, Jakarta.

Nugroho (1967), *Indonesia: Facts and Figures*, Jakarta: Biro Pusat Statistik.

O'Brien, L. (1983), 'Four Paces Behind: Women's Work in Peninsular Malaysia', in L. Manderson (ed.), *Women's Work and Women's Roles: Economics and Everyday Life in Indonesia, Malaysia and Singapore*, Development Studies Centre, Monograph No. 32, Canberra: Australian National University.

_____ (1984), 'The Effect of Industrialization on Women: British and Malaysian Experience', *Kajian Malaysia*, 2(1): 38–58.

Oey-Gardiner, M. (1991), 'Gender Differences in Schooling in Indonesia', *Bulletin of Indonesian Economic Studies*, 27(1): 57–79.

Ong, A. (1987), *Spirits of Resistance and Capitalist Discipline: Factory Women in Malaysia*, Albany: State University of New York Press.

_____ (1988), 'Industrial Development and Rural Malay Households: Changing Strategies of Reproduction', in C. Vlassoff and B.-e-Khuda (eds.), *Impact of Modernization on Development and Demographic Behaviour: Case Studies in Seven Third World Countries*, Ottawa: International Development Research Centre.

Palmore, J. A. and Singarimbun, M. (1991), *Marriage Patterns and Cumulative Fertility in Indonesia, 1987*, East–West Population Institute, Working Paper No. 64, Honolulu.

_____ (1992), 'The Conflicting Effects of Delayed Marriage and Declining Divorce Rates on Cumulative Fertility in Indonesia', *Asian and Pacific Census Forum*, 6(1): 5–26. ·

Pang, E. F. (1982), *Education, Manpower and Development in Singapore*, Singapore: Singapore University Press.

Pastner, C. M. (1980), 'Access to Property and the Status of Women in Islam', in J. I. Smith (ed.), *Women in Contemporary Muslim Societies*, Lewisburg: Bucknell University Press, pp. 146–78.

Peletz, M. G. (1988), *A Share of the Harvest: Kinship, Property and Social History among the Malays of Rembau*, Berkeley: University of California Press.

Penny, D. and Singarimbun, M. (1973), *Population and Poverty in Rural Java: Some Economic Arithmetic from Sriharjo*, Ithaca: Department of Agricultural Economics, Cornell University.

Pitsuwan, S. (1985), *Islam and Malay Nationalism: A Case Study of the Malay-Muslims of Southern Thailand*, Bangkok: Thai Khadi Research Institute,

Thammasat University.

Prentice, D. J. (1978), 'The Best Chosen Language', *Hemisphere*, 22(3): 18–23.

Prodjodikoro (1967), *Hukum Perkawinan di Indonesia* [Marriage Law in Indonesia], Bandung: Sumur Bandung.

Prothero, E. M. and Diab, L. (1974), *Changing Family Patterns in the Arab East*, Beirut: American University of Beirut Press.

Rachapaetayakom, J. (1983), 'The Demography of the Thai Muslims: With Special Reference to Fertility and Nuptiality', Ph.D. thesis, Australian National University, Canberra.

Raffles, T. S. [1817] (1978), *The History of Java*; reprinted Kuala Lumpur: Oxford University Press.

Rahman, F. (1982), *Islam and Modernity: Transformation of an Intellectual Tradition*, Center for Middle Eastern Studies, No. 15, Chicago: University of Chicago Press.

_____ (1987), 'Islam: An Overview', in M. Eliade (ed.), *The Encyclopedia of Religion*, Vol. 7, New York: Macmillan, pp. 303–22.

Ramli Ismail (1991), 'Poligami Tidak Buruk Jika Wanita Faham', *Utusan Malaysia*, 4 September.

Rasjid (1954), *Fiqh Islam* [Islamic Interpersonal Law], Jakarta: Attahirijah.

Raybeck, D. A. (1974), 'Social Stress and Social Structure in Kelantan Village Life', in W. R. Roff (ed.), *Kelantan: Religion, Society and Politics in a Malay State*, Kuala Lumpur: Oxford University Press.

Reid, A. J. S. (1988), *Southeast Asia in the Age of Commerce, 1450–1680*, Vol. 1, *The Lands Below the Winds*, New Haven: Yale University Press.

Robertson, J. F. (1971), 'Very Young Brides', *Brunei Museum Journal*, 2(3): 31–8.

Roff, W. R. (1970), 'South-East Asian Islam in the Nineteenth Century', in P. M. Holt, A. K. S. Lambton, and B. Lewis (eds.), *The Cambridge History of Islam*, Cambridge: Cambridge University Press.

_____ (1974a), *The Origins of Malay Nationalism*, New Haven: Yale University Press.

_____ (ed.) (1974b), *Kelantan: Religion, Society and Politics in a Malay State*, Kuala Lumpur: Oxford University Press.

Roose, H. (1963), 'Change in the Position of Malay Women', in B. E. Ward (ed.), *Women in the New Asia*, Paris: Unesco, pp. 287–94.

Rudie, I. (1983), 'Women in Malaysia: Economic Autonomy, Ritual Segregation and Some Future Possibilities', in B. Utas (ed.), *Women in Islamic Societies: Social Attitudes and Historical Perspectives*, London: Curzon Press.

Ryder, N. B. (1964), 'The Process of Demographic Translation', *Demography*, 1(1): 74–82.

Sanyoto, N. (1974), *Undang-undang Perkawinan Berikut Peraturan Pelaksanaan dan Penjelasannya*, Jakarta: Bp. Karya Bani.

Sarwono, S. W. (ed.) (1981), *Seksualitas dan Fertilitas Remaja* [Adolescent Sexuality and Fertility], Jakarta: C. V. Rajawali and the Indonesian Planned Parenthood Federation.

_____ (1990), 'Social Psychological Aspects of Health and Health Care', in J. C. Caldwell et al. (eds.), *What We Know about Health Transition: The Cultural, Social and Behavioural Determinants of Health*, Vol. 2, Canberra: Health Transition Centre, Australian National University.

Saw, S. H. (1967), 'Fertility Differentials in Early Postwar Malaya', *Demography*, 4(2): 641–56.

—— (1989), 'Muslim Fertility Transition: The Case of the Singapore Malays', *Asia–Pacific Population Journal*, 4(3): 31–40.

Shamsiah Sanin (1986), 'Kadar Cerai di Wilayah Paling Tinggi', *Berita Harian*, 22 July.

—— (1991), 'Poligami: Perlukah Kebenaran Isteri?', *Berita Minggu*, 6 October.

Shryock, H. S. and Siegel, J. S. (1971), *The Methods and Materials of Demography*, 2 vols., Washington, DC: US Bureau of the Census.

Sidhu, M. S. and Jones, G. W. (1981), *Population Dynamics in a Plural Society: Peninsular Malaysia*, Kuala Lumpur: University of Malaya Co-operative Bookshop.

Siegel, J. (1969), *The Rope of God*, Berkeley: University of California Press.

Simon, A. (1991), 'Match-Making Service for Muslims a Hit', *New Straits Times*, 30 August.

Singapore, Republic of (1973), *Report on the Registration of Births and Deaths and Marriages, 1973*, Singapore: Singapore National Printers.

—— (various years), *Yearbook of Statistics: Singapore*, Singapore: Department of Statistics.

Singarimbun, M. (1975), *Kinship, Descent and Alliance among the Karo Batak*, Berkeley, University of California Press.

—— (1984), 'Kumpul Kerbau Liar', *Tempo*, 29 September.

Singarimbun, M. and Manning, C. (1974a), 'Fertility and Family Planning in Mojolama', Institute of Population Studies, Gadjah Mada University, Yogyakarta.

—— (1974b), 'Marriage and Divorce in Mojolama', *Indonesia*, 17: 67–82.

Sisters in Islam (1990), 'Polygamy Not a Right Enshrined in the Quran' [Letter], *New Straits Times*, 20 August.

Smith, P. C. (1975), 'Changing Patterns of Nuptiality', in W. Flieger and P. C. Smith (eds.), *A Demographic Path to Modernity*, Quezon City: University of the Philippines Press.

—— (1980), 'Asian Marriage Patterns in Transition', *Journal of Family History*, 5(1): 58–96.

—— (1982), 'Contrasting Marriage Patterns and Fertility in Southeast Asia: Indonesia and the Philippines Compared', in L. Ruzicka (ed.), *Nuptiality and Fertility*, Liège: Ordina Editions.

—— (1983), 'The Impact of Age at Marriage and Proportions Marrying on Fertility', in R. A. Bulatao and R. D. Lee (eds.), *Determinants of Fertility in Developing Countries*, New York: Academic Press.

Smith, P. C.; Shahidullah, M.; and Alcantara, A. N. (1983), *Cohort Nuptiality in Asia and the Pacific: An Analysis of the World Fertility Surveys*, World Fertility Survey Comparative Study No. 22, London.

Smith, T. E. (1961), 'Marriage, Widowhood and Divorce in the Federation of Malaya', Paper presented at the IPU Conference, New York.

Soeradji, B. (1979), 'Marriage and Divorce in Indonesia: A Demographic Study', Ph.D. thesis, University of Chicago.

Soeradji, B. and Hatmadji, S. H. (1982), *Perbedaan Umur Perkawinan antar Daerah*, Jakarta: Lembaga Demografi, Fakultas Ekonomi, Universitas Indonesia.

Stewart, J. C. (1984), 'Maguindanao', in R. V. Weekes (ed.), *Muslim Peoples: A World Ethnographic Survey*, 2nd edn., London: Aldwych Press.

Strange, H. (1981), *Rural Malay Women in Tradition and Transition*, New York: Praeger Publishers.

Sudewa, A. (1980), 'Pengaruh Pemilihan Jodoh, Umur Kawin dan Perceraian terhadap Fertilitas: Kasus Ngaglik', Mimeograph, PPS Kependudukan, Gadjah Mada University, Yogyakarta

Suhaini Aznam (1991), 'States Differ on Approach to Polygamy: Spouses and Suitors', *Far Eastern Economic Review*, 22 August.

Suprapto, B. (1990), *Liku-Liku Poligami*, Yogyakarta: Penerbit Al Kautsar.

Suryadinata, L. (1989), *Military Ascendancy and Political Culture: A Study of Indonesia's Golkar*, Monographs in International Studies, No. 85, Ohio University Center for International Studies, Athens.

Sutherland, H. (1978), 'The Taming of the Trengganu Elite', in R. T. McVey (ed.), *Southeast Asian Transitions: Approaches through Social History*, New Haven: Yale University Press.

Swift, M. (1963), 'Men and Women in Malay Society', in B. E. Ward (ed.), *Women in the New Asia*, Paris: Unesco.

Tabari, A. and Yeganeh, N. (eds.) (1982), *In the Shadow of Islam: The Women's Movement in Iran*, London: Zed Press.

Tai, C. L. (1979), 'Divorce in Singapore', in E. C. Y. Kuo and A. K. Wong (eds.), *The Contemporary Family in Singapore*, Singapore: Singapore University Press, pp. 142–67.

Tan, B. A. and Chak, C. S. (1988), 'Nuptiality', in National Population and Family Development Board, Malaysia, *Seminar on Findings of Population Surveys and Their Policy Implications*, Kuala Lumpur.

Tan, P. C. (1983), 'The Impact of Nuptiality on Fertility Trends in Peninsular Malaysia, 1957–1980', Ph.D. thesis, Australian National University, Canberra.

—— (1986), 'The Study of Marriage and Marital Dissolution in Peninsular Malaysia: The Singles', Final Report submitted to Lembaga Penduduk dan Pembangunan Keluarga Negara and the United Nations Fund for Population Activities, Kuala Lumpur.

Tan, P. C. and Jones, G. W. (1990), 'Malay Divorce in Peninsular Malaysia: The Near-Disappearance of an Institution', *Southeast Asian Journal of Social Science*, 18(2): 85–114.

—— (1991), 'Changing Patterns of Marriage and Household Formation in Peninsular Malaysia', *Sojourn*, 5(2): 163–93.

Tan, P. C.; Chan, P. T. H.; Lee, K. H.; and Nagaraj, S. (1986), 'The Study of Marriage and Marital Dissolution in Peninsular Malaysia: The Married Couples', Final Report prepared for the United Nations Fund for Population Activities, Kuala Lumpur.

Tan, P. C.; Tan, B. A.; Tey, N. P.; and Kwok, K. K. (1988), *A Cohort Analysis of Recent Changes in Nuptiality Patterns in Peninsular Malaysia*, Kuala Lumpur: National Population and Family Development Board.

Tey, N. P. and Chak, C. S. (1988), 'Fertility Trends and Differentials', in *Proceedings of the Seminar on Findings of Population Surveys and Their Policy Implications*, Kuala Lumpur: National Population and Family Development Board.

Tham, S. C. (1979), 'Social Change and the Malay Family' in E. C. Y. Kuo and A. K. Wong (eds.), *The Contemporary Family in Singapore*, Singapore: Singapore University Press.

Thani, A. M. (1979), 'Sosial Masyarakat di Cerpen Melayu', *Berita Minggu*.

Thomas, L. (1974), 'Bureaucratic Attitudes and Behavior as Obstacles to Political Integration of Thai Muslims', *Southeast Asia*, 3(1): 545–66.

—— (1982), 'The Thai Muslims', in R. Israeli (ed.), *Crescent in the East: Islam in Asia Major*, London: Curzon Press.

Tibi, B. (1991), *Islam and the Cultural Accommodation of Social Change*, Boulder: Westview Press.

Tim Peneliti, PSK–LP UNPAD (1988), 'Perkawinan dan Perceraian di Jawa Barat', Universitas Padjajaran, Bandung.

Tsubouchi, Y. (1975), 'Marriage and Divorce among Malay Peasants in Kelantan', *Journal of South East Asian Studies*, 6(2): 135–50.

—— (1976), 'Islam and Divorce among Malay Peasants', in S. Ichimura (ed.), *Southeast Asia: Nature, Society and Development*, Honolulu: University Press of Hawaii.

Tsuruoka, D. (1990), 'Fabricated Future', *Far Eastern Economic Review*, 1 November.

Tsuya, N. and Mason, K. O. (1992), 'Changing Gender Roles and Below-Replacement Fertility in Japan', Revised version of paper prepared for the IUSSP Seminar on Gender and Family Change in Industrialized Countries, Rome.

Unesco (1972), 'Education in Malaysia', *Bulletin of the Unesco Regional Office for Education in Asia*, 6(2): 115–28.

United Nations, Department of International Economic and Social Affairs (1989), *Adolescent Reproductive Behaviour*, New York.

—— (1990), *Patterns of First Marriage: Timing and Prevalence*, New York.

——, (1991), *The Sex and Age Distributions of Populations: The 1990 Revision*, ST/ESA/SER.A/122, New York.

—— (various years), *Demographic Yearbook*, New York.

Utas, B. (ed.) (1983), *Women in Islamic Societies: Social Attitudes and Historical Perspectives*, London: Curzon Press.

Villeneuve-Gokalp, C. (1991), 'From Marriage to Informal Union: Recent Changes in the Behaviour of French Couples', *Population: An English Selection*, 3: 81–111.

Von Elm, B. and Hirschman, C. (1979), 'Age at First Marriage in Peninsular Malaysia', *Journal of Marriage and the Family*, 41(4): 877–91.

Vreede-de Stuers, C. (1960), *The Indonesian Woman: Struggles and Achievements*, The Hague: Mouton.

—— (1976), 'On the Subject of the "R.U.U.": The History of a Set of Matrimonial Laws', in B. B. Hering (ed.), *Indonesian Women: Some Past and Current Perspectives*, Brussels: Centre d'Etude du Sud-Est Asiatique et de l'Extrême-Orient.

Wallerstein, J. S. (1991), 'The Long-Term Effects of Divorce on Children: A Review', *Journal of the American Academy of Child and Adolescent Psychiatry*, 30(3): 349–60.

Wallerstein, J. S. and Blakeslee, S. (1989), *Second Chances: Men, Women and Children a Decade after Divorce*, New York: Ticknor-Fields.

Wan, F. K. and Saw, S. H. (1974), *Report of the First National Survey on Family Planning in Singapore, 1973*, Singapore: Family Planning and Population Board.

Wayachut, J. (1993), 'Trends and Differentials in Female Age at First Marriage in Thailand during the Twentieth Century', *Sojourn*, 8(2): 293–314.

Weekes, R. V. (ed.) (1984), *Muslim Peoples: A World Ethnographic Survey*, 2nd edn., London: Aldwych Press.

Westermarck, E. (1922), *The History of Human Marriage*, 3 vols., New York: Allerton Book Company.

340 BIBLIOGRAPHY

White, B. et al. (1992), 'Workshops and Factories: Dynamics of Production Organisation and Employment in West Java's Rural Footwear Industries', Paper presented at the 9th Biennial Conference of the Asian Studies Association, 6–9 July.

White, E. H. (1978), 'Legal Reform as an Indicator of Women's Status in Muslim Nations', in L. Beck and N. Keddie (eds.), *Women in the Moslem World*, Cambridge, Mass.: Harvard University Press.

Wibowo, S.; Gunawan, A.; Merina, D.; Anisah; and Aziz, D. (1989), *Penelitian Deskriptif Mengenai Sebab-Sebab Kota Indramayu sebagai Produsen Utama Wanita Tuna Susila*, Jakarta: Pusat Penelitian Kemasyarakatan dan Kebudayaan, Universitas Indonesia.

Widarti, D. (1991), 'Determinants of Female Labour Force Participation and Work Patterns: The Case of Jakarta', Ph.D. thesis, School of Social Sciences, Flinders University, Adelaide.

Widyantoro, N. and Sarsanto, W. S. (1990), 'Cultural Dimensions of an Indonesian Family Planning Service', in J. C. Caldwell et al. (eds.), *What We Know about Health Transition: The Cultural, Social and Behavioural Determinants of Health*, Vol. 2, Canberra: Health Transition Centre, Australian National University.

Wilder, W. (1970), 'Socialization and Social Structure in a Malay Village', in P. Mayer (ed.), *Socialization*, London: Tavistock.

—— (1982), *Communication, Social Structure and Development in Rural Malaysia*, LSE Monographs in Social Anthropology 56, London: Athlone Press.

Williams, L. B. (1990a), 'Marriage and Decision-Making: Inter-Generational Dynamics in Indonesia', *Journal of Comparative Family Studies*, 21(1): 55–66.

—— (1990b), *Development, Demography, and Family Decision-Making: The Status of Women in Rural Java*, Boulder: Westview Press.

Wilson, P. J. (1967), *A Malay Village and Malaysia: Social Values and Rural Development*, New Haven: HRAF Press.

Winstedt, R. O. (1961), *The Malays: A Cultural History*, 6th edn., London: Routledge & Kegan Paul.

Wolf, A. P. and Huang, C.-S. (1980), *Marriage and Adoption in China, 1854–1945*, Stanford: Stanford University Press.

Wolff, D. L. (1990), 'Factory Daughters, the Family, and Nuptiality in Java', *Genus*, 46(3–4): 45–54.

—— (1992), *Factory Daughters: Gender, Household Dynamics and Rural Industrialization in Java*, Berkeley: University of California Press.

Wong, A. K. (1976), 'Women as a Minority Group', in R. Hassan (ed.), *Singapore: Society in Transition*, Kuala Lumpur: Oxford University Press.

—— (1981), 'Planned Development, Social Stratification, and the Sexual Division of Labor in Singapore', *Signs*, Winter.

Wong, A. K. and Ng, S. M. (1985), *Ethnicity and Fertility in Southeast Asia: A Comparative Analysis*, Research Notes and Discussion Paper No. 50, Singapore: Institute of Southeast Asian Studies.

World Bank (1987), *World Development Report, 1987*, New York: Oxford University Press.

—— (1990), *World Development Report, 1990*, New York: Oxford University Press.

—— (1993), *World Development Report, 1993*, New York: Oxford University Press.

_____ (various years), *World Tables*, Washington, DC.

Wrigley, E. A. and Schofield, R. S. (1981), *The Population History of England: A Reconstruction*, London: Edward Arnold.

Xenos, P. and Gultiano, S. A. (1992), *Trends in Female and Male Age at Marriage and Celibacy in Asia*, Papers of the Program on Population, No. 120, Honolulu: East–West Center.

Young, M. L. (1991), 'Circuits of Migration: A Structural Analysis of Migrations in Peninsular Malaysia', Ph.D. thesis, Australian National University, Canberra.

Young, M. L. and Salih, K. (1986), 'Industrialization, Retrenchment and Household Processes: Implications of the Recession', Paper presented at the Himpunan Sains Sosial IV, Persatuan Sains Sosial Malaysia, University of Malaya, Kuala Lumpur.

Zainab Mohd. Ali (1987), 'Tidak Tahu Tanggungjawab Punca Terbesar Berlaku Perceraian Suami Isteri', *Utusan Melayu*, 1 April.

Zainah Anwar (1987), *Islamic Revivalism in Malaysia: Dakwah among the Students*, Petaling Jaya: Pelanduk Publications.

Zainal A. (1991), 'Emosi Terkawal Rumahtangga Kekal', *Berita Harian*, 16 April.

Zalaluddin bin Abdullah (1979), 'Perkahwinan dan Perceraian (Satu Kajian Dibuat di Kampung Belukar, Mukim Ulu Sat, Machang, Kelantan)', Graduation Exercise, Faculty of Economics and Administration, University of Malaya, Kuala Lumpur.

Zelnik, M. and Shah, F. K. (1983), 'First Intercourse among Young Americans', *Family Planning Perspectives*, 15(2): 64–70.

Zeng Yi and Vaupel, J. W. (1989), 'The Impact of Urbanization and Delayed Childbearing on Population Growth and Aging in China', *Population and Development Review*, 15(3): 425–45.

Zeng Yi; Tu Ping; Guo Liu; and Xie Ying (1991), 'A Demographic Decomposition of the Recent Increase in Crude Birth Rates in China', *Population and Development Review*, 17(3): 435–58.

Zuidberg, L. C. L. (ed.) (1978), *Family Planning in Rural West Java: The Serpong Project*, Amsterdam: Institute of Cultural and Social Studies.

Index